Business Law
In the News

Business Law
In the News

Jeffrey F. Beatty
Boston University

Susan S. Samuelson
Boston University

Little, Brown and Company
Boston New York Toronto London

Copyright © 1996 by Jeffrey F. Beatty and Susan S. Samuelson

All rights reserved. No part of this book may be reproduced in any form or by any electronic or mechanical means including information storage and retrieval systems without permission in writing from the publisher, except by a reviewer who may quote brief passages in a review.

Library of Congress Catalogue No. 95-82434
ISBN 0-316-77110-4

MV-NY

Published simultaneously in Canada by
Little, Brown & Company (Canada) Limited

Printed in the United States of America

Contents

Preface ix

Unit 1 The Legal Environment 1

Chapter 1 Introduction to Law 3
Administrative Law 4
Jurisprudence 8
Legal History 10
Comparative Law 14

Chapter 2 Dispute Resolution 17
Alternative Dispute Resolution 18
Voir Dire 22
Expert Witnesses 25

Chapter 3 Common Law, Statutory Law, and Administrative Law 29
Bystander Rule 30
Lobbyists 32
Administrative Agencies 34

Chapter 4 Constitutional Law 43
Judicial Review 44
Free Speech 46
Takings Clause 52

Chapter 5 Intentional Torts and Business Torts 57
Emotional Distress 58
Liability 59
Privacy and Publicity 60

Chapter 6 Negligence and Strict Liability 65
Duty 66
Breach 67
Foreseeability 71

Chapter 7 Crime 75
Mens Rea 76
Insanity 79
Fraud 81

Chapter 8 International Law 87
Child Labor 88
Arms Export 90
Trade Disputes 93
Foreign Sovereign Immunities Act 95

Chapter 9 Business Ethics and Social Responsibility 97
Employee's Responsibility 98
Organization's Responsibility to Its Customers 103
Organization's Responsibility to Employees and the Employee's Responsibility to the Organization 105
What Is Ethical Behavior? 107

Unit 2 Contracts 113

Chapter 10 Introduction to Contracts 115
Purpose of Contract 116
Subjects of Contracts 117

Chapter 11 Agreement 125
Acceptance 126
Counteroffer 128
Promissory Estoppel 130

Chapter 12 Consideration 135
Concept of Consideration 136
Adequacy of Consideration 138
Accord and Satisfaction 140

Chapter 13 Legality 143
Illegality Generally   144
Investments   145
Noncompete Clauses   149

Chapter 14 Capacity and Consent   153
Minors   154
Misrepresentation   156
Fraud   161

Chapter 15 Written Contracts   163
Sale of Land   164
Not Performable Within One Year   166

Chapter 16 Third Parties   169
Third Party Beneficiaries   170
What Rights Are Assignable?   171

Chapter 17 Performance and Discharge   175
Conditions   176
Material Breach   180
Impossibility   183

Chapter 18 Remedies   185
Injunctions   186
Special Issues of Damages   189

Unit 3 Commercial Transactions   191

Chapter 19 Introduction to Sales   193
Mixed Contracts   194
Unconscionability   196

Chapter 20 Ownership and Risk   199
Bona Fide Purchaser   200
Creditor's Rights   202

Chapter 21 Warranties and Product Liability   205
Warranties   206
Negligence   209
Strict Liability   210
Future Laws   213

Chapter 22 Performance and Remedies   217
Usage of Trade   218
The Parties' Agreement   220
Cure   222
Impossibility and Impracticability   224

Chapter 23 Creating a Negotiable Instrument 229
Promissory Note   230
Checks   232

Chapter 24 Liability for Negotiable Instruments   235
Negligence   236
Crimes   237
Dishonor   238
Employee Indorsement Rule   241

Chapter 25 Banks and Their Customers   243
Wrongful Dishonor   244
Bank's Duty To Pay   245
Stop Payment Orders   247
Electronic Fund Transfer Act   249

Chapter 26 Secured Transactions   251
Protection of Buyers   252
International Perspective   254
Repossession   255

Chapter 27 Bankruptcy 257
Introduction to Bankruptcy 258
Chapter 7 259
Chapter 11 263

Unit 4 Agency and Employment Law 267

Chapter 28 Agency: The Inside Relationship 269
Creating an Agency Relationship 270
Duties of Agents to Principals 274

Chapter 29 Agency: The Outside Relationship 279
Apparent Authority 280
Acting Within the Scope of Employment 281
Principal's Liability for Torts 284

Chapter 30 Employment Law 289
Public Policy 290
Employee Privacy 291
Sexual Harassment 294
Age Discrimination 296

Chapter 31 Labor Law 299
Organizing 300
Collective Bargaining 303
Strikes 306

Unit 5 Business Organizations 311

Chapter 32 Starting a Business: Limited Liability 313
General Partnerships 314
Limited Partnerships 319
Limited Liability Companies 321
Franchises 323

Chapter 33 Life and Death of a Partnership 327
Creating a Partnership 328
Partnership by Estoppel 331
Dissolution 334

Chapter 34 Partnership in Operation 341
Fiduciary Duty to the Partnership 342
Right To Bind the Partnership 346
Joint and Several Liability 347

Chapter 35 Life and Death of a Corporation 351
Incorporation Process 352
Piercing the Corporate Veil 353

Chapter 36 Corporate Management 357
Duty of Care 358
Business Judgment Rule 360
Takeovers 362

Chapter 37 Shareholders 365
Shareholder Meetings 366
Rights of Shareholders 368
Right to Protection from Other Shareholders 374

Chapter 38 Securities Regulation 379
Public Offering 380
Liability 381
Insider Trading 383

Chapter 39 Accountants' Liability 387
Liability to Clients 388
Fraud 391

Unit 6 Government Regulation 395

Chapter 40 Antitrust: Law and Competitive Strategy, Part I 397
Price-Fixing 398
Cooperative Strategies 399

Chapter 41 Antitrust: Law and Competitive Strategy, Part II 401
Monopolization 402
Predatory Pricing 404
Tying Arrangements 406

Chapter 42 Consumer Law and Truth in Advertising 411
Right to Privacy 412
Credit Cards 415
Consumer Product Safety Act 417

Chapter 43 Environmental Law 421
Clean Water Act 422
Clean Air Act 423
Superfund 426

Unit 7 Property 429

Chapter 44 Intellectual Property 431
Ownership of Intellectual Property 432
Intellectual Property in Cyberspace 435
Patents 437

Chapter 45 Real Property 441
Sales 442
Adverse Possession 445
Eminent Domain 448

Chapter 46 Landlord-Tenant 451
Creation 452
Use 454
Crime 457
Rent 459

Chapter 47 Personal Property and Bailments 463
Conditional Gifts 464
Bailments 465

Chapter 48 Estate Planning 469
Wills 470
Living Wills 472

Chapter 49 Insurance 475
Specialized Insurance 476

Preface

Law is a powerful force that affects each of us, every day of our lives. The purpose of this reader is to share with students our excitement about the law and to demonstrate what an immediate impact it has on all of us. The newspaper and magazine articles compiled in this book illustrate the far-reaching scope of the law. These articles also offer concrete examples of theoretical concepts. Students who read about the Iraqi invasion of Kuwait (page 224) will understand, and remember, the concepts of impossibility and impracticability in contracts long after they would have forgotten a simple memorized list. Both students and faculty will enjoy the lively classroom discussions that these articles prompt.

Many faculty already use newspaper articles to supplement their texts, but the process of obtaining permissions is cumbersome (and expensive). By collecting our favorite articles in one volume, we save other faculty the time-consuming permissions process. We will update the book regularly to keep articles current.

This reader was compiled as a companion to our textbook, *Business Law for a New Century* (also published by Little, Brown & Company). The text itself contains many short excerpts from articles. This reader offers the opportunity to include entire articles. The chapters in this reader are keyed to the chapters in our textbook, but this book could easily be used to supplement any business law text.

We hope that everyone who reads this book, whether studying law for the first time or teaching it for the fiftieth year, will find these articles enlightening, fascinating, and even entertaining.

Finally, we are grateful to Rick Heuser for his creativity and for his leadership of the talented Little, Brown team: Betsy Kenny, Jessica Barmack, Virginia Pierce, Maureen Kaplan, and David Bemelmans. Our thanks to them all. We would also like to thank Ori Ben-Chorin who provided invaluable research assistance.

Jeffrey F. Beatty
Susan S. Samuelson

Business Law
In the News

Unit 1

The Legal Environment

Chapter 1

Introduction to Law

Administrative Law

Jurisprudence

Legal History

Comparative Law

Administrative Law

A group of commentators proposes a "manifesto" that urges dismantling much of the federal bureaucracy and increased emphasis on individual responsibility.

Manifesto for Culture Warriors of the Right
Larry Arnn, *Washington Times*

> The foundation of our national policy will be laid in the pure and immutable principles of private morality. [T]here is no truth more thoroughly established, than that there exists in the economy and course of nature, an indissoluble union between virtue and happiness.
>
> George Washington, First Inaugural Address, 1789

It is sometimes said that the principles of American democracy offer little or no support for morality. But this belief reflects an inadequate understanding of those principles. Indeed, this agnosticism about the moral underpinnings of democracy is a fairly recent arrival on the American political landscape. It was not always so.

The Founders of America built the first nation dedicated explicitly to the rights of all men under the "laws of nature and nature's God." This law is a moral law, because it prescribes something more than rights—it prescribes also responsibilities. For this reason, it is truly the anchor of our liberty; as Abraham Lincoln said, it is "the father of all moral principle, in us." Under its influence, religion has flourished in America hand in hand with religious liberty. Under it our society has been both good and great, its goodness the cause of its greatness.

Our problem today consists simply in this: Many of our leaders—intellectual, cultural and political—have abandoned the moral and natural law. If we do not repudiate this error, we will suffer a collapse that is both complete and irrecoverable.

That government should be limited is essential for this restoration of morality. It is hardly surprising that the vast administrative state that has grown up in the past several decades is one of the greatest sources of moral corruption in American society. Continued expansion of this administrative state inevitably diminishes the spheres of self-governing citizenship and responsible personal morality. America cannot recover its moral health, pub-

---

Copyright © 1995. Reprinted with permission from *Washington Times*, Nov. 19, 1995, p.B4. Larry Arnn is president of the Claremont Institute in Claremont, Cal.

lic or private, without largely dismantling these ruinous bureaucracies, which act to sever immoral action from its consequences. We must recognize that the administrative leviathan is an enemy not only of freedom but of virtue.

But much of the work to restore America's cultural and moral health must be done outside the realm of government. Indeed, government tends to take its direction from those ideas, mores, and "causes" most respected by the intellectual and cultural leaders of civil society. Therefore, without forgetting the key role of laws in shaping civic character, we must encourage the development of a vibrant and virtuous civil society, and resist the baleful influence of those who preach that there is no truth or virtue.

The relativists have indeed their own comprehensive moral agenda. Repugnant alike to the claims of reason and revelation, it is built upon hollow preferences or naked will. It threatens our liberty and our goodness alike, because it destroys the basis for both, and offers in their stead only dissolution and misery—underwritten by government.

The culture conflict confronting America is a struggle over which of these two visions of America shall prevail. We are convinced that the traditions of Western civilization and the principles of the American founding will, in the long run, triumph over the shallow, self-loathing, and nihilistic counter-morality of relativism.

The dominant liberalism of the past half-century has gone far toward replacing the American vocabulary of virtues with the ersatz vocabulary of "values." We must seek to restore a healthy public discourse on first principles by appealing to the characteristically American idea of "responsibility." Individual and civic responsibility are the key elements of that spirited self-government and self-assertion that must complement the exercise of rights and the natural pursuit of self-interest. Responsibility is the antidote to the ethic of irresponsibility that is the moral essence of the welfare state—both in its middle class and dependent class variants.

Nor should we be content merely to revive the minimum elements of civic morality, however great an accomplishment that would be in the current reduced moral state of the nation. Let us also champion the moral grandeur of our Washingtons and Lincolns; they contrast favorably with the vapid and hollow individuals celebrated today by the "politically correct."

Finally, in this endeavor we must not rely solely on arguments based on self-interest, important as these are to a sound understanding of our economic institutions. We must above all advance arguments based on justice. For this purpose, too, the principles of the Declaration of Independence and the Constitution remain both relevant and authoritative.

The developing conflict over culture is a battle for the soul of America. We call upon all like-minded Americans to fight it, and to win it.

The other authors of the manifesto are as follows:

Richard Brookhiser, senior editor, National Review; Angela "Bay" Buchanan, chairman, Buchanan for President; Edwin Meese, Ronald Reagan Fellow, the Heritage Foundation; Linda Chavez, president, Center for Equal

Opportunity; Angelo Codevilla, professor of political science, Boston University; Edward J. Erler, professor of political science, California State University at San Bernardino; Heather Higgins, senior fellow, the Randolph Foundation; Charles R. Kesler, director, Salvatori Center, Claremont McKenna College; Alan Keyes, American Enterprise Institute (on leave); John Marini, professor of political science, University of Nevada at Reno; Michael Medved, film critic, Sneak Previews; Tom Minnery, vice president, Focus on the Family; Ralph Reed Jr., executive director, Christian Coalition; William A. Rusher, chairman of the Advisory Board, John M. Ashbrook Center for Public Affairs; Bret Schundler, Mayor of Jersey City; Thomas G. West, professor of politics, University of Dallas. (Affiliations are listed for identification purposes only.)

Administrative Law

Many people believe that federal administrative agencies are bloated political bodies that drain tax money while interfering with private enterprise. This columnist takes sharp exception to that view, arguing that much of the work these agencies do is vital to the health and safety of almost everyone.

Abroad at Home: Bare Ruined Choirs
Anthony Lewis, *New York Times*

The radical Republicans in Congress like to say that they are cutting and changing for the sake of our children. "Our goals are simple," Newt Gingrich said. "We don't want our children to drown in debt. . . ." What kind of America will our children in fact inherit if the Republican Congress meets its declared goals? If the legislation now in process is finally enacted?

It will be an America of caveat emptor, buyer beware. The assurance of safety that we take for granted in buying food, drugs and industrial products will be gone. Instead of a community effort to assure safety—that is, Government programs—the burden will be on individuals to see to their own safety.

Copyright © 1995 by The New York Times Co. *New York Times,* July 10, 1995, §A, p.13, col. 1. Reprinted with permission.

The Agriculture Department will be forbidden to inspect meat products by modern scientific methods. It will be up to individual families to make sure the hamburger meat they buy is not tainted by dangerous bacteria.

The Food and Drug Administration's testing requirements for new medical drugs will be drastically curtailed. The drugs will go on sale, and over time the marketplace will decide whether they are safe and effective. Of course ordinary people cannot know whether meat is poisoned or new drugs are safe. So the consequence of reducing regulation will be that more people will die: more children especially. As it is, five million Americans a year get sick from tainted meat, and 4,000 die.

The victims of damaging drugs or bad food will also find it much harder to sue for damages, because of civil law "reforms" now going through Congress. So will the victims of securities fraud.

The new America will be a more divided society. Income disparities, already the greatest in the developed world, will increase as the tax code is changed to benefit the rich. The development of an elite class, living in protected areas and attending its own schools, will be accelerated. The dangerous division between black and white will be exacerbated. There will be no more efforts to bring the deprived children of the ghetto into mainstream America.

Crime will have grown even as authorities made the criminal law ever harsher. Prisoners, deprived of the hope that used to be given by the chance for education, will be more desperate—and prisons more violent schools for crime.

Elements of the safety net that now keeps the poor from utter destitution and hunger will be gone. School lunches, nutrition support for poor pregnant women and other such programs will have been abandoned or transferred to the states. And with states competing in tax reduction, many will drop the programs.

It will be a country with strikingly fewer areas of natural serenity and beauty. Old-growth forests will be clear-cut, and logging trails bulldozed through national wilderness areas. Controls protecting sensitive areas will have been removed. Wetlands will shrink because the Government will be required to compensate owners for not developing them—and Congress will not appropriate the money. Grazing limits on Federal land used by ranchers will have been relaxed, and grassland will increasingly turn to dust bowls.

Air and water pollution, so strikingly reduced in the years before 1995, will have grown steadily worse as regulations were repealed by Congress or made unenforceable by interminable judicial review. Many species of fish and animals will have disappeared.

Is that grim vision of the American future a realistic one? Absolutely. The glimpses shown are only a few examples of the changes that will result from pending legislation. And the legislation will almost certainly pass unless President Clinton finds the backbone to veto it.

All this is being done, we are told, to liberate "the people"—to free us from domination by the Federal Government. So goes the battle-cry of ascendant right-wing populism. The truth is the opposite. What is being done is for the benefit not of the many but of an elite few: the chemical and tobacco and drug companies, the accountants and agribusinesses and financial houses that want freedom to make money without concern for the public health or welfare. They make the contributions, and they call the tune.

We are heading for the atomization of America. Radical Republicans are intent on destroying the power of the community, expressed through government, which makes modern industrial society bearable.

Jurisprudence

When commentators analyze contemporary legal issues, they often invoke philosophers and jurists of other ages. This author takes an impassioned look at contemporary problems. Is his perspective accurate?

Selfish Behavior To Blame for Chaos in Society
Charles R. Hosler, *Chapel Hill Herald*

In 1651 the English philosopher Thomas Hobbes published his great work "Leviathan" that offered a political philosophy that called for the abolition of civil insurrection through "adherence to the law," a basic requirement of a nation's political structure. Hobbes focused on the civil right of personal security, to be guaranteed by the state as long as individuals obeyed the law. Hobbes' theory has contributed to our present infatuation with "rights."

Later another Englishman, John Locke, offered a more lenient version of Hobbesian thought, wherein citizen devotion to the state was not always necessary. However, both Hobbes and Locke agreed that personal security was fundamental to safeguard individual rights within any society. Scholars seem to agree that Locke's influence on America's Founding Fathers and the early colonists was profound, as reflected in the language of the Declaration of Independence, Constitution and Bill of Rights.

England's great jurist Sir William Blackstone synthesized the theories of Hobbes and Locke by listing three principal rights that the Estate must pre-

Copyright © 1995 by the Durham Herald Co. *Chapel Hill Herald,* May 13, 1995, p.4. Reprinted with permission. The writer is a retired meteorologist who worked for the Environmental Protection Agency.

serve: personal security, personal liberty and private property. Of these, Blackstone insisted that personal security, which "consists in a person's legal and uninterrupted enjoyment of his life, his limbs, his body, his health and his reputation," is the most important for the state to provide. Blackstone's masterful synthesis of British common law, contained in his "Commentaries on the Laws of England," sold in the colonies prior to the Constitutional Convention in 1787, had a major influence on American law, as expressed by James Madison, Alexander Hamilton and John Jay in the Federalist Papers.

Unfortunately, during the last half of this century America has disregarded the warnings of Hobbes, Locke, Blackstone and our Founding Fathers—all recognized that society cannot view all rights as created equal, since none take precedence over the primary right of personal security. In recent decades Americans have come to think that all individual rights should have equal demand; the public's lack of distinguishing between primary and secondary rights has led to a profound misunderstanding of government's most basic responsibility.

Today our conception of rights is primarily the result of our Supreme Court that, through its liberal interpretation of the Constitution, has written hundreds of new rights into law that have enhanced egoism, resulting in the weakening of the right of personal security. When the rights of the accused were expanded, the police and courts lost some of their traditional methods of keeping the peace; judicial interpretation of the Eighth Amendment's proscription of cruel and unusual punishment has contributed to greater instability of our prisons. The disregard of personal security, for a substitution of individual rights by our judges and juries, has been documented by Andrew Peyton Thomas in his 1994 book, "Crime and the Sacking of America." Thomas provides ample documentation that our government's failure to ensure personal security has been a major factor in contributing to our rising crime rate in recent decades.

America has become a nation obsessed with individual rights, infecting both liberal and conservative ideologies. Our country, state, community, yes, even our families, have disintegrated into factions of self-interested individuals who care little about the concerns for others and have little regard for the law. The flight of adults from family responsibilities exemplifies our society's egotistical sickness. Today, almost everything that our society does, sees, hears or reads encourages selfishness, directly or indirectly; these encourage crime, the most extreme form of selfishness.

Unfortunately, we have placed the blame for our increased crime on inanimate and impersonal things, such as guns, drugs, poverty, environment, etc. This is a copout, since any real soul-searching would reveal that our present social chaos results from our selfish values that we as a people have adopted in recent decades. Crime has grown because a majority of Americans are concerned primarily with their economic interests.

Even in a democracy, when a majority of its citizens are unwilling to obey the law, that nation cannot survive. While civilization was created to constrain egoism, Western philosophy and history has taught us that civilization cannot be fostered without religion, which will continue to be our most important means of criminal control. No amount of money or rights can appease or mend the souls of criminals. Accordingly, we must begin to resist the current denigration of religion and religious values by our society's opinion leaders—academia, media, entertainment industry, public schools and even our Supreme Court. As Andrew Peyton Thomas said, "We must again know what it is like to worship something more sublime than ourselves."

Legal History

We can all take pride in our legal traditions, as demonstrated by this celebration of a court's 300th anniversary.

Rotunda Shows History of the Supreme Court
Norman Goodman, *New York Law Journal*

On May 6, 1991, we celebrate the 300th anniversary of the New York Supreme Court, the oldest continuously sitting trial court in the United States. As an institution, it is 85 years older than the nation itself. Steeped in tradition and visionary in law, this court traces its roots back to our Anglo-Saxon origins. As Franklin Delano Roosevelt wrote on the occasion of the Court's 250th birthday in May 1941, "In the days of the early beginnings of the Court, there was practically no other place, except England and some of the British Colonies, where justice, in any form approaching our modern concept of the term, was freely administered. A judicial system free from domination by the Crown, more or less open to all who might seek to enter—where judgments were rendered by one's peers rather than by political rulers—was virtually then unknown except in the Anglo-Saxon world."

The Supreme Court of Judicature, its original name, was created by an act of the Assembly of the Province of New York passed on May 6, 1991, so that all inhabitants " . . . may have all the good, proper, and just ways and means for the securing and recovering their just rights and Demands. . . . " It was composed of five justices appointed by the governor with a quorum consisting of the Chief Justice and two Associate Justices. It met only in

Copyright © 1991 by the New York Law Publishing Co. *New York Law Journal,* May 6, 1991, p.S-6. Norman Goodman is the County Clerk and Clerk of the Supreme Court, New York County.

New York City Hall on the first Tuesday of April and October and could hear and try both civil and criminal actions.

Chief Judge of the Court of Appeals Irving Lehman on the occasion of the 250th anniversary of the court said that "the Supreme Court of New York . . . has been open continuously to all who sought protection for their rights and liberties . . . and has measured rights and administered justice in accordance with the ancient traditions, rules and practices of the common law of England brought to the Colony in the 17th Century and developed here to meet new conditions and new problems. . . . " This synopsis, eloquently stated by Judge Lehman, is reflected and copiously documented in over 70,000 cubic feet of records deposited in the Office of the New York County Clerk.

First Session

The Court opened its first session on Oct. 6, 1691 at the Stadt Huys (the first City Hall) with Chief Justice Joseph Dudley presiding. The minutes of this first session, now on display in the rotunda of the New York County Courthouse, were badly damaged over the years, but through private funding a professional conservator was hired and the remaining portions of the manuscript saved. The business of the first days were both civil and criminal, and the practices and procedures of the Court were established. In fact, Dudley realized that this Court would Americanize in some fashion the English laws for he wrote "We must not think the laws of England follow us to the ends of the earth." Unfortunately, he could not remain Chief Justice. Alas, he was a Massachusetts resident who refused to relocate to New York and, thus failing to meet this early residency requirement, had to give up his office.

With England 3,000 miles away and practicing a policy of "salutary neglect" towards her colonies, the Supreme Court of Judicature began to exercise a degree of independence from the Crown and the royal governors. Cases were heard and decisions rendered which reaffirmed colonial rights in opposition to the governor. In 1735, as clearly recorded in the Supreme Court minutes of the day, a New York jury found John Peter Zenger "not guilty" of libel in printing pamphlets criticizing the governor and his policies. This precedent-setting decision resulted in "freedom of the press" begin affirmed in our First Amendment. A further search of our records, many of them in the shape of rolled animal skin parchments, finds the case of Forcey v. Cunningham N.Y. Sup.Ct. Minute Book 1763 in which the justices ruled that a jury's determination of fact cannot be reviewed by an appeals court.

Therefore, the Revolutionary leaders who met in Kingston in April 1777 to establish a permanent state government did not express dissatisfaction with the courts. The first state constitution provided for the continuation of the Supreme Court and the enforcement of the laws in effect up until then. An examination of our minute books for this Court show this continuity. Only minor changes such as the substitution of the phrase "State of New

York" for "Province of New York" and the introduction of dating records since the year of independence can be found. Overall, the format and legal practices remained the same.

The Legal Community

The legal community who practiced in the court also produced many of the leaders of the state and nation during the early national period. John Jay, a prominent New York lawyer and supporter of the Revolution, was appointed the first Chief Justice of the New York Supreme Court. Eventually, John Jay would be named by George Washington as the first Chief Justice of the U.S. Supreme Court. Jay was only one of many attorneys and judges of the state Supreme Court who assumed this leadership role. An inspection of our roll of attorneys admitted to practice before the court reads as an honor roll of luminaries that helped shape our future. On this scroll will be found Alexander Hamilton, Aaron Burr, Henry Brockholst Livingston, Richard Varick, DeWitt Clinton, Egbert Benson (New York's first Attorney General) and others. They practiced extensively in the court and the many cases in which they were involved both as litigants and attorneys can be found in the Archives of the County Clerk. The authors of the multi-volume works on the legal careers of John Jay, Alexander Hamilton and Aaron Burr used these records extensively. . . .

New State Constitution

In 1846, a new state constitution shortened the official name of the court to "Supreme Court," but as our records show, this had already been a common practice among judges, clerks and attorneys for years. In addition, the Court of Chancery was abolished in the state and its equity jurisdiction was assumed by the Supreme Court. Divorce, among other equity matters, now became part of the jurisdiction of this court.

Our court, during the turbulent era prior to the Civil War, can take pride in that it dealt with the slavery question in a direct, forthright way. In 1852, a New York Supreme Court judge freed eight slaves who had escaped while being transferred from Virginia to Texas. In his ruling which can be read on our records People v. Lemmon 20 NY 562, the judge ignored the federal fugitive slave statutes on the basis that, under natural law, New York State's laws were sufficient to deny the former owner a right to the possession of slaves in this state. This ruling in the case was upheld on appeal.

The court continued to remain the protector to whom people turned in defense of their rights. During 1909, in the matter of In Re Mary Mallon (a.k.a. Typhoid Mary) N.Y. Sup.Ct., N.Y. Ct. Cl. WRM258, a writ of Habeas Corpus was sought from the court for her release from confinement in Riverside Hospital. The New York City Department of Health had determined that she was a typhoid carrier since wherever she worked, an epidemic had broken out. Fortunately, Supreme Court Justice Mitchell Erlanger, after examining the medical evidence and affidavits in her file, as can any research today, denied the request. Once freed by the Department of Health after repeated assurances that she would not work with food, Mary Mallon returned to her avocation as a cook. Typhoid again broke out and she was reconfined for the rest of her life to Riverside Hospital.

In 1916, seeking relief from censorship Theodore Dreiser brought suit against his publisher for withdrawing from publication his novel The Genius. The Society to Suppress Vice claimed the book was obscene. The Supreme Court sided with the author in Dreiser v. Lane 183 App. Div. 773.

Even international issues reach the New York Supreme Court. In 1986, the Philippine government of Corazon Aquino brought an action against former President Ferdinand Marcos and his associates to prevent them from selling property they owned in Manhattan in Philippines v. Marcos N.Y. Sup.Ct., N.Y. Ct. Cl. 4476/86. The Philippine government claimed that this property was purchased with money allegedly embezzled by Marcos from the government. The filings in the case were numerous and the affidavits copious before the case was eventually moved to the federal court.

In 1988, the court was even called upon to decide who had won the America's Cup. The Mercury Bay Boating Club of New Zealand claimed that the San Diego Yacht Club had fielded an ineligible craft in the competition. The litigation was voluminous and protracted but eventually the San Diego claim was upheld in Mercury Bay Boating Club v. San Diego Yacht Club 76 NY2d 256.

Fifty years ago, the distinguished attorney John W. Davis said of the New York Supreme Court that it " . . . stands watch upon the ramparts to guard the rights and liberties of the people of the State of New York. Long may it live!" We reach that proclamation. The proud history of the Supreme Court so minutely documented in our records, reflects the dedication of the judges, attorneys and court personnel, together with the people of the State of New York in seeking a just society.

Comparative Law

Diverse cultures approach similar legal issues in dramatically different ways, as indicated in this comparison of the law in the United States, the United Kingdom, and the European Economic Community.

Trap Lies in Superficial Similarity
A. H. Hermann, *Financial Times*

Three legal systems meet in London, both historically and geographically. Institutions imported by the U.S. from England have been modified by continental influences and by the exigencies of a rapidly developing dynamic society. English law and the machinery of justice, although sticking to the traditional paraphernalia of law in dress and in procedure, has also been changing to meet the needs of world-wide commerce and, more recently, to absorb the law of the European Communities, based on civil law concepts. The obvious differences are no great obstacle; it is the superficial similarity disguising fundamental divergence of approach which creates dangerous pitfalls for the foreign lawyer and his clients.

To start with, the constitutional setting is all different. In England the supremacy of Parliament is absolute (and there is no dichotomy between Parliament and a majority Government) and the judges cannot reject laws because they seem to them contrary to the constitution or a fundamental principle of law. In the U.S. by contrast, the decision of every issue important for the individual or the nation can be ultimately sought in courts of law. To a large extent the U.S. seems to be ruled by judges who can review the acts of legislature for conformity with the constitution, and are often filling in the gaps, if President and Congress cannot agree. In continental Europe judicial review is more specialised. There are, as a rule, separate administrative courts for dealing with the citizen's complaint of the decisions taken by the executive, and one constitutional court which has the monopoly of dealing with complaints that an act of Parliament infringes constitutional principles or fundamental laws.

The European Communities generate law which has precedence over that of member states. In its peculiar system the European Parliament has only a consultative role, and legislation is thrashed out by the Commission supposed to represent the collectivity and the Council composed of ministers representing member states.

Copyright © 1985 by The Financial Times Ltd. *Financial Times*, July 15, 1985, §I, p.10. Reprinted with permission.

There is a striking difference between the continental and the UK judiciary. While in the UK judges are selected from barristers (or advocates in Scotland) who reached the top of their profession, in continental Europe lawyers join the judicial service at the beginning of their career, and the most able work their way up to the top. This has several important consequences. There are practically no junior career judges in England. All minor criminal cases are decided by magistrates, and most of the commercial disputes are decided by arbitrators. The political influences on the selection of judges can come into play on the continent only when judges are promoted to the top posts. In England they are discreetly present right from the beginning of the judge's career.

Things are very different in the U.S. Federal judges are as a rule appointed for life by the executive after screening and approval by Congress. The higher the appointment is the more it is exposed to party politics. The appointment of judges of individual states is very much in the hands of the governor. In the majority of states judges are elected for fixed periods from six to fifteen years. In a minority of states they are merely confirmed by the legislature. The general tendency seems to be to re-elect or confirm for the following period. Whoever is in the control of the executive, both federal and state, may have an important lever in the appointment of chief judges. In addition, many lower courts seem to be exposed to the influence of the smaller territorial units on which they depend for their budgets and often for the enforcement of their decision. The court's clerk seems to have an importance unknown in England or Europe, maintaining good relations between the court and the local bar, administration and political factions.

The source of law, the drafting of statutes and their interpretation, also differ greatly. The case law retains its original function in England, where there is a great reluctance to codify, although the proliferation of decisions makes the selection of precedents more arbitrary and the results less certain. The avalanche of precedental decisions issuing from the appellate courts of the U.S. has made it necessary to streamline common law by a selection of leading cases and by restatements of law—in both respects the influence of academic thinking and legal logic is strong. The purposive interpretation of both common law and statutes leads to a greater readiness to abdicate from the specific functions of a lawyer, as conceived in England, in favour of policy-making based on the results of other disciplines—economic, sociology and psychiatry, for example. In this respect continental Europe and the U.S. are closer to each other than they are to England.

Procedure too could not be more different. While on the continent the judge is in firm control of the proceedings which are mainly written, the English judge still thinks of himself as an umpire leaving all initiative to the parties in dispute who are virtually free to determine the pace of the proceedings which are almost entirely oral. In the U.S. they seem to have a mixture of the two. The adversary system flourishes, but written proceedings replace oral proceedings as one ascends the hierarchy of the courts, and in the appellate courts the presiding judge will actuate a red light after 30 minutes to stop the attorney's speech-making—a device very much missed in English courts.

These different legal cultures breed different legal professions. The absence of codification and the predominantly oral procedure help to perpetuate in the UK a divided profession, where solicitors hold the client by the hand and do most of the writing, while barristers and advocates talk to court and "think on their feet." Both leave it to the accountants and merchant bankers to provide corporate clients with the global and strategic guidance which a U.S. corporation expects from its lawyers, who also do the lobbying and law compliance work for them. The continental law firms are only learning, but have a better start because theirs is not a divided profession. This, and their greater familiarity with multi-national business corporations opens great opportunities for U.S. law firms in Europe.

Chapter 2

Dispute Resolution

Alternative Dispute Resolution

Voir Dire

Expert Witnesses

Alternative Dispute Resolution

Alternative dispute resolution is a thriving business. What parties have a vested interest in litigation? In alternative dispute resolution?

A Kinder, Cheaper Route to Justice
John H. Kennedy, *Boston Globe*

Soothing seascapes hang on the walls and turquoise carpet is underfoot. In conference rooms named for peacemakers Martin Luther King Jr., Gandhi and Ralph Bunche, business enemies settle into comfortable chairs to settle their disputes. Here, at the Boston office of Endispute Inc. and at other private companies like it, you can see the face of a kinder, gentler—not to mention an often quicker, cheaper—justice. No gritty courthouses, Dickensian delays, surly bureaucrats and scorched-earth litigation. Companies like Endispute, as opposed to the public courts, aim to get combatants to say "yes" rather than to pursue what can be costly, public and sometimes traumatic verdicts.

Alternative dispute resolution [ADR], of which mediation and arbitration are key pieces, has arrived. ADR companies lay claim to helping foment a quiet revolution in the legal industry. They plan to become to the civil justice system what Federal Express is to the Postal Service. And now some of the national companies, including Endispute, are considering taking their companies public within the next year or two. In fact, over the next decade, mediation and arbitration could cut in half the millions of lawsuits filed by Americans annually, said James Henry, president of the Center for Public Resources, a nonprofit group that promotes ADR for business and public disputes. "That, I don't think, is a fantasy. It's a real prospect," said Henry. "It has commenced to chip away.

But the fledgling industry has not been without critics, growth pains and uncertainty. Some say a private system will drain the public courts of support and resources, setting up a better brand of justice for those who can pay. "I worry about this," said Frank E. A. Sander, a Harvard law professor and ADR guru. "I'd like to see more people of goodwill, power and influence help to improve the public justice system instead of devoting so much energy into developing private alternatives."

There appear to be only a handful of national players in the business at the moment. The largest and oldest is the American Arbitration Association, a New York-based nonprofit group founded in 1926. It offers a range of

Copyright © 1993 by the Globe Newspaper Co. *Boston Globe*, Dec. 26, 1993, p.81. Reprinted courtesy of The Boston Globe.

ADR services, but has historically relied on arbitration, in which one party typically wins. Three other for-profit companies appear to be positioning themselves as practitioners of the more flexible mediation, in which a "neutral" attempts to bring parties to an amicable agreement that is nonbinding:

- California-based Judicial Arbitration & Mediation Service Inc. calls itself the biggest for-profit private provider, with an estimated $30 million in revenue. It relies on 275 former judges in 21 offices to provide its ADR services, said John P. Unroe, president and chief executive.
- Endispute Inc., with about $10 million in revenue, is based in Washington, but has its biggest office in Boston. It uses judges, lawyers and nonlawyer mediators. Founded in the early 1980s by Jonathan B. Marks and Eric D. Green, a Boston University law professor, Endispute established a larger West Coast beachhead this month by merging with San Francisco-based Bates Edwards Group.
- Seattle-based US Arbitration & Mediation Inc. has 43 offices in the United States, including Boston. While its revenue is between $6 million and $7 million, it touts broader coverage than Endispute and Judicial Arbitration & Mediation, with local offices that are often franchises. "It gives ownership on the local level and has worked well," said Michael S. Gillie, executive director who owns a majority share of the company.

Of course, ADR is not a panacea. Mediations and arbitrations break down, and the parties head to the courts for a ruling. In addition, ADR is not the proper place for a variety of disputes, including civil rights cases and constitutional questions. In fact, some critics say the behind-closed-doors nature of ADR slows the evolution of the law, which relies on decisions by public juries and judges.

But the private companies are unabashedly optimistic about ADR and its place in the legal landscape. (The three big for-profit companies project growth ranging from 20 percent to 30 percent in 1994.) At times, they sound like enthusiastic practitioners of a new religion. "Today, even the most ardent died-in-the-wool traditionalist concedes that ADR has taken over," Green said.

To gain clients, and credibility, private ADR firms are turning increasingly to retired judges. In Massachusetts, Endispute uses a half-dozen, including James P. Lynch Jr., a respected jurist and former chief of the Superior Court. Perhaps a dozen others are working in mediation for smaller companies, including former Superior Court Judge Paul G. Garrity, one of the first Massachusetts judges to jump into for-profit ADR. And that doesn't include vast number of lawyers and mediators, both privately and in government, who work in smaller operations.

Lynch, who left the bench when he reached mandatory retirement age of

70 in 1991, now serves as a mediator, special master and arbitrator for Endispute. He relishes the flexibility he never had as a judge, often using an informal, friendly style to find common ground. And at times he is asked to bluntly assess the merits of a case. "You can bring a dash of objectivity—a reality check—to the process for the first time," said Lynch, sipping coffee in the Alva Myrdal room, named after the 1982 winner of the Nobel Peace Prize.

There is even catharsis. While litigants often face years and hundreds of thousands of dollars of legal expenses before they get their cases before a judge and jury, within weeks they often sit across the table from those they feel wronged them. (The large providers say their services run between $200 to $400 per hour.) During a recent mediation, Lynch turned to a libel plaintiff and asked him whether he had anything to say. Across the table was a top official from a New England newspaper. "He talked for 45 minutes, nonstop," said Lynch. "After that, the case was settled in a few hours. Simply because he could tell the editor what he thought." Adds Ericka B. Gray, a senior mediator at Endispute: "This is the only field where I've ever heard of someone getting a thank-you note from all sides. I've never heard of that in litigation. I've never heard of that in the courts."

The ability of the private companies to sell their services to the insurance industry has helped fuel growth. But other large companies are turning to ADR to settle disputes, as a method to cut legal costs. "We actively consider it in each and every piece of litigation we have, because the transaction costs of litigation are so incredibly high," said Jack Douglas, general counsel of Reebok International Ltd., the Stoughton footwear company. "It would be irresponsible not to pursue a lower cost method to resolve disputes."

But private providers like the American Arbitration Association, Endispute, Judicial Arbitration & Mediation and US Arbitration probably won't be alone in the array of providers. Courts, while captive to erratic public funding, have reacted to the private services and promise to take a more visible role. They are also concerned about getting co-opted. (In fact, they were jolted last year when a private provider asked to rent courtroom space in Cambridge on Saturdays.)

Massachusetts courts use ADR, although the programs vary from county to county. The Supreme Judicial Court his month appointed an ADR panel to help the court develop standards for its own programs, and look at the relationship between the courts and private providers. "How this whole thing will shake out among these giants, like Endispute and JAMS, is very hard to predict," said Sander, the Harvard professor who is vice chair of the new panel. "If the public system ever got up to speed, it might well reduce the demand in the private system."

Another brake on the industry's growth could be a move to regulate private mediators. Currently, virtually anyone can hold himself out as a mediator.

Lawyers and law firms, part of the problem for an advocacy system that is too slow and expensive for many litigants, want to be part of the solution. Lawyer Gordon T. Walker nearly started his own ADR business before joining the Boston office of McDermott Will & Emery, the large national firm based in Chicago. He says lawyers should be doing more than just advise clients about ADR and help them through the process. Law firms themselves should provide "neutral" services—as arbitrators and mediators—just as Judicial Arbitration & Mediation and Endispute do. "Law firms should be players," says Walker. "Not only do law firms have the litigation expertise, they also have business expertise. They have persons who are very much acquainted with problems of specific industries or businesses."

While Endispute and JAMS have an eye toward taking their companies public, there is no certainty of success. They need only look to another ADR company called Judicate Inc., based in Philadelphia. Judicate went public in 1985, but its stock has floundered. Its experience raises the question whether such an ADR company can support a large and expensive administrative staff necessary for publicly traded companies.

"The issue is can you commit millions of dollars on the marketing side and create any sort of return for outside investors?" asked one industry official, who spoke on the condition he would not be identified. "The one concrete model we have of that is Judicate. But at the moment they don't see much tangible benefit." Judicate, the official said, has been able to tap into the "McJustice" end of the business—smaller disputes, with lower profit margins—but hasn't made dramatic inroads into the "gourmet" market—the larger, more complex cases. Company officials did not return several telephone calls.

Of course, success of any large company depends on how well it explains its product and, more importantly, why people need it. "I think the biggest hurdle is there isn't anyone else like us out there," said Unroe of Judicial Arbitration & Mediation. "If you are an investor and trying to understand what this is like, there is no category to put us in. And the other biggest hurdle? To understand the value it brings."

Voir Dire

Some observers claim that permitting too many peremptory challenges during the *voir dire* gives an advantage to a party that can outspend its opponent.

Ideal Juror for O. J. Simpson: Football Fan Who Can Listen
David Margolick, New York Times

Men rather than women, black men if possible. Older people rather than younger. Discerning rather than deferential. Shepherds rather than sheep, football buffs rather than football widows, fans of "L.A. Law" rather than "NYPD Blue." And though there are no longer any blank slates when it comes to O. J. Simpson—"If you get people who don't know anything about this case, they must be total idiots," Gerry Spence, the high-profile defense lawyer, remarked—it's better that they get their news from "MacNeil/Lehrer" or Newsweek than "Geraldo!" or Star.

Among lawyers and jury consultants that is the consensus prescription for Mr. Simpson's ideal juror, the type his legal team should seek on Monday, when jury selection in the case is scheduled to begin. Yesterday, the judge in the case described news organizations as "irresponsible" and said they were disseminating incorrect and "prejudicial" information to the public.

Jury selection, experts agree, is perhaps the crucial phase of the case—matched, said Roy M. Black, a prominent defense lawyer in Miami, only by Mr. Simpson's potential appearance on the stand. "Everything else in the case is not even in the same universe," said Mr. Black, who successfully defended William Kennedy Smith against rape charges in 1991. "You've got to put people on the jury who are willing to listen to what he has to say."

But these rules of thumb on jury selection in this case, while widely shared, are by no means universally held. Jury selection remains one of the last refuges of ethnic, racial and sexual stereotypes, a process in which political correctness has no place. In deciding who will decide Mr. Simpson's fate, however, these stereotypes are often contradictory.

Women, particularly white women, particularly those who know bad marriages or abuse, may be more likely to empathize with the slain mother of two small children, but they could also be more likely to fall in love with a dashing male defendant. Blacks may be more wary of law enforcement,

Copyright © 1994 by The New York Times Co. *New York Times,* Sep. 23, 1994, §A, p.1, col. 5. Reprinted with permission.

more inclined to think that Mr. Simpson was set up. But they may be just as inclined to resent such assumptions and assert their independence.

Law-and-order types may favor the prosecution, but they, more than others, could be offended by what the defense has characterized as bungling by the Los Angeles Police Department. Younger jurors may be more conservative than the aging alumni of Woodstock Nation, more inclined to see Mr. Simpson as huckster and hack actor than hero, but their minds are supple enough to attend to tedious testimony, and thereby spot cracks in the state's case. So would more intelligent jurors, but too much scientific sophistication may make them easily dazzled by the results of DNA tests.

"Anyone who tries to sell you on the idea that jury selection is a science is jerking your chain," said Robert Hirschhorn, a jury consultant in Galveston, Tex., and co-author of a leading text on the subject. "What you're trying to do is match your client, your case and your lawyer with your juror. At best, it's 20 percent science, 80 percent art."

In a sense, "jury selection" is a misnomer. It is more a matter of de-selection, damage control, forensic triage. Each side may challenge an unlimited number of candidates as being biased, but only 20 without explanation—so-called peremptory challenges. "You're not selecting people but eliminating those you find offensive," said Gerry Goldstein of San Antonio, president of the National Association of Criminal Defense Lawyers. "What you get is what's left over, the people who don't tell you very much."

Neither side is sparing any expense. The defense team, led by Robert L. Shapiro, has brought in Jo-Ellan Dimitrius of Pasadena, Calif., a veteran of the Rodney G. King, Reginald O. Denny and McMartin Preschool cases. The Los Angeles District Attorney's office has retained Decision Quest of Los Angeles, which assisted Pennzoil in its celebrated battle against Texaco.

To lawyers like Mr. Spence, it is a waste of money. Lawyers, he believes, can do the job just as well using little more than instinct. "I don't care whether jurors are rich or poor, black or white, male or female, old or young or what they do," he said. "I want to know if it's someone I can bare my soul to, someone who will listen to me, someone I can be a friend to, or if it's some cynic or jerk who's full of hate."

But to Mr. Black, it is money well spent. Because the case is so extraordinary, he said, all conventions about picking jurors are inapplicable. Candidates must be asked the standard questions—about the people they admire, the books they read, the television programs they watch, the bumper stickers on their cars—plus others particular to the Simpson case: their views on interracial marriage, for example. They must also be asked questions about particular evidence, arguments or personalities in the case that emerge only by staging simulated trials before focus groups or mock juries, as the defense has presumably been doing and the prosecution did earlier this month in Arizona—much to its chagrin when word of the panel's distaste for the prosecutor, Marcia Clark, and her case leaked out.

Just what all those questions will be, and who will ask them, remains to be determined. Both sides have submitted proposed jury questionnaires to Judge Lance A. Ito, highlighting the queries they deem most important. After consulting with counsel, he will amalgamate the two, and ask those candidates for whom three to six months of jury duty would not impose a disabling hardship to fill out the resulting form.

In many states, lawyers conduct the questioning process known as *voir dire* themselves. They use it not only to select jurors but also to establish rapport with potential panelists and lay out their cases. To the dismay of defense lawyers, who believe that by asking open-ended, touchy-feely questions, they plumb subterranean psychological strata that judges miss, a California law adopted by referendum four years ago authorizes courts to question jurors entirely by themselves. But state law also authorizes judges to let the lawyers take part should the lawyers demonstrate "a significant possibility of bias because of the nature of the case or its participants." Judge Ito is expected to allow both sides to participate to some degree. For each it could be critical: for the prosecution, because a single Simpson sympathizer can produce a hung jury; for the defense, because of the need to ferret out subtle, pro-prosecution biases.

Mr. Hirschhorn and Mr. Black said Ms. Clark should seek out female jurors. "Women are more likely to bond with a female prosecutor and more likely to be sympathetic to the abuse angle of the case, particularly if they've had any problems with men—and there are very few who haven't," Mr. Black said. But Linda A. Fairstein, chief of the sex crimes prosecution unit of the Manhattan District Attorney's office and the prosecutor in the Robert Chambers "preppie murder" case, strenuously disagreed. "In general, and across all racial borders, when the defendant is attractive, articulate and a celebrity, women more than men tend, unfortunately, to base their verdict on external appearances," Ms. Fairstein said. "It's one of the saddest lessons I've learned in doing this work." Female jurors, she added, tend to judge female victims harshly, a factor that could prove crucial in this case, where the defense is expected to depict Nicole Brown Simpson as a habitué of life's fast lane.

Mr. Hirschhorn joined Mr. Fairstein in also challenging the widely held notion that black jurors, feeling kinship with Mr. Simpson and disdain for the white establishment, would favor the defense. "If that's what the defense is thinking, O. J.'s going to go from Hall of Fame to the halls of San Quentin," Mr. Hirschhorn said. "African-Americans become leaders when other blacks are on trial, and they may very well judge them more harshly."

Mr. Black advised the defense to stay away from young jurors. "People who went through the 1960s are probably a lot better, and older people would know O. J. better," he said. "To people in their 20s, O. J. is ancient history." Ms. Fairstein thought the prosecution should stay away from younger jurors as well, but for different reasons. "Young jurors have trouble putting people behind bars for a long incarceration," she said. "And young jurors tend to waffle. They're not leaders in the jury room."

However long it lasts and however much they may participate, the *voir dire* will provide the lawyers a chance to shape—or reshape—their images. Ms. Clark, for example, can humanize herself, Mr. Hirschhorn said, thereby avoiding the fate of Moira K. Lasch, the wooden, icy and ultimately unsuccessful prosecutor in the William Kennedy Smith rape case. And if he were defense counsel, Mr. Hirschhorn said, he might want to abolish some of the polish. "I'd be a little worried about coming across as slick," he said. "I would not wear double-breasted suits, I would not wear a shirt of any color other than white or blue, I'd stay away from the power collars, cuff links, tie bars and pinkie rings."

Expert Witnesses

Expert witnesses are common in trial. Do they provide useful information or do they supplant the jury?

Courts' Call for Experts on the Rise; Complexity of Cases Fueling the Demand
Paul Langner, *Boston Globe*

They are the hired guns of the court scene, the expert witnesses called to explain complex matters to juries and judges. Lawyers find them indispensable, and they are becoming more so as scientific testimony becomes more subtle and technical. Expert witnesses, said attorney John J. Bonistalli, who has handled the defense in some prominent criminal cases, "can be incredibly useful to your side of the case. They can help the jury understand things beyond their own experience or their own ability to evaluate." And, said John C. McBride, a criminal attorney, "criminal law is getting more complicated, and there is going to be a need for more expert witnesses."

A criminal trial can become a duel of expert witnesses, as was shown during the recently concluded murder trial of David Azar in Middlesex Superior Court. Azar, 34, was convicted on July 28 of second-degree murder in the killing of his daughter, Geneva, who died after her head was slammed against a hard surface in her home last Nov. 27. During the two-week trial, two medical expert witnesses called by Assistant District Attorney Elizabeth Keeley—

Copyright © 1989 by the Globe Newspaper Co. *Boston Globe,* Aug. 6, 1989, p.25. Reprinted courtesy of The Boston Globe.

state medical examiner Dr. Joanne Richmond and child abuse specialist Dr. Paul K. Kleinman—testified that the evidence convinced them that the girl had battered child syndrome and shaken infant syndrome, and that her injuries could have come only from being slammed "willfully" into a hard surface. Two medical expert witnesses called by defense attorney Robert A. George—Rhode Island medical examiner Dr. William Sturner and former New York City medical examiner Dr. Michael Baden—said that the same evidence convinced them that the injuries could have been inflicted accidentally.

Criminal trials can turn on how believable the expert witnesses are, defense attorneys say, but prosecutors are less certain. One is more likely to see expert witnesses in civil trials, where, civil attorneys say, everything may hinge on how believable an expert witness has been. Criminal prosecutors usually affect detachment when asked how valuable expert witnesses are. Said Assistant Middlesex District Attorney David Meier, "They're important, no question. But I wouldn't say a case hinges on experts. It all depends what the experts testify to. It depends on the subject matter. If it is strictly forensic evidence, yes, that makes a big difference. But if it is, say, psychiatric evidence, I don't think it does."

Most expert witnesses have to recite their qualifications under questioning, and the opposing attorney may introduce evidence that the witness is not qualified. The judge makes the determination. In a few cases, attorneys may acknowledge the witness' expertise to save time. For example, in cases such as that of Dr. George Katsas, who reckons his autopsies and court appearances in the thousands, defense attorneys often say, "I stipulate to Dr. Katsas' expertise," saving the hour it would take to recite the septuagenarian's qualifications.

And what of the juries for whose benefit the expert witnesses are brought into a case? Judges give jurors a short speech before that witness testifies, to the effect that even though the witness has been qualified as an expert, the jurors are free to believe all of his or her testimony, none of it or some of it. From what can be learned from those jurors who talk after a verdict has been brought in, they are prepared to be convinced, but don't always end up accepting everything an expert witness says.

In the Azar trial, for example, juror A. Leo Silvestrini said afterward that the jurors had difficulty believing Baden, who testified for the defense, because, Silvestrini said, Baden could not tell the child's cause of death. This same point was brought out by Dr. Brian Blackbourne Friday during the WBZ-TV program "People Are Talking," when he asked Baden what he thought the cause of death was if not blunt trauma to the head. Baden, taking part in the show by telephone link, said it could not be determined from the evidence, and that he still felt the child may have died accidentally. This position provoked a condemnation from Dr. Eli Newberger, also a child abuse expert and specialist in family development. "I was concerned hearing such testimony of people with important reputations, one the Rhode Island state medical examiner and the other a former New York City medical examiner," said Newberger during an interview Friday. "I was concerned to see this group distort and pervert the clinical findings for the benefit of the defense who are paying them handsomely. This is very troubling."

Another juror for the Azar trial, speaking on condition of anonymity, said he and others put "a lot of weight on the doctors' testimony because that was the first hard evidence we had about what happened in that house that day." The two defense expert witnesses, he said, had the same evidence, "but it seemed as if they were funneling their testimony over into the side of the defense version of what happened. They seemed to have had the choice of saying it was a willful act or an accident and they chose to say it was an accident." This same juror said the jurors had been "most highly impressed with the testimony of Dr. Kleinman because he was the most professional sounding of the group and the most unbiased. At least it appeared that he had no ax to grind."

Richmond, the juror said, while offering "very credible testimony," was not as detached as Kleinman. While he "was trying to just give us the facts, this was not as true of Dr. Richmond, who had a point of view, almost an ax to grind." However, some courtroom observers felt Richmond's testimony was restrained to the point of being passionless, while the younger Kleinman seemed to struggle to conceal his outrage, and barely succeeded.

Expert witnesses' testimony is expensive. A source close to the case said each of the two defense expert witnesses in the Azar trial were paid about $5,000. This is not out of the ordinary, says McBride. Between getting a doctor to review the evidence and having him testify, the bill usually runs between $2,500 and $5,000, he said. "Like with different lawyers, the fee will vary with the ability of the experts."

Sometimes the fee is increased by travel expenses, since it is rare that an expert witness is locally available. Courthouse folklore has it that the farther away the witness lives, the weaker the defense's case. And after all the expense and travel, the hired gun may backfire on the attorney. This happened in 1987 in the trial of Violet Amirault and her daughter, Cheryl Amirault LeFave, who were accused of sexually molesting children in the Fells Acres day-care center in Malden. Dr. Sherry L. Skidmore, a psychologist, had been flown in from Los Angeles by defense attorney Joseph Balliro to testify that children will fantasize about sex abuse, and that if they don't answer every time they are asked, that would show the abuse did not happen. On cross examination, the prosecutor, Laurence Hardoon, asked Skidmore if it wasn't true that children "clam up under pressure." Replied Skidmore, "I know of no research to substantiate that." "But," said Hardoon, "doesn't common sense tell you that this is so?" Said Skidmore, "I am not here to use common sense. I am here as an expert."

Prosecutors, too, may get answers they did not expect from their own expert witnesses. After laboriously questioning a young chemist about his qualifications, Assistant District Attorney Thomas Brennan asked him how many times he had testified in the courts of Massachusetts. Replied the visibly nervous chemist, "Approximately once."

Jurors are never told of facts about expert witnesses that may reduce their stature in the eyes of laymen who do not distinguish between the expert witness's expertise and his or her history or private life. Thus, the jury for the Azar trial never learned that Baden had been fired from the medical examiner's office for what a spokesman for Mayor Edward Koch called "a colorful and celebrity-studded history." He did not elaborate.

Chapter 3

Common Law, Statutory Law, and Administrative Law

Bystander Rule

Lobbyists

Administrative Agencies

Bystander Rule

When should the law require a bystander to act? The question gets no final answer—in civil *or* criminal law.

Why Alleged Onlookers to Rape Cannot Be Charged; Under Virginia, Maryland and D.C. Law, Standing By and Watching Is No Crime
Ruth Marcus, *Washington Post*

Fairfax County Prosecutor Robert F. Horan Jr. said his hands were tied. He said he found it "morally reprehensible" that four or five teen-agers would watch as a 15-year-old Fort Hunt High School student was raped in a school bathroom. But he said he could take no legal steps against the youths. "There is nothing to charge them with," Horan said Wednesday, when he announced that two other youths were being charged with rape in the Oct. 3 incident in which rape is alleged. "If the public wants that changed, the place to do that is the legislature, not the commonwealth's attorney's office," said Horan. Another man, Jeffrey Lewis, 19, was charged last month with abduction with intent to defile in the same case.

"I feel angry," Susan G. Wibker, a sexual assault therapist at the Fairfax County Victim Assistance Network, said of the onlookers' escape from legal liability. "It's a statement to the victim that it's nothing to make a big deal out of, it's not that important." The legal situation in Virginia is not unique. Under the law in Maryland, the District and all but three states, bystanders have no legal duty to step in to stop a crime—or even to pick up the phone to alert police.

"In our system of law, we're not our brother's keepers . . . ," said George Washington University law professor Gerald M. Caplan. "The common law has a cold, heartless quality to it." Law professors' favorite classroom example is that of the Olympic swimmer who sees a baby drowning in a shallow pool of water. Under the traditional American rule, derived from centuries of English law, the swimmer has no legal responsibility to rescue the child. "Conscripting people to do good runs against very strong traditions in the American legal system," said New York University Law School Professor David A. J. Richards, who favors a change in the law. "The law ends up really reinforcing the worst impulses of citizens."

Most European countries take a different approach. In West Germany,

Copyright © 1984 by The Washington Post. *Washington Post,* Nov. 16, 1984, p.D1. Reprinted with permission.

for example, a bystander can be sentenced to up to a year in prison for failure to render aid in an emergency situation where "he would not subject himself to any considerably danger" or violate another legal duty. "Just about every Western country has a duty-to-assist law," said Harold Takooshian, a Fordham University psychologist who has studied the problem of bystanders' inaction and organized a three-day conference earlier this year on the 20th anniversary of Kitty Genovese's murder. Genovese was stabbed to death outside her New York apartment building as 38 of her neighbors ignored her cries for help.

Until recently in this country, only Vermont had such a duty-to-assist law, imposing a $100 fine for failing "to reasonably assist" a person in grave danger. Last year, Rhode Island and Minnesota enacted similar laws, spurred by reports of the rape at Big Dan's tavern in New Bedford, Mass., where four men raped and sodomized a woman on the bar's pool table as the bartender and four patrons looked on. Two of those patrons were later charged with aggravated rape because prosecutors said they cheered the attackers on, but they were acquitted.

In Rhode Island, witnesses to a rape who fail to notify police immediately face fines of up to $500 and imprisonment for as long as one year. The Minnesota law provides a $100 penalty for failure to render "reasonable assistance" to anyone who is "exposed to or has suffered grave physical harm." It also allows victims of the crime to file civil damage suits against witnesses who failed to come to their aid. "It doesn't mean you have to jeopardize your own life, but at minimum you must call the police," said state Rep. Randy Staten, who sponsored the Minnesota measure. None of the three laws has yet been enforced, according to Takooshian. But, he said, they serve an important moral function simply by being on the books. "Once something becomes a law, that strengthens the moral statement," he said.

Not everyone favors such statutes, however. "It creates the danger of people who take desperate acts because they're afraid they'll be in trouble with the law," said Robert Kane, a prosecutor in the Big Dan's case. "To be a coward is not to be a criminal," he added. "There are some weak and timid people out there."

Whatever the legal situation, some social scientists suggest that the problem of bystander inaction is particularly prevalent in crimes such as rape. "When there's a man attacking or fighting with a woman, what bystanders generally do is make an assumption that the two people know each other," said R. Lance Shotland of Pennsylvania State University. "Once having decided that, they tend to say he's not really hurting her, she doesn't really want help."

Lobbyists

The chapter's discussion of "unseen players" focuses on lobbying in Washington. But lobbyists are active—with their checkbooks—in all state capitols as well.

Teachers Union Outspends Other Capitol Lobbyists

Tom Precious, *Times Union (Albany)*

Lobbying continued to be a growth industry in this city last year, with special-interest groups spending $39.1 million to influence policymakers, state officials said Wednesday. That's up from $38.5 million in 1993. Those totals, however, don't include the millions spent on lobbyists hired to try to win contracts from state agencies. Such information doesn't have to be disclosed under state law.

Lobbyist spending has risen each year since it began being tracked in 1978, the annual report by the state Temporary Commission on Lobbying shows. The New York State United Teachers checked in first among all special interests in money spent on lobbying, at $638,434. Wilson, Elser, Moskowitz, Edelman & Dicker, whose partners include former top Assembly aide Kenneth Shapiro, was the top lobbying firm, taking in nearly $2 million in fees.

Government watchdog groups, releasing their own statistics including how much special-interest groups spent on campaign contributions, said reforms are needed. "What we're saying is you [shouldn't] have to pony up millions of dollars to be a player in the political process," said Andrew Greenblatt, executive director of New York Common Cause.

Along with the New York Public Interest Research Group and the League of Women Voters, Common Cause said the top ten special-interest groups its so-called fat cats list spent more than $11 million to influence lawmakers and the governor during 1993 and 1994.

NYSUT also headed that list. Combining lobbying fees and campaign contributions, the groups said the teachers union spent $3.3 million in the two-year period on its Albany influencing operation. A hospital trade group was next, at $1.036 million, followed closely by the Public Employees Federation at $1.035 million and the Civil Service Employees Association at $977,000. The group's numbers, however, don't include individual contribu-

Copyright © 1995 by The Hearst Corp. *Times Union (Albany)*, March 16, 1995, p.B2. Reprinted with permission of the *Times Union*.

tions made by doctors or lawyers, for example, that would show more money being spent by those special interests.

Calling for such reforms as public financing of campaigns, the groups said money increasingly decides the fate of legislation. "We now see a rather perverse form of democracy by the highest bidder," said Barbara Bartoletti, a lobbyist with the League of Women Voters. Pointing to a weak anti-smoking bill approved last year, Bartoletti recalled that lawmakers opened their doors to industry lobbyists.

Lobbyists, not surprisingly, took a different view. In fact, last year's top lobbying firm went so far as to put out a press release boasting of its showing. The Wilson, Elser firm said it succeeds "because of the respect we have for those who serve, regardless of political affiliation, and the high standards to which we hold ourselves."

Milton Mollen, the lobbying agency commissioner, said that tight state budgets lead to an increase in lobbying expenses as special interests compete for a slice of the fiscal pie. As in past years, Mollen again proposed rules to give the agency more power to investigate possible lobbying abuses. The commission also wants to require lobbyists to detail specific bills they try to influence. But the agency's influence in the Legislature has been limited at best: After 17 years in existence, the agency has been unable to get the word temporary removed from its name, meaning it needs annual approval from lawmakers to keep operating. "We always live in hope," Mollen said when asked if he thought reforms were any more likely under the new Pataki administration.

Lobbying to win state contracts is thought to be a major business, though it's impossible to say how much is spent because that information isn't reported. Illinois, for example, last year began requiring disclosure of such contacts with state agencies; in the first six months the amount of reported lobbying spending doubled, according to officials.

In New York last year, 1,930 lobbyists were registered, representing 1,099 clients, ranging candy companies to the New York Yankees to McDonald's. More money ($5.4 million) was spent by health and mental health interests than any other industry. Trade groups were second, spending $5.3 million, the commission said. A quarter of the money was spent by the top ten lobbying firms, whose partners include numerous former top lawmakers as well as legislative and administration staff members. Comparing the New York lobbying industry to "political insider trading," NYPIRG lobbyist Blair Horner said, "We believe these huge sums . . . are at the heart of what's wrong with state government."

The government reform groups have been pushing to require the state Board of Elections to computerize its operations, thereby making it easier to track the role of money on government policy decisions. The lobbying commission recently computerized its information. Mollen said the agency is exploring ways to put the data out over the Internet, the worldwide computer network, so anyone with a computer and modem can look up lobbying information.

Administrative Agencies

One of the many powerful—and controversial—federal agencies is the Food and Drug Administration. The first of three articles on the agency examines some of the current fights over its mission. Is there a better way for society to do the work now done by agencies?

Prodding the FDA / Both Sides Say Lives Are at Stake
Doug Levy, USA Today

The radio announcer offers a sober warning: "Every year tens of thousands of Americans die while the Food and Drug Administration—the FDA—delays approval of drugs readily available in Europe." So says the commercial from the Citizens for a Sound Economy Foundation. But Dr. Sidney Wolfe, director of Public Citizen Health Research Group, offers another side to the story. His organization says the FDA has kept at least 47 dangerous drugs off U.S. shelves, including one pain reliever sold in Britain and Germany that was pulled there after causing 36 deaths.

Depending on who's talking, the FDA either saves people or it kills them. Critics view the agency as a power-hungry behemoth whose over-regulation drives small businesses into oblivion and keeps life-saving medical products from dying patients. Boosters say without the FDA, unscrupulous companies would sell and promote untested products, giving desperate patients false hopes—or worse, killing them. As with almost every political issue, the truth lies somewhere in between. Members of Congress hope to find the facts in hearings starting later this month.

As one of the largest federal agencies, the FDA and its 9,300 employees have jurisdiction over processed food, seafood, drugs and cosmetics, meaning its regulations affect virtually every person throughout every day. Now, well-financed lobbying groups are running ads, holding news conferences and stirring up opinions. In a newspaper ad for the Washington Legal Foundation, a picture shows a coffin awaiting burial: "The FDA can delay medications and

Copyright © 1995 by *USA Today,* March 7, 1995, p.1D. Reprinted with permission.

safety devices for years. Too bad it can't delay the consequences," says the caption.

The agency and its defenders say the ads are, at best, misleading. They cite:

- The claim that FDA rules bar drug companies from publicizing aspirin's ability to prevent second heart attacks. The FDA responds that drug companies can tell doctors about heart-related health effects of aspirin, but such claims are barred from consumer packages because of aspirin's potentially dangerous side effects that come from long-term use.

- The claim that the FDA is keeping a device to improve cardiopulmonary resuscitation, the Ambu CardioPump, off the market. The FDA says it halted research when it found out developers were testing it on patients without needed approval. Three studies haven't found it makes any difference in survival rates, though research continues.

- The claim that getting a drug to market in the U.S. takes two to three years longer than in Europe. The FDA says drug approval time averaged 19 months in 1994, a 21 percent improvement over 1993. "The American people want to know that the food they eat is safe and that the drugs they take or the medical devices they use are safe and really work," says FDA Associate Commissioner James O'Hara. "Rolling back the standards that protect the public is neither progress nor reform."

And consumer advocate Wolfe, frequently an FDA critic, says the FDA's lengthy review process has protected U.S. consumers from drugs that have injured or killed people overseas. "Thank goodness for slowness," Wolfe says.

On the other side are medical device makers, pharmaceutical and biotechnology firms and industrialists opposed to government interference—such as the Koch family of Wichita, Kan., billionaires who bankroll conservative groups promoting anti-regulatory philosophy. Ironically, some of these same interests were behind the laws that set up the current system. The 1962 law that requires drug companies to prove their products are both safe and effective before they are sold had the backing of major drug companies. It passed in part as a reaction to thalidomide, the anti-morning sickness drug that caused birth defects. Now, they say the FDA system is bogged down.

"Today it takes 12 years and $400 million to bring a drug from the laboratory to the patient," says Steve Berchem of the Pharmaceutical Research and Manufacturers of America. "It shouldn't take that long, and it shouldn't take that much." But Berchem says drug makers don't want to relax standards. They seek a more efficient approval process, which might use new statistical techniques or scientific methods.

FDA critics say the agency's policies stifle U.S. business by requiring too much data to establish safety and effectiveness. These critics include:

- Citizens for a Sound Economy, run by former Bush and Reagan administration officials.

- The Competitive Enterprise Institute, which advocates free market policies. It says its supporters include Philip Morris, Pfizer and others who sell products under FDA scrutiny.

- The Progress & Freedom Foundation, a conservative think tank, which funds House Speaker Newt Gingrich's college course.

"The agency has lost track of its primary mission, which is the protection of public health," says Alan Magazine, president of the Health Industry Manufacturers Association. HIMA wants to cut FDA enforcement authority over certain devices already on the market. For example, enforcement should be aimed at "intentional or repeated violations of law that threaten public health," and should give companies a chance to voluntarily correct problems, says a HIMA report.

Rep. Joe Barton, R-Texas, chairman of a House Commerce oversight subcommittee, says the FDA is not as "timely" as it should be in approving drugs and devices. But he's not ready to call for massive reforms. Neither is Thad Cochran, R-Miss., who heads the Senate subcommittee with jurisdiction over the FDA's budget. Cochran wants FDA critics to testify under oath before his committee. "I need to know whether these people have legitimate complaints or whether (the ads) are just fund-raising efforts in disguise," Cochran says.

But Barton, Cochran and other lawmakers recognize that the agency has enormous power to affect public health, and if there are problems, they need to be addressed. "The FDA may be unique" because its decisions may have "life or death consequences," Barton says. "If they were to approve a defective drug, it could kill people. Other regulatory agencies don't have as immediate a negative impact."

Administrative Agencies

The second article on the FDA is written by an Oregon congressman, who claims that lobbyists are unfairly attacking the agency.

FDA: The Extremists Have It All Wrong
Washington Post

In the months since the November election, a consortium of far-right think tanks, lobbyists and public relations gurus have concocted a new mythology: the Food and Drug Administration, responsible for the safety of countless products used or consumed by Americans daily, is in fact an engine of death and unemployment. The message of their well-funded, multi-media advertising campaign is corrosive and blunt: "If a murderer kills you, it's homicide. If the FDA kills you, it's just being cautious."

The new mythology is being stoked by pseudo-facts and half-baked conjecture. And although rational observers can make reasonable criticisms of the FDA, the complete laundry list of complaints by these extremists reads like Grimms' Fairy Tales as rewritten by Stephen King.

Myth 1: The FDA drags its heels at the expense of dying Americans when entrepreneurs bring them experimental new drugs.

Fact: Patients can begin using an unapproved drug or device as soon as the manufacturer makes an investigational new drug (or device) application to the FDA. All the company typically has to do is present information that the drug or device is not inherently dangerous. The FDA and the maker of the product work together to assess the results. When the clinical evidence is solid, commercial distribution is usually approved. For example, Eli Lilly and Co. received approval earlier this month for an anti-cancer drug under a new, accelerated decision process fashioned specifically for lifesaving products.

Myth 2: The FDA's bureaucracy-driven approval system kills jobs and softens America's competitive edge.

Fact: For small companies, the FDA certification of effectiveness is a guarantor of sales success at home and abroad. It provides small, undercapitalized firms that have tied their future to a single product with a Good Housekeeping seal of approval. Ask small manufacturers if their FDA approval helped them in overseas markets. Device sales alone have created a $4.7 billion U.S. trade surplus.

Copyright © 1995 by The Washington Post. *Washington Post,* March 14, 1995, p.A17. Reprinted with permission. This op-ed piece was written by a Democratic representative from Oregon.

Myth 3: The FDA approval process has kept scores of effective, life-saving products off the market.

Fact: The agency process has kept many unsafe, ineffective and potentially dangerous products from U.S. consumers. In the case of the anti-cancer agent Interleukin 2, FDA trial requirements exposed significant safety problems that even the company eventually agreed were legitimate and reasonable.

In the case of the Sensor Pad, a device for detecting breast cancer tumors, FDA's critics suggested that the U.S. agency had been unreasonably tough while Canadian counterparts had let the device on the market there. As it turns out, neither statement was correct. In yet another example, FDA's much-criticized approval process kept a new Alzheimer's drug off the market until investigators could figure out treatment methods that would not fatally damage patients' livers.

Myth 4: Industry and independent health experts overwhelmingly believe that a radical overhaul of FDA is warranted.

Fact: While few in the industry will argue FDA's perfection, most accept the fact that independent, unbiased and rigorous assessment of new products by the agency creates a gold standard necessary for global competitiveness.

Lisa Raines, vice president of government affairs for Genzyme Corp., says her company "is not interested in tearing FDA down" but wants to "take a good agency and make it better." Alan Magazine, president of the Health Industry Manufacturers Association, wants process reform, but adds, "I don't think that dismantling the FDA is in the best interests of citizens or the industry." The American Heart Association, writing to the New York Times last month to protect the use of its name in an anti-FDA advertisement, stated "while we do not always agree with the FDA on particular issues, we believe it is committed to promoting and protecting the public's health."

Myth 5: The FDA's time-consuming, ever-slowing, rope-a-dope approval system is creating huge backlogs and a stymied industry.

Fact: In some cases, the FDA process has been slow. But the numbers have improved dramatically over the past several years. Despite spurious claims to the contrary, the agency's evaluation time for breakthrough drugs has been cut by 51 percent in the pat year alone—from 23.4 months to 12.2 months. The approval time for drugs seemed potentially lifesaving averaged 10.4 months. By 1997, the FDA expects that the approval time for breakthrough drugs, or for drugs with lifesaving potential, could be down to six months.

There's no agency on earth that can't be improved, and the FDA is no exception. Some devices and non-critical applications ought to be dropped from the regulatory system entirely. Requirements for early phase trials could be significantly reformed and streamlined as has been done in Europe. Entrepreneurs could save time and money if more of the agency's approval process were moved out of the Washington-based bureaucracy and into private, third-party reviews.

These and other ideas mark a path for constructive FDA reform. Alternative, myth-shrouded proposals being offered by the extremists would tear the fabric of the world's safest and most effective health care system.

Administrative Agencies

The final article on the FDA demonstrates that problems—and crimes—may dwell in places we least expect them, such as a bottle of fruit juice. If there were no administrative agencies, would there be more cases like this?

Adulteration of Fruit Juices Still Widespread
Diana B. Henriques, *Houston Chronicle*

The clandestine production and sale of adulterated fruit juice is a widespread and profitable practice, a review of court cases filed across the country shows. The practice costs consumers about $1.2 billion a year and exposes them to undisclosed and unapproved chemicals, the federal government says.

Regulators at the Food and Drug Administration, which oversees the food industry, said they had hoped that tainted juice would become less common after the federal prosecution in 1987 of Beech-Nut Nutrition Corp. Beech-Nut paid a $2 million fine for illegally selling "apple juice" that was nothing more than sweetened water and chemicals. But the recent cases involved activities that continued long after the settlement.

While federal officials say they are committed to pursuing adulteration cases, court exhibits and interviews with investigators and juice industry executives show that enforcement efforts are haphazard. The enforcement is plagued by inadequate resources and an institutional tradition that has put a low priority on cases that, at least until recently, were not considered a threat to public safety.

FDA Commissioner David A. Kessler said the agency was determined

Copyright © 1993 by The New York Times Co. Printed in *Houston Chronicle*, Oct. 31, 1993, §A, p.12. Reprinted with permission. All rights reserved.

to prosecute juice adulteration cases when it could muster evidence to support a criminal case. "And these are serious prosecutions," Kessler said. "People are going to jail." He conceded that despite past efforts, the juice industry remained a troubling exception to the agency's generally successful efforts to combat food adulteration. "We still have to be vigilant," Kessler said. "In most cases of adulteration, it turns out to be just economic and nobody gets hurt—but there is always that potential."

Chemists, who specialize in testing food samples, estimate that about 10 percent of the country's $12 billion pure fruit juice industry is adulterated. About half of the industry is made up of orange juice processors, he said. The most common adulterants are sugar or watery orange byproducts, but in some recent cases, manufacturers used preservatives not approved as safe for use in juice.

Many manufacturers cited in court cases were important wholesalers to food producers such as Borden and Land O'Lakes, and grocery chains like Kroger, Safeway and Alpha-Beta markets. There have been no federal claims that those grocers knew they were selling adulterated juice. The recent defendants include:

Peninsular Products of Warren, Mich.; Flavor Fresh Food Corp. of Chicago; and eight individuals, who pleaded guilty to indictments in February. The federal charges alleged an eight-year conspiracy to add sugar and illegal preservatives to more than 32 million gallons of juices sold under private labels in several states. Court records allege the juice contained unapproved preservatives. The states involved are: Arizona, Connecticut, Georgia, Illinois, Indiana, Iowa, Kansas, Kentucky, Louisiana, Maryland, Michigan, Minnesota and Missouri. Also involved are Nebraska, North Carolina, North Dakota, Ohio, South Carolina, South Dakota, Tennessee, New York, Pennsylvania, Virginia, West Virginia, Wisconsin and the District of Columbia.

Paramount Citrus Association, of Mission Valley, Calif., a unit of the private investment partnership that owns Teleflora Inc., the flower delivery service, and the Franklin Mint, a collectibles retailer. In April, Paramount and its plant manager pleaded guilty in Philadelphia to selling adulterated juice to the federal government since 1985. The defendants also paid nearly $7 million to settle civil claims by the government.

Seven executives of Sun Up Foods Inc. of Benton, Ky., which before its bankruptcy in September 1990 claimed to be one of the country's largest juice wholesalers. The defendants, who denied the allegations and are to go to trial in April, were accused of adding liquid sugar to juices with equipment hidden in a secret room in their factory.

Meanwhile, Everfresh Juice Co., which from 1987 until 1992 was owned by Canadian brewing firm John Labatt Ltd., and American Citrus Products Corp., doing business as Home Juice in Melrose Park, Ill., have paid more than $2 million to settle lawsuits in Chicago. John Labatt Ltd. owns the Toronto Blue Jays baseball team. The lawsuits accuse the firms of using sugar and illegal preservatives in juices for more than a decade. The cases, filed in 1990 under a secrecy order, were settled in April.

Kristen Chadwell, who until July was general counsel for the Florida Department of Citrus, said unscrupulous manufacturers had long cut corners by diluting juice with cheap, generally harmless ingredients like beet sugar and pulp wash, watery residue obtained by soaking squeezed oranges in water and squeezing them a second time. Diluted, sweetened juice is more prone to spoilage, officials say. Chadwell said the industry's search for less detectable chemical preservatives may be outstripping regulatory efforts to protect consumers. "These are complicated, white-collar crimes, and the potential for profit is enormous."

In sworn statements filed in the litigation against Everfresh, witnesses testified they suspected the secret solution contained diethyl pyrocarbonate, or DEPC, banned as hazardous by the FDA in 1972. That speculation has not been substantiated by laboratory tests, federal officials said. The FDA's efforts to find and analyze samples of the compound have been unsuccessful, officials said.

Federal investigators in the Michigan case found a 1987 formula that listed the solution's active ingredients as natamycin and two enzymes called glucose oxidase and catalase. While not as dangerous as DEPC, none is approved by the FDA as safe for use in beverages, officials said.

Chapter 4

Constitutional Law

Judicial Review

Free Speech

Takings Clause

Judicial Review

Every four years we hold a presidential election, and every four years the candidates debate how much power the Supreme Court should exercise. Should the Court be the final word on *what the law is,* or should Congress and the President also be allowed to proclaim the law?

Robertson Says High Court Not Preeminent; Prospective Candidate Cites Founding Fathers on Equal Power of Judiciary and Congress
David S. Broder, *Washington Post*

Republican presidential prospect Marion G. (Pat) Robertson said yesterday that "a Supreme Court ruling is not the law," and neither Congress nor the president has a duty to obey judicial rulings with which they disagree. The Virginia Beach television evangelist, who said he will decide on a formal declaration of candidacy for the 1988 GOP presidential nomination in mid-September, said that all public officials "are bound to support the Constitution as they see it," but asserted that the Founding Fathers never intended the Supreme Court to be "paramount over the other two branches."

Robertson, a graduate of Yale Law School, made his comments in an interview with reporters and editors of The Washington Post. His interpretation appeared to be at odds with a line of decisions, extending back 183 years, in which the Supreme Court has asserted the power to declare acts of Congress and presidential decisions unconstitutional. But Robertson, who came to the meeting with a notebook of pertinent quotations, cited statements by Andrew Jackson and James Madison in support of his position.

The head of the Christian Broadcasting Network and host of the popular "700 Club" television show was asked about his readiness as president to uphold the Supreme Court decision on abortion rights, to which he is vehemently opposed. The questioner referred to the controlling case upholding a right to abortion, Roe v. Wade, as "the law of the United States." "I take issue with your premise," Robertson replied. "A Supreme Court ruling is not the law of the United States. The law of the United States is the Constitution, treaties made in accordance with the Constitution and laws duly enacted by the Congress and signed by the president. And any of those things I would uphold totally with all my strength, whether I agreed with them or not."

Copyright © 1986 by The Washington Post. *Washington Post,* June 27, 1986, p.A3. Reprinted with permission.

"I think Roe v. Wade is based on very faulty law," he said. "It had no precedent to it whatsoever. . . . Abortion is a state matter." Robertson said he would not seek to overturn the decision by executive order "because you don't have the power," but left the impression that he would not feel bound to enforce it either. He quoted Andrew Jackson as saying: "The court, the Congress and the executive must each be guided by its own opinion of the Constitution. . . . The opinion of the court has no more power over Congress than . . . Congress has over the court."

Asserting again that Supreme Court decisions "are not the law," Robertson said that as a private citizen today, "I am bound by the laws of the United States and all 50 states . . . but I am not bound by any case or any court to which I myself am not a party."

He said he would enforce the Supreme Court's 1954 basic school desegregation ruling because it was an "appropriate" interpretation of the Constitution. "No question they ruled correctly," Robertson said. But as a general proposition, he added, "I am concerned, as I think millions of others are, when those justices say 'the Constitution is what we say it is.' I trust the people and I trust the people's representatives . . . and I don't think the Constitution reposited in five people, who are often governed by the shifts of politics, the total domination of this society. I think that is a mistake. I don't think the Congress of the United States is subservient to the courts. . . . They can ignore a Supreme Court ruling if they so choose."

The Supreme Court asserted its power to overturn acts of Congress in the 1803 Marbury v. Madison case, in which Chief Justice John Marshall said, "It is emphatically the province and duty of the judicial department to say what the law is." Under that doctrine, the Supreme Court has struck down more than 100 laws and has ruled a variety of executive decisions invalid as violating the Constitution. Justice Marshall based his Marbury v. Madison decision in part on provisions of the Constitution that say that the power of the federal judiciary "shall extend to all cases . . . arising under this Constitution," and that the Constitution represents "the supreme law of the land." Robertson said that he believed the original assertion of judicial review was "very limited . . . a very small concept, but over the years it's been run to excess."

Free Speech

Free speech is important; no one would question that. Does speech include panhandling?

Panhandling As Free Speech; Judge's Ruling Debases the First Amendment
William Murchison, *Texas Lawyer*

Strolling in downtown Fort Worth on a sunny winter afternoon, I was approached by a man with an apparent aversion to bath tubs. He asked me if he might have the use of three dimes and two pennies. Why? For coffee. I have been hit up for more—much more—and on this occasion I was amenable. I stood and delivered.

In the 1990s such an exchange is commonplace enough. But then I remembered something. This, our brief transaction, at the corner of Main and Eighth, has been invested with radiant new meaning by the federal judiciary. I was not being panhandled. My odoriferous friend was exercising his constitutional right to free speech. He was sending a massage about poverty and need. He was, you might say, preaching to me. What did I signify by forking over—agreement with his premise? Whatever, U.S. District Judge Leonard Sand of Manhattan says that's the law. We peasants are supposed to knuckle our foreheads gratefully.

Judge Sand, in late January, ruled unconstitutional the Metropolitan Transportation Authority's ban on subway panhandling. "The simple request for money by a beggar or a panhandler," Sand said, "cannot but remind the passerby that people in the city live in poverty and often lack the essentials for survival. Even the beggar sitting in Grand Central Station with a tin cup at his feet conveys the message that he and others like him are in need. While often disturbing and sometimes alarmingly graphic, begging is unmistakably informative and persuasive speech."

It is also unsightly, sometimes coercive and—in the judgment of the Metropolitan Transportation Authority—disruptive of the subway system's campaign to clean up and so avoid losing riders. Judge Sand set these considerations at naught, however urgent they might be to the larger community. "Free speech" considerations overrode them all. Panhandlers are free to make New York's subway the Bourse of beggary, with a coat of arms bearing the outstretched palm.

William Murchison is a reporter for *Texas Lawyer*. This article is republished with permission from the 2/12/90 issue of *Texas Lawyer*. Copyright © *Texas Lawyer*.

Judge Sand's writ fortunately does not run in Texas; nor is it the last word even in New York. A recent decision in which he fined Yonkers councilmen until they voted his way in a housing case was reversed by the Supreme Court, but Sand suffers from no lack of social inspiration. He does get one thinking. Mostly he gets one thinking about how ridiculously the First Amendment is stretched these days—thanks to judges like Sand, and to complacent (if not positively beaming) lawmakers and shapers of opinion. Panhandling is free speech? Come off it. The claim is ludicrous. But, then, as we know, pornography is regarded as free speech. Flag-burning is free speech. These things are ludicrous, too, and they are also the law of the land, by judicial ukase. Judge Sand has applied himself, with skill and ingenuity, to a popular pastime—debasing and trivializing the First Amendment. Judge Sand accords more freedom of expression to panhandlers than, in the housing case, he did to elected representatives of the people.

What does it mean, freedom of speech? To the Founders it clearly meant something other than what it means to Judge Sand. James Madison, speaking in the House on Aug. 15, 1789, when the Bill of Rights was under consideration, said: "The right of freedom of speech is secured; the liberty of the press is expressly declared to be beyond the reach of this Government; the people may therefore publicly address their representatives, may privately advise them, or declare their sentiment by petition to the whole body; in all these ways they may communicate their will."

No brief representation may do justice to the range of possibilities available under a charter of free speech, but it is clear the Founders thought they were shielding speech, real speech. The idea, broadly speaking, was to protect the right to speak and write on questions large and small. This was before the age of "symbolic speech." For that age's advent the educational system may be partly to blame. Madison and the Framers presupposed a populace able to summon up and deploy the English language, on paper or the stump. The less American students learn in school today—and seemingly they don't learn much—the greater grows the desire to speak not with the tongue but the body. Maybe I exaggerate the connection, but it seems a point worth examining.

At any rate, that's what beggars do, speak with their presence, their tongues—which shape their actual requests—being secondary. Sand suggests they're telling us it's a hard life, folks. Actually the beggar I spoke with said he wanted a cup of coffee. His appearance didn't discommode me, but the presence of legions of beggars, such as formerly inhabited the New York subway, is something else again. A local government entity should have the right, without cavil or second-guessing from the courts, to assert a public interest in unimpeded access to transportation. The subway, when it banned begging, asserted such an interest because the beggars and homeless people have been driving away riders and injuring the subway's finances.

New Yorkers have a right to a self-sustaining and clean transit system, wouldn't you say? I would say, but, then, I'm not a federal judge. I don't wake up every morning wondering what part of the Constitution I'm going to rewrite today in order to express my own heightened personal vision of the Social Good. Judge Sand is such a judge, and while it gives one the willies to realize he sits on the federal bench, it's consoling to remember he is in the lowest division thereof. His superiors have the right to rebuke him. In fact, in the subway case, they have the positive duty to rebuke him. Not for the first time, he's completely off the track.

Free Speech

The law always struggles to keep pace with technology, and nothing illustrates that more clearly than the battles concerning free speech on the Internet.

Business Technology; No More "Anything Goes": Cyberspace Gets Censors
Peter H. Lewis, *New York Times*

Freedom of expression has always been the rule in the fast-growing global web of public and private computer networks known as cyberspace. But even as thousands of Americans each week join the several million who use computer networks to share ideas and "chat" with others, the companies that control the networks, and sometimes individual users, are beginning to play the role of censor. Earlier this month, the American Online network shut several feminist discussion forums, saying it was concerned that the subject matter might be inappropriate for young girls who would see the word "girl" in the forum's headline and "go in there looking for information about their Barbies," a spokeswoman said.

Users on other networks have been banished, censored or censured this year for the widespread posting of messages like "Jesus Is Coming," "Make Money Fast" and "Your Armenian Grandfathers Are Guilty of Genocide." The third case brought to cyberspace the long conflict between Turks and Armenians, and, according to some network users, produced a counterattack by an unknown Armenian sympathizer who programmed his or her com-

---

Copyright © 1994 by The New York Times Co. *New York Times,* June 29, 1994, §A, p.1, col. 1. Reprinted with permission.

puter to sniff out any message on the system containing the word "turkey" and substitute "genocide," even in forums discussing Thanksgiving meals.

On Prodigy, the country's largest commercial network, with more than two million users, supervisors have been expanding the use of what they call "George Carlin software," which finds messages with certain objectionable words and warns those who sent them to erase them or their messages will be censored. The nickname refers to the comedian who does a monologue about censorship in broadcasting titled "Seven Dirty Words." Prodigy's list of offending words has grown into the dozens.

A University of Florida student's access to the giant network known as the Internet was revoked this month after the student used university computers to repeatedly post copies of a political polemic. Outrage and calls for censorship arose among users of the Usenet network after racist messages appeared on forums set up to discuss O. J. Simpson's arrest on murder charges.

Then there is the case of Arnt Gulbrandsen, a 25-year-old Norwegian computer programmer who was enraged earlier this month when he saw that a Phoenix law firm, Canter & Siegel, was once again advertising its services over the worldwide Usenet computer network, despite pleas from many users to cease and desist. From his keyboard halfway around the world, Mr. Gulbrandsen launched the electronic equivalent of a Patriot missile: each time the law firm sent out an electronic advertisement, his computer automatically sent out a message that caused the network system to intercept and destroy the firm's transmissions. "I was somewhat surprised that I only got positive feedback," Mr. Gulbrandsen said. "I expected more than a little 'flaming,' " as personal attacks and complaints, transmitted electronically, are known among network users.

Troublesome Issues

Even longtime network users who applaud such a use of what they call a "cancelbot" acknowledge that the situation raises broad and troubling issues about censorship in cyberspace. But because the wide use of computer networks is so new, no established case law moderates the debate over censorship in such cases, the way it does for publishing, broadcasting and speech.

For some networks, the legal questions hinge on whether they are to be considered common carriers, much like telephone companies or even bookstores, which are not responsible for the content of the messages they carry, or to be regarded as private networks that have the right to establish and enforce standards of language and ethics for all users.

In recent court cases involving the computer network Compuserve, a division of the H & R Block Company, the network has argued that it is protected as a common carrier. But that raises the question of whether Compuserve has been right to enforce its own standards for content.

No One Source

The responsibility for any censorship rests not with a central authority but with the administrators of the thousands of private and public computer networks. Many of those administrators offer guidelines for users, but enforcement is usually left to peer pressure—criticism from others using the network. While some networks will act to stop a potentially objectionable message before it is distributed, others will take action only after a message is posted and users complain about it.

Because of their international nature, the networks operate outside the framework of First Amendment protections familiar to most Americans. "What First Amendment?" Wolfgang Schelongowski, a Usenet user in Bochum, Germany, transmitted during a network debate on such issues. "No such thing here, or in any country besides the U.S.A."

Laurence A. Canter and Martha S. Siegel, the lawyers who are Mr. Gulbrandsen's target, said his actions amounted to censorship. "What does this mean, that everyone on Usenet will have to meet the standards of this Gulbrandsen guy or he will take it upon himself to cancel their messages?" Ms. Siegel asked. "If anything is going to bring down the net, it'll be things like robot cancelers and self-styled censors."

The conflict is most intense on Usenet, a cooperative anarchy of private and public computers comprising more than 8,000 discussion groups, used by an estimated six million people worldwide. Usenet is most commonly reached through the Internet, an even larger web that links some 25 million people worldwide.

A Shift in Purpose

The technology that enables messages to be canceled was built into Usenet originally to allow an individual to withdraw a message he or she had written. As a safeguard, the command was designed so that only the writer could withdraw a message. In practice, however, canceling was occasionally used by computer system administrators to remove offensive or outdated messages.

Canceling someone else's message is controversial, said Ron Newman, a programmer who helped develop a technology used on many Internet computers, "because the person who issues the cancel message has to write a message claiming, falsely, to be the sender of the original message." In other words, the canceler must commit electronic forgery. "The cancel facility was not intended to be used this way, and it could easily be abused by people who want to set themselves up as censors," Mr. Newman said.

Mr. Gulbrandsen and Internet technical experts acknowledged that it would be easy to create "cancelbots" that wipe out messages from a given company, or even a certain country. But even with its potential for abuse, Mr. Gulbrandsen's action against Canter & Siegel seems to have met with popular support among users, many of whom object to advertising on the network.

"C. & S. illustrates a potential vulnerability of the net," Mike Godwin, legal counsel for the Electronic Frontier Foundation, a lobbying group in Washington, said of the law firm. "They're pushing it to the extreme. If everyone did what they did," the system would be clogged with unwanted messages and there would be "nothing worth reading." Mr. Godwin added: "The E.F.F. believes very strongly that censorship is the wrong way to approach net problems. But we also believe there are rules of the road that limit what you can do on the net, rules that don't amount to censorship."

Daniel P. Dern of Newton Center, Mass., author of "The Internet Guide for New Users," said even well-intentioned action could drift into censorship. "There is a danger of the cancel wars shifting from inappropriate resource use to canceling based on 'I don't like your opinion,' " he said. "At what point does somebody say, 'I don't like this person, and I'm going to cancel them'?"

To most users of the Internet, unbridled freedom, even anarchy, are guiding principles. "Usenet has principles, it has a social structure, but it has no government," said Brad Templeton, publisher at the Clarinet Communications Corporation, an electronic-newspaper company in San Jose, Calif. "People who study such things have said that a real anarchy, like a commune, starts breaking down at about 100 people. Somehow we have managed to grow a community of several million people. Now people see the fringes of that system breaking down. Is the answer to impose a government, or is the answer to be found within the system? The idea of a cancelbot is actually something working within the system."

Takings Clause

In the first of two articles on the takings clause, the author excoriates what he considers the excesses of environmental regulation.

Do Rights of At-Risk Rodents Override Landowners'?

Joseph Perkins, *Atlanta Journal/Constitution*

A California man owned a piece of coastal property, part of which was upland, the rest of which was wetland. He wanted to develop the entire property, so he applied for a permit to fill in the wetland portion. The U.S. Fish and Wildlife Service surveyed the property and informed the owner that the salt marsh harvest mouse, an endangered species, lived in the wetlands. But not only did the federal agency designate the wetland area a "critical habitat"—rendering it off limits to development—it also declared the upland portion of the property undevelopable. There may be a global warming trend, it explained, which will cause the polar ice caps to melt, and the property owners' wetland will be inundated. The salt marsh harvest mouse would then be forced to the upland area.

This regulatory horror story illustrates the lengths to which misguided government regulators often go to deprive landowners of full use of their property. In an effort to restore some balance between the rights of property owners and those of harvest mice, House Republicans (joined by one-third of Democrats) recently approved a bill that requires that the government compensate landowners when their property is devalued 20 percent or more by regulation.

Passage of the "takings bill" provoked predictable yelps from environmentalists, who somehow believe the government has absolute authority to restrict use of private property. But the Fifth Amendment declares that private property shall not be "taken for public use, without just compensation." In recent years, courts have held that the takings clause applies when government regulations leave property in private hands but restrict its economic potential.

Both the Supreme Court and Congress have found it necessary to curb takings because government bureaucrats have used such well-intentioned laws as the Clean Water Act and the Endangered Species Act to abrogate individual property rights. For instance, the Clean Water Act originally

Copyright © 1995 by The Atlanta Constitution. *Atlanta Journal/Constitution*, March 15, 1995, p.11A. Joseph Perkins is a columnist for *The San Diego Union-Tribune*. Reprinted with permission by *San Diego Union Tribune*.

applied to rivers and didn't even mention a "wetland." So federal regulators have arbitrarily decided that a piece of property may be considered a wetland if it is dry as many as 350 days of the year and if the wet area is as small as a puddle. Similarly, the Endangered Species Act was intended to protect bald eagles, mountain lions and other prominent creatures. Not in their wildest dreams did lawmakers imagine that federal regulators would restrict development on millions of acres of private property to ensure the comfort of kangaroo rats and snail darters and salt marsh harvest mice.

With a takings law on the federal books, the apparatchiks at Fish and Wildlife, at the Environmental Protection Agency and in the Army Corps of Engineers will still be able to regulate "nuisances"—like air or water pollution—without compensation to private property owners. But absent such threats to public health or safety, they will have to weigh the costs vs. the benefits of regulating property owners in coastal areas, wetland areas and areas in which some endangered critter or another may reside.

That is much more fair than telling a property owner he cannot develop his land because a rodent will have no place to go when the ice caps melt.

Takings Clause

In the second article on the takings clause, the author criticizes what he regards as private gain achieved at the expense of public good.

"Takings" Is the Most Terrible Idea of All in the Contract with America
Donella Meadows, *News & Record (Greensboro)*

Say goodbye to environmental protection if the "takings" section of the GOP Contract becomes law. I'm going to turn my farm into a gold mine. Old rumors about gold circulate around this town. Maybe some of it is under my farm. I plan to blast out the bedrock, grind the rubble, and run cyanide through the grindings to dissolve out the gold. I think I can find as much as $6 million worth.

What, you say the land isn't zoned for mining? The town well is just

Copyright © 1995 by News & Record. *News & Record (Greensboro)*, Mar. 13, 1995, p.A5. Reprinted with permission. Donella Meadows is a professor of Environmental Studies at Dartmouth College.

downstream? A third of my farm is protected wetland? The cyanide runoff will kill the endangered dwarf wedge mussel in the Connecticut River? Well, too, too bad. If you block my mine, you're impeding my private property rights. Under the Fifth Amendment of the Constitution ("nor shall private property be taken for public use without just compensation") that's a "taking." If you want me to preserve wetlands or keep water pure, pay me. Otherwise I'll sue the town (zoning), the state (water regulations) and the feds (Endangered Species Act). Collectively you owe me $6 million.

That's not a crazy scenario. One like it just hit the courts in Colorado. The owners of the Summitville gold mine, having extracted $6 million in gold and poisoned 17 miles of the Alamosa River, are demanding compensation for a "taking" because their cyanide heap has been declared a Superfund site, and they can no longer mine the land, nor sell it.

"Takings" is the most terrible of all the terrible ideas in the Contract with America. Takings laws are also being pushed at county and state levels, backed by oil companies, timber companies, mining companies, developers. Shucks, let's name a few: Weyerhaeuser, Exxon, Du Pont, Boise-Cascade, Texaco, the National Cattleman's Association, the American Mining Congress and the National Association of Realtors. You don't hear about those corporate interests in the takings rhetoric. You hear only about little guys. A man's got a right to do what he wants with his land. The Founding Fathers. The sacredness of private property. The stupid government won't even let you make a buck anymore.

The real message is: If I can make money doing something—if I can even imagine making money doing something—no one has a right to stop me. Money in my pocket is more important than public safety, clean air, clean water. Pay me not to pollute. In fact pay me if you want me to do anything for the public good. Here are some takings cases that have come to the courts:

- A motel operator demanded compensation because the Civil Rights Act required him to rent to people of color, diminishing his business, he says.
- A dial-a-porn company sued the Federal Communications Commission for regulations that prevent children from using its service.
- A tavern owner sued the state of Arkansas because its highway sobriety checks cause people to drink less.
- A coal company mining an underground seam caused land to subside, ruptured a gas line, collapsed a highway, and destroyed homes. The Office of Surface Mining told it to stop. The company said, pay us for the value of the coal you won't let us mine.

- The owner of a plumbing supply store sued when the city told her she couldn't pave her parking lot unless she left 10 percent of her land free (the land was in a floodplain) to reduce downstream flooding.

The courts threw out the first four of those claims and, unfortunately, granted the last one.

Legal interpretations of the Fifth Amendment takings clause started in 1887, when a beer brewer argued that a Kansas prohibition law was a taking. The Supreme Court said, "a government can prevent a property owner from using his property to injure others without having to compensate the owner for the value of the forbidden use." Since then the courts have generally ruled that you need be compensated only when a public action takes most or all of your property. If the state wants your land for a highway, it has to buy it at a fair price. If it wants you to stop dumping sewage into a stream, it doesn't owe you a thing.

With increasingly conservative courts, the "takings" line has been pushed further toward the individual good and away from the public good. The Contract with America pushes it even further. Originally it defined a taking as any regulation that reduces property value by even 10 percent. The current version, passed by the House, now in the Senate, says 20 percent. Either way, the real purpose of this legislation can't be to protect property rights. If it were, there would be some concern for the homeowners along the poisoned 17 miles of the Alamosa River, those downwind from polluting factories, those whose property value is diminished by ugly development.

The purpose can't be to redress private versus public imbalances, either. Takings advocates are strikingly silent about public givings—royalty-free mines on public lands, subsidized logging roads, underpriced grazing permits, tax breaks for oil drillers, publicly funded roads, bridges, and water projects that give some private property virtually all its value. The property rights folks have never, as far as I know, offered to share private gains that come at public expense.

Rather, their purpose, readily admitted by some, is to make environmental laws go away. If the cost of clean water is to pay every gold-crazed landowner her fantasy earnings from her land, so much for the Clean Water Act. So much for regulating toxic wastes, food safety, strip mining. Goodbye endangered species. You can see why developers and resource-extracting industries love this idea. You can see why no sane nation would allow it.

The Capitol phone line is 202-224-3121. You don't even need to know your senators' names (though you should!); just ask the operator for the senators from your state.

Chapter 5

Intentional Torts and Business Torts

Emotional Distress

Liability

Privacy and Publicity

Emotional Distress

Two articles look at the intentional tort aspects of AIDS. In this article, a state corrections officer had a stronger basis than most plaintiffs for an AIDS-fear claim, and he won. Is it right to award damages for emotional distress when a plaintiff can demonstrate no physical injury?

N.Y. Corrections Officer Awarded $99,000 by State Jury for Fear of Contracting AIDS
BNA Occupational Safety & Health Daily

A state corrections officer who was accidentally sprayed in the face with the body fluid of a prisoner with AIDS was awarded $99,000 in damages by a state Supreme Court jury in Glens Falls, N.Y., Oct. 19 (Esser v. Glens Falls Hospital, NY SupCt, No. 26731, 10/19/94).

The officer, Alfred Esser, never contracted AIDS, but sued for the "negligent infliction of emotional distress" in connection with the fear of getting AIDS, according to his attorney, Thomas O'Malley of the Albany firm of Mahoney, O'Malley, Nugent & Alexander. Esser sued Glens Falls Hospital and the nurse who accidentally sprayed him while he was guarding a prisoner in the hospital's prison ward.

O'Malley said the case is unique because there was no physical injury attached to the emotional distress, simply the fear of getting AIDS. He said the jury appeared to have been influenced by expert medical testimony that Esser could have contracted AIDS as a result of the accident. "They felt his fears were genuine and justified, under the circumstances," O'Malley said.

Anne M. Hurley, an attorney for the defendants, said it was significant that the Warren County jury declined to award any damages for future suffering by the plaintiff. The defendants have not decided whether to appeal the case, Hurley said. Hurley is with the Albany firm of Carter, Conboy, Bardwell, Case, Blackmore and Napierski.

The case stems from an incident that occurred in the prison ward of Glens Falls Hospital in December 1987. A nurse accidentally sprayed Esser with the fluid from a syringe used to clear the intravenous line of a prisoner with AIDS. Esser was sprayed in the eyes, nose, mouth, and face with the fluid. He subsequently experienced an anxiety disorder in connection with the incident and received workers' compensation benefits, according to O'Malley.

Reprinted with permission from *Occupational Safety & Health Reporter*, vol. 25, no. 22, p.1186 (Oct. 24, 1994). Copyright © 1994 by the Bureau of National Affairs, Inc. (800-372-1033).

Liability

This AIDS article looks at two issues: concealing AIDS from a sexual partner, and the potential liability of insurance companies.

Aetna Wins Rock Hudson Case; Actor's Estate Not Entitled to Coverage for Payment to Ex-Lover
Jim Doyle, *San Francisco Chronicle*

A federal appeals court ruled yesterday that Rock Hudson's insurance company does not have to reimburse his estate for a multimillion-dollar settlement to the actor's boyfriend, who said the Hollywood star had concealed the fact that he had AIDS. The U.S. Court of Appeals in San Francisco unanimously upheld a lower court decision that Hudson's homeowner policy with Aetna Casualty & Surety Co. did not cover such acts by Hudson as misrepresenting his physical condition and "willfully exposing" his lover, Marc Christian, to the AIDS virus. Hudson's estate has already paid Christian his settlement. Yesterday's ruling means that the estate will not be reimbursed by Aetna, according to Roy Weatherup, a Santa Monica lawyer representing Aetna.

Christian, a bartender, lived with Hudson for two years at the actor's home in Beverly Hills. The two were lovers in June 1984, when Hudson learned he had AIDS. The screen star died of complications of AIDS the following year at the age of 58. Soon after, Christian filed a lawsuit against Hudson's estate, accusing the actor of concealing the fact that he had AIDS. Although he had not tested positive for HIV, the virus that causes AIDS, Christian insisted that Hudson's misrepresentations about his health caused him severe emotional distress.

In 1989, a Los Angeles Superior Court jury awarded Christian $21.75 million in damages, finding that Hudson had intentionally misrepresented his condition to induce his lover to continue having high-risk sex with him. A state appeals judge later cut the jury award to $5 million. The case was settled in 1991 by Christian and several insurance companies. Aetna's lawyer said the settlement amounted to several million dollars.

Aetna, meanwhile, went to federal court seeking a declaration that—because of Hudson's misrepresentations to Christian about his health—it had no obligation to indemnify the jury verdict. Hudson had an Aetna home-

Copyright © 1993 by The Chronicle Publishing Co. *San Francisco Chronicle*, Apr. 1, 1993, p.B10. Reprinted by permission.

owner's policy with "bodily injury" coverage for visitors to the actor's property—except in cases of fraudulent conduct.

"It is undisputed that Hudson knew that he was infected with the AIDS virus," Judge Cynthia Holcomb Hall of Pasadena wrote for the appellate court. "Hudson put Christian's health in jeopardy during an eight-month period by willfully exposing Christian to the deadly AIDS virus."

Lawyers for Hudson's estate argued that although the actor may have been reckless, he never intended to infect Christian with the AIDS virus or cause him emotional harm. They also pointed out that Christian had voluntarily consented to high-risk sex with Hudson on hundreds of occasions before learning of the actor's diagnosis. But the court said Hudson's motives were far less important than the "inherent harmfulness" of the actor's conduct. Hall added: "While Christian consented to have sex, he did not consent to be intentionally exposed to AIDS."

Privacy and Publicity

When Vanna White isn't spinning the wheel of fortune, she is suing those who impersonate her—and winning.

CA Fed. Jury Awards Vanna White $403,000 over Robot Ad
Entertainment Litigation Reporter

Right of Publicity: White v. Samsung.

A federal jury in Los Angeles on Jan. 20 ordered Samsung Electronics America, Inc. and advertising agency Deutsch/Dworin Inc. to pay Vanna White a total of $403,000 for misappropriating her likeness, for their use of a Vanna White-looking robot in a print ad for a Samsung VCR without her permission (White v. Samsung, CD CA, No. CV-886499-RSL).

White, the hostess of "Wheel of Fortune," has capitalized on her fame from the show by marketing her identity to various advertisers. A humorous Samsung print ad campaign showed 21st century scenes where today's Samsung products are still working, including a Samsung VCR ad showing a robot dressed in a wig, gown and jewelry consciously selected to resemble

Copyright © 1994 by Andrews Publications. *Entertainment Litigation Reporter*, Feb. 25, 1994. Reprinted with permission.

White's hair and dress, standing next to an instantly recognizable Wheel of Fortune game board, posed in a stance for which White is famous. The caption read: "Longest-running game show. 2012 A.D." The defendants themselves refer to the ad as the Vanna White ad but, unlike other celebrities used in the campaign, White never consented to the ad nor was she compensated for it.

White sued Samsung and ad agency David Deutsch Associates, Inc. (now Duetsch/Dworin) under: California Civil Code 3344, which provides in part that any person "who knowingly uses another's name, voice, signature, photograph, or likeness, in any manner . . . for purposes of advertising or selling . . . without such person's prior consent . . . shall be liable for any damages sustained by the person or persons injured as a result thereof"; the California common law right of publicity; and 43(a) of the Lanham Act, 15 U.S.C. §1125(a), which provides in part that any person "who shall . . . use, in connection with any goods or services . . . any false description or representation . . . shall be liable to a civil action by any person who believes that he or she is likely to be damaged by the use of any such false description or designation."

The district court rejected White's claims under 3344 and 43(a) and granted summary judgment to Samsung on White's common law right of publicity claim. White appealed and the Ninth Circuit held that genuine issues of fact remain as to whether Samsung violated White's common law right of publicity. The court affirmed the district court's dismissal of White's 3344 claim and it found the lower court had erred in rejecting White's Lanham Act claim at the summary judgment stage. Samsung sought a rehearing, but the Ninth Circuit unanimously voted to deny Samsung's motion.

In its petition for writ of certiorari, filed with the U.S. Supreme Court on April 9, 1993, Samsung argued, "A parody should not be stripped of its First Amendment protection merely because it appears in a commercial advertisement. . . . In any event, the ruling below that summarily rejects any First Amendment defense of 'garden-variety commercial speech' is contrary to the decision of this Court in Central Hudson Gas & Elec. v. Public Serv. Comm'n, 447 U.S. 557 (1980)."

In *Central Hudson*, the Supreme Court set forth a four-part test in commercial speech cases, saying the court must:

(1) determine whether the expression is protected by the First Amendment;
(2) then determine whether the asserted government interest is substantial;
(3) then determine whether the regulation directly advances the governmental interest asserted;
(4) then determine whether the regulation is not more extensive than is necessary to serve that interest.

In her May 11 brief in opposition, White argued, "No 'special and important' reasons justify Supreme Court attention to this case. . . . Petitioner's arguments below directly contradict those they attempt to raise here. . . . The Court of Appeals addressed and properly decided the issues mentioned in the petition."

On June 1, the Supreme Court let stand without comment the Ninth Circuit decision and the case returned to the district court for trial. On Jan. 11, White testified that she never gave Samsung permission to use her likeness in advertisements for the VCR, that she works hard to maintain her image and that she does not take product endorsements lightly. On Jan. 14, White's attorney claimed she deserved millions of dollars for the misappropriation of her likeness, while a defense attorney maintained that the ad was a spoof of game shows and did not fool consumers into believing that White had endorsed Samsung products.

On Jan. 20, the jury awarded White $205,000 in compensatory damages from Samsung and $198,000 in compensatory damages from Deutsch/Dworin. Neither defendant commented on the verdict, though Deutsch/Dworin said it would not appeal.

Privacy and Publicity

A celebrity's *likeness* is her own property—but does she also own her *life story?* Elizabeth Taylor answers, "yes!" If a celebrity can prohibit others from telling her story, does that mean a scholar could be barred from writing contemporary history?

NBC Turns Unauthorized, Warts-and-All Book into Liz Miniseries; Taylor Unmade
Dave Walker, *Arizona Republic*

TV critics didn't get preview copies of *Liz: The Elizabeth Taylor Story* for one of two reasons. One: It stinks! Or, two (which is the reason NBC is giving): The network didn't want to fuel further legal action by Taylor, who has tried to slap injunctions on this project and the book it's based on as if legal documents were so many pink Post-it notes.

And no wonder. The best-selling source book, *Liz: An Intimate Biogra-*

Copyright © 1995 by *Arizona Republic*, May 19, 1995, p.D1. Dave Walker. Used with permission. Permission does not imply endorsement.

phy of Elizabeth Taylor, by C. David Heymann, is chock-full of salacious tales of boozing, (I suppose we should say alleged) dope taking and, worse, serial marrying. Take, say, the facing pages of 248 and 249. On this spread alone are accounts of:

- Adultery (during the filming of *Cleopatra*, Taylor openly downshifts from Eddie Fisher to Richard Burton);
- Liquor guzzling (bombed and spouting Shakespeare, Burton shows up at Fisher's house to taunt his cuckolded rival);
- One zany, apparent suicide attempt (while brooding over her messy love life, Taylor inexplicably bolts toward a second-floor plate-glass window, only to bounce off a divider and fall down);
- One even zanier non-suicide attempt (in the middle of the night after the window incident, a friend awakes to discover Taylor in the kitchen holding a big knife!—with which she is making a cheese sandwich);
- And one not-so-zany, legitimate suicide attempt (30 sleeping pills . . . stomach pumping . . . the studio spun the incident as a case of food poisoning).

Great miniseries meat, in other words.

"It's a well-documented, footnoted work," said executive producer Lester Persky, who earlier this year discussed the miniseries' legal standing with TV critics. "We have more facts than we can deal with. This is a battle I would go down in flames fighting because I don't believe that because an individual is wealthy and well-connected and can afford lawyers, people should be intimidated and prevented from writing about them." Or filming a four-hour, two-part, May-sweeps miniseries. Taylor evidently contended that such a work would violate her right to control the telling of her life story, as well as her right to privacy.

"A miniseries . . . is definitely recognized as protected free speech," said Persky, who learned the case law as producer of the miniseries biopics *A Woman Named Jackie* and *Poor Little Rich Girl*. "And I think defending the right to make a movie is more than a legal right, it a moral right." As for the privacy issue, Persky said, "I don't think people who . . . are among the most famous celebrities in the world, who don't hesitate to have very public involvement in their lives and don't live their lives in secret . . . can claim privacy unless they practice privacy. "I think the movie's task is to elucidate, to shed light in an impartial way, on the subject. That's what it's all about. What is art but the re-creation, in a meaningful manner, of life? And there's no better life than someone who's lived a vivid one."

The task of portraying Taylor's vivid life fell to Sherilyn Fenn, whose offbeat career includes roles in several movies (from soft-core porn early on to the Gary Sinise-directed version of John Steinbeck's *Of Mice and Men* to the more recent disaster *Boxing Helena*), but who is probably best-known for her weird work as Audrey Horne in *Twin Peaks*, the 1990-91 ABC series from Mars. Fenn was cast as Taylor just days before meeting with the same group of TV critics.

"It's pretty frightening, to be honest with you," she said in January. "There was a lot of excitement leading up to it. And when they actually said that everything had been confirmed—I'm really overwhelmed. It's one thing to play a character that's fictitious. It's quite another to play somebody who is alive and well—and fighting it. But I've always been drawn to challenges, and I just think she's an amazing woman and an amazing character."

Fenn said she used Taylor's films, as well as archival interviews with the star, to gain insight on the life. "I've always been moved by *Who's Afraid of Virginia Woolf?*" she said. "I think that was the most raw I've ever seen Elizabeth Taylor. I love that she came up as such an incredibly beautiful woman and just ripened before our eyes, got better and better in terms of her work. I'm doing as much research as is possible. But at the end of the day . . . I believe I just have to go inside of myself as a woman and try to sort of understand some of the parallels (between her own life and Taylor's) and hopefully expose them as honestly as I can."

Ironically, Fenn wouldn't discuss those parallels. "Too personal to talk about," she said.

Chapter 6

Negligence and Strict Liability

Duty

Breach

Foreseeability

Duty

The element of *duty* focuses on whether the defendant could have foreseen harm to this particular person. Here, the plaintiff has left the defendant's taxi, but injury is still foreseeable. Would the defendant be liable if the plaintiff had been robbed?

Cabbie Faces Claim for Errant Trip—Passenger's Fall
David Bailey, *Chicago Daily Law Bulletin*

A woman ejected from a taxicab by a confused driver may proceed with her claim that his failure to take her to her destination was responsible for injuries she suffered walking home, a divided 1st District Appellate Court panel ruled Thursday. The taxicab company and its driver may not have owed Maria Trevino the highest protection once she exited the taxi, but it had an obligation to protect her from foreseeable risks caused by a wrongful ejection, the majority concluded in affirming and reversing in part a summary judgment in favor of the defendants.

Trevino contended that Flash Cab Co. and driver Lewis Carmichael should be held liable for the injuries she sustained in the January 1991 incident. Trevino fell about a block after exiting the taxi, which she had summoned for a four-block trip from Illinois Masonic Medical Center to her home. Carmichael had made several wrong turns after declining Trevino's offer of directions, which she renewed after each error. When the taxi reached Racine Avenue and Diversey Parkway, five blocks from her home, Carmichael stopped the vehicle and ordered Trevino out, she contended.

In their summary judgment motion, Flash and Carmichael contended that they had no liability for injuries sustained by falls on natural accumulations of ice and snow, that their duty to Trevino ended after she left the taxi and that they were not the proximate cause of her injury. Cook County Circuit Judge Odas Nicholson agreed, and Trevino appealed.

"In this case, the plaintiff was neither taken to her desired destination nor an intermediate transfer point," Justice Thomas E. Hoffman wrote in the majority's 13-page decision. Rather, she was wrongfully ejected at a location of the defendants' choosing, subjecting her to the very perils she sought to avoid by engaging their services. "The carrier-passenger relationship imposes a duty of care on the carrier," Hoffman explained. "We can per-

Copyright © 1995 Law Bulletin Publishing Co. *Chicago Daily Law Bulletin,* June 8, 1995, p.1. Reprinted with permission.

ceive of no compelling reason why this duty should not encompass an obligation on the part of the carrier to protect its passenger from a foreseeable risk of harm in the event of a wrongful ejection. . . . "The magnitude of guarding against such a risk is minimal and the only consequence of placing such a burden upon a carrier is to cause it to refrain from wrongfully ejecting its passengers," Hoffman added.

With Justice Sheila M. O'Brien concurring, Hoffman also found that a jury should decide whether Trevino's ejection from the taxi was reasonably related to her fall and whether the action amounted to willful and wanton misconduct.

Justice Robert Cahill dissented, finding no reasonably close connection between the wrongful discharge of this passenger, and the harm it originally threatened, with her subsequent fall. "To be sure, the weather was what one expects in the dead of a Chicago winter, but the area where she left the taxi was safe, the cleared driveway of a gas station," Cahill wrote in his 3-page dissent. "There is no evidence in the record that the neighborhood or hour was dangerous, or that the weather was so severe that exposure to it alone was a hazard. That evidence might yield a different result."

Breach

The element of *breach* is concerned with whether a defendant's conduct was reasonable. In this case, an old rule of law is applied to a very contemporary problem.

Makers of Weapons Face Consequences
Phoenix Gazette

Gian Luigi Ferri entered the elevator of the office building at 101 California Street in San Francisco dressed in a dark business suit. He pushed the button that took him to the 34th floor, the law offices of Pettit & Martin. But this was no ordinary office visit. On that Thursday, July 1, 1993, Mr. Ferri was carrying large-capacity detachable ammunition magazines and two TEC-DC9 assault pistols. Both weapons were equipped with Hell-Fire trigger systems that substantially accelerate the rate of fire of a semiautomatic

Copyright © 1995 by *Phoenix Gazette,* Apr. 17, 1995, p.B6. Used with permission. Permission does not imply endorsement.

firearm. He stepped off the elevator, turned toward the office conference room, and opened fire.

Stenographer Deanna Eaves was struck in the right arm. Attorney Sharon Jones O'Roke was hit in the head, chest and arm. Brian Berger, a law partner was hit with another burst of gunfire and Allen Berk, a labor specialist, was gunned down in his glass-walled office. Meanwhile at the other end of the floor, John Scully, a 28-year-old attorney with the firm, ran down an interior stairwell to the 33rd floor, where his wife, Michelle, an attorney not employed by Pettit & Martin, was working. As they made their way toward the elevators, Mr. Ferri appeared on the 33rd floor. John Scully used his body to shield his wife and was fatally wounded. His wife was shot in the shoulder and chest.

Mr. Ferri ran into a stairwell where he encountered two police officers. He put a gun under his chin and fired a bullet through his head.

On that July day Gian Luigi Ferri killed eight people and wounded six others with the efficient help of the weapons and the accessories he carried. Survivors of four of the victims subsequently filed lawsuits against the manufacturers and distributors of those devices, including Navegar Inc., a Florida corporation that manufactured and sold the two TEC-DC9s used in the shooting; USA Magazines Inc. a California corporation that sold high-capacity ammunition magazines used in the shooting; Hell-Fire Systems Inc. a Colorado corporation that manufactured and sold the trigger device that Ferri used on his weapons; and Super Pawn, a Las Vegas pawnshop where Ferri purchased one of the TEC-DC9s.

The victims' case was ingenious and compelling. With the free assistance of four of San Francisco's major law firms, along with the Center to Prevent Handgun Violence and its highly respected attorney, Dennis Henigan, the plaintiffs alleged that the sale to the general public of a weapon like the TEC-DC9 is actionable negligence. Such negligence, they argued, violated a legal duty of reasonable care owed by the gun industry to the general public not to sell firearms that have no legitimate civilian use and are literally designed for crime. The lawsuits allege that sales constitute an "abnormally dangerous activity for which Intratec should be strictly liable in damages to those injured by the activity."

The argument is straight negligence law, applying the oldest principles of tort law, says Mr. Henigan, which is if you fall below a standard of reasonable care in your conduct, whether it is driving a car, working a machine, or manufacturing a gun, you are liable for the foreseeable injuries for that conduct."

A few days ago that argument found root in a courtroom. California's Superior Court Judge James L. Warren ruled that Navegar can be held liable under California law now because earlier rulings that favored gun manufacturers did not apply inasmuch as they were made before 1989—when California passed the Roberti-Roos Assault Weapons Control Act. The judge said the TEC-DC9 was just a modified version of a weapon banned by the act and that when Navegar introduced the gun into the general market "it could have foreseen that it might eventually make its way into California and be used for criminal purposes."

Mr. Henigan reminded those interested in this case that the TEC-DC9 was designed for close-range, multiple killings of the sort committed July 1, 1993 and that Intratec's own advertising boasts that its weapon is as "tough as your toughest customer," and that the pistol was advertised as having a finish "resistant to fingerprints."

These are products whose entrance into the marketplace should chill America's soul, whose murderous use now faces appropriate consequences for those foolish enough to push them toward the public.

Breach

When a tragedy occurs we tend to look for someone to blame. But if no one behaved *unreasonably*, there is no negligence.

Clermont Cleared in Drowning; Sammekia Arthur's Parents Claimed City Negligence Caused Their 8-Year-Old Daughter's Death. A Jury Disagreed
Jill Jorden Spitz, *Orlando Sentinel*

The city of Clermont is not to blame for the death of a little girl who drowned four years ago at Jaycee Beach, a jury decided Friday. The parents of the girl, 8-year-old Sammekia Arthur, sued, alleging the city's negligent hiring, training and supervision of lifeguards caused her death. They claimed that lifeguards were playing football rather than watching the beach, and that they failed to give Sammekia cardiopulmonary resuscitation to revive her after other beachgoers pulled her from the water.

After a weeklong trial, however, the jury of three men and three women took just less than three hours Friday to determine the city was not negligent. An attorney for the girl's parents had asked the jury to award between $100,000 and $1 million each to Sam Arthur and Dolores Douglas, who

Copyright © 1994 Sentinel Communications Co. *Orlando Sentinel*, Aug. 27, 1994, p.1. Reprinted with permission.

were never married. Douglas, a maid who lives in Wildwood, dissolved into tears when the verdict was read. Arthur, a Groveland auto detailer, said afterward that he had hoped the result would be different, but that he would endure with the help of his faith. "I'm disappointed," he said softly. "Very disappointed."

"I just don't quite understand how the jury could determine there was no negligence on the part of the city," said James McMaster, the attorney who represented Sammekia's parents. "The only thing I can think of is that they bought their (the city's) argument that nobody saw the little girl go under the water and since nobody saw her, nobody could have done anything to save her."

Steve Lengauer, who represented Clermont, agreed that the lack of any distress behavior on Sammekia's part was probably a major factor in the jury's decision. Nobody at Jaycee Beach on June 13, 1990, saw the girl flailing or heard her yelling for help. Her body was spotted by a little boy swimming to retrieve a football. Most likely, Sammekia—who had low blood pressure and anemia—lost consciousness and slipped under the water, Lengauer said. "Obviously this is a difficult decision for the jury to make," he said. "Saying to these folks who have lost a child that there is no one at fault takes a great deal of courage."

According to testimony presented during the trial: Sammekia and three of her cousins went to Jaycee Beach the day of the incident after Marcella Rhodes Hardwick—the boys' mother—told them not to go. At the beach, the boys swam and played in the water while Sammekia, who could not swim, built sand castles with some other children. After her playmates left, someone saw Sammekia floating on a blue raft, wearing her street clothes. She was not seen again until she was pulled from the water. In dispute was whether a lifeguard tossing a football when Sammekia drowned was on duty or on a break, and whether one or two of the beach's three lifeguards were playing football. Also contested was whether the lifeguards began CPR when Sammekia was pulled from the water.

Since the incident, the only change at the beach is a sign saying children younger than 12 must be supervised, Lengauer said. "The city has taken the position that its lifeguards acted appropriately and it guarded Jaycee Beach adequately," he said. "No changes have been made, and none are needed."

Foreseeability

The plaintiff's harm can be legally foreseeable even though the defendant never foresaw the precise way in which it occurred.

Hotel Liable for Arson Injuries of Guests; Set Fire Is Called "Foreseeable" Risk
Mark A. Cohen, *Massachusetts Lawyers Weekly*

A hotel that had inadequate lighting and exits was liable for injuries suffered by guests in a fire set by an arsonist, the Appeals Court has ruled. The hotel owner argued that it owed no duty to the guests because the damage caused by the arsonist was not a foreseeable risk. But the Appeals Court disagreed, saying the defendant owed a duty to protect guests from a deliberately set fire.

"The [trial] judge was warranted in finding that the corporation's failure to provide adequate lighting and egress created a foreseeable risk that a fire, however started—innocently, negligently, or by criminal act—would cause harm to its guests," Judge Gerald Gillerman wrote, affirming a judgment against the hotel owner.

However, the court reversed judgments against two officers of the corporation that owned the business and the realty trust that leased the property on which the hotel was operated. There was no evidence that the trust or the corporate officers breached any duty owed to the plaintiffs, Gillerman said.

The 11-page decision is Addis, et al. v. Steele, et al., Lawyers Weekly No. 11-082-95.

Plaintiffs' attorney Steven B. Rosenthal of Boston said that he was pleased with the court's determination that "foreseeability is not contingent on the manner in which the fire is started." The duty owed "was to provide against harm by providing a means of safe egress," Rosenthal stated. However, Rosenthal said he was disappointed that the judgments with respect to the corporate officers and the trust were reversed. The corporation is out of business and was not insured, Rosenthal noted.

Defense attorney Evan T. Lawson of Boston said that the court would have been warranted in finding an arsonist's fire to be unforeseeable because it is qualitatively different from an accidental fire. "While [the innkeeper] could foresee a fire, it could not foresee that the spread of the fire would be accelerated by gasoline [as it was in this case]," Lawson said. The inn-

Copyright © 1995 by Lawyers Weekly, Inc. *Massachusetts Lawyers Weekly,* May 1, 1995, p.1. Reprinted with permission.

keeper's sprinkler system would have put the fire out if gasoline had not been used, he asserted.

Lawson said the portion of the decision finding that the trust was not liable upholds the "corporate separateness" doctrine. "There are ongoing attempts to make individual officers and directors liable for corporate torts," Lawson noted, adding the issue was very important in this case because the innkeeper was not insured.

Inn Flamed

During the early morning hours of Oct. 2, 1989, a fire started by an arsonist broke out at the Red Inn in Provincetown. Plaintiffs Deborah J. Addis and James E. Reed were guests of the hotel that night. They were awakened by the fire alarm and ran down a flight of stairs. The premises were dark and full of smoke. The hotel's dining room was on fire. The plaintiffs, who were husband and wife, tried to exit through a door and found it locked. When other efforts to escape the fire proved unsuccessful, they ultimately jumped out of a second-story window and were injured.

Subsequently, the plaintiffs brought suit against the trust that owned the hotel property, the company that operated the hotel and two beneficiaries of the trust (who were also officers of the hotel corporation). The plaintiffs alleged that the defendants negligently failed to provide a proper and safe means of exiting the hotel. A jury-waived trial was held in Brookline District Court. At the close of the plaintiffs' case, the defendants moved for dismissal. Judge John A. Pino denied the motion. On Feb. 12, 1993, Pino found for the plaintiffs against all defendants. Pino concluded that the defendants were negligent in failing to:

- have someone on duty at night;
- maintain sufficient or emergency lighting; and
- provide access to exits that were clearly marked and easily opened.

Pino also determined that the defendants "could have foreseen that a thirdparty wrongdoer could commit an intervening criminal act," and that the defendants could have reasonably anticipated the fire. The judge awarded $98,000 to the wife and $22,000 to the husband. The defendants appealed to the Appellate Division of the District Court, which affirmed the judgment on Jan. 18, 1994.

Harm Foreseeable

The Appeals Court ruled that the trust and the hotel officers could not be liable for the plaintiffs' injuries as a matter of law. The trust merely rented the premises to the hotel company, Gillerman noted, adding that the lease provided no basis for liability. While the officers of the company were also beneficiaries of the trust, this fact did not impose upon them a duty to the plaintiffs, the judge said.

Turning to the hotel company's liability, Gillerman noted that "while innkeepers are not insurer's of their guests' safety, . . . they do owe a duty to take steps to protect their guests against unreasonable risk of physical harm." That duty "is grounded on the 'special relationship' that exists between a hotel and its guests," Gillerman wrote. Under the state building code, the company was required to take precautions to protect guests in the event of a fire, such as providing adequate lighting and clear access to exits, Gillerman noted.

"We have no doubt that the corporation owed the plaintiffs a duty of care and that by failing to provide adequate lighting and a clear and obvious exit path from the building in the event of fire, the corporation failed to perform its duty of protecting the plaintiffs against an unreasonable risk of injury," Gillerman wrote. "But whether that failure is sufficient to fasten liability on the corporation is correct in arguing that because the fire was set by an arsonist, the corporation did not have to protect the plaintiffs from the criminal activity of a third person."

This question "boils down" to the issue of foreseeability, Gillerman stated. If the harm caused by the fire set by the arsonist was foreseeable, the company can be held liable for the resulting damages, the judge said. Since it was foreseeable that a fire could occur at the inn, it made no difference whether the fire was started accidentally or set in determining the company's liability, Gillerman concluded.

Chapter 7

Crime

Mens Rea

Insanity

Fraud

Mens Rea

Prosecutors considered the following case one of fraud, but supporters of the defendants claimed they lacked *mens rea* and were forced to commit their acts by an inadequate health care system. Should we consider the suffering of a criminal defendant in assessing his guilt?

For Love of a Friend, He Lands in Prison
St. Petersburg Times

Benny Milligan thought it was a matter of life and death, so he lied to save his best friend. Now both are going to prison today, and Milligan's wife is under house arrest. Prosecutors called it insurance fraud and conspiracy. Supporters of the three call them heroes and say their plight is a dramatic example of the health-care crisis in America: where a person has to lie about health insurance because he is afraid medical treatment will be denied.

It all began July 8, 1990, when Milligan and his wife, Tammie, of Pearl River, La., went with James McElveen and three other friends to see the waterfall at Fall Hollow along the Natchez Trace National Parkway in Tennessee. Milligan, 31, and McElveen, 32, had been best friends since high school. They played on the same championship softball team; they worked together in McElveen's father's construction company; they joined the Navy together; and McElveen was best man at Milligan's wedding.

Suddenly, a day in the park turned into a nightmare. McElveen tripped and fell over the 30-foot cliff. Milligan and another friend hurried to the bottom, where they found McElveen unconscious and covered with blood, his body smashed and twisted against the rocks, face down in the water.

They got him back up the cliff and into a car, and drove 20 minutes to the nearest hospital, Lewis County Community Hospital in Hohenwald, Tenn. Nearing the hospital, Milligan remembered that McElveen, who worked as a painter for a small construction company, had no health insurance.

Their friends, Justin and Tabitha McCaleb, who lived in Hohenwald, recalled stories of patients without health insurance being turned away from hospitals. Among the friends, there was concern that McElveen, who had no discernible vital signs, might be denied care and die.

At the hospital, a doctor and nurse began examining McElveen in the back of the car. Right behind them, clipboard in hand, came a woman from

Copyright © 1993 by *St. Petersburg Times,* Jan. 8, 1993, p.1A. Reprinted with permission.

the admissions office. It was then that Milligan made the snap decision that would change their lives. Milligan, an engineer who had worked eight years with Martin Marietta Corp. and whose health insurance was provided by NASA, switched identities. McElveen was admitted as Milligan—a fully insured patient. Milligan immediately told his wife about the switch, and she signed the forms admitting McElveen into the hospital as her husband.

"I know what I did was wrong, but looking back on it, I did what I had to do," Milligan said Thursday. "I don't feel as though I'm a criminal in the sense of being a rapist and a robber and a mugger, but I do realize that I broke the law."

Gordon Bonnyman, a Legal Aid lawyer who testified at the trial, said the friends had good reason to be worried that McElveen would be denied admission. "The law is that he must be treated, but the practice is that he might not be treated," Bonnyman said. A 1985 federal law forbids hospitals that receive any federal funds, including treating Medicare or military veteran patients, from turning away patients in danger of immediate death, regardless of whether they have insurance. But Bonnyman noted that a 1987 report in the Journal of the American Medical Association indicated that 250,000 patients a year are turned away from hospitals because they lack insurance. He said he did not know of any specific cases in which emergency patients were denied admission at Lewis, but he knew of many such cases throughout middle Tennessee.

McElveen's injuries were severe. A few hours after being admitted to Lewis, he was transported to Maury Regional Hospital in Columbia, Tenn., where he was diagnosed with a burst vertebra and other spinal trauma. Two days later, as he was regaining consciousness, McElveen was transferred to Vanderbilt University Medical Center in Nashville. A doctor told him he needed surgery to fuse his lower vertebrae. With immediate surgery, he stood a 30 percent chance of being partially paralyzed. If he delayed the surgery three months, the chances of paralysis jumped to 90 percent. By the time McElveen gave his approval for the surgery, he knew about the deception and went along with it.

The surgery was successful. He was not paralyzed. But his medical bills had reached $41,107.45. Without Milligan's insurance coverage, Bonnyman said it's not likely McElveen would have received the necessary surgery at Vanderbilt, which has a policy of discouraging uninsured treatment unless it contributes to the hospital's teaching role. He said there is no law requiring hospitals to provide treatment beyond that necessary to stabilize a patient in danger of immediate death. And despite his pain and the medication, McElveen said he realized "that I was in this fantastic hospital and getting this fantastic treatment because I was under (Milligan's) fantastic insurance."

But Milligan's conscience was bothering him. He made an appointment with a social worker employed by Martin Marietta with the intention of confessing and seeking help. But when he got into the session, he became worried about losing his job and hastily ended the conference without disclosing the switch.

Milligan and McElveen both said they intended to pay back the insurance. But the deception was discovered by NASA's inspector general, possibly on a tip from McElveen's estranged father. Milligan was fired from his $12-an-hour job on Sept. 19, 1990. Since then, he has worked at a variety of jobs, most recently as a stevedore unloading ships at less than $8 an hour. He often does not work a full 40 hours a week. In addition, Milligan and his wife lost their health insurance when Milligan was fired. Their three young daughters—ages 6, 4 and 14 months—recently qualified for Medicaid.

The three friends were arrested in May 1991 and went on trial a year later. A 12-member federal jury convicted the Milligans of four counts of mail fraud, one count of wire fraud and one count of conspiracy to defraud the U.S. government. McElveen was convicted on all but one count of wire fraud because he was unconscious when the first deception was made. They faced five years in prison for each count.

At the sentencing hearing in July before District Judge Thomas A. Higgins, McElveen pleaded to take the sentence for all three defendants. "My friends saved my life," McElveen recalled telling the judge. "They thought they were doing what they needed to do. They lost everything. . . . I'm the one who made out on this deal. I benefited everything. He lost everything and he's losing more." McElveen said the experience has made his friendship with Milligan closer. "I don't think anybody else in the world would have done that for me except Benny. A lot of best friends don't get a chance to be tested, and he was tested and he came through."

Apparently moved by McElveen's statement, Higgins delayed sentencing until Nov. 23. He ordered Milligan to serve nine months in prison and three years probation, McElveen to serve seven months in prison and three years probation, and Mrs. Milligan to serve four months under house confinement—her movements restricted to work, shopping and taking her three daughters to school or the doctors. All three were ordered to pay restitution.

Mrs. Milligan began serving her sentence Dec. 8. As a convicted felon, she lost her job as a waitress in an off-track betting establishment that paid about $75 a day. Now she works in a diner making about $100 a week. She has been ordered to pay restitution at the rate of $300 a month—money she says she doesn't have.

Milligan and McElveen are scheduled to report to the federal penitentiary in Carville, La., this afternoon. Although their case is under appeal, they do not expect the sentence to be deferred.

Their plight has been championed by Families USA, a health care reform advocacy group. "To me, Benny and Tammie are heroes, not criminals," said Ron Pollack, executive director of Families USA. "The real crime is a health care system that forces good people like Benny and Tammie into this kind of moral dilemma. They had to choose between James's life and their own future." Pollack, who plans to be with Milligan and McElveen when they arrive at Carville penitentiary, sent letters Thursday to President Bush and President-elect Bill Clinton urging them to pardon the three friends. "In no place in the Democratic Western world could this be a crime," Pollack said, noting that virtually every other advanced country provides insurance to all citizens. "It's only in the United States where (health care) is not a right, but a privilege."

Insanity

This is a famous case of "temporary insanity." Does that defense humanely distinguish guilty defendants from those with mental illness, or does it demonstrate a legal system gone awry?

Mrs. Bobbitt Acquitted in Spouse Attack; Temporary Insanity Cited
Jerry Zremski, *Buffalo News* Washington Bureau

Instead of spending the next 5 to 20 years in prison for slicing off her husband's penis, Lorena Bobbitt will spend the next 45 days in a mental hospital. A jury of seven women and five men Friday found Mrs. Bobbitt to be temporarily insane when she maimed her husband, Town of Niagara native John Wayne Bobbitt, last June 23. The jury acquitted her of a charge of malicious wounding, agreeing with the defense argument that after suffering years of abuse and a rape at the hands of her husband on that June morning, Mrs. Bobbitt felt an "irresistible impulse" to strike back.

The jury returned the verdict late Friday afternoon after a two-week trial and a day of deliberations. As the verdict was read, a spectator shrieked, but Mrs. Bobbitt appeared confused, leaning over to one of her attorneys and saying: "Is that good?"

"And I said, 'Yes, it's good,' " said Lisa Kemler, the attorney.

Mrs. Bobbitt immediately escaped the media throng in front of the courthouse by leaving through a back door. In a statement read by a friend, Janna Bisutti, Mrs. Bobbitt said she hoped her case would inspire other bat-

Copyright © 1994 by The Buffalo News. *Buffalo News,* Jan. 22, 1994, p.1. Reprinted with permission.

tered women to seek help. "Your lives are probably filled with fear and no hope of escape," the statement said.

John Wayne Bobbitt and his family had checked out of their Manassas hotel and could not be reached for comment. But Bobbitt's attorney, Gregory Murphy, was furious about the verdict. "I would like someone to explain to his family how someone can do this and get away with it," said Murphy, who lashed out at prosecutors who acknowledged during this trial that Mrs. Bobbitt was raped even though a jury acquitted John Wayne Bobbitt of that rape charge two months ago.

The same prosecution team—Prince William County Commonwealth Attorney Paul Ebert and his assistant, Kenmore native Mary Grace O'Brien—handled both cases. That left those lawyers in the unusual position of siding with Mrs. Bobbitt in November and John Wayne Bobbitt in January. But Ebert insisted that wasn't a factor in the jury's decision—which, he said, stemmed from Mrs. Bobbitt's convincing self-portrayal as a frail, disturbed and mistreated young woman. "The message this verdict sends concerns me, though," Ebert said. "Certainly I have some sympathy for Lorena Bobbitt, but that doesn't excuse what she did."

At a news conference, Ebert said he had no choice but to call Bobbitt, a 26-year-old ex-Marine and bar bouncer, to the witness stand. During his testimony, Bobbitt frequently contradicted his own statements about his marriage and the events of last June 23. Mrs. Bobbitt, 24, a manicurist from Ecuador, contradicted herself, too. In this trial, she said she couldn't remember severing her husband's penis—even though she described the act at her husband's trial two months ago. Ms. Kemler, Mrs. Bobbitt's attorney, said the jury saw far beyond such details. "This case was not about a penis," she said. "It was about a life."

During nearly a full day of testimony, Mrs. Bobbitt catalogued four years of abuse at the hands of her husband, saying he beat her, raped her, forced her to have anal sex, and practiced Marine torture techniques on her. That harrowing, tear-filled testimony contrasted sharply with the carnival-barker atmosphere that surrounded the trial. John Wayne Bobbitt was himself partly responsible for that atmosphere: T-shirts bearing his autograph were for sale in the court parking lot, and Bobbitt made fun of his own plight on Howard Stern's radio show.

The end of the trial—which was broadcast live by Court TV and CNN—won't mean the end of the publicity. Lawyers for both the Bobbitts say their clients are now sifting through dozens of television, movie and book offers. For Mrs. Bobbitt, though, the next 45 days will be spent out of the limelight. After the trial, she was immediately whisked away to Central State Hospital in Petersburg, where she will be evaluated by state doctors for 45 days, as is required in insanity-plea cases in the state of Virginia. Doctors will then issue a report to the judge in the case, Herman A. Whisenant Jr., saying what kind of treatment she needs.

Her husband, meanwhile, won't know for another two years if he'll ever be able to have sex again. Mrs. Bobbitt took his penis with her when she fled their Manassas apartment the night of the attack, and later flung it along the side of a highway. Police recovered the organ and doctors reattached it in 9½ hours of surgery. In wake of the trial, the Bobbitts also have one last legal matter on their agenda: The couple has filed for divorce.

Fraud

Fraud costs billions annually. This article highlights the work of fraud investigators.

Fighting Back Against Fraud
Bill Day, *Business Record*

It's 7 A.M. While most of the neighborhood is just getting up, the private investigator has already been on the job for an hour. He's parked in a nondescript car four houses down from where a woman is recuperating from a fall at work. The woman is supposedly unable to get around. She's receiving a workers' comp check from her employer's insurance company while she relaxes at home.

At 7:30, she hustles her kids outside and into her car. The investigator captures her smooth gait on video. When she arrives at the school, he tapes her standing outside for 30 minutes, talking with the other moms. By that afternoon, the investigator has footage of the supposedly hobbled woman going to the grocery store and walking the dog. When she shows up at her workplace a week later—this time sporting a leg brace and crutches—she's confronted with the tape. She has no choice but to drop her workers' comp claim.

Until recently, the woman might have gotten away with her scam. But insurance companies, believing up to 15 percent of all claims are fraudulent, now employ teams of investigators to check suspicious claims.

Private investigator Gordon Gratias, who has worked with insurance companies in Des Moines for 26 years, has spotted people working on their houses, bowling, laying carpet, changing tires, lifting heavy objects, moving to a new house and working other jobs—after they claimed injury and

---

Copyright © 1995 by *Business Record*, Apr. 24, 1995, vol. 91, no. 17, §1, p.10. Reprinted by permission The Des Moines Business Record.

started collecting workers' comp. "There's a huge amount of money that insurance companies are getting frauded out of," Gratias said.

Thomas Gorgen, executive vice president of Silverhawk Investigations, can rattle off fraud cases like baseball fans rattle off batting averages. There's the person who filed workers' comp claims against several companies under several aliases for the same injury. There's the guy who was supposedly laid up but was working a second job roofing houses. There's the construction company executive who banged his knee on a desk and claimed total disability. "We toasted him real good," Gorgen said. The man was videotaped coaching his sons' baseball team when he was supposed to be in bed recuperating. Gorgen said footage of the man jumping over a four-foot fence was especially damning.

"People who commit fraud think they are very, very smart—and a lot of them are," Gorgen said. "But more and more, the people who think they're smart aren't, and they make a mistake."

Winning "The Lottery"

People cheat on insurance claims for the same reason people rob banks, executives say: That's where the money is. "I think some people today look at workers' comp as the lottery," Gorgen said. "They think there's a big pot of money to be made from that injury."

Des Moines property and casualty insurers provide every type of coverage in every part of the country, and have combined assets exceeding $4.2 billion. As an example of how much damage fraud can do, executives compare the $20 billion to $40 billion lost each year to fraud to the $17 billion lost in the nation's worst hurricane.

But insurers are fighting back. Some special investigative units, like the one at the Allied Group, are made up of former police or federal investigators. Others, like those at Preferred Risk Mutual Insurance Co. and Employers Mutual Casualty Co., are staffed by former claims adjusters with a nose for suspicious claims. Investigators say there are two types of insurance thieves: the professional, who stages accidents and fires to collect on policies, and the opportunist, who has a legitimate claim but pads it to make extra money.

Suspicions Confirmed

The first signs of fraud usually show up when a claim is filed. Adjusters are trained to recognize red flags. In a workers' comp or personal injury case, adjusters may become suspicious if the claimant is a disgruntled employee or if about to retire or be laid off. Adjusters are also wary of short-term employees or those with financial difficulties.

The incident report is also checked to see if it happened at an odd time or in a place where there were no witnesses. In an automobile accident claim, an adjuster will make sure the claimant's story matches the police report.

If enough doubts are raised—company investigators won't reveal how much suspicion it takes—the adjuster will refer the case to the company's special investigation unit. The unit's first step is to check several national databases, like the National Insurance Crime Bureau's. The NICB database is so sophisticated, spokesman Jon Hoch says, it was able to identify the van carrying the bomb used in the World Trade Center bombing two years ago. Even though investigators found only a partial vehicle I.D. number in wreckage at the scene, NICB was able to match it to a van reported stolen from a rental company, leading to the arrest of several suspects.

If the claimant's name shows up in the database, the insurance company will likely check to see whether claims for the same incident were filed with other companies. Investigators will also check whether the claimant has a criminal record, and whether he or she is undergoing some kind of personal turmoil, such as a divorce. In workers' comp cases, if investigators believe the claim is fraudulent, they will spy on the person, trying to get video of the claimant doing things he supposedly is medically unable to do.

Tom Peterson, executive vice president at IMT Insurance Co., tells of a 23-year-old man who filed a claim after supposedly being totally disabled. Investigators taped him doing a handstand while riding his motorcycle down the street. The claim was dropped.

But Dave Wiggins, an attorney who represents claimants in injury cases, cautions that video doesn't really tell the whole story. "The problem with surveillance is it's like a political campaign—you can't tell what the problem is in a 30-second bite." Wiggins says by the time injury cases get to an attorney, it should be apparent whether fraud exists.

Arson is more difficult and costlier to prove. Some units have their own arson specialists—the Allied Group has a former fire department captain in its unit—but most hire outside contractors. Adjusters working an arson claim ask whether the building was up for sale at the time of the fire. They also examine the owner's financial status. If valuables or pets were inexplicably out of the structure during the fire, that raises red flags. New policies or recent increases in insurance coverage also prompt inquiry. If a fire is of suspicious origin, insurers will being in specialists to determine how and where the flames started.

Another way investigators are clued into fraud is through anonymous tips. The National Insurance Crime Bureau has a toll-free hot line (800-TEL-NICB) where people can report those who have cheated insurance companies. Jon Hoch of the NICB said cars reported stolen have been found buried in compost piles, at the bottom of swimming pools, sunk in lakes and even stashed in an attic after nosy neighbors alerted investigators.

Honest Claims vs. Obvious Fraud

Because policies include a "cooperation clause" that amounts to the property owner's permission to investigate claims, insurers don't need search warrants. They do, however, need probable cause. Insurers have to be suspicious, but they also have to respond quickly to settle legitimate claims. Because many questionable claims are later determined valid, insurers must be careful in starting investigations. Acting in bad faith or delaying settlement of honest claims can lead to lawsuits, company executives said. One likened the threat of a bad-faith lawsuit to a sword hanging over his head.

Marc Kelly, coordinator of the special investigation unit at Employers Mutual Casualty Co., said until there is a "documentable suspicious element" to a claim, investigators don't touch it. This can include anonymous tips, a certain number of red flags, or information gleaned from databases.

At the National Insurance Crime Bureau, only 4 percent of the thousands of inquiries received each year lead to investigations. And Tom Farr, vice president and general counsel at Red Risk Mutual Insurance Co., says his company's investigators are busier screening suspicious claims than investigating them. "The cases they keep (for investigation) are not numerous," he said.

If a claim is sufficiently suspicious but no clear evidence of fraud is found, insurance companies will usually try to negotiate a reduced settlement. But when a claim is proved fraudulent, companies must decide whether to simply deny the claim or pursue criminal charges.

Many companies prefer not to go to the trouble and expense of prosecuting, especially in states where penalties are lenient. "Prosecution of every claim would be a futile attempt," Kelly said. "In an appropriate case, certainly we would not hide from the possibility of being a criminal complainant. But our real goal is to make the claim disappear."

The point, companies say, is to make sure the costs of fraudulent claims don't result in higher premiums.

Money To Be Saved

Insurance executives have a hard time calculating how much money they save by investigating false claims, but they all say it's a lot. Even so, Kelly said the best investigative units catch only about 2 to 5 percent of fraudulent claims. Some units profess to save $5 to $8 for every dollar they spend. Kelly says that for too long, investigators have tried to foil the "glamorous" frauds: professional theft rings, major arson and staged accidents. He thinks investigators should focus more attention on "opportunistic" fraud—when there is a valid claim but the claim is padded to make up for a deductible or just to cash in. It's a philosophy he acknowledges is only now catching on with insurance investigators, especially those with a background in law enforcement who are used to going after big-time criminals. "Some of them are beginning to realize that perhaps their targeting is wrong," he said.

Hoch is among those who disagree with Kelly. "Rings have been involved in fraud in excess of millions of dollars," he said. "You've got to concentrate on the guys that are hurting you the most first."

Donna Smith, a vice president at the Allied Group, said her company doesn't try to determine how much money its investigative unit saves because it knows the effort is worth the expense. Besides, says Tom Peterson of IMT, deterrence value can't be measured in dollars. "It's a situation where you know you would be losing if you didn't have experts attacking the problem."

Getting Tough With Fraud

Executives with Des Moines-based insurers, whether they do business regionally or nationally, agree the Midwest is not the country's biggest problem area for fraud. But they say fraud is on the rise here, and they started their investigative units just in time.

EMC Co.'s Marc Kelly says databases will improve to the point where, in five or 10 years, companies will be able to prevent fraud before it happens by screening policy applicants. In addition, a number of states are requiring that insurers establish anti-fraud policies and set up special investigative units. And state legislatures are getting serious about imposing stiff penalties on people convicted of fraud.

Even if an insurance company doesn't think it's worth it to prosecute, the NICB's database makes it possible to compile that person's previous frauds. The best policy, says IMT's Tom Peterson, is to be a customer-oriented business. "We're lucky, because we know our customers very well. I think that's a deterrent for fraud."

Chapter 8

International Law

Child Labor

Arms Export

Trade Disputes

Foreign Sovereign Immunities Act

Child Labor

One of the grim realities of a "shrinking world" is that some of the clothes we wear or household items we use may have been manufactured by children who live in conditions of virtual slavery. If you strongly suspected that an item you wanted had been produced by child labor, would you buy it?

Trapped in a Hellhole; Lost Futures: Our Forgotten Children
Stan Grossfeld, *Boston Globe*

The brass factories are all unmarked, down alleyways framed by streams of urine baking under windows covered by bars. This is the 19th century revisited. Furnaces belch molten lava and acrid smoke attacks the eyes and throat. On the edge of the darkness, a 10-year-old boy, his brown body turned black with soot, is making a brass angel while living in hell. For this, he is at least paid a pittance every week, 30 rupees, or about a dollar. But for the 10 million children who toil throughout India as virtual slaves, there is no compensation.

"I was kidnapped," says eight-year-old Laxmi Sada at Mukti Ashram, a home for freed slaves. "Me and three more boys were playing outside the village and some people came and gave us something to eat and said they had even better things to eat. They took us in a bus. I didn't even know what a carpet factory was. I started crying. Many times I was beaten. It was the master who first hit me with the punja a comb-like tool, and the blood came down . . . then they would put matchstick powder on the wound and light it to stop the bleeding. I never saw the sun rise." Sometimes Laxmi went to the bathroom in his pants. "If you got up, you'd get beaten."

Laxmi's father came to the factory to rescue him, but factory goons intercepted him. "I saw my father being beaten. He could not recover. My father wanted to take me and put me on his lap. Why did he have to die? I was there one year. Now I say, long live the revolution, stop child slavery. I want to kill the master. Because of him I couldn't see my father."

Some 50,000 children toil six days a week for a few dollars a month in factories throughout Moradabad, four hours east of New Delhi. The chil-

Copyright © 1994 by Globe Newspaper Co. *Boston Globe,* Dec. 29, 1994, p.A8. Reprinted courtesy of The Boston Globe.

dren choke on noxious fumes that carry tuberculosis and other respiratory diseases.

"Nobody lives to be 40," says Karan Singh, a human rights worker. Behind these doors, children make miniature Statues of Liberty, and busts of John F. Kennedy. The irony is that India—the world's largest democracy—is doing virtually nothing to enforce a 1986 law that prohibits children younger than 14 from working.

"It's very frustrating," said Kailash Satyarthi, chairman of the South Asian Coalition on Child Servitude, an umbrella organization responsible for the rescue of 26,000 children. "The law is there but the government doesn't want to implement it. Sometimes the fine is less than $2. So you're using a child's life for a $2 fine."

"They say the parents need the children to work to get by, but that's not true because there are 50,000 children working here while 50,000 adults are unemployed. We need to give those jobs to the adults and let the kids go to school," says Ashutosh Chakrapani, a coalition worker.

The International Labor Organization estimates there are some 200 million child laborers under the age of 15 worldwide. Many of these are bonded laborers, that is, unpaid slaves. They don't get paid wages, they don't get paid on a piece-work scale. They are lured away from their parents, who are told they are going to go to school to be trained for a job. The parents are given a small loan with high interest that they can't repay. Sometimes they are given nothing.

Udai Ram, 9, of Bihar says, "A middleman came to my village and told my father I would be taken to school to learn things. They promised him a 50-rupee advance. He never got it. "When I went in there the first time there was a thick cloud. I saw this beautiful carpet and I wanted to sit on it and I was beaten. I worked till 12 midnight. The master was teaching and I made many mistakes. The master would hit my finger with a very sharp knife. Once he cut the small tip off."

Udai said he worked with 11 other boys in a factory with three looms. "I always wanted to cry. I'd think about a beautiful forest and a river with my friends making balls of sand. My master is free. While I was working, I saw he got a new car and a new truck. It was like being in a cage. Have you seen birds fly? Now I'm out of the cage. I have never seen an adult make a carpet."

"Nimble fingers? That's bullshit," says Satyarthi, rebutting the claim that child weavers make smaller knots and thus produce higher quality rugs. "Nimble fingers have nothing to do with the knotting. The more knots in the less space, the finer the carpet. Tighter knots are made by strong men." Satyarthi has supported U.S. Senator Tom Harkin's "Child Labor Deterrence Act," which calls for a ban on importing goods produced with child labor under age 15, and provides money for rehabilitation. The U.S. imported more than $170 million worth of carpets from India in 1993, but importers and retailers say it is impossible to certify that the carpets are made without child labor. And with the passing of GATT, the Iowa senator's bill is technically illegal.

"If people keep buying carpets, they are guilty of perpetrating child slavery," says Satyarthi. "We're telling people that with these shining carpets, most of the shining comes from the blood of the children."

Arms Export

When arms export laws fail, the result may be that weapons designed by Americans are used to fire upon . . . Americans.

U.S. Found To Have Eased Way for Iraqi Supergun
Douglas Frantz, *Los Angeles Times*

The Bush Administration approved export licenses for computers and software that helped design Iraq's notorious supergun and a ballistic missile capable of reaching Israel and other Middle East countries, according to documents and congressional investigators. The export license for the computers was granted in the fall of 1989 to a Maryland company controlled by artillery wizard Gerald Bull, who was assassinated six months later outside his apartment in Belgium. Often called the world's greatest artillery designer, Bull had ties to U.S. intelligence and had served time in jail for violating U.S. export laws.

A prototype of the supergun designed by Bull for Iraq was discovered in the mountains north of Baghdad after the Persian Gulf War. United Nations inspectors said the 360-foot-long howitzer had been tested and was capable of firing nuclear, chemical and biological warheads.

The Commerce Department's approval for export of technology used by Bull adds a new element to the campaign debate over whether U.S. export policies played a role in building up Iraq's military arsenal. Critics have accused the Administration of permitting Iraq to obtain sensitive U.S. equipment as part of its effort to influence the regime of Saddam Hussein.

After claiming for months that no U.S. material was used in Iraq's weapons program, President Bush acknowledged last week that some U.S.

Copyright © 1992 by The Times Mirror Co. *Los Angeles Times*, Oct. 27, 1992, pt.A, p.5, col. 1. Reprinted with permission.

technology sold for commercial uses had been shifted illegally by Iraq to military programs. Previous disclosures have shown that U.S. technology was used in Iraqi nuclear and chemical weapons programs. Documents provided to The Times show for the first time that U.S. technology also played a role in designing the supergun and, according to sources, refining Iraq's long-range ballistic missile.

Bull's Maryland company claimed in its application for a license to export the computers that they were destined for Iraq's state automotive factory. However, a separate license request for the software said the computers would be used in Belgium for "analysis of designs for military and heavy construction vehicles, lorries, satellites, missiles."

Sources familiar with Bull's operations have told congressional investigators and The Times that the computers designed elements of the supergun and the ballistic missile, which was test-fired by Iraq in late 1989 and was also being refined when Bull was murdered. "It was a surprise to me when the government approved the license for the computers," said one former Bull associate in an interview Monday. "It appeared that the United States would have exercised more prudence."

Rep. Henry B. Gonzalez (D-Tex.), who has been investigating the Administration's Iraq policy, is scheduled to describe details of the Bull episode today at a hearing of the Senate Banking, Housing and Urban Affairs Committee. Brent Scowcroft, Bush's national security adviser, and former Commerce Secretary Robert A. Mosbacher have ignored invitations from the Banking Committee to appear as witnesses at the hearing, according to a staff member of the panel.

In March, 1990, Bull was shot to death outside his Brussels apartment. The killer shot the 62-year-old scientist twice in the back of the skull but did not take $20,000 in his pockets. The murder remains unsolved. Bull's family has charged that it was carried out by Israel in retaliation for Bull's work for Iraq. Israel was particularly alarmed by the supergun, but its government has denied any involvement in the murder.

Two weeks after Bull's death, British customs agents seized eight huge steel tubes designed to form a 180-foot howitzer barrel. Labeled oil pipes, they were awaiting shipment to Iraq. Additional components were found elsewhere in Europe.

Bull's Space Research Corp. had developed extended-range artillery shells in the 1960s and 1970s for the Canadian and U.S. military. He also sold $30 million worth of arms to South Africa, a violation of U.S. export laws that led to his imprisonment for six months in 1980. A congressional report later concluded that Bull had met the South Africans through a CIA official.

After his release, Bull moved Space Research Corp. to Brussels. He also opened an affiliate with the same name in Baltimore, headed by his son, Michael. The Baltimore company applied for an export license in 1989 for two Iris super 380 computers and associated hardware with a total cost of

$161,080, according to documents. The company said the computers were for Iraq's State Enterprise for Automotive Industries. The license was approved on Sept. 22, 1989. Because of the sophistication of the computers, the approval specified that they could not be used for nuclear purposes.

A few months earlier, Swanson Analysis Systems in Houston, Pa., had received U.S. approval to sell software for the Iris computers to Bull's Brussels company. That application said the computers would be used to test such military goods as missiles and military vehicles for stress. It specified that the software was bound for Belgium, a permissible destination. "We sought and were granted the appropriate licenses," said John Swanson, the company's president. "Our contract said that the technology could not be exported to any other country."

Sources close to Bull's operation said the computers and software were used both in Belgium and Iraq to work on the supergun and Iraq's long-range missile. They also said the computers helped design self-propelled howitzers for Iraq's army.

A spokeswoman for the Commerce Department's Bureau of Export Administration said she could not comment on either license because of privacy laws.

Intelligence documents indicate that work began on the supergun in 1988 and information about the project circulated in intelligence circles in 1989 and 1990. On Nov. 6, 1989—less than two months after the computers were approved for export—a CIA report identified Space Research Corp. as a component of Iraq's worldwide arms-buying network.

After the Gulf War, Iraqi officials initially denied possessing a supergun. However, they later acknowledged work on the project and U.N. inspectors found a tested prototype and components for four more guns. They were later destroyed by the U.N. team, as were the components of Iraq's ballistic missile program.

Trade Disputes

Trade disputes never stop. A few days after American and Japanese trade negotiators settled a potentially devastating dispute over automobile tariffs, a new dispute arose concerning film.

U.S. Probes Japanese Photo Trade
Robert Trautman, *Calgary Herald*

The United States said Monday it would investigate complaints by Kodak that Fuji controls the Japanese market for film and photographic paper, potentially opening another trade rift with Japan just days after settling a major dispute over cars.

U.S. Trade Representative Mickey Kantor acted on the petition by Eastman Kodak Co., which charged that rival Fuji Photo Film Co. and the Japanese government engaged in anti-competitive practices in the Japanese market. "American manufacturers of photographic film and paper should be able to compete on a fair basis in the Japanese market, just as Japanese firms can here," Kantor said in a statement.

Kodak said in its own statement, "We are one step closer to finally correcting years of anti-competitive behavior in Japan regarding consumer photographic film and paper." Kodak estimated that Japanese market barriers have cost it an estimated $5.6 billion in lost sales since the mid-1970s.

Kantor's office said that, according to Kodak's petition, Fuji enjoys a 75 percent share of the Japanese market for photographic film, while Kodak's share is only 7 percent. Kodak said this contrasts with its 43 percent share in Europe and 44 percent throughout the rest of the world. It said there was a similar discrepancy in the market for photographic paper, with Fuji enjoying an 86 percent share in Japan and Kodak 8 percent.

Kantor's statement echoed the open-market arguments the United States made in the tense, long-running dispute over trade in cars and parts that was settled last Wednesday when the two sides reached an accord in Geneva hours before U.S. sanctions on Japanese luxury car imports were due to start.

"It is critical that U.S. firms achieve full access to Japan's market, a market roughly comparable in size to that of the United States," Kantor's statement said Monday. "I hope that we can work constructively with Japan to ensure that Japan's market is open to U.S. film products."

Investors applauded the U.S. action, sending Kodak's shares higher, but

Copyright © 1995. *Calgary Herald*, July 4, 1995, p.D3. Reprinted with permission of Reuters.

the dispute over film could take longer to resolve than the auto trade dispute, industry analysts said. "This could well be a long haul, and tougher than the auto issue," said Jeffrey Pittsburg at Goldis Pittsburg Institutional Services.

Kodak's stock added $1.75 to close at $62.375 on the New York Stock Exchange.

Kodak's petition cited decades of exclusionary practices, largely involving Fuji, including price-fixing in trade associations and trying to control financially struggling wholesalers and retailers through cash payments to them. Fuji has answered Kodak's complaint by saying that annual reports by the U.S. trade office on closed markets worldwide had never cited problems in Japan's photo market. It also said that while it had a 70 percent share of the Japanese market and Kodak 10 percent, that was reversed in the United States where Kodak has 70 percent and Fuji 10 percent. Fuji said the two had similar market shares elsewhere.

In response to Kodak's petition, the United States will seek talks with Japan on opening markets. While no deadlines were stated, U.S. officials say tariffs could be imposed on Japanese film and paper if there was no timely resolution.

This action adds a new dimension to the continuing troubled U.S. trade relations with Japan. Besides the auto trade dispute resolved June 28, the two nations are to open talks next Wednesday on a civil aviation dispute, in which Washington claims Tokyo is breaking a bilateral accord by not allowing increased cargo flights by an American carrier. The United States has said it would restrict some Japanese cargo service if the dispute was not resolved. It said specific markets for the sanctions would be selected after a public comment period ended July 14.

Foreign Sovereign Immunities Act

The Foreign Sovereign Immunities Act can bar a lawsuit even in the most compelling of cases. Does it make sense to respect the integrity of another nation regardless of what that country has done?

Holocaust Survivor Blames U.S. for Court Ruling on German Suit
Matthew Dorf, *Jewish Telegraphic Agency*

Fifty years ago today, Hugo Princz, a U.S. citizen, was languishing in the Dachau concentration camp and feeling abandoned by the American Government. On Tuesday, only hours after the Supreme Court ended his legal fight to win reparations from the German Government, the 71-year-old survivor said he is "being stabbed in the back" by the same government which, he believes, refused to come to his aid, both then and now. Without comment, the Supreme Court on Tuesday refused to hear an appeal of a lower court ruling that Princz, a Highland Park, N.J. resident, cannot sue Germany.

In March 1992 Princz filed a lawsuit seeking $17 million from the German government. Last summer, a federal appeals court ruled that the Foreign Sovereign Immunities Act of 1976, which limits the rights of U.S. citizens to sue foreign governments, prevents Princz from taking Germany to court.

When the United States declared war against Germany, Princz and seven members of his family, all American citizens, were living in Czechoslovakia, where they were turned over to the Nazis. Princz, who later spent three years in Auschwitz, is the only member of his immediate family who survived the Holocaust.

Liberated by U.S. forces at the end of the war, he was taken to a U.S. military hospital, thereby bypassing the displaced persons camps. As a result, he was never registered as a Holocaust victim. Despite Germany's policy of paying thousands of dollars in reparations to victims of the Nazis, the German government had denied reparations to Princz because, the Germans say he did not meet the requirement that recipients be "stateless."

Princz blames the U.S. government both for his fate during the war and his lack of compensation today. "This is a repetition of what happened to my father in 1939," Princz said, explaining that his father had tried to secure safe passage from Prague for his family, but U.S. officials had been denied the necessary papers. Today, Princz and his attorney, Bill Marks, say the

Copyright © 1995 by *Jewish Telegraphic Agency*. January 18, 1995, p.7. Reprinted with permission.

State Department has "abandoned" them in their legal quest. They say the State Department refused to file a brief on his behalf in the court case.

Furthermore, in papers filed with the Supreme Court, Germany claimed that the State Department "implicitly agreed" with its position that Princz is not entitled to reparations, Marks said. The State Department's "silence may well have sent a signal to the court that the German assertion was correct," Marks said. "It is a dark chapter in the history of America when our government can not side with an American citizen in a case like this," Princz said. President Clinton did raise the matter in a private meeting with German Chancellor Helmut Kohl last year, but no details were revealed at the time.

While the court's decision ends Princz's legal quest, two other avenues remain to fight his battle. One avenue is legal, the other legislative. In addition to filing for legal recourse against Germany, Princz is seeking to sue the four German companies he was forced to work for during the Holocaust. A series of legal complications and motions have delayed the judge's decision on whether he has the right to sue. A ruling is expected in the coming weeks.

But Princz's best hope, according to his attorneys, lies with Capitol Hill. In the final moments of the last Congress, the Senate ran out of time to vote on a bill that would have allowed Princz to sue the German Government. The House had unanimously approved the same measure, which would amend the Foreign Sovereign Immunities Act to allow victims of genocide to sue foreign governments.

Rep. Charles Schumer (D-N.Y.) announced after the Supreme Court decision that he will reintroduce the bill next week. "In the interest of fairness and justice to Mr. Princz for the horrors he suffered during the Holocaust, Congress must act quickly and allow him to claim his just reparations," Schumer said. Calling the court's decision "disappointing," Schumer urged President Clinton to "announce his intention to sign the bill into law" to help garner support on Capitol Hill.

Senate Majority Leader Bob Dole (R-Kan.) expects to co-sponsor the legislation in the Senate, but he will not commit until he sees the final language of the bill, an aide to Dole said.

The Anti-Defamation League plans to lobby aggressively for Congress to pass the new legislation. "We were disappointed that the administration did not intervene. This underscores the need to pass this legislation," said Jess Hordes, ADL's Washington director.

Calling the battle for reparations a "game of cat and mouse," Princz supporters say they hope swift action by Congress and the White House support will prompt the German government to settle the case out of court. In any case, Princz vowed to "go on fighting as long as I have breath. I'm not asking for special treatment," the survivor said. "I'm asking for what an average German national would get."

Chapter 9

Business Ethics and Social Responsibility

Employee's Responsibility

Organization's Responsibility to Its Customers

Organization's Responsibility to Employees and the Employee's Responsibility to the Organization

What is Ethical Behavior?

Employee's Responsibility

On an airplane flight, a Texas Instruments sales person discovers a confidential document left behind by a competitor. What should he do?

Businesses Toe the Ethics Line; "Pond-Scummy, Immoral Behavior" Can Be Costly
Daniel Fisher, Arizona Republic

When the Texas Instruments Inc. salesman settled into his seat on the airliner, he discovered a golden opportunity—and an ethical dilemma—staring him in the face. Stuffed into the seatback pouch in front of him, among the in-flight magazines and instruction cards, was a document with a competitor's logo, stamped "confidential."

What to do? Legally, the salesman was free to keep the document and then use it against his competitor, and many employees would have done just that to bolster their own value to their companies. But at TI, that course of action wouldn't be wise. If the salesman had used the document, he might have been fired. TI is one of a growing number of companies that have hired ethicists to make policy out of philosophical quandaries like the one facing the salesman. And at TI, the salesman's temptation was a no-no.

"If you are in possession of confidential information about a competitor, you need to return it," said Carl Skoogland, chief ethics officer at TI. "We have ethical obligations to our competitors as well as our customers." Hard-bitten executives may snicker, but according to the Center for Business Ethics at Bentley College in Waltham, Mass., a third of Fortune 500 corporations have ethics officers, and 90 percent of U.S. business schools now have ethics programs, up from just a handful 15 years ago. One reason for this upswing: Bad ethics can be costly.

In 1991, when a Navy officer inadvertently left a document that contained information about a Bath Iron Works competitor in the company's boardroom, executives at the defense contractor ordered subordinates to copy it. Word leaked out about the incident, and Bath's reputation with the government, its key customer, was shattered. Though Bath had done nothing illegal, it took the company months of hard work to repair its standing, including installing a board-level ethics committee and firing the chairman and two vice presidents.

Ford Motor Co. paid an even heavier price for its ethically bankrupt decision to save money on the design of the Pinto subcompact in the early

Copyright © 1993 by *Arizona Republic,* Nov. 15, 1993, p.E1. Daniel Fisher. Used with permission. Permission does not imply endorsement.

1970s. The car displayed a tendency to catch fire in rear-end collisions. "They did not violate any regulation or law, but in every civil lawsuit they faced after somebody was killed or burned severely in that car, they lost," said Michael Hoffman, director of the Center for Business Ethics. "Juries felt, essentially, that they did an unethical act by putting that car on the road."

The price of some ethical transgressions is more subtle than that. Take the case of Jose Ignacio Lopez de Arriortua, the former purchasing czar at General Motors Corp. His tough tactics at the automaker in the 1980s reportedly included distributing sensitive information to suppliers about rivals in order to play them off against each other. "Besides being pond-scummy immoral behavior, what does that do to your supplier relationships?" asked Norman Bowie, an ethics professor at the University of Minnesota's Carlson School of Management. "It introduces all kinds of inefficiencies because nobody trusts you any more."

Some ethicists believe that their job is to counteract the "if it's legal, do it" attitude of the 1980s, which they say led to abuses in takeovers and the junk-bond market. "I think a lot of people now realize the law is inadequate to deal with all these ethical issues," said Diana Robertson, an assistant professor at the University of Pennsylvania's Wharton School of Business.

An argument recently has erupted among ethicists over whether businesses truly can be considered ethical if their behavior isn't completely altruistic. "You've got to walk the walk, talk the talk," Bowie said. "You simply can't do it in order to increase your profits."

These kinds of discussions are way too ethereal, other ethics experts say. In a controversial article in the May issue of the Harvard Business Review, Andrew Stark accused some of his colleagues, including Bowie, of failing to provide concrete advice to managers. "My complaint is business ethicists all too often say something is wrong and then walk away without participating in some kind of effort to deal with the situation," said Stark, an assistant professor in the Faculty of Management at the University of Toronto.

That doesn't seem to be the case at TI, however. Skoogland, a 57-year-old former quality-control engineer who became the company's ethics officer in 1987, views the job as anything but hands-off. Sometimes, the job demands difficult decisions. For example, Skoogland's department was instrumental in banning TI from contracting with suppliers owned by relatives of employees. This was to reassure suppliers that contracts weren't awarded on the basis of insider relationships.

However, that rule was brought into question two weeks ago when purchasing managers discovered that a TI employee's wife owned one of the company's minority contractors. That squeezed the ethics office, because another of its mandates has been to use contractors run by minorities. After much discussion, Skoogland and the managers said they had reached what they think is an ethical decision: The contractor will be let go, because bending the nepotism rule would cause more harm than good.

If U.S. companies continue to make creative and ethical decisions like that, the image of corporations relying solely on greed to survive could become as out of favor as junk bonds.

Employee's Responsibility

Michael Lewis (who wrote the best-seller *Liar's Poker* about his experiences as an investment banker) argues in this article that disloyalty to the boss is the worst sin an employee can commit. The disloyal employee becomes virtually unemployable. Lewis says that's why "everyone talks about business ethics, no one does anything about them." Is Lewis right? Is it better to cheat on an expense account than be disloyal to your boss?

The Good Rat
Michael Lewis, *New York Times Magazine*

About once a month I get a call from some businessman who says that he wants me to help him write a scathing exposé of his company. In six years or so as literary counsel to the disillusioned, I have heard from employees of every major Wall Street firm and another dozen large American companies. The stories often sound riveting and plausible, despite the breathless tone common to those who tell them. Wherever you turn in corporate America, it seems, evil pays generous dividends. My role, I have learned, is to listen encouragingly to the problem until the disillusioned businessman comes to his senses. Invariably, this is what happens:

Disillusioned Businessman: . . . anyway, this thing is not just a book. It's a movie. I see Pacino playing the chief executive officer.
Me: Me, too.
D.B.: There's just one thing I'm worried about, now that I have thought it over.
Me: What's that?

Copyright © 1995 by the New York Times Co. *New York Times Magazine,* Oct. 29, 1995, "The Capitalist." Reprinted with permission.

    D.B.   I want to stay in the industry. I mean, after we've nailed the s.o.b.
    Me: You know, the industry is not going to like the movie deal.
    D.B.:   *(long pause)* No . . . you're right. Tell you what. I'll call you back.

That is how we part: me without a book to ghostwrite; him without a movie deal. The disillusioned businessman concludes that his reputation for loyalty is too important to discard for a long shot at immortality. He no longer *feels* loyal, of course. He senses that his job prospects will suffer if he proves himself capable of independent thought and action. He is right, at least to judge from the way we treat those who lack the instinct to keep mum.

On Oct. 2, *Business Week* published the story of John Swanson, who left Dow Corning after 27 years to help a journalist, John A. Byrne, write a book about the company. Swanson ran Dow's ethics program when Dow was burying research on animals that linked the company's silicone breast implants to cancer. In the early 1970s, Swanson even wrote a pamphlet about business ethics called "A Matter of Integrity." As he worked away on business ethics, his wife, Colleen, received Dow's silicone implants, and spent the next 17 years feeling strangely sick.

In June 1991, the Swansons discovered that the company had been less than forthright about its research. Colleen filed a lawsuit a year later. John—ever the company man—remained with Dow. He made a brief effort to change its ways and then, having failed, recused himself from the silicone business. In August 1993, he took his retirement benefits and set out to tell his story.

His gesture was not entirely selfless. He is to receive half the royalties from the book. He stands accused by Dow of demanding payment from the company *not* to write the book. The Swansons, viewed by many people as sleazy opportunists, picked up and left their home in Michigan for Indiana where, it said in *Business Week,* John "hoped to establish himself as an ethics consultant." (Read: The royalties had better be good.)

A month before the Swanson article appeared in *Business Week, Fortune* published a similar "inside" story by Mark Whitacre. Whitacre had spent the previous six years working for Archer-Daniels-Midland, the grain company that makes those ominous-sounding ingredients that appear in fine print on the packages of some foods. Three years into his job of producing lysine (it tastes like chicken), he was encouraged by his chief executive officer to collude with his competitors. At the insistence of his bosses, he maintains, he met with Japanese lysine manufacturers in a Mexican hotel room and discussed fixing prices. But Whitacre felt uneasy breaking the law. He says that he seriously considered leaving his job, though he was first in line to be the next president of Archer-Daniels.

Meanwhile, the company's chairman had asked the F.B.I. to investigate possible sabotage of one of the company's lysine plants. During this investigation, the F.B.I. naturally questioned Whitacre. He brought up the unrelated matter of price fixing and suddenly found himself the mole in a F.B.I. sting. He moled away for several years, until he made the mistake of confiding in an Archer-Daniels attorney. Betrayed by the attorney, he was fired and then accused by his former colleagues of having stolen millions of dollars from the company. Forsaken and scandalized, Whitacre moved from Minneapolis to Chicago with his family to become, as he was recently quoted in *The Wall Street Journal,* "chief executive officer of a start-up biotechnology company." (Read: All job offers from competitors have expired.)

It is sometimes pointed out that although everyone talks about business ethics, no one does anything about them. Why should anyone? A man who pursues his own socially dubious interests within a large corporation may easily wind up the subject of flattering profiles and weepy eulogies. A man whose corporate betrayal emits the slightest whiff of self-interest is reviled and suspected of opportunism. Neither Swanson nor Whitacre is better off than he was before he came clean. Neither man seems to have landed a real job. Both seem to have felt the need to leave town. Their motives are now viewed more cynically than they would have been if they had remained loyal to their companies.

The fact remains that even if all the charges against the men were true, society should be better off for their betrayal of their bosses. Yet society does not see it that way.

Loyalty is more often an excuse than a virtue. Or it makes a virtue out of not thinking very much about why you do what you do. If a cause were naturally just, its leader would have no need to demand loyalty from his followers, or so you might think. Most business leaders clearly don't agree, for loyalty is more highly valued in business than in any place but the Mafia and the military (where followers in both must be prepared to kill for the boss).

The writer knows that he can betray friends and family to great fanfare. The political operative (James Carville and Mary Matalin, Peggy Noonan) knows that he can drum up new business with a memoir, even if the book makes his boss look like a fool. As soon as the midlevel businessman takes up his Dictaphone, however, he becomes a commercial untouchable. He may fib on his expense reports; he may jump to a competitor; he may cheat on his wife; he may even vote for a liberal. But if he wishes to remain employable by big American corporations, he must never, ever, rat on the boss. If he does, no matter how greatly we benefit from his act of treason, we will always suspect that he is scum.

Organization's Responsibility to Its Customers

R. J. Reynolds created Joe Camel, a hip cartoon character, to advertise cigarettes. As a result, the company now controls one-third of the cigarette market for children under 18. Why is it worse to sell cigarettes to children than to adults? Is it right to work for a cigarette company at all? Are there some industries in which it would be unethical to hold any job?

FTC Staff Takes Aim at "Joe Camel"; Reynolds Denies Ad Campaign Is Aimed at Enticing Teens to Smoke
Stuart Auerbach, *Washington Post*

The Federal Trade Commission staff wants to kill the six-year-old Joe Camel advertising campaign because the smoothly hip cartoon character has been too successful in enticing teenagers and young adults to smoke Camel cigarettes. The FTC staff has formally recommended that the five commissioners ban the ads. If the commission follows the staff recommendation, it will start an administrative process that will likely take several years and almost definitely end in court if the recommendation is upheld.

The staff proposal was reported yesterday by the *Wall Street Journal* and confirmed by a spokeswoman for RJR Nabisco Holdings Corp., owner of R.J. Reynolds Tobacco Co. The spokeswoman declined to elaborate on the case. "Our discussions with the FTC are confidential," she said. An FTC spokeswoman declined to comment. The issue pits the desire of the FTC staff to protect the health of Americans by making it harder for cigarette companies to market and sell their products, which have been scientifically linked to cancer, heart disease and other life-threatening illnesses, against a company's First Amendment right of free speech.

It is sure to be contested vigorously by R.J. Reynolds, which has benefited greatly from the aggressive advertising campaign's appeal to young smokers. Largely as a result of that campaign, Camel was one of the few non-discounted cigarettes to increase its market share last year. Further, Camel now holds about one-third of all sales to youths under 18 years of

Copyright © 1993 by The Washington Post. *Washington Post,* Aug. 12, 1993, p.D9. Reprinted with permission.

age, and its market share among 18- to 24-year-olds has almost doubled since the campaign started in 1987, according to studies compiled by a coalition of health groups that filed a complaint against the Joe Camel ads with the FTC two years ago.

The coalition argued that the ads promote smoking among teens because Joe Camel cuts a glamorous figure, depicted as sexy, athletic, debonair and heroic. "This campaign represents one of the most egregious examples in recent history of tobacco advertising targeted at children," the health coalition said in its 1991 petition.

Word of the FTC staff recommendation was cheered by the American Medical Association, whose past president, John L. Clowe, said he hoped the FTC commissioners "act with great haste." "If the tobacco industry had any shred of humanity or sense of business ethics, 'Old Joe' [as Joe Camel is fondly known around R.J. Reynolds] would have been set out in the desert back in 1991," Clowe said. "Once again, the world has seen the true face of tobacco conglomerates. It is a ruthless face of greed, disease and addiction."

"If we believed for a minute that Camel advertising induces children to smoke, we would not wait for the FTC or anyone else to act. We would immediately change the campaign," Reynolds countered in a statement yesterday.

FTC observers said any commission action is months away at best. To prove its case and win a ban on Joe Camel advertising, the FTC will have to expand the "unfairness" doctrine to a degree that legal experts said will be very difficult. R.J. Reynolds says that Joe Camel ads are aimed at young adults, but the FTC is expected to claim that the ads are unfair because they are trying to get underage youth to do something that they are not legally allowed to do—buy cigarettes.

The FTC previously has won cases using the unfairness doctrine against 900-number calls on the grounds that it is unfair to target children in advertisements when they are not the ones who will have to pay the bill for the phone calls. In past years, the FTC has won consent decrees against advertising that it considered unfair, but since the companies involved decided against contesting the complaints, the agency's power in that area has never been tested by the courts.

Organization's Responsibility to Employees and the Employee's Responsibility to the Organization

Do two wrongs make a right? Is it right for a woman to keep her pregnancy secret, knowing that if she discloses it, the company won't hire her? Is it right for a company to refuse to hire someone because she is pregnant?

Pregnancy, Gender Issues Pose Questions of Ethics
Gail Schmoller, *Chicago Tribune*

It could happen to almost any woman. You are up for a promotion or interviewing for a new job and find out you're pregnant. Do you withhold the fact from the employer for fear of being disqualified? Revealing a pregnancy might not have been an ethical dilemma in the predominantly male workplace 30 years ago, but today many moral questions facing employers and employees stem from situations involving women in the work force.

"The relationship between women and men as actors in the business enterprise has been undergoing a transformation, changing sets of roles which alter expectations that the genders have of one another," says Lawrence Gene Lavengood, a professor of business history at the J.L. Kellogg Graduate School of Management at Northwestern University.

The situation may be changing, but business ethics is still generally questions of truth and justice, says Father Thomas McMahon, director of the Loyola University's Center for Values in Business. In the case of revealing a pregnancy to an employer, he says the right of an employer to know the whole situation supersedes an individual's right to privacy. Otherwise, he says, any promotion or job will be offered "under false pretenses."

Sharon Kinsella, director of Nine to Five, a national women's employment problems hotline, would disagree. Because employers historically are less likely to offer a woman a job or promotion if she is pregnant, concealing such information is ethical, Kinsella says. "It's nobody's business except yours and the person who helped you conceive," she says. "If feeding your family is the No. 1 priority, then that's the ethical choice you have to make."

Such thinking is an example of the "end justifying the means," says McMahon, when asked about the hypothetical situation. McMahon says

Copyright © Chicago Tribune Company. All rights reserved. *Chicago Tribune,* Sept. 15, 1991, p.9.

such shortsightedness is one of the tougher lessons he tries to get across to students. "When all is said and done, it's better to (be) above board."

However, Kinsella says that the workplace often does not offer women an opportunity to act ethically if they want to keep their job. Steve Priest, executive director of the Center for Ethics and Corporate Policy, a non-profit organization in Chicago that encourages ethical leadership in business, would agree with Kinsella. A saleswoman being sexually harassed by someone on her account may get a mixed message from her boss about his concern for her plight and his desire that she not lose the account, Priest says. If the woman is not willing to sacrifice her integrity for her job by not complaining, Priest says, "then it becomes a prudential decision: What should she do? What should she tell her boss?"

The woman's moral dilemma is generated by a larger ethical question facing the employer, Priest says: "How do we promote a climate in a corporation so that a woman can be honest with her boss?" Change can come gradually through seminars and sensitivity training in companies, he says.

The public doesn't have much faith that business can respond to such questions, says Charles Watson, author of *Managing with Integrity* (Praeger, $26.95). "One popular superstition that grips many lives in our time is the belief that success in business requires greed, deceit and unfeeling ruthlessness," he says. Watson's book suggests ways managers can set a general tone of ethical conduct from the top:

Send a "strong and unambiguous message" informing all employees as to "what is and what is not acceptable behavior" and enforce standards. "When an infraction of ethical standards occurs, there can be a tendency to want to let it go by," Watson says, an approach that conveys a message that the rules are just for appearances.

Individuals can create a framework for their own ethical behavior by developing loyalty to a cause, Watson says.

Workers also should maintain concern for customers and other employees, the book says.

Watson and McMahon say that the business world could not survive if most workers were unscrupulous. "Business requires trust," McMahon says. "The whole world is based on trust."

What Is Ethical Behavior?

The Conference Board asked senior business executives and M.B.A. students to analyze three ethical questions. Who's right—the students or the executives?

Bad Judgment or Inexperience? Business Students' Ethical Decisions

Ronald E. Berenbeim, *Across the Board*

That's what an executive might wonder, looking at the way business students arrive at ethical decisions.

Do you think that the M.B.A. candidates your company hires this year—its next generation of senior executives—will handle difficult ethical problems in the same way as you and your colleagues would?

— How would you treat a colleague's former confidences if you were now in a position to give him an important promotion?
— How would you respond to requests from Latin American distributors for help in circumventing local tax laws?
— How would you react if you discovered that your predecessor had authorized questionable disbursements?

The Conference Board asked senior business executives and M.B.A. students to analyze these three ethical questions. The U.S. executives were surveyed by mail; 186 responded. The 98 students answered these hypothetical questions after a presentation by Pete Townley, The Conference Board's president, at New York University's Stern Graduate School of Business Administration. Townley appeared there as the 12th annual Stovall Fellow, a program inaugurated by Robert Stovall, president of Stovall/Twenty-First Advisers Inc., a money-management firm.

The senior executives, all of whom work for medium-size to large corporations, were asked for their own views rather than for a statement of their company's policy. Besides being asked to choose from various options for dealing with the ethical problems, the executives and the students were told to rank the three factors that most influenced their thinking. Their answers follow.

Copyright © 1992. Reprinted with permission from *Across the Board,* Oct. 1992, vol. 29, no. 10, p.43.

Does Confidentiality Have Limits?

In 1985, Bob Spicer, a 15-year veteran salesman for Archer Corporation and a frequent winner of annual performance awards, told his boss, Joe Sampson, that "I have been drinking a lot because I'm depressed about my personal problems." Sampson referred him to Archer's employee-assistance program, which offers counseling for alcohol and substance abuse and psychiatric problems.

Since that time, Spicer's job ratings have remained consistently superior. The company does not have access to his medical records and does not know whether he has ever obtained or is currently receiving counseling for depression. Joe Sampson, the manager whom Spicer consulted, is now CEO of Archer.

In November 1990, Spicer applied for the high-stress position of vice president of sales, a job that warranted serious consideration of his past performance.

In making their decisions, M.B.A. students tended to focus on giving employees a fair opportunity to be promoted. Senior executives emphasized the company's interest, and, to a lesser but significant degree, their own perceptions of Spicer's interest. More than half of the M.B.A. candidates agreed that "his personal problems are irrelevant in making the promotional decision." A larger percentage of executives believed that Spicer should be asked whether he is still depressed.

The differences between students and senior executives are best illustrated by their rankings of the three factors that most influenced their responses. Both groups agreed that the employee's performance record and general principles of fairness were the two most important considerations, but the students attached a higher priority to employee rights than to the relevance of a medical complaint to job requirements.

"Demonstrated performance is the principal element of job selection," said one M.B.A. candidate. "An employee's civil rights must always be kept in mind." Another student said that using the information would "create an unfair situation for people who are open about personal problems."

One student distinguished between the relevance of health complaints to job performance and the disabling effects of certain conditions. "Health complaints should be considered only when it is known that a person cannot perform a certain function," he argued.

The need for Spicer to understand the high-stress requirements of the new position was a recurring theme among executives who thought the depression incident ought to be discussed. They maintained that such an exchange was in Spicer's best interest. "It would be unfair for a candidate not to seriously consider the potential harmful effects of increased stress," said the personnel manager of a manufacturing company. This arguably paternalistic rationale was rarely cited by students.

Both students and executives who recommended a discussion of the incident cited the relationship between Spicer and Sampson as a justification for it. "Since Spicer was able to talk to Sampson," a financial-services executive said, "the two men obviously have an ideal open relationship. My choice might be more difficult if there was a lower level of trust in the prior relationship." Ultimately, both groups considered Spicer's job performance the decisive factor.

What Price "Accommodation"?

> Dagonet, a diversified manufacturer, is undertaking a major effort to introduce its products in Latin American markets. The company has been asked by several potential distributors to overbill and remit the differences of their companies' accounts in Switzerland and the Cayman Islands. The practice is customary in these countries, because local taxes are confiscatory and the local exchange rates make it very difficult for local distributors to achieve profitable results. Dagonet has received similar requests in the past from American and European firms, and has always refused.

The students' responses to this scenario were less dependent on conventional standards of honesty and fidelity to company policy than were the reactions of the senior executives. Consequently, the students were more likely to recommend that the company accede to the local distributors' request and to favor allowing the local subsidiaries the latitude to formulate policies based on regional customs and practices.

The students generally challenged the assumption that a corporation should unilaterally establish ethical business principles in a competitive global environment. The M.B.A. candidates ranked "profitability and sound business practices" third among the factors that most influenced their responses. The students were also much less sensitive than the senior executives to the potentially corrupting effects of agreeing to the distributors' terms. Executives ranked "integrity and morale of company employees" second among the important considerations in making their decision, while students rated it sixth and last.

Reflecting her group's greater concern with profitability in world markets, one student said, "As long as the firm's practice is in line with the local standards, it's fine. We can't wait for the rest of the world to reach universally acceptable ethical standards before business begins to expand overseas."

The senior executives, on the other hand, considered well-established company policy to be the most important consideration. One M.B.A. candidate shed light on why the students were less likely to factor company policy into their decision. A single policy, he said, might be a luxury that only a large company could afford; "Having one policy worldwide means ignoring all the political, economic, and cultural differences. If Dagonet is a very large and powerful company, such a policy could be feasible; otherwise, probably not."

The students who said that they would deny the distributors' request rejected it for pragmatic rather than principled reasons. The real question, they said, was not what the right or wrong course of action was, but what the effect on the company would be. One student said, "If you allow it, your U.S. and European sales forces will undoubtedly find out and demand equal treatment for their distributors." Another student warned that "it would be foolish to follow local customs in Latin America because the customs might change and the company could be admonished and thrown out when a new dictator rolls in."

Although senior executives also pointed to the need for flexibility and respect for local customs, their responses suggested that ultimately a company must follow its internal moral compass. A manufacturer's government-business affairs counsel put it this way: "A company should be consistent; its managers should not rely on 'situation ethics.'" A general counsel for a bank put it this way: "Without trying to pass judgment on others, ethics decisions must be based on the company's standards."

If there was one point on which the students and the senior executives agreed, it was that it's a lot easier to take a principled stand on a theoretical dilemma than on a real one. "I have no overseas experience," said a vice president of human resources. "I might be less highminded if I had."

Should Questionable Disbursements Be Investigated?

> Lily Bart's mentor, Lawrence Selden, is promoted, and Bart assumes his post as vice president of the general-services division of Newland Inc. Bart continues to report to Selden. In familiarizing herself with the responsibilities of her new job, Bart discovers that there have been questionable disbursements for travel and entertainment expenses in the past. The company's general counsel assures Bart that there has been no illegal conduct, and that both Selden and his predecessor routinely approved such reimbursements despite their apparent violation of the company's ethics code.

Although students and executives were more likely to agree here than in the two previous scenarios, the M.B.A. candidates showed less enthusiasm for investigation of past practices and a broad interpretation of the general counsel's role in enforcing ethical policies and principles. The students were also less likely than the executives to agree that Bart was confronting ethical as well as business or managerial issues.

Students showed a preference for education and clarification over investigation and enforcement. "The most effective way to correct this kind of misconduct," said one, "is to educate the people involved and increase the awareness of ethical codes among all employees."

Although more of the executives favored investigation and broad powers for the general counsel, many agreed with the students that a non-accusatory approach should be taken. A bank's senior economist argued in favor of corporate due process: "The travel and expense abuses are 'apparent'—but not facts. Proving that consistent abuse occurred appears difficult and could be disruptive." Even a utility executive who favored an investigation cautioned that "the intent should be to establish a new practice, not to search for the guilty."

One student who said that Bart's career was the most important consideration warned that "for Bart to make too big a commotion about this might be political suicide, in which case she would have no impact on changing the questionable behavior." Executives rated the effect on Bart's career last, and gave it the lowest approval level of any proposed rationale in the three case studies.

Where Generations Differ

Students appear to be more concerned than executives about how ethical decisions actually affect people. Will Spicer be judged fairly in his effort to obtain a promotion? Can the manager of the Latin American subsidiary compete for business in his region and for companywide recognition against the heads of U.S. and European units? Should Lily Bart risk her career to enforce the company's policies?

In each of the three cases, the students accorded greater weight to the interests of the individual than did the executives, who were more inclined to emphasize the interests of the company and to be more concerned about exposing it to risk. The Spicer promotion decision best illuminates these contrasting views. Senior executives commented that a discussion of the earlier drinking problem would benefit Spicer because it would help him to understand what the new job required and to determine whether he would be able to handle the stress. Not one student advanced such a rationale for discussing the incident with Spicer. The students' assumption seemed to be that because Spicer had worked for the company in the sales area, he knew the demands of the position he was applying for, and that any further discussion of stress was unnecessary.

It appears, then, that ethical priorities depend on where you sit. If you are responsible for promoting and protecting the company, you are likely to attach the highest priority to the organization's welfare. If you are an ambitious student aspiring to business leadership, you are most concerned that a company offer you opportunity and judge you according to the contribution that you make.

Unit 2

Contracts

Chapter 10

Introduction to Contracts

Purpose of Contract

Subjects of Contracts

Purpose of Contract

The author of this article injects a strong note of morality into a mortgage contract. Is his attitude justified?

"Lock In" Means There's No Turning Back
Bob Kerlin, *Washington Times*

A month ago, we signed a lock-in agreement on a 30-year fixed loan at 7⅞ with two points. Then the rates started to drop; now we can get the same loan at 7⅜ with two points. Wanting to save money, we contacted our mortgage company about lowering our rate. The company has refused to do so. We are thinking about having our loan transferred to another company, but the current company also has refused even to do that. We are to go to settlement in two weeks and want the current rate. What can we do?

—James, Annandale

A commitment is a two-way street. Honor your commitment.

At loan application, a borrower is given two choices, to lock in the interest rate, usually for a 60-day period or to float the rate until he elects to lock in the rate. The borrower always has those two options, and most lenders let the borrower decide.

When a borrower elects to lock in the rate on his loan, he has the benefit of knowing what interest rate he will have at settlement—no matter what happens to the interest rates. Most lock-in agreements have wording to this effect: "After the loan is locked in there can be no change in the rate, discount points or loan amount." This makes sense from the standpoint that the lender has to know at what program and interest rate the loan is to be underwritten.

The mortgage market is a very fickle mistress, and the rates can change hourly. The advantage of a lock-in is that the borrower does not have to worry about the uncertainty of the daily fluctuations and can be assured of the rate he will have at settlement.

Let's take a look at the other side of the coin. If the rates were to rise and a lender did not honor its commitment, a borrower would raise holy hell—and rightly so. An analogous situation would be in the stock market. Orders are received daily to buy or sell a stock, and the trade is executed

Copyright © 1995. Reprinted with permission from *Washington Times*, June 23, 1995, pt. F, p.26. Bob Kerlin is a local mortgage banker and real estate consultant with Prosperity Mortgage.

immediately with payment within a week. If you place a buy order for IBM at 52 and it drops to 48, you are expected to honor the agreement at 52.

A similar situation would be with the purchase of a home. Both buyer and seller sign a contract stating that the house will convey for a certain price, say $200,000. This is a bilateral contract between two parties agreeing on the price of the home. Before settlement, if oil is found on the property, the seller cannot unilaterally change the price to $400,000. Likewise, the buyer cannot lower the price after contract if a home down the block sells for less. A contract is a contract.

If the rates had gone up, you would not have written this letter but would have told all your friends how you had outsmarted the market. Honor your agreement.

As to the idea of having your loan transferred, it is not yours. The information you provided the mortgage company was for it to make a credit determination on your loan. The file is the mortgage company's property, and it does not have to give it up. It is the same as a job application that you fill out though you never take the job; you can't have it transferred from one employer to another. Nothing can stop you from making another application with another company. Just don't call me; I only deal with honorable people.

Subjects of Contracts

Contract claims can cover diverse subjects, such as this case about college credits.

College Can't Revoke "Life Experience" Credits; Court Upholds Agreement as a Valid Contract
Melissa A. Davey, *Legal Intelligencer*

Joseph Britt objected to a classroom exercise in which another male student was asked by their professor to make sexual advances toward him. According to a lawsuit filed by Britt, after he voiced his objections, the professor tried to ruin his academic reputation. Britt sued the professor and Chestnut Hill College, where he was enrolled. Following preliminary objections, the trial court struck Britt's claim for breach of contract, ruling that the

Copyright © 1993 by Legal Communications, Ltd. *Legal Intelligencer,* Oct. 26, 1993, p.3. Reprinted with permission.

college was entitled to revoke credits it had previously promised him for "life experience."

"Contractual Obligation"

But a three-judge panel of the state Superior Court has reversed that decision, ruling that "such a holding ignores the fact that an institution may make a contractual obligation to a student which it is not free to later ignore." The panel also affirmed the trial court's decision to grant defendants' objection to Britt's claim of intentional infliction of emotional damage, ruling that the plaintiff did not present necessary medical evidence of the emotional damage he alleged.

Britt, a detective, enrolled in a master's degree program at Chestnut Hill College in 1987 and planned to graduate in May 1990, according to Judge Joseph A. Del Sole's 11-page opinion for the panel. Britt enrolled in a one-week "gender stereotyping" course in June 1989 in order to fulfill requirements for his degree, according to the Oct. 13 opinion. The course was taught by Thomas Earl Klee.

Britt claimed that, as part of a classroom exercise, Klee directed another male student to make physical advances toward Britt. The student, who Britt claimed was a "known" homosexual, complied by telling Britt he was attracted to him and touching him above the knee. Britt said he rejected the student's advances. According to Britt's complaint, the next day, Klee assigned the student to serve as a "facilitator" to "deal with [Britt's] anger," according to the opinion.

Objection To Exercise

Britt said he then objected and told Klee he thought the exercise was improper. He said Klee became openly critical of his attitude and classroom performance and gave him a "C" grade for the course.

Britt claimed that, following the incident, Klee did "everything within his power" to sabotage his reputation and academic career. He alleged that Klee arranged to have himself assigned as Britt's academic adviser and then "personally revoked, and successfully persuaded other instructors to revoke, certain pre-approved credits that had been granted to [Britt] upon admission to the college," Del Sole wrote. According to Britt, because those credits were revoked, he was not able to graduate in May 1990 as he had planned.

Britt filed a six-count complaint against Klee and Chestnut Hill College, alleging defamation and slander, breach of contract, civil conspiracy, assault and battery, sex discrimination and intentional and malicious infliction of mental distress. Preliminary objections were filed by Klee and the college.

The trial court denied objections to Britt's defamation and slander claims, but granted the objections "in the nature of a demurrer" to the assault and battery, sex discrimination and intentional infliction of mental distress counts. The court also sustained a preliminary objection to the civil conspiracy claim and granted the defendants' objections in the nature of a motion to strike with respect to the breach of contract count. This appeal followed.

Appealable Issue?

Del Sole wrote that, before the court could discuss the nature of Britt's claims, it must first decide whether the issues Britt raised were appealable. He explained that, under Meinhart v. Heaster, decided earlier this year, an order dismissing some but not all counts of a complaint usually cannot be appealed immediately. However, he added, quoting *Meinhart,* "if a dismissed count states a cause of action that is separate and distinct from the remaining counts, the order dismissing that count is final and appealable."

In the immediate case, the court found the breach of contract claim "clearly separate and distinct" from the remaining defamation claim. While the court found the question of whether Britt's claim for intentional infliction of emotional distress was different from the defamation claim "more difficult to answer," it too was ruled final and appealable. "The torts in question are separate and distinct," Del Sole wrote. "Furthermore, the nature of the damages suffered by a plaintiff as a result of their commission are not alike."

According to the opinion, the lower court decided to strike Britt's breach of contract claim without looking at the defendant's preliminary objection to the claim, which asserted that the claim did not comply with Pa.R.C.P. §1019. "Instead, the trial court held that [the] college was entitled to revoke the credits in question because [Britt] did not have a vested right in receiving a degree," Del Sole wrote.

But the Superior Court disagreed, rejecting the lower court's decision that the college was "entitled to revoke credits previously granted for work performed out of school." "It is apparent to this court that such a holding ignores the fact that an institution may make a contractual obligation to a student which it is not free to later ignore," Del Sole wrote. "The economic reality is that colleges and universities are competing to attract non-traditional age students and many of those institutions have designed programs to cater to them," he continued "Through advertising and recruitment campaigns, an increasing number of colleges and universities are promising students who wish to return to school flexible schedules, evening and weekend classes and academic credit for life experience. Students, in turn, attracted by these options, may seek to apply to a particular institution and inquire as to the requirements they will have to meet in order to achieve their degree," he added. "Where an individual is induced to enroll in a university or college based upon an award of certain life experience credits, the institution cannot then, after the student's enrollment, revoke those credits."

Not An Infringement

Del Sole added that the court's decision does not represent an infringement on schools' rights to develop their curricula and set requirements for the degrees they offer. But an institution that promises a student "life experience credits," which will allow the student to graduate at an accelerated rate, cannot then renege on that promise. Therefore, the Superior Court reversed the trial court's order striking the breach of contract claim.

Britt also questioned the trial court's grant in the nature of a demurrer of preliminary objections to the claim for intentional infliction of emotional distress. "Our court has consistently held that a preliminary objection in the nature of a demurrer should only be granted in cases that are free from doubt," Del Sole wrote.

On this portion of the appeal, the Superior Court agreed with the lower court's decision that Britt's presentation of the facts was "insufficient" to support his allegation of intentional infliction of emotional distress. According to the opinion, Kazatsky v. King David Memorial Park, the state Supreme Court concluded that, when a plaintiff makes a claim of intentional infliction of emotional distress, "at the very least, experience of the alleged emotional distress must be supported by competent medical evidence." "From our review of the complaint, it is apparent that [Britt] has failed to allege that [the defendant's] conduct caused him to seek medical treatment," Del Sole wrote. The Superior Court affirmed that trial court's order dismissing Britt's claim for the intentional infliction of emotional distress.

Subjects of Contracts

Contracts often concern public issues and public money. Political leaders who inherit a deal made by their predecessors may be unhappy about it. Would it make sense to allow public entities to escape from contractual obligations? What advantages would that have, and what problems would it create?

$100m Vow for Logan Area Upheld; Community Groups Win Suit for Deal To Buffer Expansion
Meg Vaillancourt, *Boston Globe*

Community groups in East Boston and Winthrop won a major victory yesterday when a judge ruled the Massachusetts Port Authority must honor an earlier promise to spend as much as $100 million to cushion the impact of Logan Airport's $1.2 billion modernization and expansion program. The money would go for parks, day-care facilities, noise reduction and programs to reduce the impact of traffic on surrounding neighborhoods.

The mitigation agreement was approved in 1993 by a Massport board dominated by appointees of Gov. Michael S. Dukakis. The current board, controlled by Gov. Weld, has resisted its implementation for nearly two years. Internal Massport estimates indicate the mitigation agreement's price tag could exceed $100 million.

"Vindication is sweet," said Mary Ellen Welch, a member of Airport Impact Relief, an East Boston group that was a plaintiff in the suit along with Friends of Belle Isle Marsh, which has members in Winthrop, East Boston and Revere. "The new Weld-dominated regime at Massport refused to recognize our agreement and that was a clear injustice," she said.

The ruling is a big loss for the Weld administration. Weld's Massport chief, Stephen P. Tocco, had refused to honor significant portions of the 1993 agreement, arguing that a Massport board dominated by Dukakis appointees could not bind the current board now controlled by Weld appointees. Tocco yesterday declined to say whether Massport would appeal the ruling and issued a written statement that appeared to attempt to marginalize the two groups that successfully sued his agency. "We disagree with the decision of the lower court," Tocco said. "We regret that two small groups have suc-

Copyright © 1995 by Globe Newspaper Co. *Boston Globe,* June 9, 1995, "Metro/Region," p.1. Reprinted courtesy of The Boston Globe.

ceeded in delaying beneficial community programs and defying the will of the larger East Boston and Winthrop communities."

In his decision yesterday, Suffolk Superior Court Judge Patrick King ruled that the mitigation contract reached with Massport and the community groups in June 1993 "is a valid contract." Denying Tocco's central argument that a new board could not be bound by agreements reached by its predecessor, the judge ruled that "the mere fact that the board executed the mitigation agreement on the eve of a shift in its political majority is not enough to invalidate the agreement."

The 1993 agreement called for Massport to make payments of $300,000 a year for 17 years to a community foundation. The agreement also required Massport to help expand parks near the airport, provide facilities for day care, increase mass transit to and from the airport, reduce the impact of traffic on surrounding neighborhoods and increase public participation in Massport's controversial runway expansion program. Other provisions call for studies of indoor pollution, noise and sleep disturbance in surrounding communities and for a reduction in engine emissions, odors, noise and soot.

"Implementation of this agreement is essential in order to bring East Boston and Winthrop some minimal protections, which are necessary to protect these communities from continued airport growth," said Peter Koff, attorney for the plaintiffs.

But several community groups with ties to Rep. Emanuel G. Serra (D-East Boston) have signed on to a rival mitigation agreement reached with Tocco but not approved by the Massport board. That pact would give $1.5 million a year for 10 years to a coalition of East Boston community groups. However, it would not address all of the environmental concerns raised in the earlier agreement. The groups holding out for the Tocco agreement include the East Boston Chamber of Commerce, the Piers Project Advisory Committee, the Land Use Council of East Boston, the Environmental Rights Committee and neighborhood groups in Jeffries Point.

Serra, who supported the Tocco agreement, argued the community deserved more money and other considerations to make up for the airport's impact. But supporters of the previous agreement countered that Serra was looking for a pot of money over which he would have considerable control—a contention Serra has denied. "The agreement that was approved in court was a good beginning," Serra said. "But I think we can improve upon it. Maybe we can mesh the two mitigation agreements together."

An analysis prepared for Massport argues that the Tocco agreement is better because it sets lower baseline levels for future air and noise reduction programs, commits $25 million to residential soundproofing in the area, and "broadens community participation." But an analysis prepared by Koff, who successfully represented the signatories to the first agreement, found the Tocco plan "weaker" in that it does not support free shuttle service from South Station to Logan, drops agreements about community involvement in a proposed runway and scales back a commitment to new parks—especially to a "linear park" that could link the East Boston piers with Belle Isle Marsh.

Koff also argued that the "broader community participation" cited by Massport comes at the expense of the community groups' right to sue Massport if the agency does not live up to the agreement—a right that would be waived in Tocco's agreement, Koff said.

Chapter 11

Agreement

Acceptance

Counteroffer

Promissory Estoppel

Acceptance

Negotiation is a serious business, and an acceptance should not be lightly made on the assumption that it can be withdrawn.

Litigant May Get $60,000 Whether She Wants It or Not: Judge Is Forcing Woman To Settle
Ted Cilwick, *Salt Lake Tribune*

There wasn't much remarkable about Letha Robinson's slip-and-fall case—until she refused the $60,000 check her lawyer wrangled from Delta Air Lines to settle the lawsuit. The Salt Lake City woman had a change of heart, believing her case was worth more than that, and has yet to sign either the check or the settlement papers, court records show. Now, though, after a seven-month tug-of-war, a federal judge is forcing her to accept the settlement. If she doesn't capitulate by mid-November, U.S. Magistrate Samuel Alba has ordered her share of the settlement to be turned over to her.

"She's kind of an unusual client," says her lawyer, Ned Siegfried of Salt Lake City, an attorney for 11 years who specializes in personal-injury cases. "I've settled a couple thousand injury claims and usually the people can't get their money quick enough." Moreover, says Siegfried, Robinson sustained only "minor injuries" while slipping on a Delta ramp at the airport in Indianapolis—and may have come away from a jury trial empty-handed. "If we took it to trial, we had a 90 percent chance of getting no costs," he noted, in part because neither Robinson nor her mother could even identify the liquid substance she supposedly slipped on. The lawyer says he has written Robinson "dozens" of letters urging her to take Delta's money, but to no avail so far. Robinson, nearly 50, a former mail clerk for a large insurance firm, could not be reached for comment.

Court documents show that she would receive $28,956 of the settlement and her lawyers, $20,585. The rest, about $10,500, would satisfy medical liens filed against her, including Burns Chiropractic ($4,209) and Cottonwood Hospital ($3,397).

The lesson for others involved in common cases such as personal-injury suits is: If you initially direct your lawyer to accept a settlement, but later change your mind, you probably will be forced to accept the deal—even if you never signed the dotted line.

Several recent Utah cases, as well as the state Code of Judicial Administration, hold clients responsible once they signal their lawyers to enter a

Copyright © 1994 by The Salt Lake Tribune. *Salt Lake Tribune*, Oct. 16, 1994, p.C1. Reprinted with permission.

settlement, according to Delta lawyer Robert Hilder. As long as fraud is not involved and the settlements contain the basic elements—offer, acceptance and consideration (usually money), parties cannot later change their minds, Hilder wrote.

Siegfried agrees. "It would be worthless to appeal [Alba's order] to the 10th Circuit [Court of Appeals in Denver]," he says. "We really didn't have much of a leg to stand on." Alba also concurred, and left little room for Robinson to do anything but accept the settlement. He has ordered Delta to deposit the $60,000 in a court account. If Robinson persists after 30 days, he will dismiss her suit and distribute shares of the settlement.

Robinson incurred back, neck and leg injuries while boarding a Delta flight on Dec. 31, 1991. She field the lawsuit a year later. Delta initially denied her allegations and stated that the fall was due to her own negligence or others. Delta also contended that some of her injuries could not be explained by such a fall and had a neurologist lined up as an expert witness, records show.

The case was scheduled for a three-day jury trial in January 1994, but that was canceled because of ongoing settlement negotiations. Delta originally offered $32,500, then $50,000, while Siegfried demanded $90,000. The lawyers agreed on $60,000 in March, and Siegfried says Robinson told him to accept. But during the six weeks it took Delta's insurers to cut a check, Robinson changed her mind and has balked ever since. Says Siegfried: "Based on the liability situation we were up against, this probably is in the top 1 percent of the cases I've settled. . . . I've had the check in hand since the end of April."

Counteroffer

The law should focus on substance, not form. Has this court successfully looked behind the term "counteroffer" to find the truth, or has it unfairly voided a legitimate deal?

Counteroffer Encounter Leads to a No Counter in the 1st Circuit

Robert A. Feldman, *Corporate Legal Times*

Raymond Bourque made a written offer to the FDIC to purchase a piece of real estate for $105,500. The offer, made through an attorney, included an earnest money deposit of $10,000 and a signed FDIC purchase-and-sale agreement. The FDIC's account officer wrote back:

> This letter is to advise you that the FDIC is unable to accept Mr. Bourque's offer. FDIC's counteroffer is $130,000. All offers are subject to approval by the appropriate FDIC delegated authority. FDIC has the right to accept or reject any and all offers. I am returning your customer's contract of sale and earnest money deposit. If your customer wishes to accept this counteroffer, please return the amended Purchase & Sale Agreement to me.

Two days later, Bourque's attorney sent in an amended Purchase & Sale Agreement for $130,000. The FDIC deposited the original $10,000 earnest money check. Subsequently, the FDIC substituted a new account officer. She advised that the FDIC had received a higher offer, and the property was sold to a third party for $253,000. Bourque sued to obtain the benefit of his bargain. After the lawsuit was filed, the FDIC changed the macros on its computers so that "counteroffers" would no longer be sent out. The new FDIC documentation invites another offer.

Working with the facts as they then were, the FDIC and a co-defendant nevertheless maintained that no contract had been formed with Bourque. They moved for summary judgment. Their motions were successful, and the 1st Circuit affirmed on appeal. Bourque v. FDIC, 42 F.3d 704 (1st Cir. 1994.)

Some additional facts: Prior to the initial offer, Bourque's attorney had written to the FDIC account officer, asking whether he was the person han-

---

Copyright © 1995 by Corporate Legal Times Corp. *Corporate Legal Times*, June, 1995, "Contractually Speaking," p.9. Reprinted with permission. Robert A. Feldman served as in-house counsel for more than 20 years, most recently at Comshare Inc., Ann Arbor, Mich. He is now in private practice in Ann Arbor. Additionally, he offers consulting services and in-house seminars and workshops on contract drafting and negotiations.

dling the asset and whether he had authority to discuss the property. An assistant confirmed that the account officer was the person handling the property. The assistant apparently did not indicate that there were any limitations on the account officer's authority to sell the property.

The FDIC said it made a mistake by cashing Bourque's earnest money check. Another mistake was failing to follow policy by sending back a standard FDIC document with the "counteroffer." The document explained that the account officer did not have the authority to sell. On the other side of the ledger, there was some evidence that Bourque's attorney had a prior dealing with the FDIC and hence may have been aware of authority limitations.

Although the FDIC said, not once but twice, that it was counteroffering, named a specified sum and invited acceptance, there was, according to the federal appeals court, no counteroffer. Indeed, the evidence was so one-sided in favor of the FDIC that "no reasonable person could decide to the contrary." Hence summary judgment was appropriate.

The case, whether rightly or wrongly decided, serves as a useful review of some fundamentals regarding contract formation. While these issues may come up with more regularity in a first-year contracts class than in the commercial world, there is the occasional odd case, such as *Bourque,* to remind us that even the elementary can be complex enough to occupy nine pages of judicial explanation in the Federal Reporter.

In determining whether there is an offer, the use of words like "offer" and "counteroffer" are given weight but are not controlling. An offer may be really an invitation to make an offer. A reservation of the power to close a deal indicates there is no offer. That, according to the *Bourque* court, is what happened here. While conceding that the language was "hardly a model of clarity," the court concluded the only reasonable interpretation was that the FDIC had simply extended an invitation to submit an offer.

Notwithstanding the outcome here, a sound contract practice is to say what you mean. Call out, in unequivocal words, an invitation to submit an offer or a request for a proposal and state that there is no obligation to accept (if that is the case). The FDIC, liquidator of assets and guardian of the taxpayer's dollar, is frequently blessed in its litigation efforts. Private litigants should not place too much reliance on the precedential value of its many victories.

Promissory Estoppel

In this important case, the court was faced with an unusual promise—one of confidentiality. It had to consider traditional contract law and also promissory estoppel.

Court Restores Cohen Award
Margaret Zack, *Star Tribune*

The Minnesota Supreme Court has reinstated a $200,000 award against two Twin Cities newspapers that broke promises of confidentiality to a news source. In a decision to be filed today, the court ruled that Dan Cohen had a legally enforceable promise when reporters for the *Star Tribune* and the *St. Paul Pioneer Press* promised him anonymity in exchange for information about Marlene Johnson, who was the DFL candidate for lieutenant governor at the time.

The case began during the waning days of the 1982 gubernatorial race, when Cohen approached the reporters with documents that showed that Johnson had been charged in 1969 with unlawful assembly and convicted in 1970 of shoplifting. Cohen had ties to the campaign of Wheelock Whitney, Independent-Republican candidate for governor, and the papers' editors overruled their reporters' promises, publishing stories that named Cohen. The editors said that the source of the documents was as newsworthy as the contents. After the stories were published, Cohen was fired from his job with an advertising agency.

Elliot Rothenberg, Cohen's attorney, said today's decision means that a promise is a promise. "No person or institution is above the law that a promise once made must be honored," he said. "Any person or institution who violates a promise is liable for injuries."

The *Star Tribune* released a one-line statement yesterday from Tim McGuire, executive editor, who said, "We are obviously disappointed in the decision, but we respect it." Paul Hannah, the lawyer representing the *Pioneer Press,* said, "The only official comment is our disappointment at the results."

In its unanimous ruling, the court said it was significant that the *Star Tribune* and the *Pioneer Press* editors who decided to break the reporters' promises believed they generally must keep such promises. "It was this

Copyright © 1992 by Star Tribune, Minneapolis-St. Paul. *Star Tribune,* Jan. 24, 1992, p.1A. Reprinted with permission.

long-standing journalistic tradition that Cohen, who has worked in journalism, relied upon in asking for and receiving a promise of anonymity," wrote Justice John Simonett. The case has been closely watched nationally because of the question it raised about the reporter/source relationship. Rothenberg said the decision is good for reporters, because it means that a promise is backed not only by moral obligations but also by legal principles.

Under an agreement with the Supreme Court, its decisions are released to the news media the day before they are filed, with the understanding that reporters may contact the attorneys involved in the suit but not parties to it.

In a prepared statement, Cohen said, "The message of this case is clear. Minnesota juries and courts will not protect intentional lies by even those as rich, powerful and politically correct as the *Minneapolis Star Tribune* and *St. Paul Pioneer Press.*"

The case began its journey through the courts in 1988 when a District Court jury awarded Cohen $700,000, which was later reduced to $200,000 by the Minnesota Court of Appeals. Cohen appealed and in June 1990 the Minnesota Supreme Court ruled that the First Amendment protected the newspapers against damages in the case, saying that a journalist's promise is not a legally enforceable contract. Cohen then appealed to the U.S. Supreme Court, which ruled in June 1991 that the First Amendment did not prevent a lawsuit against the newspapers under the doctrine of "promissory estoppel." Promissory estoppel infers that a legal agreement similar to a contract exists if failure to fulfill a promise results in an injustice.

The case was sent back to the Minnesota Supreme Court. Attorneys for the newspapers asked the court to use the Minnesota Constitution to find broader press protection than the First Amendment provided. The court declined to do that in today's decision, and said that the state constitution's guarantees of freedom of the press did not prevent Cohen's case from being considered under the theory of promissory estoppel. The court said Cohen released his information to reporters only after being promised confidentiality, and then lost his advertising job as a result of that promise being broken.

Cohen's case had first been argued as a breach of contract, but in its 1990 ruling in the case, the state high court decided the reporters' promises were not legally enforceable contracts. The newspapers argued that they should not be punished for publishing the whole truth. But the court disagreed, saying, "Veiling Cohen's identity by publishing the source as someone close to the opposing gubernatorial ticket would have sufficed as a sufficient reporting of the 'whole truth.' "

The court characterized the evidence at trial as the pot calling the kettle black, with each side insinuating that the other's behavior was unethical. "Neither side in this case clearly holds the higher moral ground," the court said. But it then went on to say that the importance of honoring a promise of confidentiality and the lack of evidence of a compelling need to break that promise demanded that Cohen be compensated.

Here is a chronology of the *Cohen* case:

Oct. 27, 1982—Reporters for the *Minneapolis Star Tribune, St. Paul Pioneer Press,* Associated Press and WCCO-TV are contacted by Dan Cohen, supporter of Independent-Republican gubernatorial candidate Wheelock Whitney. In exchange for anonymity, Cohen gives them court records showing that DFL lieutenant-governor candidate Marlene Johnson had been convicted of shoplifting in 1970.

Oct. 28, 1982—The story about Johnson's previous misdemeanor record is published. Cohen is named as the source of the information in the *Star Tribune* and *Pioneer Press.* The Associated Press does not use Cohen's name, and WCCO-TV does not use the story.

Oct. 28, 1982—Cohen resigns as public relations director for Martin-Williams Advertising Inc.

Dec. 15, 1982—Cohen sues Cowles Media Co., parent company of the *Star Tribune,* and Northwest Publications Inc., parent company of the *Pioneer Press,* claiming fraud and breach of contract for naming him as the source in the Johnson story.

July 5, 1988—The trial starts in Hennepin County District Court. Judge Franklin Knoll presides.

July 6, 1988—*Star Tribune* and *Pioneer Press* attorneys call Cohen a dirty trickster who was trying to defeat former Gov. Rudy Perpich's 1982 gubernatorial candidacy by giving the information on Johnson to the media.

July 22, 1988—The six-person jury rules in Cohen's favor, awarding him $200,000 for the loss of his job and $500,000 to punish the newspapers for failing to protect his identity. The damages are divided equally between the papers.

Aug. 23, 1988—Lawyers for the newspapers ask Knoll to set aside the verdict. They argue that the $500,000 in punitive damages cannot be supported because no fraud or misrepresentation had occurred.

Nov. 19, 1988—Knoll refuses to set aside the verdict and rules that there are no grounds for a new trial. The papers continue with plans to appeal.

Sept. 5, 1989—The Minnesota Court of Appeals rules 2-1 that the *Star Tribune* and *Pioneer Press* committed breach of contract when they published Cohen's name but that he is not entitled to punitive damages. The justices let stand the $200,000 award for actual damages.

March 13, 1990—Lawyers for both papers argue their cases before the Minnesota Supreme Court.

July 20, 1990—The state Supreme Court rules 4-2 that the *Star Tribune* and *Pioneer Press* were not liable for damages. The justices rule that enforcing a promise of anonymity would violate the newspapers' First Amendment rights and that keeping the promise might be a moral obligation but not a legally binding one.

Dec. 10, 1990—The U.S. Supreme Court agrees to hear the Cohen case.

March 27, 1991—Lawyers for both sides present arguments.

June 24, 1991—The Supreme Court rules 5-4 that reporters' promises of confidentiality are legally enforceable, despite the U.S. Constitution's free-press protections. The high court says Minnesota's Supreme Court should restudy its ruling that threw out the $200,000 award against the two newspapers.

Dec. 3, 1991—The state Supreme Court hears arguments. It has two options: It can reinstate Cohen's damages or rule that such a breach of promise is overridden by the state constitution's free-press guarantees.

Jan. 23, 1991—The state Supreme Court rules that Cohen had a legally enforceable promise of confidentiality and should be awarded $200,000 in damages.

Chapter 12

Consideration

Concept of Consideration

Adequacy of Consideration

Accord and Satisfaction

Concept of Consideration

This article looks at athletic scholarships and suggests that schools make misleading promises. If some schools abuse athletes, should the problem be attacked by contract lawsuits, or legislation—or not at all?

Playing Ball with Colleges
David Salter, USA Weekend

As high school football stars decide which colleges they'll play for, and basketball players receive their first visits from college recruiters, this is a good time to reflect on the plights of Kevin Ross and Bryan Fortay. In a first-time legal action settled in 1992, Ross sued Creighton University for breach of contract. He contended that the Omaha school had failed to fulfill its promise to educate him in exchange for playing four years of Bluejays basketball. The suit further said Creighton had denied Ross tutoring and directed him to a worthless degree. Education experts later determined that Ross read at the second-grade level. (The terms of a $30,000 settlement prohibit the university, Ross and his attorney from commenting on the case.)

In a more celebrated, still pending case, Fortay, a quarterback for Rutgers University, filed a lawsuit last year against the University of Miami, his former school. The suit alleges that Miami's football coaches failed to fulfill their recruiting promise to install Fortay as starting quarterback for the Hurricanes. He said it might have cost him the chance to play professional football.

Those legal actions highlight a dilemma many top high school athletes will face: College sports is a high-stakes game in which recruiters promise the world—and athletes rarely get what they expect. Instead of focusing on how their college choice can lead to a career in the pros, students and parents should take a hard look at the numbers and start thinking about the part that's most likely to matter in the long run: a good college education. Just consider these alarming statistics:

- One-third of professional athletes are functionally illiterate. They can't read well enough to understand the contracts they have signed.
- There are about 948,000 high school football players and 517,000 high school basketball players. Each year, of that number, 150 make it to the NFL after college; 50 make it to the NBA.

Copyright © 1994 by Gannett Company, Inc. *USA Weekend,* Jan. 23, 1994, p.8.

- Not even 2.5 percent of college seniors will make it even one year in professional basketball.

An athletic scholarship is renewable annually. It is not the guaranteed four-year deal that people believe it is. A coach can revoke a scholarship any time. This amounts to slavery, because a coach holds the power to blackmail an athlete to do whatever he or she desires. This is particularly alarming for poor and minority students who might not otherwise be able to go to college.

Despite proclamations in the National Collegiate Athletic Association manual that academic quality is a high priority, many student athletes are exploited by the schools they represent. The Division I coaches are paid to win games, fill stadiums and win post-season competition. In the '92-93 school year, $33.9 million was awarded to schools by the 19 football bowl games. Athletic departments depend on that revenue for survival. But they don't graduate most of the players who win the games: Only 43 percent of the men who play Division I basketball graduate, and just 46 percent of the football players graduate.

The NCAA has discussed reform for a long time. But it is only rhetoric. A true reform model is right under the NCAA's nose. The smaller schools that compete in Division III have the ingredients for successful sports programs: The schools' presidents, not their athletic departments, control athletic budgets, precluding a lust for revenue. Coaches are not evaluated solely on win-loss records. Players don't get athletic scholarships; they must earn admission like any other student.

Let's use Division III as a model for NCAA athletics so we can educate the student athletes who entertain us every weekend. Then we can wish them good luck as they walk across the stage in a different uniform: a cap and gown.

What To Ask Recruiters

For scholastic stars who still dream of a pro career, here's what you face: The odds against a high school football player eventually making it to the pros are 6,318 to 1. The odds against a high school basketball player: 10,345 to 1. To put that in perspective: If you filled Duke University's Cameron Indoor Stadium to capacity with NBA hopefuls, then squeezed in 1,000 more, only one would make the NBA. So high school athletes and their parents need to ask specific questions:

- What is the graduation rate of the athletic program, and of the team?
- What academic support services will be provided? Will these services be available during the playing season?
- How does the coach monitor the academic progress of his or her athletes?

- What action is taken if an athlete fails to meet academic requirements? Are the requirements clearly explained? In writing?
- How many academic advisers are available? Do they work for the athletic department or for academic affairs?

What the NCAA Says

There's no question that as an athletic program becomes larger, and the competition becomes greater, the dollars involved increase and the risk of exploitation increases, says NCAA spokesman Francis Canavan. The concern about exploitation of student athletes is one the association has come to address.

Adequacy of Consideration

Although courts seldom inquire into the *adequacy* of consideration, nonetheless both parties must give *some* consideration. Why do courts regard consideration as fundamental to a contract?

Dead Man's Act Doesn't Bar Testimony: Court
David Bailey, *Chicago Daily Law Bulletin*

A woman's estate may seek to collect the $125,000 promissory note found among her papers, but the couple who signed it can testify that she never gave them money, the 1st District Appellate Court ruled Tuesday. The justices reversed and remanded a Cook County Circuit Court judge's finding that the paper did not constitute an enforceable contract, reviving the estate's claim to the note. But the divided panel also ruled that the Dead Man's Act cannot be used by the estate to stop the couple from testifying that the deal was never consummated.

A dissenting justice contended, however, that the majority's decision to sanction "direct testimony regarding the deal in effect judicially repeals" the Dead Man's Act.

Robert F. Smith sought to collect on the note, signed in 1986 by Craig T. Haran and Judy M. Haran, that was among the papers he found while

Copyright © 1995 by Law Bulletin Publishing Co. *Chicago Daily Law Bulletin,* June 27, 1995, p.1. Reprinted with permission.

reviewing his mother's estate. Barbara A. Smith had died in 1991, leaving, among other things, the note, a deed to a house she owned, insurance papers and jewelry. The note stated, in part, that the Harans used a house and property as collateral for the $125,000, which was to be repaid within 12 months with 10 percent interest. The Harans contended they had only considered transacting business with her and never received the money. No payment had been demanded until the estate sought it in 1992.

Judge Paddy McNamara found that the instrument failed to create an enforceable contract because it lacked any consideration. McNamara also noted that no paper trail documented an exchange of funds, there was no evidence the venture ever started and no testimony had been taken from bankers or attorneys who would normally have been involved in such a deal. Smith appealed.

The justices ruled that the note contained a promise to pay, and the estate may recover on it unless the Harans establish that no consideration was given. The majority also found that Barbara Smith's alleged failure to give the Harans money did not qualify as an event "that would be excluded from discussion by the Dead Man's Act. If the testimony was to be that decedent did indeed give them money at some specific point in time, that would clearly qualify as an event," Justice Gino L. DiVito wrote. "But decedent's failure to give the Harans money at any point in time cannot be so characterized."

The estate could also be considered to have waived the bar of the Dead Man's Act, the majority found.

"The note in question here, to be where it was found, must have been given to the deceased (an event in her presence) and, since it is unrealistic to assume that it was merely given to her without any communication whatsoever, there must have been conversation about it," DiVito wrote. "Indeed, the estate relies entirely on its inferences—on the existence of the instrument, its having been retained by decedent, and its having been kept by her in a special place—as evidence that consideration was given."

Barring the Harans' testimony would disadvantage the living, and the trial court's barring of the testimony was an abuse of discretion, the majority found. Justice Carl J. McCormick concurred.

Justice Allen Hartman dissented, finding that the Harans should not be allowed to testify that they never received money in exchange for the promissory note. "The resulting testimony, upon which the majority stamps its imprimatur, places the parties on unequal footing," Hartman wrote.

The estate also did not waive the protection of the Dead Man's Act, nor were the Harans in any way disadvantaged. Hartman wrote. "The Dead Man's Act does not entirely preclude the Harans from defending or rebutting the presumption of consideration in the retrial of the case. The Harans may produce income tax or bank records detailing their business ventures, list investors and contributions made and provide bank records that could shed some light on whether any funds were exchanged for the instrument," Hartman wrote.

To sanction the Harans' direct testimony that no money was ever exchanged, however, clearly and impermissibly defeats the purposes of the Dead Man's Act and judicially repeals its provisions," Hartman wrote.

Accord and Satisfaction

A new Ohio statute is designed to make the old remedy of accord and satisfaction readily available to consumers. Are there any dangers to the new program?

New Law Helps Consumers in Bill Disputes
Armond Budish, *Plain Dealer*

You have a dispute over a bill. Maybe you just had some repairs done around the house, but the bill came in much higher than was promised or justified. Or perhaps you had your car in the shop for repairs and the bill reflects work that you believe was never done.

How can you handle bill disputes? If you just refuse to pay, the creditor may threaten to destroy your credit rating. You could go to court, but that's always a hassle (although Small Claims Court should be easier than a regular court to navigate). A new Ohio law gives consumers a great weapon to fight disputed bills. This consumer protection device is called accord and satisfaction.

Q. What is accord and satisfaction?

A. Here is how accord and satisfaction works: You pay the amount you feel is appropriate, not the whole bill. On the check itself, or in an accompanying note, you should clearly state that your payment is "payment in full" or "in full satisfaction" of the bill. If you follow the rules discussed below and the creditor accepts your payment (cashing the check is acceptance), then you are off the hook for the rest of the bill.

Accord and satisfaction actually is the rebirth of an older consumer protection device. An Ohio court case decided six years ago had severely undercut the value of accord and satisfaction by allowing the creditor to cross out

Copyright © 1995 by Plain Dealer Publishing Co. *Plain Dealer,* June 25, 1995, P.3I. Reprinted with permission.

your "Payment in Full" language, keep your partial payment and still hold you responsible for the balance. Now, if the creditor keeps your money for at least 90 days, you're off the hook.

Q. What rules do I have to follow for accord and satisfaction?

A. First, you must have a bona fide dispute over the bill. You can't simply decide that you don't want to pay the entire bill. But if you have a legitimate gripe over the charges, you can use accord and satisfaction. Second, you must state clearly, either on the check (on the memo line) or in an accompanying note, that your payment is payment in full satisfaction of the bill.

The company may send you a notice indicating that payments or communications concerning disputed debts must be sent to a designated person, office or place. Businesses do this so they know when accord and satisfaction is being used against them, and can then decide whether to accept your payment or go after the full amount they claim is due.

If a business sends you a notice telling you where to send disputed payments, send your check to that person or place. If you don't follow the instructions, your remaining balance will not be discharged. But if you do send your payment to the right place and the business accepts it, you don't owe any more.

If the business doesn't send you a notice concerning disputed payments, send in your partial payment in the normal manner. The business has 90 days to return your payment or it will be stuck with your partial payment as payment in full.

Q. What if the company continues to harass me after accepting my payment?

A. If you have followed the rules discussed, you might first try explaining that you have "paid in full" through the accord and satisfaction law—the business may not realize that you have done that or may not understand what it means. Maybe sending a copy of this column will help.

If you still get dunned, you may want to check your credit record on file with the major credit bureaus (listed in the telephone book). As long as no harm is done to your credit rating, you can ignore the threats. But if your credit is harmed, you can write an explanatory letter to include in your credit file, and you may have to go to court to collect damages caused by the creditor.

Chapter 13

Legality

Illegality Generally

Investments

Noncompete Clauses

Illegality Generally

The lawyer for American Express indicates that if the debtor is right, there will be a flood of such cases. Is he right? (Research has located no reported case between these parties, indicating it probably settled out of court.)

Call Girl Credit Won't "Do Nicely"
Ian Ball, *Daily Telegraph (London)*

A man being sued by American Express for not paying his bill claimed in a counter-action yesterday that he does not owe the money because he used the charge card to pay for an illegal act—hiring prostitutes. "It is axiomatic that a contract which has as its purpose an underlying illegality cannot be enforced by either of the parties," said Mr Thomas Waxter, his lawyer. "It's the oldest profession and an old rule of law—they go together as far as I'm concerned." His Baltimore client, Mr Michael Gianakos, said he used the credit card in July and August 1987 to pay for the services of prostitutes at the Club Pussycat and the Jewel Box in a red-light district of downtown Baltimore known as The Block. The women allegedly were paid by the two clubs. Bills submitted to American Express showed the $6,700—£3,900—in charges were for champagne. Both clubs have denied that prostitution takes place on their premises.

Mr Waxter said yesterday that American Express was responsible for deciding which businesses can accept its credit card. "American Express sends out sales people," he added. "Those people and the company make a judgment about who's going to get a card. The place is called the Pussycat Club—they had to know what kind of business it was." The lawyer pointed out that the Maryland Court of Appeals had ruled several times that contracts based on illegal sexual acts are unenforceable.

Yet paying a prostitute or call-girl by credit card has become fairly common in the United States, according to police vice-squads—at least in the upper echelons of the profession. Almost all the call-girl services that advertise heavily on late-night soft-porn channels on cable television in New York and other large cities talk of accepting credit cards. The slips the cardholder receives with his monthly bill—and which in some cases may find their way on to a company expense-account sheet—bear the imprint of a company with an innocuous name.

Copyright © 1989 by The Daily Telegraph plc. *Daily Telegraph (London)*, Mar. 22, 1989, p.3. Reprinted with permission.

Mr Sidney Friedman, representing American Express in the case, declined to discuss the company's legal strategy. "But if he's right, everyone is going to be lined up in The Block with their charge cards in their hands," he commented.

Investments

The crisis at Barings Bank highlights the dangers of derivatives. Should governments restrict the use of derivatives?

Derivatives Bring Down a Bank and People Wonder What's Next
Alex Brummer, Patrick Donovan, and Mark Milner,
San Diego Union-Tribune

The global banking crisis brought about by the failure of Barings Bank, the patrician bank which handles Queen Elizabeth's personal fortune, could have been lifted straight from a publicity blurb about a forthcoming financial blockbuster. It's a catastrophe which was never meant to happen. Yet it was clear that the world's financial markets have become so vulnerable that they can be thrown into disarray by just one series of unlucky dealings in complex financial products. At the center of this drama is one banking executive who works for the Singapore branch of Barings, a key player in the British financial world.

The immediate losses are known to be more than $800 million—more than the entire market worth of Barings Bank. But the real liabilities could be far higher as it has yet to count the cost of other derivative contracts now coming to light. In other words, Barings looks in danger of being swallowed up in a black hole of potentially unlimited trading losses.

Like every other major bank, Barings has leaped into the market for derivatives: financial instruments which effectively involve "betting" against changes in the financial markets. Companies buy them to insure themselves against changes in interest rates or currency movements, for example. But they're also used as tools for speculation on their own account.

Copyright © 1995 by The San Diego Union-Tribune. *San Diego Union-Tribune*, Mar. 5, 1995, p.G-4. Reprinted with permission. Brummer, Donovan, and Milner wrote this article for the Manchester Guardian Service of England.

Huge fortunes are to be made if traders call the risks well. But call the markets wrong, and the potential losses are far greater than the initial investment.

Barings employs 4,000 people, around half outside of Britain. It's a pivotal player in the financial market, helping arrange everything from stock market flotations to big takeover deals. Its blue-blooded background has provided it with special access to some of the fastest growing markets of the Pacific, including Singapore and Tokyo, where the losses have been run up.

So interconnected are the financial markets, however, that the collapse of Barings is having a huge knock-on effect throughout the rest of the world. The British merchant bank has a 40 percent stake in Dillon Read, one of the biggest players on Wall Street. More seriously, this will cause huge damage to the credibility of the British financial institutions.

As the crisis deepened, it raised worrying questions about the extent to which the financial markets are vulnerable to these derivatives contracts, for this is not the first time that a major player has been stung by big losses in this sophisticated area of financial trading. Last year, Orange County in California was rendered technically insolvent because of derivatives losses. Big companies like Royal Dutch/Shell also have been hit.

Many commentators have openly questioned the wisdom of markets taking the huge risk of what is essentially gambling on movements in market prices. Other losses could be shrugged off as one-time incidents. Yet this is the first time that a major merchant bank, a potent symbol of the City of London's commercial traditions, has been brought to the brink by derivatives trading.

Anyone reading this and enjoying a glass of orange juice, slice of toast or cup of coffee is taking part in the world of derivatives trading. Such fragile commodities as the Florida orange crop, wheat from the American Midwest or Brazilian coffee beans, have long been traded across derivatives markets.

At the heart of any derivatives contract is what will happen in the future. Take oranges. An orange orchard is not an industrial production line where output can be trimmed or accelerated. The farmer cannot, on a day-to-day basis, change the number of oranges his trees are going to produce. If the weather is kind and fruit abundant, then the price of oranges goes down. Good news for the consumer, but not necessarily for the farmer. On the other hand, a frost at the critical time could reduce the crop, pushing prices sharply higher.

But it is very hard to run a business on the back of not knowing what the price will be for a once-a-year crop until the day you get it to the buyer. Tough, too, for orange juice makers, bakers and coffee grinders who cannot predict what they might have to pay on the day. In a bid to curtail such uncertainties, markets grew up where "soft" commodities were traded in advance of the crop being ready to harvest. Price and delivery were agreed for some specified date in the future—hence the name given to one of the main means of derivatives trading, the futures contract. For producers and consumers, such markets provided a way of insuring against sharp price movements. Contracts were a "hedge" against the full blast of events beyond their control.

So-called "soft commodities" were not the only ones traded in such a way. London's Metal Exchange, set up in 1877, provided a similar function for the producers and consumers of metals such as tin and copper—another area where there was (and remains) potential for productive capacity and demand to move sharply out of balance.

New tin mines and copper smelters are not to be had overnight, nor, once they have been closed down, can they easily and swiftly be brought back into production. Such markets have known their own shocks. For example, the great tin crisis—when the price of the metal was kept artificially high by producers buying back their own output through the market—rocked the metal exchange less than a decade ago.

What has made derivatives notorious, however, is a relatively new development: the application of contracts initially developed for commodities to financial products—to stocks, bonds, interest rates, currencies. Indeed, there seems no end to the ingenuity of derivatives designers. To complicate matters further, the range of derivatives contracts has expanded. In addition to the "future," there is the "option," an agreement which gives one party to the deal the right (but not the obligation) to buy or sell oranges, currencies or whatever, at a set date in the future. Then there's the "swap," where firms agree to exchange obligations. A company which has to pay interest on a loan at a fixed rate may swap with another firm whose interest rates can change.

From such relatively simple tools, financial derivatives designers have managed to come up with products of fiendish complexity. What keeps the regulators, like the Bank of England, awake is the potential scale of the problems financial derivatives can cause. Someone physically buying, say, $100,000 worth of stocks or bonds has to come up with $100,000. But the buyer of a futures contract initially only has to put up part of the money—say 10 percent—called the margin. So someone with $100,000 could buy a futures contract on $1 million worth of shares. But if the market had moved up when the buyer had expected it to go down, or vice versa, his losses would also be 10 times as high. Regulated markets counter the problem by asking those involved to put up more money during the life of the contract to take account of price movements. But in the huge market among the world's big financial institutions there are no such safeguards. Losses can mount unchecked until the contract falls due—by which time there may not be enough money to pay.

The 1995 crisis at Barings, even though it involves these new-fangled financial tools, follows a classic historic pattern. Almost all the financial panics of the last 100 years—including the Baring Brothers' gamble in Argentine bonds exactly a century ago—have occurred after a long run when the financial markets and the strength of the global economy have appeared immutable. And they have begun with the unexpected—in this case, an allegedly renegade dealer in Singapore.

What distinguishes the present crisis is that it has occurred at a bank with a modern reputation for probity and whose clients reach to the highest level in British society; and that it occurred in the emergent markets of the Pacific Rim, which have the jump on the rest of the world, in that their markets open first, and where volumes now rival those on the more mature markets of Europe and North America. (They are also about as far as possible away from the Bank of England, which in this case is the responsible regulatory authority.)

What is of concern to the regulators on such occasions is not that any particular institution is wiped out but concern that the disaster could spread. Initially, such a panic spreads by diminishing confidence in the banking system, causing investors to withdraw money and sell the shares of other banks which operate in similar style, because of concern that they may have been caused difficulty.

When problems occurred in the British consumer credit markets in 1973–95, the Bank of England, together with the ordinary commercial banks, stepped in with a billion-pound-plus rescue package in an effort to prevent the scare spreading to other banks—but not before NatWest, the largest British bank, was required to issue a disclaimer about its own position.

The Barings problem is bound to lead global investors to question not just whether there is a problem in Tokyo but in other Far Eastern markets, and in London, too. The pound is already extraordinarily weak because of Prime Minister John Major's political difficulties and the preference of foreign investors to put their funds into Germany. The possibility now looms of a stampede of sterling, which could further destabilize the prime minister.

Losing Big Money

The Barings Bank derivatives losses are only the fourth largest in the past 15 months.

Top 5 Derivatives Losses past 15 Months:
- *Japan:* Refiner Showa Shell writes off two-year losses—$1.7 billion
- *U.S.:* Orange County, California, bankrupt after derivatives losses—$1.69 billion
- *Germany:* Industrial Group Group Metallgesellschaft—$1.5 billion
- *Singapore:* Britain's Barings Bank collapses—$1 billion or more
- *U.K.:* Drug company Glaxo—$207 million

Noncompete Clauses

Noncompete clauses are common, and at times may affect even the high and mighty. When a court decides whether to enforce such a clause, should it consider the employee's sophistication?

Business and the Law: The Admen's New Suit— The Battle Between the Saatchi Group and Its Former Employees
Robert Rice, *Financial Times (London)*

The ousting of Mr Maurice Saatchi as chairman of Saatchi & Saatchi, the advertising group, and the subsequent resignation of three senior executives, has sparked off what promises to be a protracted and bitter legal battle. Writs are flying in both directions. The company is anxious to protect its position. Key clients such as British Airways and Mirror Group have already severed relations. Others are threatening to desert. The share price has fallen from a high of 146p before the Saatchi brothers sold their remaining 1.8m shares at the beginning of January to a low of 97p. US shareholders are considering suing for damages.

Last Thursday, the company issued a writ against Mr Saatchi and the three executives, Mr Bill Muirhead, Mr Jeremy Sinclair and Mr David Kershaw, alleging conspiracy to injure the business of Saatchi & Saatchi, and accusing Mr Saatchi of inducing the three to breach their employment contracts. It is also seeking an injunction preventing the three executives from joining a new agency to be set up by Mr Saatchi or any other competing business for a year. The company intends to hold them to their employment contracts and to enforce restrictive covenants, preventing them from setting up in competition, soliciting clients and poaching other Saatchi employees. Mr Saatchi and the executives intend to counter-claim against the company.

The company appears to have a strong case against the three executives. In general, where an executive leaves without serving notice, it amounts to a repudiatory breach of contract. The employer can accept the repudiation or not. According to Mr Fraser Younson, vice-president of the Employment Lawyers' Association and partner of Baker & McKenzie, the international law firm, if a company does not accept the repudiation, it must make it clear in writing to the employee that he or she is expected to continue to turn up for work. If the employee refuses, the company can sue for damages and

Copyright © 1995 by The Financial Times Ltd. *Financial Times (London)*, Jan. 17, 1995, p.16. Reprinted with permission.

obtain an injunction to prevent that person working for anyone else until his or her notice period has expired, providing the contract has clauses in it dealing with issues such as competition and confidential information.

Courts are powerless to compel anyone to continue to work in accordance with his or her contract, but are prepared to restrain someone from committing further breaches of the contract terms.

If the employee decides to work out the period of notice, the company must pay him or her. Alternatively, the company and employee may reach an agreement on "garden leave." In this case, the employee is not required to work, but continues to be paid and is banned from working for anyone else or setting up in competition until the notice period expires. The only way an employee can avoid being tied down in this way is if he or she can show that the resignation came in response to the employer's repudiatory breach of the contract of employment. Hence the intention of Mr Muirhead, Mr Sinclair and Mr Kershaw to counter-sue for constructive dismissal.

The outcome will depend on the reasons they advance to substantiate their claims. From their resignation letters published in the press last week, all three seemed to base their decisions to quit on the Saatchi board's decision to remove Mr Saatchi as chairman, contrary to their express advice. Mr Muirhead wrote of feeling "totally compromised" by the board's decision. Mr Sinclair said the company was in the grip of people who did not understand the business and seemed prepared to ignore the advice of those who did. Mr Kershaw wrote that Mr Saatchi's removal was "commercial vandalism" and made it impossible for him to continue.

Whether the board's behavior amounted to a repudiation of their individual employment contracts or breach of some implied term is for the courts to decide. But employment lawyers expressed some doubt whether removal of a third party by itself would be enough to establish wrongful dismissal.

If the three succeed in establishing repudiation of their employment contracts by the company, that would defeat any restrictive covenants in their contracts not to compete. The only way the company could then enforce covenants would be if the employment contracts expressly provided that the restraints should apply irrespective of how termination of the contract came about. Even then, the courts might refuse to enforce them. Lawyers point out there are few hard and fast rules in the area of restraint of trade. The courts tend to treat each case according to its facts.

In general, however, restraints are void unless they are both reasonable and in the public interest. The burden is on the employer to show that a restraint is reasonable. It must seek to protect the employer's legitimate business interests, either its trade secrets, goodwill or trade connections. If the restraint is wider than reasonably necessary to protect legitimate business interests, the courts will not enforce it. In deciding whether the restraint is too wide, the court will look at the geographic area it covers, its duration, the nature of the business and the precise terms of the restriction.

Few courts will enforce restraints lasting more than a year, for example. Clauses banning employees from soliciting clients are generally only enforceable to the extent that the employee has had direct, recent contact with a client. On the other hand, courts will generally enforce non-solicitation clauses that ban employees from accepting work from or dealing with the employer's clients. That makes it unnecessary for the employer to show that the employee induced clients to transfer their business. Clauses prohibiting the poaching of other employees generally have to be directed at certain classes of employee, such as account managers or creative directors in the case of an advertising company. Courts will not enforce a general restriction on poaching of employees.

Taken at face value, the company's case against Mr Saatchi looks less solid. By removing him as group chairman, it is technically in repudiatory breach of his service contract, thereby rendering any restrictions on him setting up in competition unenforceable. In normal circumstances, a "golden handshake" to reflect the unexpired term of the service contract might give an employer leverage to negotiate a "non-compete" agreement. But if Mr Saatchi leaves the courts to decide if he was wrongfully dismissed and, if so, what level of compensation he should receive, the company would appear powerless to prevent him setting up a new agency.

The situation is complicated, however, by accusations against Mr Saatchi that he conspired to damage the business of the company and solicited the three executives to breach their employment contracts. If the company can establish that Mr Saatchi solicited employees prior to his removal by the board, and while still employed by the company, he would be in breach of fiduciary duty and the implied duty of loyalty owed to the company. In those circumstances, the company could sue him for damages and enforce any non-compete clauses in his contract preventing him from setting up a new agency. A court battle looks inevitable.

Chapter 14

Capacity and Consent

Minors

Misrepresentation

Fraud

Minors

In this contract dispute involving a minor, the emotional and financial stakes rise because a parent is involved.

Bank Wrong To Let Mother Guarantee Loan
Claire Bernstein, *Toronto Star*

There are some loans banks should never make. They are immoral and illegal. And when banks make them, courts should punish them by awarding punitive damages. To protect guarantees signed by wives for loans by their husbands, banks require the wives to seek ILA—independent legal advice: "Before you sign, Madame, go see a lawyer who will explain the consequences of your guaranteeing your husband's business loan. And if you don't want to go, please sign this waiver."

Actually, the whole concept of independent legal advice is a sham. What is this independent lawyer going to say? "If you don't sign, your husband won't get the loan. If you do sign, and he can't pay back the loan, you will lose your home." The wife knows that already. What she really needs is her mother: "Daughter, you've got to decide: Is the marriage worth the risk of losing your home? If it isn't, get out now, with the home in your hands, not in the bank's."

Now, the truth is that, while some of these guarantees are the result of emotional blackmail, many are simply a matter of cold, hard cash. The wife who guarantees her husband's loan stands to profit if his business is a success. The house was put in her name in the first place to prevent its falling into the hands of creditors—an advantage to both partners. That's why it's understandable that the courts recently threw out the appeal of three wives who tried to get their guarantees invalidated because they didn't get independent legal advice. It was obvious to the court they knew what they were getting into by guaranteeing the loan.

But here is one guarantee that stands a good risk of being regarded by the courts as unconscionable: the guarantee of a mother put into the position of helping her son or daughter. That's what a mother's role in life has been. And no amount of ILA will make her withstand this strong emotional pressure: "Ma, please sign this guarantee for me. I need you. I love you."

A recent judgment that has upset the financial community threw out the guarantee of a 57-year-old part-time nurses' aide and waitress with a Grade

Copyright © 1995 by Toronto Star Newspapers, Ltd. *Toronto Star*, Apr. 3, 1995, p.B3. Reprinted with permission. Claire Bernstein is a Montreal lawyer and syndicated columnist.

8 education—even though she had waived her rights to independent legal advice. Her daughter had asked for help. She and her common-law husband needed a bigger trailer to have room for all his children from his former marriage. The bank wouldn't give them the money unless the mother co-signed the loan. The bank wasn't stupid. Daughter and dolt couldn't manage money. They were in over their head. They owed thousands. But the bank was ready to lend them money—with the mother's collateral: her condo, worth $160,000. And the mother couldn't resist her daughter's entreaties. The bank lent the couple $45,000, to cover not only the trailer, but also all the couple's credit-card debt. As collateral, they put a mortgage on the mother's condo. The inevitable happened. The couple didn't pay. The bank claimed the condo. The mother went to court. And the court invalidated the mortgage on her condo.

As lawyer Cindy Biondi with Toronto firm Fraser & Beatty observes: "Unequal bargaining power with an unfair contract creates a presumption of undue influence." The mother's plea that she didn't know what the consequences could be from her co-signing was credible because she needed her son's help with her finances. Motherly love in certain situations is the equivalent of undue influence. Certain mothers can't resist pressure from their children, no matter what financial imbeciles the kids are.

It is in these situations that banks have a societal duty to protect people driven by their emotions, and not lend to credit-unworthy offspring even if mom is willing to sign. And it is in these situations that the courts must punish the banks by imposing punitive damages if they fail to carry out this duty.

Misrepresentation

As schools compete for students, they make more promises. These students claim the school's promises were false. Is there equal bargaining power between a university and a high school student?

Barrage of Student Lawsuits Aimed at Vocational School

Jeanne Sather, *Puget Sound Business Journal*

Disgruntled former students have filed at least four lawsuits against Pima Medical Institute, the Seattle branch of an Arizona-based vocational school chain. The suits claim the school misrepresented its programs, painted an overly rosy picture of graduates' job prospects and gave inflated estimates of the salaries they could hope to earn. Three suits have been filed since December.

Students, who paid thousands of dollars for the courses, also complained about the quality of the teaching. "What a joke of a program," said former student Shelly Kniestedt, 24, who settled a separate lawsuit with Pima in September. Kniestedt said that in the veterinary assistant program she took, she practiced injecting a Nerf ball but never laid a hand on a real animal.

The Seattle school, housed in a nondescript office building on Eastlake Avenue East, has about 350 students, director Walter Greenly said in an interview. It is one of five such schools operated by Tucson, Ariz.-based Pima Medical Institute. The schools offer programs to train students for jobs in medical fields, such as physical therapy aide or veterinary assistant.

A group of 12 former students in Pima's ophthalmic medical assistant program filed suit in King County Superior Court in mid-January. Another student in the same program, Randall Hashimoto, filed a similar suit later in the month. The first suit seeks reimbursement of tuition and $10,000 in punitive damages for each plaintiff under the state Consumer Protection Act. Hashimoto's suit was for breach of contract and misrepresentation.

The dozen plaintiffs in the first suit were students in the nine-month ophthalmic program which began in August 1992. Hashimoto enrolled in the program in a later session, in February 1993. Victoria Vreeland, an attorney representing the group of 12 plaintiffs, said that the program was brand-new when her clients enrolled. Pima director Greenly said the 12 plaintiffs were members of a class of 16.

Copyright © 1994 by Puget Sound Business Journal. *Puget Sound Business Journal*, Feb. 11, 1994, vol. 14, no. 39, §1, p.4. Reprinted with permission.

The complaints say students were told the program would lead to a well-paying job in a field of health care that was in great demand, as an assistant to an optometrist or ophthalmologist. They were also promised that after 55 weeks of classroom training, they would be placed in 25-week "externships" for on-the-job training and then placed in jobs paying $11 to $16 an hour.

However, the suits assert, the school was not properly equipped to train students in this field and as a result, the students were not qualified for employment. Vreeland said the students were told that externships were already lined up for them, but more than half were never placed in training programs. Greenly disputed this, but provided no numbers.

According to Hashimoto's complaint, all courses in the ophthalmic program were taught by Shawn McKinney, the program director, who was a certified ophthalmic medical technician. Students had numerous complaints about the quality of his teaching. Greenly said that McKinney has since been fired.

Another suit was filed against Pima in December by Christopher Jackson, who paid $3,920 for a physical therapy technician/aide program at Pima.

Pima settled Kniestedt's lawsuit by reimbursing the tuition she'd paid in 1992 to attend the 27-week veterinary assistant course. Her suit said the school claimed graduates of the program earned starting salaries of $8 to $10 an hour, and that 90 percent of graduates were placed in jobs with veterinary clinics. In fact, Kniestedt's attorney, Lowell Dale Young said, only registered veterinary technicians who have graduated from a two-year program and passed state board exams would get a starting salary in that range. Veterinary assistants, for whom no formal training is required, typically make about $5 an hour. "But they didn't make the distinction between technicians and assistants," he said. Greenly disputed that, saying that the school tells prospective students they can expect a starting salary of $5.50 to $8 an hour.

According to Young and Kniestedt, admissions officers at Pima continually compared their program to the one at Pierce College, a Tacoma community college that runs a two-year veterinary technology program certified by the American Veterinary Medical Association. This program is in high demand, with about 120 applicants each year for 40 spots.

"There's no comparison," said veterinarian Tim Lawson, director of Pierce's program. After completing the program and passing the state and national exams, Lawson said, his students go to work as veterinary technicians at a salary of about $10 an hour. Lawson said it was his understanding that Pima told its students they would be eligible to sit for the state board exam, when in fact they can't because the program they attend is not certified by the veterinary association. "It's also spendy," he said of Pima's $4,363.85 price tag for the 27-week program. Pierce students pay about $4,000 for two years' tuition.

Kniestedt's attorney asked the school to prove its claims about salaries and job placement by providing the names of former students and information about the jobs they had obtained, but the suit was settled before Pima turned over this information. "They misrepresented the whole program; they promised all these big things," said Kniestedt, who now works for Federal Express and does dog grooming on the side.

Misrepresentation

The seller of land must disclose known problems, but buyers have some obligations, too.

A Closer Look; Make Sure You See the Whole Picture Before Buying Land
Kathleen Furore, *Chicago Tribune*

Robert and Barbara Freitag thought their dream had finally come true: They had purchased almost 10 acres of land and were building the rural home for which they had been saving for years. But their dream turned into a nightmare before they even moved into their house near Prairie du Chien in the picturesque bluffs area of southwestern Wisconsin.

When the couple lived in Elk Grove Village, "we had been looking for some inexpensive land and saw a newspaper ad for some land in Wisconsin," says Barbara Freitag. "We called the 800 number, talked to a gentleman and came here to see the land. We fell in love with it immediately, and bought 9 1/2 acres in May of 1989. We only visited the property once in the spring and once in the fall, then came up the following spring and got to talking with some of the neighbors. When we mentioned that we'd been told by our developer, Woodland Farms, that the county would start maintaining the road up to our property—it's the only road that goes up that hill—they said: 'You haven't been to any township meetings, have you? We have, and it's not the county's obligation.' "

That revelation proved just the beginning of the Freitags' problems. They've also had to dig a 360-foot-deep well and have poles installed for electric wires, even though Barbara Freitag says the developer assured them there was underground electricity and water 100 feet below ground on their property. "The land was inexpensive, but that's where the economy

Copyrighted © Chicago Tribune Co. All rights reserved. *Chicago Tribune*, Apr. 11, 1994, "Your Money," p.1. Used with permission.

stopped," she says. "We're paying for the electric work on a five-year plan, and we had to take out a separate mortgage just to dig the well."

Jack Ebben, general counsel for American Investment, a company that works with real estate brokers, said he knows of only one complaint against Woodland Farms (which Ebben said ceased operations in May 1993) for road maintenance problems, offered to show 39 evaluation forms and letters from satisfied customers of Woodland Farms and wondered whether many complaints stem from misunderstandings rather than salespeople's misrepresentations.

And Tom White, who was a general partner and broker for Woodland Farms, questions the accuracy of the Freitags' complaints. "Our company had a long-standing policy of making any representations in writing," he said. "If there is access by a private road, we disclose the existence of a private road easement (which means the road is not public property and won't be maintained by rural governments). If we say there's electricity, we put it in writing.

"And it is our policy to never make any representations about the depth of water. If someone suggests someone made any representation about water depth, I don't believe it because there's no way to estimate the depth here before drilling because of the rock strata."

According to Bonnie Jansen, a representative for the Federal Trade Commission, land-sale problems became prevalent in the 1970s and early '80s and continue today. So common are instances of overpricing, overselling and misrepresenting facts about land and the area in which it is located that the FTC's Bureau of Consumer Protection/Office of Consumer and Business Education has published a brochure that tells whom to talk to, which questions to ask and things to watch for before buying any property.

Here is some of the FTC's advice:

- Don't buy property "site unseen." Talk to area residents and ask if they're satisfied. Just think of what the Freitags would have discovered had they spoken with their neighbors before investing.

- Contact state or local offices to confirm who is required to develop and maintain roads and put in utilities for water, electricity and sewerage. "We should have gone to a township meeting, and we could have gone to the local postmaster, who would have advised us who to get in touch with," admits Barbara Freitag.

- Ask about zoning regulations or environmental land-use restrictions that could prohibit you from building on the property or would make construction costly. The Freitags' neighbor, Carol Higgins, for example, says a state agency has controlled what is built on the bluffs of the river near her family's property since 1989.

- Talk to local real estate agents to learn more about area land values and the resale market. Also, compare prices of similar properties listed in local classified ads. And check with the tax assessment and county recorder offices to find out about appraisals and sales prices of area lots.

- Contact the U.S. Department of Housing and Urban Development, your local or state consumer protection office, the chamber of commerce or the Better Business Bureau for information about the developer or sales agent. Also, check with the local county clerk's office to learn of any civil actions brought by or against the seller or developer.
- Check with HUD to determine if the property is registered. The 1968 Interstate Land Sales Full Disclosure Act, which generally applies to developers selling or leasing 100 or more unimproved lots through interstate commerce, requires developers to register their subdivisions with HUD. It also mandates that developers provide consumers with a summary of the registration in a statement called a property report before a contract or agreement is signed. The report lists distances to nearby communities over paved or unpaved roads; present and proposed utility services and charges; and soil and foundation conditions that could cause construction or septic tank problems.
- Ask about cancellation rights before signing a contract. If the property is subject to the Full Disclosure Act, the contract should specify a "cooling-off" period of one week—or longer if allowed by state law—during which the customer can cancel the deal. If the land isn't covered by the act, check the cancellation clause in the contract.
- Keep copies of any promotional materials you received at the sales presentation and newspaper articles about the development along with your contract. They could be important if you want to cancel the contract because of misrepresentations made at the time of purchase.

If you believe you are the victim of a land sale scam, the FTC advises complaining in writing to the seller. If no progress is made, you should contact the local or state consumer protection office. If you want to determine if you have rights under the Full Disclosure Act, send details of your complaint to the Department of Housing and Urban Development, Interstate Land Sales Registration Division, 451 7th Street, S.W., Washington, D.C., 20410. Include the developer's name, name and location of the subdivision, and copies of any documents you signed. You also can file a complaint with the FTC, which normally does not handle individual cases, but looks for patterns of violations, by writing Correspondence Branch, Federal Trade Commission, Washington, D.C. 20580.

Fraud

When does an aggressive sales job become fraud?

Advertising Contract With Publisher Of Yellow Pages Voided Due to Fraud
Small Corporation Update

Advertising in the "Yellow Pages" used to have one universally recognized meaning. Nowadays, it's a good idea to check out the company before you place your phone directory advertisement. The slogan "Let your fingers do the walking" is an unprotected trademark, used by many Yellow Pages publishers.

Iva Kinimaka, president of Kinimaka Enterprises, Inc., a catering company, found this out the hard way. Kinimaka had advertised in GTE's Hawaii Telephone Company's Yellow Pages directory for over five years. GTE had contacted Kinimaka about renewing the ad. While he was awaiting a personal visit from a GTE sales representative, a saleswoman from the Island Directory Company, Inc., a competitive Yellow Pages publisher, stopped by Kinimaka's office. She said she was "from the Yellow Pages" and, using Kinimaka's ad from the GTE directory, discussed the copy with him.

After agreeing to some wording changes, Kinimaka received an important phone call. While he was on the phone, the saleswoman placed a contract entitled "Application for Advertising" in front of him, and he signed it without reading. (Had he read the document, he'd have seen the words in bold print: "**This is not a telephone company publication.**") A few days later, the GTE rep contacted Kinimaka. He then realized that the saleswoman who'd called on him wasn't from GTE. But he had no idea whom he had been dealing with: She hadn't left a copy of the contract or a business card.

Several months later, he received a proof of his ad with the Island Directory Company. He returned it with a handwritten note canceling the ad. Island refused to cancel and sued to recover $5,132.06, the amount due on the contract. The trial court found Kinimaka had signed a valid, non-cancelable contract and told him to pay.

But on appeal Kinimaka was let off the hook. The Hawaii Court of Appeals agreed that he'd signed a contract with the Island Company, but it held the contract voidable due to the saleswoman's fraudulent misrepresentation. By using Kinimaka's GTE ad, introducing herself as being "from the

Copyright © 1994 by Fred S. Steingold. *Small Corporation Update*, March 1994, vol. 5, no. 3, p.13. Reprinted with permission.

Yellow Pages," not leaving a business card or a copy of the contract, and handing him the contract to sign while was on the telephone, said the court, Island's representative misled Kinimaka into believing he was contracting with a GTE representative.

Chapter 15

Written Contracts

Sale of Land

Not Performable Within One Year

Sale of Land

This "how-to" article points out that disputes over fixtures and personalty are best avoided with a clear written contract.

Confirm the Fixtures You Want Included in Sale of House
Dian Hymer, *Sacramento Bee*

Defining a few real estate terms may help you to determine what's included in the sale if the purchase contract is vague. Real property, or real estate, is the land and anything that's permanently attached to it, such as a house, trees, shrubs and a fence. Personal property refers to movable items which are not permanently attached. Furniture and clothing are personal property.

A fixture is an item of personal property which has been converted to real property by permanently attaching it to the real property. A furnace is personal property when it's sitting in a contractor's warehouse. The furnace becomes real property when it is installed in (and attached to) a house. Pre-printed real estate purchase contracts usually include clauses that discuss what is included in the sale. Real property is obviously included. Fixtures are also usually included, unless they are specifically excluded. Personal property is usually excluded unless it is specifically included.

The "fixtures" clause may require the sellers to include such things as window coverings (including drapery rods), fireplace equipment, pool and spa equipment, built-in appliances, television antennas, light fixtures, attached floor coverings and mailboxes. But these clauses vary, so read the one in your contract carefully.

Sometimes sellers will exclude fixtures from the sale of their property. The most common exclusions are light fixtures and built-in shelving units. Ask the sellers to patch holes and paint after they remove items they are excluding. If an excluded light fixture is the only source of light in a room, you may want to ask the sellers to replace the fixture with another one or credit you a reasonable amount of money.

First-time tip: There's no harm in being redundant in the purchase contract if it removes ambiguity and prevents after-closing disputes. For instance, let's say the master bedroom drapes match the sellers' bedspread. The sellers have not excluded the drapes and the boiler plate in the contract

Copyright © 1995 by McClatchy Newspapers, Inc. *Sacramento Bee*, Feb. 5, 1995, p.H20.

requires the sellers to include window coverings. Regardless of this, the sellers may assume that because the drapes match their spread, they will take them when they leave. If you want the drapes, state so in the contract, even though it's covered in the fine print. This way, you won't be unpleasantly surprised when you move in and find out you don't have any window coverings in your bedroom.

Most contracts include a space for the buyer to write in items of personal property they would like the sellers to include in the sale. Requesting items of furniture can annoy a seller. Ask your agent to check with the sellers, or their agent, before you start asking for personal property, other than appliances.

Built-in appliances are usually included in the sale. Sellers may include freestanding appliances such as a washer, dryer, refrigerator, or stove (which are technically personal property), if the buyers request them, and the sellers don't need them in their new home. Free-standing appliances are often included in their "as is" condition and without warranty. Make sure these appliances are in good working order by asking the sellers to disclose any defects.

The closing: Don't make the mistake of assuming that free-standing appliances will be included in the sale. Unless they're included in the written purchase agreement, the sellers aren't obligated to leave them for you. If there are free-standing appliances on the property that you don't want, and you're afraid the sellers will leave them, be sure to put in the contract that the sellers will remove the items by closing.

Not Performable Within One Year

An employment contract for half a million dollars per year, for five years? It sounds almost too good to be true.

CA 2 Rules Contract with Brokerage Unenforceable under New York Statute
Securities Regulation & Law Report

Applying New York law, the U.S. Court of Appeals for the Second Circuit declined to reinstate a foreign exchange trader's contentions that he was fired by defendant Salomon Brothers Inc. in violation of an oral employment agreement (Zaitsev v. Salomon Brothers Inc., CA 2, Docket No. 94-9335, 7/27/95).

The alleged oral contract was unenforceable under the New York Statute of Frauds, the court concluded.

Guaranteed Bonus

Judge Joseph McLaughlin recounted the pertinent facts as follows. Plaintiff Michael Zaitsev, a citizen of the former Union of Soviet Socialist Republics, was hired by Salomon in 1990 as a foreign exchange trader. Allegedly, at the time, Zaitsev and two Salomon officials entered into an oral employment agreement for a minimum of five years with an annual salary of $100,000 and a guaranteed annual bonus of at least $400,000.

According to Zaitsev, the agreement also provided that he could resign for any reason with 60 days' notice, the court related. However, Zaitsev maintained, he could be fired only if: Salomon failed to obtain the requisite visa or employment certification on his behalf; he engaged in conduct that resulted in the revocation of such visa or certification; or he committed intentional misconduct or gross negligence in connection with his employment.

Fired 14 months later, with no bonus, Zaitsev filed suit in federal district court, alleging breach of contract, state labor law violations, unjust enrichment, and other causes of action. Salomon, in turn, denied the existence of any oral contract. Rather, it claimed Zaitsev was an employee at will with an annual salary of $100,000 and no guaranteed bonus.

Concluding that the oral agreement was barred by the Statute of Frauds,

---

Copyright © 1995 by The Bureau of National Affairs, Inc. (800-372-1033). Reprinted with permission from *Securities Regulation & Law Report*, vol. 27, no. 31, p.1308 (Aug. 4, 1995).

the lower court granted Salomon's summary judgment motion. Zaitsev's appeal followed.

Statute of Frauds

Affirming, the court advised that under New York law, to be valid, a contract must be in writing if it is not to be performed within a year. "A contract that is 'capable' of being performed within one year of its making is outside the statute," the appeals court noted.

Zaitsev, it continued, argued that the contract was capable of being performed within one year. First, the court noted, he argued that Salomon might have been unable to obtain the requisite visa and therefore could have terminated the agreement. However, the court rejoined, rather than being capable of being performed within one year, under that circumstance, "the contract would be incapable of being performed at all."

Similarly, the court disagreed that if the contract were terminated because Zaitsev engaged in conduct that resulted in the revocation of his visa, it would not be covered by the statute. In that connection, the court noted that under New York law, where—as here—performance within one year "depends upon an act solely within the control of the party seeking to enforce the oral agreement, the Statute of Frauds remains applicable."

Last, the court noted Zaitsev's argument that Salomon could have withdraw his visa application "at any time and for any reason, thereby terminating the contract. The contract alleged by Zaitsev, however, contains no such provision," the court responded. "To the contrary," it noted, the alleged oral contract "fairly contemplates that Salomon would make a good faith effort to obtain the work visa for Zaitsev."

In other matters, the court rejected Zaitsev's argument that other writings, "when cobbled together, are sufficient to satisfy the" statute. Such writings—a letter inviting Zaitsev to work for Salomon and various letters from Salomon to immigration officials—do not contain essential terms of the alleged oral agreement, the court concluded. As such, it said, the statute of frauds is not satisfied.

Rejecting Zaitsev's remaining arguments, the court concluded that the complaint properly was dismissed below.

Chapter 16

Third Parties

Third Party Beneficiaries

What Rights Are Assignable?

Third Party Beneficiaries

Wisconsin football fans were ecstatic when their team earned a rare visit to the Rose Bowl. But some of those who travelled west never got to see the game, and they sued.

Badgers Fans' Suit Rejected; Judge Sees No Contract with PAC 10
Ed Treleven, *Wisconsin State Journal*

A Dane County judge tossed out a lawsuit Thursday against UCLA by Badger football fans who claimed they were illegally denied tickets to the Rose Bowl. Judge P. Charles Jones said in a written decision that Badger fans who went to California with the promise from tour promoters that tickets awaited them were not parties in a contract between the Big Ten and Pac 10 conferences that governs the Rose Bowl and cannot recover damages because of a breach of that contract. "I do not believe any of the terms of the agreement manifest an intention that tour package purchasers of Rose Bowl tickets are beneficiaries of the agreement with rights to recover damages from a breach of the agreement's provisions," Jones wrote.

The class-action lawsuit filed on behalf of about 1,000 Badgers fans had claimed that UCLA encouraged ticket scalping by selling 4,000 extra tickets to athletic booster Angelo Mazzone instead of giving the tickets to the Big Ten Conference as it was required to do. The lawsuit against UCLA sought compensation and punitive damages. A lawyer representing the fans is recommending that they appeal.

The Rose Bowl contract allowed UCLA to sell extra tickets to "season ticket holders, alumni, faculty, students and the like." Jones noted that had the extra tickets been given to the Big Ten, there was no guarantee the Big Ten would have sold the tickets to tour promoters.

"(They) not only lacked standing to sue for any breach, and even if they had standing it is illogical to conclude that the travel agents would have received any Rose Bowl tickets under the agreement," said Richard Ninneman, a lawyer with Quarles and Brady in Milwaukee who represented UCLA in the matter. "We are pleased that Judge Jones agreed with the arguments advanced by the California Regents and its Los Angeles campus," he said.

"I'm very disappointed," said James Olson, a lawyer representing

Copyright © 1994 by Madison Newspapers, Inc. *Wisconsin State Journal*, Nov. 18, 1994, p.1C. Reprinted with permission.

plaintiffs in the case. He said he thought there was strong precedent to demonstrate the fans were third party beneficiaries under the Rose Bowl agreement." [Jones] didn't agree with us," he said.

Olson said letters are being sent to plaintiffs explaining the decision to them. He will meet with them sometime in the next few weeks to decide whether to appeal the decision but said he is tentatively recommending that it be appealed. Jones' decision also allows UCLA to renew a motion it made in September, seeking lawyer's fees and other costs associated with the case. Ninneman said he didn't know whether UCLA would refile the motion.

Fans are also suing several travel agencies that sold airline tickets, lodging and game ticket packages to Badger fans headed to Pasadena for the Rose Bowl. Olson said those actions are still proceeding, though no court dates are set.

What Rights Are Assignable?

Most states that have lotteries prohibit assignment of the proceeds. Is that right? This legislator doesn't think so. Is there a legitimate reason for a state to make the restriction, or do governments do this simply to keep more cash for themselves?

Option To Assign Lottery Winnings to Others OK'd
Howard Fischer, *Arizona Business Gazette*

Lawmakers are sending a message to the Arizona Lottery: If someone wins, it's their money to spend. Senate Bill 1308 would allow lottery winners to assign their rights to future payments to someone willing to give them up-front cash. The annual checks then would go to the new owner of the rights. Several winners thought they already had that right. After all, the state still pays out the same amount of money. But they were wrong—which is why it is going to take a change in the law.

Anyone who plays Lotto now must choose at the time of the ticket purchase whether to go for the whole amount of the prize, paid out over 20

Copyright © 1994 by Phoenix Newspapers, Inc. *Arizona Business Gazette*, Mar. 10, 1994, p.25.

years, or opt for a single cash payment. The latter usually winds up being about half as much as the advertised jackpot. Before March 1992, however, the only option was the annual installment.

Dennis Bedford and Albert Monteverde split a winning lottery ticket they bought in 1987. They won $579,624, which was to be paid out at the rate of $28,000 a year, minus taxes, from an annuity purchased at the time by the state. Last year, though, the pair contracted with Woodbridge Partners Group to buy out the last 13 payments—with a face value of $364,000—for $125,000 in cash. As part of the deal, Woodbridge wanted the future lottery checks made out to the partnership, something the Arizona Lottery refused to do.

Ed Kiyler, an assistant lottery director, said the pair lack the authority to assign their rights. Why? The annuities belong to the Arizona Lottery. "The people who win are the beneficiaries," he said. "They can't assign something that doesn't belong to them."

The pair eventually got a court to order the transfer. Sen. Bill Hardt, D-Globe, figured that shouldn't be necessary. His bill would allow winners to seek permission to sell their beneficiary rights. The bill has cleared the Senate. But, before voting, lawmakers added one more caveat: The prize winner must provide a notarized affidavit that he or she "is of sound mind, not acting under duress and has received independent financial and tax advice concerning the assignment."

The measure awaits House action.

What Rights Are Assignable?

Should a bulk purchaser of "800" telephone numbers be permitted to assign the numbers—for a profit?

800 Numbers Appear on Black Market
Steve Caulk, *Rocky Mountain News*

A black market in the toll-free telephone business has sprung from a growing demand for "800" numbers. While the Federal Communications Commission rations the popular numbers, opportunists plot ways to capital-

Copyright © 1995. Reprinted with permission of *Rocky Mountain News,* Aug. 7, 1995, p.37A.

ize on the desperation of business people who need the numbers sooner than long-distance carriers can provide them.

AT&T Corp. refers to the on-the-side sale of 800 numbers as "brokering," and the company considers it unethical. "A person buys up blocks of 800 numbers and resells them," said AT&T spokesman Mike Lordi. "We feel it's a violation of our FCC tariff. It is a concern." Spokeswoman Susan Sallet of the FCC said the agency has heard "allegations" of brokering, but has never uncovered evidence. The FCC says it is up to the carriers to pursue the "violations."

Berith Jacobsen of Denver sells custom-made golf bags, and she received a call from a man willing to sell her an 800 number he happened to have—800-GOLF-BAG. If his timing had been better, she might have accepted. She had spent 10 months trying to get the 800 number that best suited her business: 800-B-ACTIVE. Her line of products includes other sports-related luggage. "I bet I talked to 25 people before I finally got it (800 number)," she said. "It had belonged to a wheelchair company that went out of business, and then somebody in AT&T in Denver had picked up the number."

So by the time a Southern California man called her, she had her number—which probably saved her a good bit of money. He had seen an advertisement for her company in a golf magazine, and he offered to sell her 1-800-GOLF-BAG for $2,500. "When he first started talking, I thought, 'Well, maybe he'll say $500,'" she said. "I thought $2,500 was kind of outrageous."

Brokers can arrange a private transfer of an 800 number simply by alerting the long-distance carriers involved, said Lordi. A transfer of rights to a toll-free number is acceptable, he said, when there is no profit involved. "We're talking about a process where a broker buys huge blocks of 800 numbers with the express intent of marketing and selling them," Lordi said. "That's a bit different from a company calling another company because the company has a number you're interested in."

Chapter 17

Performance and Discharge

Conditions

Material Breach

Impossibility

Conditions

When is news *news*? Even that issue can be controlled by contractual conditions.

Networks Wage Latest Battle for the "First" Powell Interview

Elizabeth Kolbert, New York Times

The tightly orchestrated media campaign for Gen. Colin L. Powell's autobiography, *My American Journey*, took another unscripted turn today when Tom Brokaw, the NBC News anchor, said that he would broadcast an interview with the General on Friday evening, a few hours before a much-publicized meeting with Barbara Walters appears on ABC. Mr. Brokaw's decision to broadcast his interview three days earlier than planned was greeted with howls of protest at ABC, which had been pursuing General Powell for more than a year and had obtained an agreement granting the network his first interview. "What NBC is pulling is beyond me," said Joanna Bistany, a vice president of ABC News.

The competition between the two networks illustrates just how hot a media property the former Chairman of the Joint Chief of Staff has become as he considers a possible Presidential run. As Mr. Brokaw noted, even the fighting over who broadcasts the first interview serves General Powell's purposes. "The fact is," he said, "it's great for the book, and it's great for Colin Powell."

But the contretemps between ABC and NBC also demonstrates just how elaborately the General and his publisher, Random House, have tried to arrange his self-described re-emergence into public life. The book's publication date is Sunday, but it will be in bookstores on Friday.

As a condition of interviewing General Powell or getting an advance copy of his book, news organizations, including *The New York Times*, have had to sign agreements with Random House stipulating when their stories can be made public. In case the news organizations were tempted to stray from their agreements, several of them received a sharply worded fax from Random House's president, Harry Evans, on Wednesday night warning that such action would constitute a "material breach of contract."

"Everybody was set up to go at a certain time," said Carol Schneider, vice president of publicity at Random House, "and we're expecting everyone will honor their obligations."

Copyright © 1995 by The New York Times Co. *New York Times*, Sep. 15, 1995, §A, p.30, col. 1. Reprinted with permission.

Such is the level of interest in the General, however, that at almost every turn, media competition has threatened to upset Random House's best-laid plans. First, even though Time magazine had purchased exclusive rights to excerpt General Powell's book—which it did this week—Newsweek magazine obtained a copy and published a cover article on it last week. In an effort to placate Time—and keep the story on the magazine's cover—General Powell granted the magazine an interview to go with the book excerpt.

At that point, Ms. Bistany said, ABC considered its agreement with Random House, which called for Ms. Walters's interview to be broadcast after the book's excerpts appeared in Time, to be void. But ABC decided not to move up the broadcast date. Instead, ABC News broadcast two minutes of Ms. Walters's interview as part of a larger story on the General on Monday night. Ms. Bistany said that the segment was used as a promotion.

Mr. Brokaw said that his arrangement with Random House called for NBC Nightly News to be the first evening news program to broadcast an interview with the General and that the agreement was abrogated when ABC presented its segment on Monday. He said he doubted that Peter Jennings, the ABC News anchor, considered the report on the General to be merely a promotion. "They pulled kind of a flim-flam," he said of ABC.

Mr. Brokaw had been scheduled to broadcast his interview on Monday; instead, he is planning to present it during Friday's newscast, which is seen in most of the country at 6:30 P.M. Ms. Walters's interview will be broadcast 10 P.M. Friday on the magazine program *20/20*.

Newspaper interviews with General Powell were granted on the ground that the articles not be published until Sunday. On Monday, General Powell is scheduled to appear on the CNN program *Larry King Live*. Also on Monday, the NBC news program *Today*, is scheduled to broadcast the first of three installments of an interview with the General by one of the program's hosts, Katie Couric.

Jeff Zucker, executive producer of *Today*, said that despite Mr. Brokaw's decision, he planned to stick to the original schedule. "We feel we gave our word," he said.

Conditions

This "how-to" article reviews many of the condition clauses that may arise during the negotiations of a property sale.

Sale's Fudge Factor Gets Sticky; Contingencies: Safety Net or Headache?
Ilyce R. Glink, *Chicago Sun-Times*

Contract contingencies can be a buyer's best friend and a seller's worst nightmare. By definition, a contingency is a provision in a real estate contract that sets forth one or more conditions that must be met before a deal can be closed. Usually buyers will insert a contingency into a contract to protect themselves in case something goes wrong before closing. For example, a home buyer may want the right to back out of the contract if he or she can't get a mortgage or if the home inspection reveals a material defect.

There are many different types of contingencies. The three most common include the financing or mortgage contingency, approval of the home inspection and the attorney approval rider. But local circumstances may dictate the need for other contingencies. In California, which has been plagued by earthquakes, floods, fires and mudslides within the past year, it has become increasingly difficult for home buyers to purchase hazard insurance. Because lenders won't give you a mortgage without hazard insurance, a hazard insurance contingency now pops up regularly on contracts.

While contingencies offer buyers and sellers a way out of a serious situation, they're not to be used lightly. If you simply change your mind about the purchase, and tell your attorney to, say, disapprove the contract, you could be opening yourself to even bigger problems.

Remember, just because a contingency has been attached to a contract doesn't mean sellers have to accept all of them. Whether or not sellers allow a contingency to stand will depend on local market conditions and how easily they believe you will satisfy it. And, depending on local custom, sellers may have the right to continue to show their property until some or all of the contingencies have been met.

Mortgage or Financing Contingency. A mortgage contingency gives buyers the right to back out of the contract if they can't find a lender who will give them a commitment at an agreed-upon rate by a certain date. The contingency should state the type of mortgage and interest rate the buyers

Copyright © 1995 by Ilyce R. Glink. Distributed by Real Estate Matters Syndicate. Reprinted with permission.

are seeking, both of which should be at or around the prevailing market rate. It should also limit to 30 or 60 days the amount of time you have to get your mortgage approved.

Home Inspection Contingency. This contingency gives the buyers the right to have a professional house inspector or third party examine the property within a certain period of time after the contract has been signed. The buyer may also ask that the inspection contingency cover other types of inspections, including radon, asbestos, lead, toxic substances, water, soil sample and pests. Inspection contingencies are commonly worded to allow a buyer to cancel the contract if a serious defect is discovered. But it may not help if you decide to back out because the inspector found some broken window panes.

Attorney Approval Rider. Depending on the state, buyers and sellers may want the right to have the contract approved by the attorney, who will negotiate the finer points with the attorney representing the other side.

Sale of the Buyer's Prior Residence. Since most folks need the equity from their current residence to serve as a downpayment on the next property, buyers often want the right to pull out of a deal if the sale of their current residence falls through. Sellers dislike this contingency, and often continue showing their property until it has been satisfied or withdrawn from the contract.

Admittance to Clubs. If you live in a home on a private golf course, or within close proximity to a private club, a prospective buyer may ask for a contingency that gives him or her the right to withdraw from the deal if they don't receive membership in the club.

Parking. If the seller's unit does not offer any sort of parking, a buyer may ask for a contingency that allows the buyer to cancel the contract if parking cannot be secured.

Material Breach

This sports dispute illustrates how one party's claim of material breach can give rise to the other party's assertion of bad faith. Is either party here showing bad faith?

Rangers Sue Keenan, and Throw In Some Insults
Robert McG. Thomas, Jr., *New York Times*

In a vividly written complaint describing Mike Keenan as both a "great hockey coach" and a "faithless employee," the Rangers have filed suit to force Keenan to abide by the five-year contract he repudiated last Friday. The suit, which amounts to a second action by the Rangers in the Keenan case, was filed in Federal court in Manhattan late Monday afternoon, the same day Gary Bettman, the commissioner of the National Hockey League, agreed to a request by the team that he resolve the dispute. Bettman is expected to issue a ruling after a hearing next week.

The suit seeks similar remedies and more, including an immediate foreclosure of a $975,000 loan the Rangers said they extended to Keenan last year to buy his $1.3 million house in Greenwich, Conn. The loan, according to the suit, was in addition to Keenan's basic compensation set by the contract at a minimum of $5.11 million and a maximum of $8.15 million, including salary and bonuses.

Agent Also Involved

The suit, which also names Keenan's agent, Rob Campbell, as a defendant, seeks declaratory judgments upholding Keenan's contract with the Rangers and invalidating the five-year contract he signed with the St. Louis Blues.

Keenan stunned the Rangers last Friday when he announced that he considered himself a free agent, saying that the team had breached his contract by missing a substantial bonus payment due on Thursday, only 30 days after the Rangers won their first Stanley Cup championship in 54 years. After negotiating with the Detroit Red Wings and then with St. Louis, he signed a five-year, $5 million contract with the Blues on Sunday. The Rangers maintain that their one-day delay in paying Keenan the bonus did not constitute a material breach of their contract with the coach.

Neither Blues officials nor Keenan's agent returned phone calls seeking

Copyright © 1994 by The New York Times Co. *New York Times*, July 20, 1994, §B, p.9, col. 5. Reprinted with permission.

comment, but Rangers officials were outspoken in an hourlong news conference yesterday morning at which they discussed virtually every aspect of the case except the lawsuit they had filed quietly the day before. The Rangers did not announce the lawsuit, which was filed late Monday afternoon and not discovered by court reporters until yesterday morning. Ken Munoz, the general counsel of Madison Square Garden, the Rangers' parent company, later explained that the Rangers considered the lawsuit a precaution designed to assure that any suit Keenan might file after Bettman issues his ruling would be routed to the Federal court.

At the news conference, Munoz along with the Garden president, Bob Gutkowski, and the Rangers president and general manager, Neil Smith, reiterated that the Rangers regard Bettman as the proper arbiter of the dispute. The Rangers said the one-day delay in paying Keenan's season-end bonus was a minor lapse that they earnestly tried to rectify by offering to deliver the check within an hour of learning Keenan was making an issue of it on Friday. "There was no opportunity to cure the one-day late," said Munoz.

As for why the check was late, the three officials insisted it had been an innocent error, but offered various explanations. "We made a mistake," said Smith, who called it "a human error," and a "clerical error," even though, he acknowledged at one point, there had never been a plan to issue the bonus checks, including Keenan's, before Smith's return from vacation on Monday, four days after the contractual deadline. "This has never happened before," he said. "It's not something I thought of."

The three specifically rejected Keenan's claim that he and his agent had given them ample notice he would hold them to the letter of the contractual deadline. "None of us here received any phone calls from Mr. Keenan or Mr. Campbell addressing the fact that Madison Square Garden may be late about a bonus check," Gutkowski said. "There was no dialogue concerning that issue at all."

He had in fact received phone calls from Campbell in the weeks after the Stanley Cup victory, Gutkowski said, including one seeking to buy tickets to the Barbra Streisand concert at Madison Square Garden, a request, Gutkowski said, he had fulfilled with considerable difficulty. "As I recall," he said, "he was one day late with his payment."

Smith, who acknowledged "communications problems" with Keenan, said he had thought he and Keenan had worked out their differences at a meeting in Hartford in connection with the N.H.L. draft late last month and in a later telephone call in which they had discussed free agents.

Gutkowski recalled that shortly before the draft he had rejected a request from Keenan that he be allowed to seek a general manager's job elsewhere. "There was absolutely no interest to see Mike Keenan leave the organization," he explained. "He was our coach. We'd just won the Stanley Cup. We have a responsibility to our fans and we worked long and hard to get Mike Keenan as our coach and we wanted him to remain as such."

As for what prompted Keenan to bolt, nobody would venture a guess.

"He moves in strange and different ways," said Gutkowski, who noted that at the time he was hired, Keenan, who had previously been general manager of the Chicago Blackhawks, had insisted he wanted to be simply a coach. Since then, Gutkowski said, Keenan had evidently changed his mind. He had become so determined to be a general manager as well as a coach, Gutkowski suggested, that he would have found another pretext to leave the team even if his bonus had been paid on time.

Indeed, the way Gutkowski professes to see it, Keenan will not be satisfied until he arrives at a hockey position of such unlimited power and executive scope that he will be able to delay his own bonus and breach his own contract with himself. "I think Mike Keenan in his own mind will always want to be coach and general manager of any franchise he's involved in," Gutkowski said, "and the president and the secretary and anything else that he can handle—especially treasurer."

Impossibility

A simple *force majeure* clause can go a long way to protect a company that has suffered a critical accident. What difficulties are created when one party insists on a *force majeure* clause? If you were negotiating a contract, would you permit a *force majeure* clause to cover an incident like this?

Shell Plant Recovers from Explosion
Bryan Kokish, *Rubber and Plastics News*

Shell Chemical Co.'s thermoplastic elastomer plant in Belpre, Ohio, is back to full capacity a year after an explosion and fire killed three workers and closed a portion of the facility. The Houston-based firm, which shut down production of its Kraton G unit after the May 27, 1994, blast, recently lifted its declaration of *force majeure*, effective June 1. *Force majeure* serves as a notification to customers that a company can't meet contract obligations because of a crisis.

Of the five departments at the facility, the blast shut down four, severely impairing the K-1 unit, which manufactured Kraton G. About a month after the explosion, Shell restarted three units at the plant. "I'm happy to say that now we are in the position where we can meet our customers' needs," said Richard Stade, manager of Shell's elastomers business. "Also we are continuing to debottleneck our G units which allows us to meet the needs of new customers along with the long-term growth of our existing customers." Shell is the only company that makes Kraton G, which is used in road and roofing applications and some adhesive products. However, some other firms manufacture similar products.

Shell will not reveal how much the blast has cost in terms of damage to the facility and lost revenues. About 50 to 75 of the unit's 480 employees were at the factory when the blast occurred. The explosion spurred the evacuation of more than 300 people from surrounding communities. The fire began in one building and spread to at least one tank, which eventually collapsed. During the blaze, flames reached heights of 300 to 600 feet. Officials blamed the blast on an error in the mixing process.

Copyright © 1995 by Crain Communications Inc. *Rubber and Plastics News*, June 12, 1995, p.8. Reprinted by permission.

Chapter 18

Remedies

Injunctions

Special Issues of Damages

Injunctions

An employer will often use an injunction if he believes that a former employee is violating a noncompete clause. Should a court automatically grant an injunction if the employee has violated the contract, or must the court examine the fairness of the noncompete clause?

WYRK Sues WNUC Over Steve Mortenson Move
Anthony Violanti, *Buffalo News*

Steve Mortenson may be a casualty in a radio battle between country stations WYRK-FM 106.5 and WNUC-FM 107.7. Mortenson's career hangs in the balance of a lawsuit brought by WYRK against WNUC. WYRK is owned by American Radio Systems, a Boston company that owns stations throughout the U.S. John Casciani owns WNUC, one of the few locally owned stations left in Buffalo.

Mortenson left WYRK on Feb. 18, and on March 1 joined Carol Williams as part of a morning team at WNUC. WYRK claims Mortenson violated a six-month non-compete clause in his contract. Mortenson was briefly ordered off the air by a judicial injunction on March 15, Casciani said. Mortenson returned on March 27, when Casciani said a state court issued a stay of the injunction until an appeal hearing will be held in May.

Casciani said that American Radio Systems is suing his station for $1.5 million and that Mortenson is also being sued for legal damages. "We're going to fight this thing," Casciani said. "To me it seems like a classic case of David and Goliath." Casciani said that Mortenson signed the non-compete contract while WYRK was owned by Stoner Broadcasting. The station has since changed ownership.

Paul Perlman, lawyer for WYRK, said the ownership change did not matter because the non-compete contract clause included "all successors" or new owners. "There are 265 radio markets in this country, and (Mortenson) can work at 264 of them, under the non-compete contract," Perlman said. "He signed a contract and he should honor that contract."

WYRK has dominated country music in Buffalo for the past decade. The station is a ratings powerhouse and huge commercial success. WNUC went to a "new country" format about three years ago and has been struggling. Mortenson, who used to be a midmorning personality at WYRK, seems to be caught in the middle.

Copyright © 1995 by The Buffalo News. *Buffalo News*, April 14, 1995, p.9. Reprinted with permission.

"He wanted a job and I gave him a job," Casciani said. "Now we're going to fight to keep it."

Injunctions

An injunction is a powerful weapon, but like all remedies it has limitations, as this television reporter discovered. Why are courts reluctant to order an employer to give a particular job to an employee?

Precedent Prevails Over Anchor's Contract Quest
Elaine Song, *Connecticut Law Tribune*

By suing WFSB Channel 3 for reinstatement as anchor on the 6 P.M. and 11 P.M. news shows, anchor Don Lark not only challenged his employer of 14 years, but a history of legal precedent in contract law. At a bench trial that lasted more than a week, Lark's lawyer, C. Michael Budlong, of Hartford's Budlong, Becker & Murrett, urged that an exception be made to the general rule that courts do not order specific performance of contracts. Lark sought an injunction compelling the station to keep him on the air at the choice anchor times.

But in a Nov. 28 decision, Hartford Superior Court Judge Marshall K. Berger Jr. affirmed the long-standing practice. "Courts have traditionally declined to enter the workplace, in part, because of the difficulty of judicial supervision," Berger writes in his decision. He continues, "Courts have also been reluctant to force the continuation of a hostile or intolerable employment relationship." Berger essentially finds that Lark's contract requires the company to pay him for the length of his contract, which expires Aug. 1, 1995, but it doesn't have to assign him to the specific news slots stated in the contract.

Not only did Berger find support in precedent, but in the U.S. Constitution. He finds that granting specific performance would violate WFSB's First Amendment right to control its editorial content. Assuming that a news anchor takes part in the writing and presentation of the news, a station's right to control editorial content includes its selection of a news anchor, Berger

---

Elaine Song is a writer for the Connecticut Law Tribune. This article is reprinted with permission from the *Tribune*, Dec. 12, 1994, p.12. The Connecticut Law Tribune © 1994.

reasons. "A station must have the right to decide and control who writes and delivers the news," he writes.

No Middle Ground

Station officials maintain that they did what they could to avoid a drawnout court battle by offering Lark reassignment to other time slots. Station officials approached Lark with offers to extend his contract by placing him in three other news-show slots: at noon, 5 P.M. and 5:30 P.M., says Vice President and General Manager Christopher J. Rohrs.

But Lark saw no middle ground between his position and theirs, and believes the station broke its promise to him. "I had no other choice than to do what I did," he says, adding that the five-year contract he was offered included decreases in salary over time. "He was offering me five years of pay cuts," Lark says.

Berger made note of the station's offers in finding that Lark's situation didn't meet the standard needed for an injunction. Berger cited testimony finding that Lark wouldn't sustain irreparable harm if he appeared on the nightly news shows offered him.

"We just think he made a bad decision to take it to a confrontation and go into the legal process rather than to work with us," Rohrs says. "This case should not have gone to trial," says WFSB attorney, Joseph A. Moniz, of Day, Berry & Howard in Hartford. "The evidence showed that he was very marketable. He could have done other things, rather than challenge over 200 years of precedent," Moniz says.

Budlong didn't return telephone calls to his office. But Lark, who praises his lawyer's work on his case, says the decision to proceed to court was entirely his. "It was my decision. I asked him to defend my rights in this case," he says. Lark says he chose Budlong to represent him because he was his longtime lawyer and had litigated contracts before. "He's been a friend of mine for about 12 years," Lark says. "I knew him to be an experienced contract lawyer and experienced litigator."

The case centered on two clauses in Lark's contract: one clause states that Lark's duties are to anchor the news at 6 P.M. and 11 P.M. The other clause is a so-called "pay, no play" provision. Under that clause, the station successfully argued, the station had no obligation to put Lark on the air in the time slots it designated in the contract; it was only obligated to pay him. Berger found no conflict between the statement of anchor times and the pay, no play clause. "To adopt the plaintiff's position would require the court to find that the pay, no play clause is meaningless," Berger writes.

Evidence against Lark included testimony that the clause setting forth time assignments appears throughout the industry. Based on that evidence, Berger found that the clause prohibits an employer from forcing someone to perform other duties not stated in the contract.

Budlong argued that an exception exists in the doctrine that an exception exists in the doctrine that courts don't order injunctive relief in employment contracts: that is, an exception for special, unique or extraordinary personal services or acts that would make it difficult for the employer to replace the employee. But Berger finds that the exception applies to cases restraining an employee from leaving an employer. It doesn't apply to a situation in which an employee is trying to order his employer to retain him.

In the end, an 1890 precedent prevailed. Citing William Rogers Mfg. Co. v. Rogers, Berger writes: "Over 100 years ago, our Supreme Court stated, in a different fact situation, that 'contracts for personal service are matters for Courts at law, and equity will not undertake a specific performance.' "

Special Issues of Damages

A lawsuit is an unpredictable thing. Will this plaintiff recover $20 million in compensatory damages and additional punitive damages—or nothing?

"Geraldo" Suit Set for Sept. Trial
Adam Sandler, *Daily Variety*

A jury trial has been set for Sept. 26 in the $20 million lawsuit filed by actor Sonny Gibson against talkshow host Geraldo Rivera. Intent on having his day in court, Gibson could be among the few plaintiffs whose cases against Rivera proceed to trial.

Gibson, who claims he was deceived into appearing on a segment of "Geraldo" on May 3, 1994, also is suing Premiere magazine writer John Richardson, Tribune Entertainment, CBS Entertainment and "Geraldo" show exec producer Martin Berman and producer Penny Price, the latter allegedly assisting in the inducement of Gibson to appear on the show. Since filing the suit in August (Daily Variety, Aug. 15, 1994), Gibson has prevailed on three motions brought by the defendants' attorneys in an attempt to have the case dismissed. Attorneys for Gibson deposed Rivera in New York last Thursday.

Copyright © 1995 by Daily Variety Ltd. All rights reserved. *Daily Variety*, Aug. 1, 1995, p.2. Reprinted with permission.

No Protection

A court earlier this year denied a motion brought by Premiere that attempted to get the case dismissed by asserting Richardson and Rivera were protected by the First Amendment. The court found that fraud and conspiracy were not protected under the free speech doctrine and ordered that the lawsuit move forward.

The suit accuses the defendants of fraud, conspiracy, breach of contract and intentional infliction of emotional distress, among other causes of action, and seeks at least $20 million in compensatory damages, with punitive damages to be determined at trial. The defendants have denied wrongdoing.

In the 47-page complaint, Gibson claims he was brought to a satellite studio in West Los Angeles to participate as an expert in the segment "Women Who Married Men in the Mafia." But the show actually was about "Casting Couch Abuses" and featured several guests asserting that they were sexually harassed or raped by Gibson. As a result of the airing of those claims, Gibson said he has lost several acting jobs. Gibson also said the financial backers of a film in which he was to star backed out of the deal.

To support the theory he was intentionally sandbagged, Gibson points to being brought to the studio under the pretext that Geraldo was taping his show in New York, when in fact, the show was being taped from nearby CBS studios in the Fairfax district.

Unit 3

Commercial Transactions

Chapter 19

Introduction to Sales

Mixed Contracts

Unconscionability

Mixed Contracts

This "how-to" article looks at contracts that mix goods and services, and makes a sound recommendation about drafting such agreements.

Contracts Mixing Goods, Services Bring Mixed Results
Robert A. Feldman, *Corporate Legal Times*

Everyone knows that most sales of goods which take place within the confines of the United States are governed by Article 2 of the Uniform Commercial Code (UCC). Everyone also knows that most sales of services are not subject to Article 2. This is all well and good. It's refreshing to have clarity and certainty in the law.

What about a transaction that involves a mix of both goods and services? Many of the transactions we document these days are not neatly confined to goods or services. Does Article 2 of the UCC apply? Or the common law of services? Or both? More importantly, what difference does it make?

Answering the last question first, different legal results may—and often do—flow from the application of these different bodies of law. For example, the common law typically imposes a requirement of substantial performance with respect to services. The UCC has a different standard: perfect tender. The effect of this difference may be less than what appears on the surface, but it is helpful to bear it in mind when drafting or responding to such things as warranty provisions.

Different implied warranties, remedies and statutes of limitations may come into play. Different rules in other areas may fill contractual gaps differently. While a significant portion of the *Restatement (Second) of Contracts* follows Article 2 rules, there are differences. And, of course, the "Restatement" rule, even if it parallels the UCC, may not be followed by a particular jurisdiction.

Computer Consulting as a Service

The kind of decision process that a mixed contract invokes is illustrated by Conopco Inc. v. McCreadie, a 1993 case involving a cast which included

Copyright © 1994 by Corporate Legal Times Corp. *Corporate Legal Times*, Nov. 1994, p.10. Reprinted with permission. Robert A. Feldman served as in-house counsel for more than 20 years, most recently at Comshare Inc., Ann Arbor, Mich. He is now a principal in the Detroit law office of Wise & Marsac. He offers consulting services and in-house seminars and workshops on contract drafting and negotiations.

Faberge Inc., Elizabeth Arden Co., Unilever United States Inc., and Eli Lilly and Co. The defendants were partners in Ernst & Young. The dispute centered around Elizabeth Arden's allegedly defective computer system. Specific complaints included slow response time and unacceptable system errors. Ernst & Young had acted as a computer consultant in connection with the system. Among the plaintiff's causes of action was one for breach of the implied warranty of merchantability. While this implied warranty arises out of a sale of goods under Article 2, it is generally not present in a sale of services. In other words, while a sale of goods may carry a results warranty—e.g., fitness for ordinary purposes—services do not typically carry this burden. Just as the lawyer, although held to a standard, does not guarantee that the client will win the case, nor the physician that the patient will be cured.

The court found that Ernst & Young had sold services, not goods. Accordingly, and because there was no material issue of fact to present to a jury on this fact issue, the court granted summary judgment on this claim to Ernst & Young. Ernst & Young had previously lost a motion to dismiss the same claim. At that time, the court with nothing but the pleadings before it, had noted that the contract clearly fell within the ambit of the UCC.

The determination on summary judgment was based on a finding that the contract was predominantly one for the sale of services. This predominant thrust test, although not found in the UCC, is one of the more popular tests that the courts apply to a mixed goods-services contract. The same test is codified in the "U.N. Convention on Contracts for the International Sale of Goods."

Avoiding Surprises

So here we sit, drafting a mixed goods-services contract, trying to play judge and jury with a predominant thrust test or whatever other test the applicable jurisdiction may use. Will we win on a motion to dismiss? Will we win on a motion for summary judgment?

One solution may be to duck the issue. If you are a seller, assume that Article 2 applies and write your disclaimers accordingly. If you can disclaim the implied warranties, you need not worry about whether they apply. If you are a buyer, assume you don't have them and make them express. The more the parties spell out, the more likely there will be no surprises regarding substantial performance versus perfect tender, applicable remedies or any other issues.

Unconsciousability

Let your fingers do the walking through this discussion of unconscionable exculpatory clauses.

Directory Assistance: Recourse for Yellow Page Ad Problems; Legal Recourse
Fred S. Steingold, *Party & Paper Retailer*

Most businesses rely—at least to some extent—on ads in The Yellow Pages. Therefore, errors in these ads can often lead to lost profits and damage your reputation. So, what are your legal rights if the phone company leaves information out of your ad, prints incorrect information, or omits the ad all together? Many courts today are ruling that the phone company must compensate fully for losses—but the courts have not always taken this position. In past years, retailers' rights in this area were weak, since phone companies place clauses such as this one in their advertising contracts:

> The telephone company will not be liable to the advertiser for damages resulting from failure to include all or any of the advertising in the directories or from errors in the advertising printed in such directories, in excess of the agreed price for such advertising.

These clauses are often printed in small type on the back of the order form. Nevertheless, in the past, courts around the country ruled that these clauses were perfectly valid. If your store paid $2,000 for a Yellow Pages ad, the phone company could not be held liable for more than $2,000, even if you lost $50,000 worth of business. Unfair? You bet. But until fairly recently there wasn't much that could be done. The contract clause was a valid defense in a lawsuit against the phone company.

Fortunately, the tide is turning. In a number of recent cases, courts have struck down these clauses, calling them "unconscionable." Businesses have been allowed to collect the actual damages caused from Yellow Pages errors.

Insurance agent, Kenneth Allen, sued the phone company after it failed to publish his advertisement in the Flint, MI, Yellow Pages. Allen sought damages for lost business, however, the phone company pointed to the contract clause and argued: "We can't be liable for more than the customer paid for the ads." The court of appeals disagreed with the phone company, stating

---

Copyright © 1995 by Information Access Co., a division of Ziff Communications Co.; 1995 4Ward Corp. *Party & Paper Retailer*, Jan., 1995, vol. 10, no. 1, p.24. Reprinted with permission. Fred S. Steingold is a lawyer and author of Legal Master Guide for Small Business, living in Ann Arbor, MI.

that Allen and the phone company were not in positions of equal bargaining power. The Yellow Pages is the only directory of classified telephone listings freely distributed to all telephone subscribers.

The advertising contract was a "take it or leave it" proposition. Allen couldn't have advertised in The Yellow Pages unless he accepted the phone company's contract terms. The court felt the phone company's attempt to avoid the consequences of its own negligence was unconscionable. Therefore, the contract clause is not enforceable. A victory for the small business man? Yes—but only a partial one. Still ahead was the difficult task of establishing how much business was actually lost because of the phone company's error.

In a case originating in Racine, WI, the Discount Fabric House convinced a jury that it lost $9,000 worth of profits because the phone company omitted the store's trade name from a Yellow Pages ad. The phone company appealed all the way to the Wisconsin Supreme Court. Again, the defense insisted that the contract clause limited the store to collecting the amount it spent for the ad, rather than receiving the actual damages. Again, the court balked at that proposition. The court pointed out that the phone company's Yellow Pages were distributed to everyone with a telephone. No competing publications offered a similar distribution system.

The court said, "The telephone company encourages the public to 'Let your fingers do the walking.' In the present case, due to the company's negligent publication of the quarter-page ad, the public walked right by the plaintiff's ad, since it did not include the significant and commercially important words, 'Discount Fabric House.' " The phone company had to pay the $9,000 awarded by the jury.

In a New Jersey case, an aerial photographer was the victim of phone company carelessness. John Tannock, owner of John Tannock Studios, wanted his Yellow Pages ads to read: "F.A.A. Licensed & P.P. of A. Certified." In one phone book, the words were left out entirely; in another they were garbled. The trial judge turned down the phone company's attempt to limit damages based on the usual contract clause.

The judge noted that the contract clause was printed in type only one-sixteenth of an inch high in a very light color. It was on the back of a one page contract among 20 other paragraphs. "The print is too small to be read by an average person without the aid of a magnifying glass," the judge said. He ruled that it would be unconscionable to bind the photographer to the contract language.

A similar result was reached in South Dakota, where the phone company left out a Yellow Pages ad ordered by Marion Rozenboom, an electrical contractor doing business as Rozy's Electric. Rozenboom claimed that he suffered $25,000 in damages as a result of the phone company's error. The South Dakota Supreme Court held that Rozenboom was entitled to his day in court and that the contract clause could not be the barrier. Said the court: "The only way for Rozy's to realistically communicate with the same audience as his competitors, is to advertise in The Yellow Pages. Justice demands that an aggrieved party reach out and touch the cause of his grievance."

Clearly we have a trend in the making. If your business ever suffers a loss due to the phone company's carelessness in handling your Yellow Pages ad, don't be intimidated by the small print in your contract. There's a good chance that the court will allow you to recover all damages that can actually be traced to the advertising error.

And with the growing number of court decisions striking down these unreasonable clauses, you may not even have to go to trial. The phone company may settle your claim on realistic terms if you have provide good evidence of the extent of your losses.

Chapter 20

Ownership and Risk

Bona Fide Purchaser

Creditor's Rights

Bona Fide Purchaser

The buyer of this truck spent over $1,000 fixing it up, only to learn he had voidable title. The outcome isn't as bleak as it can be in such cases.

Bad-Luck Truck Is Red-Hot and Stolen
Thomas Ryll, *Columbian (Vancouver, Wash.)*

Somebody in Spokane must be mighty happy that his Ford pickup was stolen in 1988. Happy because the truck will soon be returned after thousands of dollars of bumper-to-bumper improvements by two owners, one of whom rescued the vehicle as it was destined for a wrecking yard.

Clark County resident Tom Riner learned all this the hard way. Riner bought the vehicle in April, spent more than $1,000 in repairs himself and then was told the truck was stolen. Friday, he was awaiting a mailed vehicle forfeiture document from the Washington State Patrol. The truck was already sitting in an impoundment yard, and once he signs the document the pickup will be gone.

Riner, a 57-year-old retired IBM technician who lives in Washougal, was lucky: After Riner's threat of legal action, the seller refunded the entire purchase price of the pickup, plus the money Riner spent on repairs. To the penny. Riner received a payment of $4,227.82.

Although his experience is rare, it points out the potential risk of buying an out-of-state vehicle with a questionable history. The pickup's seller held a valid Oregon title, but because the Washington State Patrol inspects all such vehicles, the red-hot nature of the vehicle was discovered. That occurred in Stevenson. Riner was notified by a Vancouver trooper that the truck was stolen.

Patrol Sgt. Mike Warren, supervisor of the Vancouver vehicle inspection station on Evergreen Boulevard, said that of the more than 800 vehicles examined there each week, perhaps two are found to be stolen. Vehicle buyers can take some precautions, but, "It's a tough thing. There's no sure way" to guard against buying a stolen out-of-state vehicle, he said. For example, in the case of Riner's truck, even if a law officer had run a computer check for a stolen vehicle with the Ford's VIN number as listed on the title it would not have come back as hot.

Riner found the 1972 Ford 4×4 advertised on a bulletin board at a store near his home. Its owner lives in The Dalles, Ore., but his sister lives near

Copyright © 1995 by The Columbian Publishing Co. *Columbian*, June 11, 1995, §A, p.4. Reprinted with permission.

the store. He negotiated a sale price of $2,850. The seller had an Oregon title issued in March 1988.

Riner took the truck home. However, before he had it inspected as part of the process of transferring the title, he had brake, starter, power-steering and front-suspension work done. "I wanted to make sure it was road-ready," he said.

In late May, he took it to the Stevenson inspection station. The trooper who looked the truck over was instantly suspicious because an information plate was missing from the door frame. However, the title's VIN number matched the number on another door-frame plate. Then the trooper checked the VIN number stamped in the truck's frame. "I didn't even know about that number," said Riner. "He took the title and wrote 'void' across the front of it. I said, What's wrong?' He said that the numbers didn't match."

Earlier this month, Riner received a call from another trooper, who disclosed the bad news: the truck was reported stolen on March 7, 1988, out of Spokane. Riner learned the person he bought the truck from had unwittingly purchased the vehicle later that month from two people who were going from wrecking yard to wrecking yard, selling pieces of the Ford. The purchase price was $100 cash and a car worth $300 in trade, Riner said.

Oregon officials, either overlooking or unconcerned about the VIN discrepancy, issued a title in March 1988 to the new owner. He then invested extensively in everything from a high-performance engine to new tires.

When Riner demanded a refund from the seller, "They just about exploded," he said. Reasoning that "part of something is better than part of nothing," he sought the return of only the $2,850 purchase price. When that was rejected, he threatened legal action. The seller apparently contacted an attorney. The seller then offered the full price, including his expenses, for which he had saved receipts.

"The gods are with me. I thank my Lord," said Riner on Friday, adding that the original Spokane owner, who had no theft insurance, "is getting a heck of a deal."

How to Prevent Auto Disaster

Although only a tiny percentage of vehicles are found to be stolen when they are inspected by the Washington State Patrol, a few precautions could prevent disaster for those buyers:

- Ensure that the VIN numbers on the existing title exactly match those on the vehicle. A mismatch could be the result of a transcription error or worse.
- VIN numbers are commonly riveted to the dashboard near the steering wheel, but they also appear elsewhere on a vehicle. Sometimes described as "secret," those numbers are in various

locations, such as stamped in the frame pan under the rear seat of the Volkswagen Beetle.
- Any evidence of tampering with numbers or identification plates is immediate cause for a red alert.
- Know the car's history. Is the seller the original owner? Does he have receipts for the period? If not, does he seem like the kind of person who will pull up stakes and leave after you buy the car?
- Your local law enforcement agency may be willing to take a vehicle's VIN number and check it against stolen-vehicle records. "We do that all the time," a Vancouver Police Department employee said.

Creditor's Rights

Selling goods on consignment carries a significant danger—you may lose the goods to the consignee's creditors.

Money Talk: Getting Caught in the Consignment Cross-Fire
Carla Lazzareschi, *Los Angeles Times*

Q: I recently consigned for sale my replica 1962 Ferrari to a Beverly Hills auto dealer. Unknown to me, the dealer owed his bank money. Now the bank, Capital Bank in Century City, has foreclosed on the dealer and attached his assets—including my car. I still have the "pink slip," but the bank has my car and refuses to give it back. I'm an innocent third party to this mess. Can the bank really do this?—M.S.

A: Yes, as your lawyers have no doubt already told you, the bank is well within its legal rights to do exactly what it has done. Theoretically, the bank, armed with the appropriate court order, could even sell your car and use the proceeds to pay off the debt owed by the auto dealer.

On the surface, this answer flies in the face of common sense and decency. After all, why should you, an admittedly innocent third party to whatever disagreement exists between the car dealer and his bankers, get

Copyright © 1991 by The Times Mirror Co. *Los Angeles Times*, May 12, 1991, pt. D, p.4, col. 3. Reprinted with permission.

caught in their cross-fire? The answer is that you didn't have to get caught at all.

Sections 9114 and 2326 of the state Uniform Commercial Code detail the conditions for consigning merchandise to brokers for sale and provide an easy escape from the mess you now face. The law says the consignor should file a UCC-1 statement proclaiming that the consigned merchandise belongs to him, not to the broker. The UCC-1 form is completed and filed before the broker is given the goods to sell.

What good is a simple piece of paper? The statement puts broker's creditors on notice that they can not attach that asset in the event of a financial or legal dispute. According to Hydee Feldstein, a Los Angeles bankruptcy lawyer, the form is designed to protect lenders making business loans to businesses that both sell new and consigned goods. The goal is to prevent misunderstandings about the health of a business on which lenders are making commercial loans by notifying them at least some merchandise in the dealer's possession does not belong to him and should not be taken as evidence that his business is thriving.

Of course, this UCC-1 form explanation comes far too late to save you any anguish. You obviously never filed one. But that doesn't mean you have no hope of recovering your car. The law allows you two other avenues to reclaim your car without throwing yourself at the mercy of the bank. You can claim that the consigned merchandise is personal, household property designed for daily use. (This might be a tough argument to make for a replica vintage Ferrari.) Or you can attempt to demonstrate that it was "generally" known by creditors that the business was "substantially" dealing in consigned goods, and that the bank should have known it as well.

This latter point is not easy to prove. According to Feldstein, you must show that the dealer's consignment operations were so well established that creditors would "generally" know to include that factor in their loan-making process.

Even if you can't squeeze through the law's loopholes, all is not lost. According to Lonnie Umbenhower, a senior vice president of Capital Bank, the bank is not interested in depriving you of your property. Umbenhower says the bank continues to hold your Ferrari, as it is entitled to do, because the matter has not gone to court. However, he observed that once the mess between the bank and auto dealer is untangled, your car will likely be returned.

Chapter 21

Warranties and Product Liability

Warranties

Negligence

Strict Liability

Future Laws

Warranties

This article reminds us that while many merchants will accept the return of an item that has no defects, they are probably not required to do so.

Retailer Refuses To Accept Return of Computer Disc
Michael Ferry, *St. Louis Post-Dispatch*

Q: A few weeks ago, I bought a computer program from a store that sells computer software and other electronic items. From what the salesman told me, I thought it would meet my needs. However, when I started using it at home, I found that it didn't. When I tried to return the program, the store said it would replace it if it was defective but wouldn't give me a refund or take it in exchange for another program. What can I do?

A: Whether it's legal probably depends, more than anything else, on exactly what the salesman told you. If we assume the salesman told you nothing that would give rise to legal rights on your part, then you are essentially saying that you didn't like the program, which has nothing wrong with it. If that's your only complaint, then you probably have no legal right to return the program or get your money back. Many retailers let people return merchandise with virtually no questions asked, but they do so as a matter of good customer relations, not because of any legal requirement.

If we assume that the salesman told you specific things about the program, then the statements could amount to a warranty. Depending on what the salesman said, he could have made an express warranty—a specific, explicit promise. Or, if the salesman knew what you needed and that you were relying on his expertise to give you the right program, what he said could be an implied warranty that the program was fit for the particular purpose you had in mind.

If there was either an express or implied warranty, you must then ask whether the seller limited the warranty by limiting the remedies available if the warranty was breached. Also, the seller may have made disclaimers, although express warranties cannot be disclaimed. Note that we're talking about warranties made by the seller, not by the manufacturer of the computer program.

You may want to pursue this through arbitration with the Better Business Bureau. That can be a good choice if your legal case is weak but your

Copyright © 1994 by St. Louis Post-Dispatch, Inc. *St. Louis Post-Dispatch*, Sep. 24, 1994, p.4D. Reprinted with permission.

factual case is strong. If the arbitrator thought that you had been treated wrongly or unfairly, the ruling could be made in your favor even if the law weren't on your side.

Arbitration rulings are generally not reviewed by the courts, so the software seller would have no appeal of a ruling in your favor. Of course, the software seller would have to agree to submit the matter to arbitration. Another option would be small claims court, which in Missouri hears cases involving up to $1,500.

Warranties

A meat wholesaler gives us a glimpse inside a company that faces defective product claims.

Spotting Claims That Are Just a Song and Dance
James M. Burcke, *Business Insurance*

While the ConAgra Red Meat Cos. receive their share of dubious liability claims, the most "exotic" came from a belly dancer. The dancer sought $20,000 from Monfort Inc., the principal unit of ConAgra Red Meat, after she chipped a tooth on a foreign substance that allegedly was contained in ground beef produced by Monfort.

"Her whole point was that this really affected her career from an appearance standpoint," says VP of Risk Management Lucky Gallagher, laughing. "Nobody was looking at her teeth. She was 51, by the way." Monfort finally settled the claim for a "very small amount" that covered the dancer's dental bills, Ms. Gallagher says.

It's not unusual for ConAgra Red Meat to pay a "nuisance value" to settle a claim like the belly dancer's that has some validity, Ms. Gallagher points out. "We do investigate every claim, because not every claim is valid," explains P. Kay Norton, VP of legal and government affairs and general counsel.

After investigating a liability claim, ConAgra Red Meat's inhouse claims staff, which administers all general and product liability claims,

Reprinted with permission from *Business Insurance,* Issue of Apr. 18, 1994. Copyright © 1994, Crain Communications, Inc. All rights reserved.

"takes a practical approach," Ms. Norton says. The first step in this approach is deciding whether the product that allegedly caused the injury could have been a ConAgra Red Meat product, since retailers like grocery stores and restaurants will often buy meat from various suppliers.

Once it is established that the product in question was produced by the company, claims handlers "take a look at the evidence, what our quality assurance people say about whether it could have been related to an action of ours" and then recommend whether a settlement offer should be made, says Ms. Norton. While this investigation is handled by the claims administration staff, Ms. Norton—in her role as ConAgra Red Meat's general counsel—will involve herself with a claim if it appears to be "legally complex, like the Jack in the Box litigation," she says.

In early 1993, two children died and nearly 300 other people became seriously ill after eating undercooked hamburgers tainted with E-coli bacteria at Jack in the Box restaurants in the Pacific Northwest (BI, Feb. 1, 1993). Jack in the Box's parent, Foodmaker Inc., is suing the company that grinds its hamburger, which in turn "is coming up the chain" to all of the companies that supplied it with meat, including ConAgra Red Meat.

"It will be a very complex matter in terms of trying to determine the origin of the bacteria," says Ms. Norton, who fears the litigation could drag on for years. A piece of meat, she says, "could be sterile when it left us but not be sterile by the time it lands on your plate in the local restaurant" because it could have been kept in an unrefrigerated area—what is known as "temperature abuse" in the trade. "A huge issue" in the Jack in the Box litigation will be identifying the suppliers of the products that caused the deaths and illnesses, Ms. Norton says, noting that "it is very unlikely if it will ever be determined."

The claims against ConAgra Red Meat in the Jack in the Box case are unique. Normally food poisoning suits are brought against grocery stores, restaurants or other retailers, not suppliers. Also, meat packing companies are seldom involved because most meat is cooked before eating and the cooking kills most bacteria, Ms. Norton says. "What happened in Washington in the Foodmaker situation involved a particularly nasty strain of E-coli bacteria and, most important, happened because the product was not properly cooked."

Much more common than food poisoning claims are what the ConAgra Red Meat risk management and legal staffs refer to as "tooth fairy claims," like the belly dancer's, that allege that bone, glass or other foreign substances in Monfort products caused dental injuries. "The traditional claim has been an allegation of bone chips or sometimes a foreign object in a product. Somebody bites into a hamburger and breaks a tooth, so we call them tooth fairy claims," Ms. Norton explains. Most complaints involve pieces of bone that were found in "boneless" products like ground beef and boneless roasts, though "some people complain even if the product wasn't represented as boneless," she says. "Of course, those are the claims that we just don't pay."

Generally, people sue the restaurant or grocery store where they bought the meat, she says. Those defendants "will kick it back to us if they think it is our responsibility." If the hamburger is ground at a ConAgra Red Meat facility, ConAgra Red Meat could be liable for the claim. However, if bulk meat shipped by ConAgra Red Meat is ground into hamburger by a retailer or a restaurant, ConAgra Red Meat will maintain it is not liable. "And, if the allegation is that there was glass in the product, it could not have come from us because we don't have glass in any of our plants due to USDA regulations," Ms. Norton explains, referring to the U.S. Department of Agriculture.

Negligence

Is a tricycle negligently designed because it is small? Is this a legitimate issue of design or a frivolous lawsuit? Would you feel differently if it had been your child on the tricycle? Should those feelings be a factor in deciding whether the manufacturer was negligent?

Family Files Lawsuit in Death of Six-Year-Old Springfield Boy
Pat England, *State Journal-Register (Springfield IL)*

The family of a six-year-old boy who died after his tricycle collided with a commercial van is suing the driver of the van, the maker of the tricycle and the store that sold the tricycle. John Heimlich was riding a Play-skool "Cycle Blaster" when he was struck June 14 by a van driven by Gerald Wayne Wood of Springfield. Wood was backing out of a driveway in the 1800 block of South Walnut Street. The boy was pronounced dead in the Memorial Medical Center emergency room from traumatic injuries to the skull and brain.

The lawsuit names Wood, Play-skool Inc. and Venture Stores Inc. In the allegations against Play-skool, the suit contends the three-wheel toy was "unreasonably dangerous, defective and unsafe." Its low-to-the-ground design made it unsuitable for outdoor use without a flag, pennant or other

Copyright © 1995 by The State Journal-Register. *State Journal-Register (Springfield IL)*, Jan. 4, 1995, p.17. Reprinted with permission.

safety warning device to enhance visibility; the noisemaker on the toy's wheel masked the sound of traffic; and the toy had an inadequate braking mechanism for outdoor use, the 10-count suit says. Citing the same factors, the suit also alleges that the toy left Venture, 2115 MacArthur Blvd., where it was purchased, in an unsafe condition.

Venture merchandise manager Tony Figueroa declined to comment. A spokesperson for Play-skool could not be reached for comment.

"We are very sorry this tragic accident has occurred, and a settlement has been approved by Mr. Wood's insurance carrier and the plaintiff's counsel," said Wood's attorney Kevin Davlin. A Springfield police officer testifying at a coroner's inquest in June said Wood was not reckless. There was no indication of excessive speed, the officer said, who noted that Wood said he looked both ways for traffic and used his mirrors in backing, but did not see the boy. A traffic ticket issued to Wood was dismissed with prejudice when no complaining witness appeared, said Davlin.

The lawsuit is seeking funeral and burial expenses, as well as a monetary award.

Strict Liability

When product liability defendants settle a case they routinely demand that the agreement be confidential, a practice that infuriates some plaintiffs. Why do plaintiffs' lawyers dislike the practice? Is it in society's interest to allow secrecy, or should the law demand that all tort agreements be made public?

The Halcion Story; Upjohn willingly settles for silence; Frequently used legal tactic succeeds in avoiding Halcion confrontations
Kim Cobb and Steven R. Reed, *Houston Chronicle*

Even William Hawal has been silenced by the Upjohn Co. As recently as a few weeks ago, Hawal was the bulldog attorney heading up the Halcion litigation group of the Association of Trial Lawyers of America. The Cleve-

Copyright © 1994 by the Houston Chronicle Publishing Co. *Houston Chronicle,* Sep. 15, 1994, §A, p.1. Reprinted with permission. All rights reserved.

land lawyer was the touchstone for other attorneys seeking ammunition in their legal battles over the controversial Upjohn drug, which became the world's most widely prescribed sleeping pill.

But Hawal is settling his three pending cases against Upjohn, apparently making the usual confidentiality agreement which the pharmaceutical company requires in nearly all such cases. The client gets a financial settlement in exchange for silence—an agreement not to discuss the case or disseminate Upjohn documents that might be useful to other attorneys.

Hawal, who talked freely several weeks ago about his cases, is suddenly tight-lipped.

Settling for silence is a tactic used by many major companies facing product liability suits. Upjohn has used it with great success in warding off potential major losses over the question of Halcion's safety. Although Halcion provides relief from insomnia for most users, other consumers and their families have blamed it for a range of adverse effects, including paranoia, hallucinations, depression and even suicide and murder. At least 100 lawsuits against the drug manufacturer are pending.

At a recent Chicago meeting of the American Trial Lawyers Association, plaintiff's attorney Gary Pillersdorf of New York used humor to demonstrate the frustration that comes with the confidentiality agreements Upjohn has made a trademark. He trotted out the old line about having good news and bad news, telling the group that the bad news involved losses in a couple of major Halcion cases. "But the good news is there have been some advances," Pillersdorf deadpanned. "Let me tell you about some cases I've been working on." He then shoved a gag into his mouth and began making muffled and unintelligible noises into the microphone.

And when Upjohn doesn't settle a case, it is a tough and savvy opponent in the courtroom. In case after case, Upjohn has been able to portray its accusers as flawed people with pre-existing conditions—raising questions about whether Halcion can fairly be blamed for any of their strange behaviors. People take Halcion because they can't sleep. If they're already depressed, anxious, nervous or paranoid and then begin to suffer suicidal thoughts—those ideas easily are attributed to existing conditions rather than Halcion.

Citing the confusion and amnesia associated with the drug, Dr. Peter Mendelis, a staff physician at the U.S. Food and Drug Administration, said in a 1984 memo that consumers were unlikely to link their "unfamiliar emotional states" to Halcion. So far Upjohn has lost only one case over Halcion's safety, and that loss was recently reversed on appeal. In a Dallas courtroom in 1992 the family of Halcion user Bill Freeman, an ex-police officer from San Angelo, was awarded $1.3 million. However, the jury denied any financial relief for Freeman, and a Dallas appeals court cited that as the reason for overturning the verdict three weeks ago.

Freeman inexplicably killed a good friend in 1987 and was sentenced to prison for murder. He and his family sued Upjohn after Halcion's potential dangers came to light a few years later. The Freeman family's attorney plans to appeal the reversal of the 1992 decision.

Another of Upjohn's most successful tactics in fighting lawsuits is its fierce resistance to producing internal documents. The company's first argument, according to attorneys who have heard it, is that the information being sought about Halcion is a protected trade secret. "The deal (Upjohn) ultimately makes is, 'We'll give them everything they ask for provided no one else can see it,' " Pillersdorf said.

"For this issue to be tried over and over again here, with teams of lawyers who can't even talk to each other about what they've found, is an absurd way to conduct litigation in the United States . . . ," plaintiff's attorney Stuart Wechsler argued in an April hearing in a class action suit in Brooklyn.

And there's the money factor. Many people simply cannot afford to try to prove "Halcion made me do it." Because documents from previous lawsuits are protected by confidentiality agreements, attorneys are forced to go on costly fishing expeditions. "The trick is you can't afford to say, 'Give me all of Dr. X's papers,' " explained attorney Pillersdorf, who recently settled a case on behalf of two Kentucky women whose husbands committed suicide while under the influence of Halcion. "You know Dr. X has said some damaging things, but to ask for (all) his memos is a needle in a haystack."

And since Upjohn, like nearly any company, charges by the page for reproducing its internal documents—those costs alone can quickly become overwhelming. Pillersdorf considered it a victory when he recently negotiated a reduction in costs for copies of Upjohn documents at about a dime less per page than other lawyers were paying. Pillersdorf estimates that a case against Upjohn can cost from $200,000 to $300,000 just to prepare.

Hawal, when he was still leading the Halcion litigation group, said someone might claim to be "a total basket case" for years because of the drug yet face the prospect of winning only $100,000 in damages.

Hawal and Pillersdorf have used the same phrase when describing Upjohn's strategy in defending Halcion: Each plaintiff must "reinvent the wheel." And if an attorney must take what amounts to a vow of silence to hammer our a settlement for a client, Pillersdorf and Hawal have both made it clear that their first responsibility cannot be to a national pool of Halcion litigants who might benefit from their knowledge. "While we all want to be Don Quixotes, the bottom line is I have a client," Pillersdorf said.

Pillersdorf expresses grudging admiration for the attorneys who have handled much of Upjohn's Halcion legal fights—the Kansas City law firm of Shook, Hardy & Bacon. "If you've got to rate their performance, they're hard-nosed," Pillersdorf said. "But they're just good lawyers. I'm not crying foul with them."

Dallas attorney Michael Mosher is not so charitable. Mosher filed a lawsuit in January alleging that corporate misconduct and regulatory indifference were part of a conspiracy that resulted in injuries to a group of Halcion users. His racketeering suit names Shook, Hardy & Bacon as a defendant along with Upjohn. According to the suit, Shook, Hardy knew by 1990 "of the grand scope of the Upjohn fraud surrounding Halcion . . . (and) engaged in a concerted effort that included lying to opposing counsel and lying to courts about Upjohn's documents."

The Kansas City firm is no stranger to such harsh attacks. This spring, in internal documents leaked to the news media, Shook, Hardy was alleged to be a conduit for a secret fund used by the tobacco industry to underwrite scientific research that often proved favorable to cigarette makers. Two years earlier, U.S. District Judge Lee H. Sarokin of Newark, N.J., said Shook, Hardy and the tobacco companies had abused their attorney-client privilege by concealing negative results in some research projects. But Shook, Hardy hasn't lost a tobacco case. And Halcion plaintiff's attorney Pillersdorf thinks the firm may have won the Halcion battle as well. "They've avoided the major, publicized hit," he said.

But there is another way to look at it, too. Sales of Halcion have dropped dramatically in recent years because doctors are prescribing the drug less. "So maybe the public has been served," theorized Pillersdorf. "The bottom line is that . . . sometimes if we just serve a wakeup call we've done the right thing."

Future Laws

The battle over tort reform rages not only in Washington but also in many state capitols.

The Tort Stage Is Set
Texas Lawyer

The opening salvos in the 1995 Legislature's tort battle were fired Feb. 2–3 before the Senate Economic Development Committee by Gail Armstrong and Houston builder Richard Weekley, founder of Texans for Lawsuit Reform. These excerpts from their testimony show how the two sides are framing the debate.

This article is republished with permission from the 2/13/95 issue of *Texas Lawyer.* Copyright © *Texas Lawyer.*

Armstrong

My name is Gail Armstrong; I'm from Dallas, I am a registered nurse, and I am the founder of the National Breast Implant Coalition. I am an affected breast implant victim. I have two silicone-affected children.

I am addressing you today not only as a voting Republican, but as a spokesperson for the thousands of women and children whose stories have filled my heart, my mind and my home for the past three years. I have heard and with my own eyes have seen damage caused by breast implants, DES, and the Dalkon Shield. How very unfortunate that our state and federal regulatory offices were unable to protect women and children from these products; and how very ominous that you are now considering making federal and state regulations the only line of defense against products like these.

The breast implant was invented in Texas, and Texas has more breast implanted women than any other state in the nation. The numbers of women who experience malfunctions and die as a result of defective breast implants grows daily, and they will continue to grow, senators, for a long, long time. I would like to make you aware that there are many more critically and terminally ill breast implant victims than anyone realizes. Some experts say 100 percent of the breast implanted women will become sick. The latency period can be 25 to 30 years—just like smoking.

This is not the first time, nor will it be the last, that a product slips through the cracks of the FDA's powers and causes harm to several generations. But it does illuminate our need for more than one line of defense against dangerous products. Whether we like it or not, product liability and punitive damages ARE our second line of defense. In a perfect world, manufacturers would not change the results of their own product research, they would spend some time and money tracking their own medical devices and issuing recalls when it becomes obvious that one of their products is threatening consumer health and safety.

But in the REAL world, product liability and punitive damages are the motivators that send product designers back to the drawing board. In the REAL world, safe infant car seats, rupture-resistant gas tanks and airbags are continually being made better and safer because of laws that hold manufacturers accountable in the courts for their products. To remove that incentive at a time when funds to state and federal regulatory agencies are being slashed simply lacks common sense.

As a Texan, I am proud of the fact that Texas courts, because of punitive damages, were responsible for bringing the 3M Corporation to the bargaining table of the Breast Implant Global Settlement. As a woman, I am truly glad to know that my state was a factor in making the largest class action in history a little more equitable for women around the world. But as a consumer, I am alarmed to realize that Texas will NEVER AGAIN lead the way to safer products if the "Tort Reform" bills which you are considering today become part of Texas law.

Weekley

Eighteen months ago, a number of business people were sitting around a table wondering how in the world our civil justice system had become so flawed. We began a massive research project, talking to everybody in the state that we could find who had been working on this project over the last 10, 15, 20 years. We also conducted a statewide poll—bipartisan, every race, every creed—which we have delivered to your office. It shows that over 50 percent of the people in the state of Texas think that the system is flawed badly.

After all this research, we came up with an 11-point program that we believe will rectify many of the flaws in the system. The bills that you are considering right now, all of them are included in this 11-point agenda.

The people of Texas and the polls want much more than is included in these 11 points. For example, loser pay, which is now being considered in Washington, is favored by the people of Texas by a 2-to-1 basis. It's not in the 11-point agenda. Abolishing contingency fees, or capping contingency fees for lawyers—85 percent of the people in Texas want that. It's not in these proposals. Punitive damages—there's not another civilized country in the Western world that has punitive damages in their civil justice system. Five states don't have any punitive damages at all. Many states have absolute caps on punitive damages. What's in our proposal? All we're saying is put reasonable, predictable caps—two times economic damages. And this, I must emphasize, is on top of totally uncapped compensatory damages.

There are many stories that we're going to hear today that are extremely sympathetic and extremely real, and need to be compensated. That is not the issue of these debates. There are not caps on compensatory damages. Pain and suffering, disfigurement, loss of consortium, and on and on—those are all to be compensated at the full scale. What we're talking about here is putting a reasonable cap on punitive damages.

The scope of the people who back this 11-point agenda is staggering, and I will just give you a sample of the groups that endorse this program. The Texas Medical Association and their 33,000 members, the National Federation of Independent Business People and their 40,000 members, the Texas Association of Realtors and their 42,000 members, and these are not big business people. These people make an average of $23,700 a year. The engineers, contractors, Texas Hospital Association, many of the chambers of commerce around the state, including the Texas Chamber of Commerce, endorse the 11-point program, industry after industry. We feel that this 11-point program represents a consensus of the business, professional and civic leadership of this state.

Chapter 22

Performance and Remedies

Usage of Trade

The Parties' Agreement

Cure

Impossibility and Impracticability

Usage of Trade

How much testing of a new software product is *enough* testing? If a software manufacturer delivers a nonconforming video game, should the buyer get her money back?

Beta-Testers Go in Search of Software, Video Game Bugs
Bruce Haring, USA Today

When a company as big as Microsoft prepares for a rollout as huge as Windows 95, it enlists an army of 400,000 to test and retest the pre-release "beta" version for gremlins. For smaller firms with more modest needs, free-lancers like Fred Sookiasian or exterminators like the Bug Police in San Francisco do nicely.

Because he worked for a desktop publishing mail-order company, Sookiasian, 23, of North Hollywood, Calif., was offered the chance to beta-test WordPerfect 5.1 and the publishing program Pagemaker. A computer hobbyist, Sookiasian played with the software on company time and at home, for his regular hourly rate, plus the offer of "free copies of the final release." The results, after spending 15 hours on the programs: a problem with numbering and adding typesetters' bullets in Pagemaker.

Software manufacturers are naturally antsy about bugs—not the creepy crawlers, but the programming nasties that can cause a video game to abort or an accounting program to calculate incorrectly. They sometimes recruit [testers] in odd places. Sookiasian won one game-testing job after a scout saw him reading an electronic games magazine at a newsstand: "They offered $250 for only an hour's work."

He was unusually lucky, says David Maxey of Virgin Interactive, who says most game companies test in-house because of piracy fears. Also, "we have shorter beta cycles in game development than in applications like Windows 95," Maxey says. "There's not a lot of turnaround time to get reliable information back." Smaller firms might use outside help, particularly genre game publishers. "They might (use) a hard-core regular following to supplement internal testing."

Qualifications for in-house beta-testers are much more specific, Maxey says. "They need a well-rounded knowledge of PC and Mac, analytical skills—verbal and in writing, to be detail conscious and thorough . . . [and] to love the type of software they're testing. They don't just test for defects,

Copyright © 1995 by *USA Today*, June 14, 1995, p.8D. Reprinted with permission.

but for game-play balance and design defects." [Beta-testers] "range 21 to their 30s," but it's not a career position. "It's a steppingstone. ... come into this area and want to be producers, designers, artists or software engineers." Pressures to bring products to market quickly have increased the number of bugs escaping, despite refinements in testing, he says. "Because we're in a culture that lives by the quarter, there's always going to be compromise."

Marjorie DeWilde, director of quality assurance for game company Spectrum Holobyte, disagrees. "I don't think programs are any worse for bugs than they used to be. They're not necessarily any better, because the world has gotten a lot more complex, and running a game on all systems is hugely difficult." Programmers have gotten better at their jobs, she says, as the audience has gotten more picky. "The original PC customers would find a bug and work around it," because they were part of the computer community. "Today's customer won't."

At Spectrum Holobyte, product testing is "a dead-end job. But we promote people to different tracks," she says. "The playability track can work into game design or associate producer positions. Some with programming skills can become programmers. People who are leaders (may) move into management."

Or beta-testers might build a career out of it. Greg Fleming, who owns the independent testing firm Bug Police in San Francisco, started by answering an ad from Sega. "I was just a gamer and really wanted to work with video games," Fleming says. "I didn't even know how to use a computer when I started." Now he employs 40 beta-testers on everything from Super Nintendo and Genesis games to PC products. His employees are "really into software," he says. "We go through a piece of software and do everything we can think of to screw it up. Computer code is so complex that even the best programmers can't detect most of the problems."

Beta-testers are entering their busy season as companies rush to get products ready for holiday sales. Game company Digital Pictures will sometimes throw 20 testers on a product just to hasten its release. "Santa doesn't move Christmas," spokesman Ken Soohoo says. And he knows what's at stake: millions of dollars spent to recall a defective product, or at the least, millions of unhappy customers.

The Parties' Agreement

Specially designed software is guaranteed—to have some problems. One way for both parties to avoid disputes is to agree in advance on how to correct product flaws.

From Small Nags to Glitches; The Right Contract Can Keep You from Losing Your Shirt in a System Crash
Raymond T. Nimmer, *Computerworld*

What if a system fails? We have all thought about this question, but most of us have never experienced a total failure. We frequently suffer the pain of seemingly random bugs or nagging inadequacies. The system never works exactly the way it should work, but somehow it avoids crashing.

The upshot is that the buyer often bears the brunt of any cost and confusion resulting from small defects unless the seller voluntarily takes back its system. For example, if a retailer sends a customer the wrong merchandise because of a bug in the program that controls its shipments, the complaints go to the retailer. If a company does not pay a supplier because of a problem with its accounting system, the letter demanding payment goes to the company that is using the accounting software.

In an ordinary transaction, a party purchasing a system has the right to expect that bugs will be infrequent and minor. It has a right to insist that the seller disclose any known bugs. The buyer can demand that the seller help eliminate a bug. However, the seller has rights, too. It can expect that the buyer will live with some flaws in a program rather than show up at its door with an angry attorney. If the buyer expects more, the agreement between the two parties must outline it specifically.

Software and hardware companies survive or fail on the basis of their reputations, and a vendor's reputation should be the buyer's first line of defense. Informal user networks and published reviews of technologies relate how well systems and software work. As a result of these resources, a developer who consistently delivers products with too many flaws will not survive. By the same token, a buyer who does not use these resources before

Copyright © 1990 by Computerworld, Inc., Framingham MA 10701. Reprinted with permission from *Computerworld,* Jan. 8, 1990, p.109. Nimmer is Foundation Professor of Law at the University of Houston, counsel to the law firm Sheinfeld, Maley & Kay and author of *The Law of Computer Technology* (Warren, Gorham & Lamont, New York).

acquiring a system is simply flying blind and takes the risk of running into problems.

However, these resources generally provide protection only when you are purchasing a product that has a track record or that has drawn the attention of evaluators. However, there are many programs, networks and hardware systems that do not fall into this category. Furthermore, for every flawed system that is marketed, someone was the first to discover the flaws, often through a painful experience.

Addressing Serious Flaws

Who has responsibility for flaws and mistakes in a computer system when the problems are serious? The answer depends on the type of deal that you make. The contract should determine whether and to what extent the buyer is covered for these problems.

To protect the buyer, a system contract should answer five questions:

1) What happens if the system never performs at all? Often, the buyer should not be required to pay any part of the purchase price, and the system developer should refund any prepayments. However, in some transactions, the system developer might incur substantial costs, and the buyer might agree to pay for some or all of the time spent in development even if the system never works.

2) What happens if the system performs for a while and then crashes entirely? Some sellers will argue that their responsibility ends when the system is delivered and performs up to initial standards. The problem, of course, is that many flaws in a complex system are not discernible until the system is used for an extended time.

3) What happens if the system performs for a while but crashes after the buyer modifies it? Does the buyer's tinkering remove all responsibility from the seller, or must the parties try to determine whose mistake caused what problem? In a complex system, it may be impossible to make that determination. Many sellers disclaim any responsibility for any problem if the buyer changes the system in some way.

4) What happens if a defect for which the seller is responsible causes serious and substantial loss to the buyer? Is the seller responsible for all the buyer's lost time, lost accounts and lost profits? Or is the seller only obligated to repair or replace the program and, failing that, to refund the purchase price?

5) What happens if the system crashes and harms a third party? You, as the user of the system, will wind up paying the third party, but can you get your money back from the system provider?

Contracts take as many different positions on these issues as one can imagine. Most sophisticated vendors pay close attention to the need to limit their responsibility in all five situations. Few willingly agree to pay for lost profits or to indemnify the user for injuries to third parties. However, some of them will accept this responsibility, and some buyers can insist that they do so.

The greatest problem is when the contract says nothing about responsibility or when one of the parties does not understand what the language of the contract really means.

Cure

Intel Corp. discovered that cure, however costly, may be commercially unavoidable.

Intel Discloses Discovery of Bug in Motherboards; Flaw Expected To Affect Fewer Users than the Celebrated Pentium One
Dean Takahashi, *Fresno Bee*

Intel Corp. has a new flaw in some of its computer motherboards to deal with less than a year after the discovery of a bug in the Pentium microprocessor that cost the company more than $475 million. The Santa Clara-based company confirmed late last week there is a flaw in a chip made by a supplier and said it believes the flaw is not as serious as the previous costly mistake. While it apparently isn't Intel's fault, the flaw nonetheless affects its customers, said Howard High, spokesman for Intel.

The bug in a PCI controller chip produces errors in data because it inadvertently shifts data from one part of the hard disk to another when more than one device, such as a modem or a floppy disk drive, are in use. The flaw can be corrected with a solution known as a software patch, High said. He said IBM is working on a patch for its software. The bug shows up in multitasking operating systems, or those geared to handle more than one task at a time, such as IBM's OS/2 operating system, Linux, and possibly other versions of the Unix operating system.

The error is in a computer chip known as the RZ-1000 PCI controller chip designed by PCTech, a Minnesota company owned by Micron Technology Inc. The chip governs traffic between permanent memory known as an enhanced IDE hard disk drive and the microprocessor.

Copyright © 1995. *Fresno Bee,* Aug. 15, 1995, p.E1. Reprinted by permission: Tribune Media Services.

The flaw revives memories of the Pentium bug, which caused errors in division. Intel's failure to acknowledge that bug, even after its discovery last fall by a Virginia math professor, brought intense criticism of the company by engineers and scientists. After enduring weeks of bad publicity, Intel offered to replace flawed chips free to anyone who wanted a replacement and it adopted a policy of disclosing serious flaws as soon as it learned about them. Word of the new bug spread first on the Internet global communications network in the last few days on a bulletin board about Intel technology.

High said that Intel had determined that a limited universe of users who use certain "multitasking" operating systems are affected. Consumers who bought the newest Intel motherboards with support chips known as the Triton chip set are not affected. "It looks somewhat isolated," High said. "It's not fully characterized yet." For instance, users of the popular Windows 3.1 and Windows 95 operating systems from Microsoft Corp. are not affected, he said.

Intel used the flawed PCTech chip in millions of its PCI motherboards, which Intel assembles and sells to mainstream computer companies such as Dell Computer Corp. High said he did not know when Intel learned about the bug, but he was notified in the last few days by technical support that 30 to 40 people on the Internet were talking about it.

Roedy Green, a computer consultant in Vancouver, British Columbia, said he believes that for those who have the problem, the bug is more serious than the Pentium bug in terms of the harm it can do to someone's data. "It is not easy to discover," he said. "But it corrupts your data, doing things like adding one to the number in your spreadsheets. The corruption may not be obvious. I believe a lot of companies have known about this for some time."

Information about the new bug can be found on the Internet on the Intel newsgroup at comp.sys.intel.

Impossibility and Impracticability

International political disputes affect commercial deals. When several countries are involved, the viability of the deal is hard to predict. Why is it essential for the parties to decide in advance what country's law will be used to settle a dispute?

The Trade Cost of the Iraqi Invasion
Ben Leach, *Financial Times*

Any international crisis involving hostilities or trade sanctions inevitably affects private traders, shipowners and others involved in the international sale and transportation of goods. Contracts become impossible or more difficult or expensive to perform. Inevitably the parties affected are rarely able to agree where the loss should fall, and litigation results. The present Gulf crisis is likely to prove no exception.

Where under English law it becomes illegal or impossible to perform a contract, that contract is frustrated, the parties are discharged from further performance and, subject to exceptions introduced by the Law Reform (Frustrated Contracts) Act 1943, which by and large have no application to commodity sales transactions and charterparties, the loss lies where it falls.

It is important to bear in mind that the law relating to frustration is concerned with acts that the contract specifically or by necessary implication provides for. It will not apply in a situation where a party's chosen or preferred method of carrying out the contract has become impossible or illegal.

This is likely to cause difficulties in the international commodity trades. Optional origins and optional destinations are frequently stipulated. This flexibility is generally reflected in chartering arrangements. Thus an oil trader chartering a vessel to load in Kuwait will normally charter on terms whereby Kuwait is but one of a number of permissible loading places. In such circumstances, even though Kuwait cargo is no longer available and cannot lawfully be loaded, frustration will not help the charterer who will have to find other employment for the vessel or pay damages to the owner if he does not.

It might be thought that the combined effect of the various rules and orders promulgated internationally in response to the Iraqi invasion of Kuwait has been such that any contract in any way involving trading with

Copyright © 1990 by The Financial Times Ltd. *Financial Times,* Aug. 23, 1990, p.11. Reprinted with permission. The author is a partner in Sinclair Roche & Temperley, London.

either country is necessarily frustrated. Such contracts are either expressly prohibited under English law or have become illegal or impossible to perform in the place of performance. A close study of the English rules, however, reveals that things are not this simple.

Except with a special licence, no goods may be imported into the UK if they originate from Iraq or Kuwait and no goods may be exported if they are going to either country. The relevant statutory instruments came into force on August 9 the same date that the Iraq and Kuwait (United Nations Sanctions) Order 1990 came into force in the UK. On the previous day, with effect from August 7, EEC Council Regulation No. 2340/90 came into force. Both the UN Order and EEC Regulation are far wider in scope than the UK statutory instruments dealing with exports and imports.

The UN Order prohibits, for example:

- dealing in goods that have been exported from Iraq or Kuwait;
- any act calculated to promote the supply or delivery of goods in any form in either country;
- the carriage of goods originating from or destined to either country on a British owned ship or British operated aircraft.

Clearly the Order applies to British ships and aircraft wherever they are located. Equally, clearly it applies to activities of British subjects and companies both in Britain and abroad. The position of foreign branch offices of UK companies and foreign incorporated subsidiaries is unclear. It may be possible for a foreign branch or subsidiary of a UK company employing non UK nationals locally to perform a sales or purchase contract with Iraq or Kuwait without any active involvement of the head office.

Conversely foreign nationals and foreign corporations with a place of business here are not covered by the Order although in practice foreign corporations will be unable to fulfil their trading commitments with Iraq and Kuwait if they employ UK nationals in positions of authority. The position of foreign banks operating in the UK gives rise to several problems.

The approach of the EEC Regulation is essentially the same. It refers to activities, the effect of which is to "promote" trade with Iraq and Kuwait. It applies to acts done within EC territory or by means of aircraft and vessels flying the Community flag and when carried out by an EC national. It appears to have extra-territorial effect in that as a matter of English law acts done in the EC by non-UK nationals are unlawful.

Thus a contract for a French company to supply French grain to Iraq if governed by English law would be frustrated both because it required performance that has become illegal according to the law of the place of performance, i.e., France, and because the performance of the contract is expressly prohibited by English law. A contract by an American company to supply US grain would only be frustrated on the former ground.

This legislation may, according to the circumstances, have no effect on contracts which are only connected with the UK because they are governed by English law and provide for English dispute resolution, i.e., in the High Court or by English arbitration. In the commodity trades such contracts are very common. Much of the world's grain is traded on the forms of contract of the Grain and Feedrade Association which provide for English law and London arbitration, as do most of the oil and dry cargo charterparties in common use.

Take, for example, the following hypothetical case:

An exporter in country "X" has a contract for the sale to Iraq of a quantity of grain to be shipped from country "Y." To perform that contract the exporter charters a vessel that is owned by an owner incorporated in country "Z" and which flies the flag of country "Z." Neither country "X," country "Y" nor country "Z" have in fact given effect to the UN resolution and none of them is an EC country.

On the face of it both the sale contract and the charterparty can be performed and no illegality arises. A good example of country "Z" would be Liberia which has one of the world's largest merchant fleets. As far as one can tell it has not given effect to the UN resolution. However when you place these hypothetical abstract arrangements in their likely practical context the problems and potential problems begin to multiply.

If the shipowner is a Liberian company it will have no presence there. It will operate solely through managers in one of the main shipping centres, such as London, New York or Piraeus. The voyage to Iraq is likely to involve the managers in unlawful acts in the way of promoting trade according to English/US/Greek law. But would the charterparty thereby be frustrated? Perhaps not since the owners have chosen to operate through managers in one of these countries. Unless the charterparty has provisions dealing with the question of management—some charters do—then at least in theory other managers could be appointed. What has become unlawful or impossible is the shipowners' chosen mode of performance, not the contractual mode provided for.

Typically the charterparty will have incorporated the Chamber of Shipping or similar war risk provisions providing for change of destination in the event of recommendations or orders of, among others, the country of the vessel's flag. The Liberian Bureau of Maritime Affairs by Marine Notice 1-050-1 issued on August 13 has advised owners, operators and masters of Liberian vessels to "respect the United Nations sanctions." Thus the Iraqi receivers might well not receive their cargo. The sale contract would not perhaps be frustrated since, typically, a CIF (Cost, Insurance and Freight) contract does not require the seller to deliver at destination. The seller fulfils his part of the bargain by arranging freight on appropriate terms, by insuring and loading the goods on board and by tendering the documents.

The charterparty will also typically provide for payment of freight to a bank in a leading financial centre. Payment of the freight would be unlawful since its receipt would be illegal. Frustration would probably apply.

Insurance cover for the vessel and for the goods—a CIF seller is usually required to insure—would be unavailable in the world's main insurance markets. Perhaps the sale contract would be frustrated but arguably the charterparty would not as insurance by the owner is not a normal charterparty requirement.

Chapter 23

Creating a Negotiable Instrument

Promissory Note

Checks

Promissory Note

Someone writes to a financial columnist to inquire about the value of a $1 million promissory note he has received in the mail. A little knowledge can be very useful indeed. No one who is familiar with Article 3 will fall for this scam.

Promises, Promises! But Will They Make You a Millionaire?
Phil Vettel, *Chicago Tribune*

Q: I received a promissory note and accompanying letter (copies enclosed). The letter attests to the legitimacy and negotiability of the note, which is for $1 million. Is this really a valid document? Can I convert this to cash before the maturity date?

A: Tell you what, sport. I'll give you two bits for the note—and I suspect strongly that I won't be making a cent on the deal.

The note you sent is made out in your name, promising payment of $1 million to you or the bearer of the note in the year 2004, or almost 20 years from now. The accompanying letter congratulates you as being "legally a millionaire" and declares the note to be a negotiable instrument that can be sold at a discount to investors and speculators. As such, the note makes you a millionaire, the letter says, although your entire investment portfolio happens to consist of one unsecured note that is 19 years from maturity.

Well, congrats! How does it feel to be wealthy? If it feels a little funny, it should because you are, at best, a paper millionaire. At worst, you may be the butt of an elaborate joke. Only a court can decide if this note is valid, but my legal sources say it seems to be properly prepared. Let's assume it is. You're still not a millionaire. I'll show you why.

Both the note and letter are signed by the same person. Because I'm as eager to avoid legal entanglements as the next fellow, we'll refer to the maker—the signer of the note—as Mr. Bux. Bux, in other words, has agreed to pay you $1 million on Jan. 1, 2004. First question: Who is Bux? Where does he live? Better still, where will he be living on Jan. 1, 2004? If you don't know the answers, you're going to have a sweet time collecting. You see, Bux isn't obligated to pay you a dime before the maturity date. Nor is he required to set aside money or property to assure prompt payment of the note when the maturity date arrives.

Copyrighted © 1985 by Chicago Tribune Co. All rights reserved. *Chicago Tribune*, Feb. 24, 1985, p.2. Used with permission.

A lot can happen in 19 years. Bux could vanish; if you intend to collect you might have to locate him. Bux could go bankrupt, making your note worthless. Bux could die; you'd have to get the money from the estate, assuming there is $1 million in it and assuming you learn about his demise in time to submit your claim before the estate is dissolved.

But let's be optimistic: Let's assume that Bux is sole heir to the $1 billion Bux Buggywhip empire, and 2004 finds Bux healthy and wealthy. You're still not a millionaire. Why not? According to Michael Spak, professor of law at Chicago-Kent College of Law, to collect, you must have given Bux something of value (the term is "consideration") in exchange for his promissory note. If you did not, the note simply is a promise of a gift, and as such is unenforceable.

"You have to give up something for it (the note) to be valid," Spak says. "If I say, 'I promise to give you my house,' that's unenforceable. If, however, I say, 'For $1,000, I'll sell you my house,' and you give me $1,000, I must give you my house."

However, Spak says, if you sell that promissory note to a third party, the note becomes collectable. That third party, Spak says, is termed the "holder in due course," and because he gave consideration (cash or other valuable property) for the note, he can collect on the note. It doesn't matter that the consideration was paid to you and not to Bux.

So you sell the note to your brother-in-law (not a bad idea, by the way). Is he a millionaire? Nope. Essentially, he has purchased the right to collect on the note, or alternately, the right to take legal action against Bux or his estate to collect. He is right where you started, except he is in a better position to collect than you were. But you have cash in hand, and he has a paper promise.

Let's remain optimistic, however. Let's assume that you did give Bux a little something for his note. And let's keep on assuming that Bux is willing and able to pay up in 19 years. You're still not a millionaire.

If you take $100,000 right now and sock it away in zero-coupon bonds or some other instrument for 20 years (assuming 12.5 percent interest), you'll have a bit more than $1 million when the investment matures. In other words, it would cost Bux $100,000 today to guarantee payment on a $1 million note in 2004. So right now, that note is worth $100,000 at the most, providing that the million will be there when the note matures.

As far as selling your note on the open market is concerned, good luck. You might find someone willing to risk $1 on the off chance that Bux hits the lottery or wins the Irish Sweepstakes. But frankly, I'll be rather surprised if anyone tops my offer.

Checks

Frances-Rose Straith deposited one of those fake promotional checks she received in the mail. And the bank paid it. Now who is liable?

Fake Check for $95,093 Fools Recipient, Bank
T. L. Henion, *Omaha World Herald*

To Frances-Rose Straith of Falls City, Neb., the check that came in her mail looked legitimate. It read: From the Office of the Treasurer to F. R. Straith in the amount of $95,093.35. So, on May 30, she endorsed the check and took it to the drive-through window at American National Bank in Falls City—her bank—and deposited it.

"The bank took it, so I figured it was good," said Ms. Straith, a 21-year-old single mother who has worked at a Falls City telemarketing firm for the past 1½ years. She wasted little time in spending her unexpected bounty. She bought a used car and a used pickup truck from two different Falls City automobile dealers. She bought diapers for her 5-month-old daughter. And she purchased clothes. In all, she said, she wrote six checks totaling $8,331 from her newly found fortune.

"I was going to pack up and move to Kansas City, join the union and become a heavy equipment operator," Ms. Straith said. "It all happened so quick, and it seemed too good to be true." It was. The check that she deposited and the bank accepted turned out to be a non-negotiable document worth nothing. The bank was alerted to the error after an employee from one of the car dealers called to make sure that Ms. Straith's check was good.

"We had a young teller take the check because it said 'non-negotiable for cash,' and that was kind of confusing," said Phyllis Krause, personal banking officer at American National. "She was worried because the amount was quite large, and she intended to make a copy of it and talk with me about it later. But somehow it got forgotten and got deposited in the account." Ms. Krause said she notified Ms. Straith the next day that the check was no good. "All she said was, 'Oh,' and that was it."

That wasn't quite it. For starters, the car dealers took back the newly purchased vehicles. The other checks Ms. Straith wrote on her account bounced. And Richardson County officials are mulling whether any charges should be filed against her.

Ms. Straith said that, if any mistakes were made in the incident, the fault lies with American National Bank. "The bank took the thing and deposited

Copyright © 1995 by The Omaha World-Herald Co. *Omaha World Herald,* June 13, 1995, p.1. Reprinted with permission.

it. It's not my liability," Ms. Straith said. "The way I see it, they cashed it and deposited it, and it's my money." Ms. Krause said the "non-negotiable for cash" was written clearly on the document.

"I didn't see anything that said that," Ms. Straith said. "All I saw was something that said not to fold, spindle or mutilate. I deposited it, and they took it. Whose fault is that? Besides, do you have any idea how humiliating it was for them to come to my house and take away my cars? They owe me something for that." No charges were filed against Ms. Straith on Monday.

Jeff Goltz, deputy Richardson County attorney, said the matter is still under investigation. "They are talking about charges against me, but I didn't do anything wrong," Ms. Straith said.

Ms. Krause said the non-negotiable check made out to Ms. Straith resembled those often found in sweepstakes envelopes that are mass mailed. Ms. Straith said the check was the only piece of paper in a plain manila envelope that she found in the mail. She said the envelope and check resembled a tax refund mailing. "It came in a plain manila envelope, and there was nothing else in there, just the check. There was no return address," Ms. Straith said Monday. She said she thought the check might be a payment from the estate of her late father.

"I kept the thing for a week, showed it to everybody," she said. "People kept telling me that it looked all right and that I ought to cash it." Ms. Krause said she found it interesting that the check was made out for such a specific amount. "Most of those sweepstakes non-negotiable checks are made out for round-figure amounts like $50,000 or such," she said. "At this point, we're still trying to determine exactly what this document is and where it came from." Ms. Straith said she had some initial doubts whether the check was good and that's why she didn't try to deposit it immediately. She said she called her mother, who lives in the Kansas City area, to seek her counsel. "She told me, 'Frances, there is nothing that you will do in your whole life that's worth $95,000,' " Ms. Straith said.

Chapter 24

Liability for Negotiable Instruments

Negligence

Crimes

Dishonor

Employee Indorsement Rule

Negligence

An elderly man signs a check but allows a stranger to fill in the amount. The stranger fills in $6,200 more than he was authorized. Did the court make the right legal decision in this case? Was its decision based on compassion or the UCC?

The Associated Press File
Sy Ramsey, *Associated Press*

A $6,200 award to an elderly man from the Owensboro National Bank resulting from a bilking by a stranger was upheld Friday by the Kentucky Court of Appeals. "The policy underlying the impostor rule is to place the loss on the party that should presumably have the best opportunity to check the identity of the impostor," the three-member panel said. "We believe (Sam) Crisp has carried his burden."

In 1975 a stranger calling himself Bill Carter stopped at the home of Crisp, who is in his late 70s, and represented himself as an employee of Southern Construction, the court said. He convinced Crisp that the lightning rod on his home needed repair and would require a part. Crisp agreed and Carter drove to Owensboro for the part, then returned to make the purported repair. Carter charged only $12.50, and due to poor eyesight or arthritis, Crisp allowed Carter to fill out his check for that amount. The court said that Crisp at the time commented that the payee space was blank and there were large open spaces to the left of both the written and numbered figures, but was assured by Carter he would fill those in when he returned to his office.

After Carter left, Crisp became suspicious and tried to call the Owensboro bank—only to learn his telephone line had been cut. Meantime, the appellate court said, Carter presented the check to the bank for payment. "The check showed no visible indication of having been altered, but now contained a face amount of $6,212.50," the judges said. "The con artist, Carter, had kept his promise to fill in the open spaces." Crisp contended that the bank should have been alert to the fact that the check was large and that Carter was a stranger with no account and no community connections. By the time Crisp reached the bank, the court said, Carter and the money were gone.

The appellate panel said the man calling himself Carter since has been apprehended, found guilty and is serving a prison sentence for duping Crisp.

A Daviess Circuit Court jury returned a verdict against the Owensboro

August 31, 1979. Reprinted with permission of Associated Press.

National Bank for the amount of the altered check and the bank appealed. The bank contended Crisp was contributorily negligent and that it had paid the check in good faith and accordance with reasonable commercial standards. But the appeals court noted among other things that the jury took into account that the Kentucky driver's license used as identification by Carter contained his place of employment, which valid state licenses do not; that it contained a black and white picture, which state licenses do not; that Carter was not asked if he had an account with the bank, and that no other identification was sought.

Crimes

E. F. Hutton may be the most famous example of check-kiting but, as this article illustrates, others have also committed the same offense.

Check Kiter May Face 20-Year Term; Jury Convicts Anchorage Man of Scheme to Cheat Key Bank for $170,000
Natalie Phillips, *Anchorage Daily News*

An Anchorage businessman who frustrated many local travelers in the late 1980s with the bankrupt Rainbow Travel Club has been found guilty of bank fraud. A 12-member federal jury deliberated for four hours before convicting Ray Kalyan on Thursday of four counts of bank fraud and one count of making a false statement in connection with a bank loan, Assistant U.S. Attorney Crandon Randell said Friday.

The 52-year-old Kalyan, who got into the barge-leasing business during the 1989 Exxon oil spill, was found guilty of setting up a check-kiting scheme that cheated Key Bank of Alaska out of $170,000. Kalyan faces up to 20 years in prison and a $1 million fine. His sentencing is scheduled for late June.

In the weeks after the 1989 oil spill, Kalyan landed a $1.4 million contract to provide Exxon with a barge outfitted as a floating camp for 142 cleanup workers. Kalyan leased the barge from a Seattle company. [He] used a $522,000 advance payment to open an account at Merrill Lynch and to buy

Copyright © 1995 by Anchorage Daily News. *Anchorage Daily News* Apr. 22, 1995, p.C2. Reprinted with permission.

a $300,000 certificate of deposit, which he used to secure a $300,000 line of credit with Key Bank, where he had a checking account, Randell said. Over the next few months, he said, Kalyan received other payments from Exxon, shuffled money between his Key Bank and Merrill Lynch accounts, and used up his line of credit.

Finally, in late November, Kalyan wrote two checks worth $170,000 on his Merrill Lynch account and deposited them in his Key Bank account, Randell said. About the same time, he wrote checks from his Key Bank account to Commonwealth Pacific Inc., which is one of his businesses. But Kalyan didn't have the $170,000 in the Merrill Lynch account to begin with. "It is a classic check kite," Randell said. "He moves money from one checking account into another checking account. This is a red flag to a banker."

In the late 1980s, Kalyan tried to start a low-cost flight service between Anchorage and Seattle. Many participants bought $170 round-trip flights to Seattle. The service never got off the ground. The club's 1989 Chapter 11 bankruptcy petition listed about 1,400 creditors.

Dishonor

Is it ethical for banks to make a profit on bounced checks?

Insufficient Funds; Banks Charge More for Bounced Checks, Raising Questions About Fees; Say They Don't Profit
Joanne Johnson, *Hartford Courant*

If you lose track of your checking account balance and bounce a check during the holiday shopping rush, your bank may slap you with a stiffer penalty this year. A growing number of banks across the nation are boosting their fees for a bounced check to as much as $30, a banking industry newsletter says. And analysts predict bad-check fees will continue to rise, saying many banks are actually viewing the penalties as an attractive profit source as they work to recover from losses. "Banks are absolutely, positively mak-

Copyright © 1993 by The Hartford Courant Co. *Hartford Courant*, Nov. 21, 1993, p.D1. Reprinted with permission.

ing money from bad checks," said Robert Heady, publisher of Bank Rate Monitor, a Florida-based newsletter that tracks interest rates nationwide.

Banks deny the charge. "Bad checks are not one of the areas where banks try to make profits," said Kenneth Weinstein, first vice president for consumer deposit products at Bridgeport-based People's Bank. The average bad-check charge for the 120 biggest banks and thrifts in the nation's 12 major metropolitan markets has jumped to $19.35 from $18.58 a year ago and about $15 in 1987, a Bank Rate Monitor survey shows. The highest bounced check fee charged by any bank in the survey was $30. Main Line Federal Savings Bank in Villanova, Pa., recently raised its bad check penalty from $25, Bank Rate Monitor said. In Connecticut, the state's five largest banks have all raised their bounced check fees to $20 from $15 or $17.50 in the past two years.

John D. Rooney, an analyst with Legg Mason Wood Walker in New Haven, agreed that bad checks are paying off for banks and said the penalties will climb steadily higher. "There's still tremendous pressure on profits at many of the banks and loan demand is not great, especially in New England, so there's no question these fees will keep going up," Rooney said.

Bankers say the increased fees are designed to discourage customers from writing bad checks, which are expensive to process. "Banks use bad-check fees to prevent people from writing bad checks and to offset the costs of processing more than anything," Weinstein said. People's last year raised its bounced check fee to $20 from $17.50.

Brent Di Giorgio, a spokesman for Hartford-based Shawmut Bank, which also boosted its bad check fee to $20 from $17.50 within the past year, said, "The penalties are a deterrent, not a profit center. The whole idea is to encourage people to be more careful with their checkbooks, to reduce the amount of time and expense the bank has to spend on processing bad checks," Di Giorgio said.

Ed Mierzwinski of the U.S. Public Interest Research Group in Washington, D.C., said it costs banks less than $1 to handle a bounced check and that the penalties are designed to earn profits. Several bank officials disputed Mierzwinski's total, although none could provide the cost required to process a bounced check. But John Milligan, executive vice president for consumer banking at Hartford-based Fleet Bank, said, "The fee doesn't even begin to cover the process." Fleet raised its bounced check fee to $20 from $17.50 in 1991.

Still, John Hall, an ABA spokesman, said many banks charge penalties that are more expensive than the cost of processing a bad check. "It's much like a speeding ticket. It doesn't cost the state $60 to write a speeding ticket. It's for the safety of the other motorists," Hall said. "It doesn't cost banks $20 to process a bad check. It's to create a deterrent and to keep the system in operation." Weinstein said, "We would rather ask only those customers who bounce their checks to pay rather than spread the fees among customers who don't overdraw their accounts."

At the same time, banks conceded that fee income has become increasingly important as they have worked to reverse heavy losses tied to problem loans. Fee income, or the money that banks earn by charging customers for such services as processing bad checks, contributes to bank earnings. So banks have steadily increased fees for consumer services as they have faced growing competition from non-bank companies that provide financial services.

Rooney noted that fee income has become more important to banks as they have tried to offset the expenses of maintaining foreclosed real estate and increased regulatory costs. Robert Donahue, vice president for marketing at Hartford-based Bank of Boston Connecticut, said "We're always looking for opportunities to generate reasonable fee income." Bank of Boston boosted its bounced-check fee to $20 from $15 in July 1991.

Heady said banks began to see bounced check fees as a profit center about 15 years ago but that the penalties have become an important revenue source over the past few years in the battered economy. The Bank Rate Monitor survey found that the average bounced-check fees ranged from a high of $28.90 in Philadelphia to $11.05 in Los Angeles. The Boston and New York markets respectively had average bounced-check fees of $18.30 and $15.60, the survey showed. The ABA said that large banks nationwide charged an average $20 for bounced checks last year while small commercial banks charged an average $15.

Bankers said while the number of bounced checks increased during the recessionary years, the penalties seem to be working in preventing people from writing checks against insufficient funds. Of the 60 billion checks written annually, Hall said, only 0.75 percent bounce. And Hall said the total is dropping, apparently because consumers are becoming more careful about their finances.

Weinstein said he has seen a similar trend at People's Bank, where the number of people overdrawing their accounts has declined since 1991. [He] said there has been a 15 percent to 20 percent drop in the number of people bouncing checks in the past two years, although those who do bounce checks seem to be doing so 5 percent to 10 percent more often.

For customers who have trouble with bounced checks, bankers and consumer credit specialists said there are several options that can help minimize the impact of bounced check fees. Bankers said consumers can get overdraft protection, a system through which a bank automatically pays a check if it bounces. Banks draw money from either a line of credit or a savings account to cover the bounced check. If the money comes from a credit line, consumers are usually charged immediately while there may be a fee if the money comes from a savings or money market account. Either way, consumers wind up spending less money than they would if they bounced a check, bankers said.

But bankers and consumer credit specialists stressed that the best solution is to avoid bouncing a check at all. "Keep track of your deposits and withdrawals and reconcile your checkbook every month," Bev Tuttle, president of the Consumer Credit Counseling of Connecticut, said. Tuttle suggested consumers leave their checkbooks at home when they go shopping so they are not tempted to write out checks for miscellaneous purchases and use cash instead. "If you don't want to pay a bad check fee, keep track of your finances and make sure you don't bounce a check," Tuttle said.

Employee Indorsement Rule

A clerk at a university embezzled nearly half a million dollars. Who is liable—the bank or the university?

UC Santa Cruz Embezzler Gets 5 Years; Maximum Sentence Imposed on College Clerk
Maria Alicia Gaura, *San Francisco Chronicle*

A clerk who embezzled $429,975 from the University of California at Santa Cruz was sentenced to five years in state prison yesterday and ordered to repay $100,000. Mary Helen Nichols, 53, swayed slightly but remained stone-faced as Judge Samuel Stevens announced her sentence—the maximum requested by District Attorney Gary Brayton. Despite evidence that most of the stolen money was spent on her children and grandchildren, not a single member of Nichols' family attended her sentencing or wrote the judge asking for leniency.

Ever since her arrest in September, the details of Nichols' case have fascinated and outraged the campus community, with people amazed at how easy it was for a low-level clerk to steal nearly half a million dollars from an institution reeling from financial cutbacks. According to a five-year trail of canceled checks, Nichols looted the accounts of UC Santa Cruz's Student Services division by approving payment to imaginary speakers for conducting nonexistent workshops. She then forged endorsements and deposited the checks into her personal bank accounts.

Nichols' unsophisticated scam never was discovered by university officials. A sharp-eyed teller at Pacific Western Bank finally noticed that Nichols had deposited eight university checks to her personal account within a

Copyright © 1994 by The Chronicle Publishing Co. *San Francisco Chronicle*, Mar. 29, 1994, p.A20. Reprinted with permission.

10-day period and alerted authorities. An investigation found that Nichols had forged 202 checks between 1989 and 1993. An audit later revealed that the UC Santa Cruz Student Services department had no budget or accounting oversight, and had never been audited in its 13-year history. Workers in the department told an auditor that they avoided questioning Nichols about accounting irregularities because "she became easily upset."

Bruce Moore, vice chancellor of student services, resigned a few weeks after Nichols was arrested, citing poor health.

Thanks to a Lloyd's of London insurance policy, UC Santa Cruz will recover all but a deductible payment of $100,000. But it is unlikely that Nichols will repay a cent of the money ordered for restitution. Her $27,000 UC retirement fund cannot be seized by the court, and investigators say she and her drug-addicted son, Michael, spent every dollar she stole.

When officers raided Nichols' Watsonville apartment, they found her son's room strewn with garbage and compact discs. According to Brayton, 28-year-old Michael Nichols had spent upwards of $30,000 at a local music store, appropriately named "Music Madness." Michael Nichols also had access to his mother's checking account, and had written checks for tens of thousands of dollars in cash. According to Brayton, much of that money "went up Michael's nose."

Nichols spent thousands on clothes, private school tuition for her grandchildren and a family vacation to Arkansas. Her telephone bills averaged $500 per month and on occasion exceeded her $1,500 monthly take-home pay, Brayton said.

Nichols' attorney, Ken Azevedo, argued for probation rather than jail time, pointing out Nichols' age, illnesses and the fact that she was the victim of her co-dependent relationships. But Brayton said testily: "It irritates me generally that in this day and age nobody is responsible for anything they do."

Chapter 25

Banks and Their Customers

Wrongful Dishonor

Bank's Duty To Pay

Stop Payment Orders

Electronic Fund Transfer Act

Wrongful Dishonor

To protect itself from liability, this bank refused to honor valid checks. The decision turned out to be very costly—paying the checks in the first place would have been cheaper.

Jury Awards $1 Million to Colusa Scrap Dealer
Yvonne McKinney, *Business Journal—Sacramento*

A Sacramento attorney whose firm represents several local banks recently won a $1 million jury verdict for a Colusa County scrap dealer against Bank of America. Sacramento attorney Hayne Moyer on July 10 persuaded a Colusa County Superior Court jury that scrap dealer Danny Kohrdt had lost more than $1 million in business during two weeks in 1989 when the bank had refused to cash his checks. The Colusa branch had frozen Kohrdt's business accounts after it learned he was getting a divorce. Kohrdt's wife had left town and the bank could not get her signature for business transactions as it had in the past.

Bank of America may appeal the $1.03 million verdict, which was one of the ten largest jury verdicts in rural Northern and Central California since January 1991, according to Jury Verdicts Weekly. "We're looking at our options, whether to file an appeal . . . or other possible motions to lower the amount of the verdict," said Peter Magnani, a spokesman for the bank's corporate legal department. The bank contends that it performed under the terms of the agreement it had with Kohrdt and was not the cause of his losing any business, according to Magnani, who declined to make any other comments about the case. The bank was represented by in-house counsel.

Moyer apparently convinced the jury that the bank had broken its written agreement with Kohrdt and had hurt Kohrdt's business reputation when it refused to cash 43 of his checks during a 14-day period in 1989. The attorney also argued that the bank had broken an oral agreement with Kohrdt and misrepresented itself when a bank manager had told Kohrdt that some of the checks would be cashed. "Had he told Mr. Kohrdt that morning that the checks were not going to be cashed, Mr. Kohrdt might have been able to lessen the damage," Moyer said.

Kohrdt, whose business is Triangle Machinery Sales and Salvage, dismantles closed-down manufacturing plants and sells the disassembled equipment as useful scrap. Based in Maxwell, about 50 miles north of Sacra-

Copyright © 1992 by The Business Journal. *Business Journal—Sacramento*, July 27, 1992, vol. 9, no. 18, §1, p.5. Reprinted with permission.

mento, Kohrdt's salvage business has torn down plants for companies as large as General Motors Corp.

Moyer argued that the bank's freezing of Kohrdt's account came at a particularly inopportune time because his client had a huge scrap auction scheduled. "Mr. Kohrdt puts all his inventory in auction every three years, but he missed holding this auction," Moyer said. Kohrdt's sales in the past have been the largest auctions in the country for electrical parts, according to Moyer.

Moyer, who is the senior partner in the Sacramento law firm of Moyer, Buechner & Towne, said he chose to present the case as simply as possible—as a loss of business profits. The eight-man, four-woman jury apparently agreed. The 11-1 jury verdict found Bank of America guilty of breach of contract, wrongful dishonor of checks and negligent misrepresentation.

Kohrdt asked his regular attorney in Colusa to make the initial filing against Bank of America. Kohrdt later asked the Sacramento firm to represent him because it specializes in banking litigation and because his attorney would be most useful as a witness. Moyer said he laughed when first asked to take the case because he "didn't think anyone was that dumb in banking anymore."

Bank's Duty To Pay

Nina deposited her check first, but the bank paid Michael's instead. Is that fair? Is it legal?

Priority of Checks
Magazine of Bank Management

A Missouri appellate court ruled that a bank had properly honored a husband's check drawn on the same business day as one drawn and dishonored by his wife on the joint account.

Michael and Nina Smock, on the verge of divorce, had a joint checking account at the Mercantile First National Bank (bank). Late Friday afternoon, after the bank's "cut-off" hour, Nina wrote an $18,000 check on the account and gave it to the bank and, in return, received $500 in traveler's checks and

---

Reprinted from *Magazine of Bank Management* May 1986 issue, with the permission of BAI, 1 North Franklin St., Chicago, Illinois 60606.

a deposit ticket reflecting a deposit of $17,495 in a new checking account which she opened in her name alone. On Monday, Michael wrote a check in the amount of $20,649 on the joint account, gave it to the bank and received $500 in cash and a cashier's check for $20,149.95. The joint account was insufficient to pay both checks but was sufficient to pay either. Both checks were taken by a bank courier after the close of Monday to the bank's processing center on Tuesday. At the processing center, the decision was made to honor Michael's check and to dishonor Nina's. The bank wired Nina in California of the dishonor and followed this up with a letter the same day. Nina sued the bank and the bank sued Michael. The trial court found in favor of Nina but only for $2,200 (the amount she was forced to borrow to live on). The bank lost its suit against Michael.

On appeal, Nina argued that she was entitled to $18,000, not merely the $2,200, and to punitive damages. The bank argued that there was no wrongful dishonor of Nina's check in that the bank had given only provisional credit to her check, subject to final payment. The court said that when an account is insufficient to pay all items, a bank may charge items against the account in any order convenient to the bank. Furthermore, the court said that Nina, as both drawer and payee of her check, could not assert a right against the bank based on "final payment" by the bank. Thus, the court said the bank was entitled to charge Nina's check against the joint account even though it was an overdraft and that Nina thereby became a debtor of the bank and the bank could set off the amount of the debt against the balance of her personal account.

Hill v. Mercantile First Natl. Bank, Missouri Court of Appeal, June 10, 1985.

Stop Payment Orders

Whether or not the bank stopped payment, this consumer would have had to pay the car dealer in the end because her contract with him was enforceable. Therefore, she suffered no real damages and the bank was not liable.

Stopping Payment on Checks a Weak Weapon in Commerce Wars
Mark Schwanhausser, *Dayton Daily News*

When Carolyn Franklin got into a scrap with an auto dealer over the terms of a car loan she'd signed the night before, she fought back the only way she could think of. She drove the car back to the showroom, tossed the keys at the manager when tempers flared, then stopped payment on the check she'd written as a down payment. Her impulsive strategy was flawed, however. What the Sunnyvale, Calif., woman didn't count on was that her bank, Glendale Federal Bank, would mistakenly cash the check, causing several other checks to bounce—including a down payment on another vehicle—and undercutting whatever leverage she thought she might have in the dispute.

But Franklin's saga underscores the reality that consumers have only limited protection when they pay for goods and services with checks, because stopping payment on paper checks can be a weak weapon in the wars of commerce. Here's why:

- Banks charge a fee to stop payment on a check. You might want to think twice if the dispute is over a small amount.
- Consumers often wait too long to block the payment, allowing their adversary time to cash the check.
- Your bank could goof. In Franklin's case, she ordered the stop payment when her branch opened the next business day after buying the car, but Glendale let the check slip through the following afternoon. Glendale initially denied its flub, so Franklin ultimately sued the bank in small-claims court.

"I told Glendale, 'You owe me, you have devastated my finances, you made me look like a fool,'" said Franklin, a 63-year-old postal clerk who teaches speech, music and theater in her spare time. "This has never happened before. It's an embarrassment and a nightmare."

Copyright © 1995. *Dayton Daily News*, Aug. 14, 1995, p.16. Reprinted by permission: Tribune Media Services.

In May, Franklin won a $75.28 judgment in small-claims court to cover some bounced-check fees, but the judge denied her request for nearly $5,000 in mental-distress claims.

- Your request to stop payment may be only temporary. If you phone in the stop-payment request, many banks will require you to put the request in writing within 14 days. If you don't, the request expires and your creditor can resubmit the check. Ask your bank about its policy if you're in a dispute. And all stop-payment requests expire in six months.

"People should be aware of that, because there are some shady characters who know that," said Ruth Susswein, executive director for Bankcard Holders of America, a consumer group based in McLean, Va. "They will hold that check for six months and a day, then put it through. And it will go through."

Most banks will consider a six-month-old check "stale" and shouldn't cash it, but that's their choice, said Mary Jones, a consumer services officer in the state Banking Department. That means you might need to renew the stop-payment order if you haven't resolved your dispute by then. Ask your bank about its policy on stale checks.

- Stopping payment on a check does not relieve you of a legal binding debt. For example, Franklin was obligated to buy the car because she had signed an enforceable contract, but the dealer compromised and let her refinance it through her credit union.

If you don't have any choice but to pay in cash or by check, Consumers Union recommends you at least try to pay in installments. That way, you can pay incrementally, for example, as a contractor makes satisfactory progress on your project.

Paying with a credit card offers more consumer protection than either cash or checks. Under the Fair Credit Billing Act, you can dispute a payment to the card issuer if, for example, you were dissatisfied with the product, the item delivered isn't what you ordered or the charge is fraudulent.

You must lodge your dispute in writing within 60 days of the postmark date on the bill. The issuer then has 30 days to notify you that it is investigating your complaint, and a total of 90 days to complete its research and make a ruling. In the meantime, interest on the disputed charge is frozen. If the issuer rules against you, you essentially have two options: pay up or keep on fighting, Susswein says. If you fight and refuse to pay, the issuer then can decide to sue you for the bill, which can impair your credit record.

"It surely is better than cash, and even better than checks in many cases," Susswein said. "But it is not a panacea."

Electronic Fund Transfer Act

Thefts at ATM machines are a serious problem for both banks and customers as criminals think up new and creative ways to steal.

ATM Loss Case Is Settled; Chase and Victims Won't Disclose Terms
Christine Dugas, Newsday

Chase Manhattan Bank said yesterday it has reached a settlement with a Connecticut couple who claimed they were victims of high-tech bank fraud. The case, first disclosed in *Newsday* last month, illustrates how the growing systems for electronic banking and bill-paying can put consumers at risk of losing their hard-earned savings, despite the systems' built-in protections.

Marco DePalma and Nadine Mahony contend they were victims of shoulder surfing. Experts say this is a technique in which criminals use a video camera with a zoom lens to observe people punching in their codes. If an ATM user also discards the receipt from the transaction, which has the account number on it, the crooks have the tools to create a counterfeit ATM card.

The couple's problem began last April when they returned from a trip, opened their bank statement and saw a series of unauthorized withdrawals from an automated teller machine in the city. By the time they were able to freeze the account, more than $10,000 was gone. They reported the transactions to Chase immediately, but the bank initially decided not to refund their money, saying in part that the couple's ATM card had not been stolen and that the individual who made the withdrawals knew the secret pin code.

DePalma and Mahony, who live in Stratford and work in Manhattan, contacted the Secret Service, hired a lawyer, and wrote to bank regulators. Their efforts finally paid off. Neither side would disclose the actual terms of the settlement. "The situation has been resolved to our satisfaction," Mahony said..

Michelle Meier, counsel for government affairs at the Consumers Union, said the couple might have prevailed in court because the law places the burden of proof in such cases on the bank. That means Chase would have had to "show that somehow the consumers made the transfer themselves or in cahoots with someone else," Meier said.

The issue is a concern for consumers because they can be held liable for some or all of the losses. If ATM card holders report a lost card or unautho-

Copyright © 1994 by Newsday, Inc. *Newsday*, Aug. 4, 1994, p.A57. Reprinted with permission.

rized transaction on their bank statement within two days, their liability cannot exceed $50. But it they wait longer, the liability increases.

As DePalma and Mahony's case illustrates, even if cardholders report a problem immediately, the bank can dispute the claim. If that happens, consumers must be prepared to fight back and hire a lawyer, Meier said. "But consumers who aren't savvy or who don't have legal resources may not fare as well," she said. "Good rules need to be put into place to protect consumers."

Banks say that ATM card frauds are rare. But law enforcement officials and industry experts say they are on the rise. And as more people begin to use ATM cards to pay for merchandise at stores, there will be more opportunity for fraud to occur. Ruth Susswein, executive director of BankCard Holders of America, says the terminals in supermarkets that allow customers to pay with an ATM card offer little privacy for someone trying to key in their code number. James Desrosier, a vice president at MasterCard, says that the industry is developing new, more secure terminals with hoods.

Chapter 26

Secured Transactions

Protection of Buyers

International Perspective

Repossession

Protection of Buyers

Innocent buyers make down payments on oriental carpets and then have the rug pulled out from under them. This is why the details of secured transaction law are important. Why should a retailer's creditor be entitled to cash paid into the store by innocent customers?

Carpet Store on the Mat
Susan Edelman, *Bergen Record*

Sandler & Worth, a well-respected and once-successful floor-covering chain, has abruptly closed its 17 stores and is auctioning off inventory, leaving a trail of unpaid suppliers and angry customers who paid deposits for carpets and rugs. The family-owned company has fallen deep into debt and may not be able to pay its creditors or compensate customers, says its lawyer, Howard Greenberg of Roseland. Customers and suppliers alike will probably have to file claims in U.S. Bankruptcy Court. But after taxes and bank debts are paid, there may not be any money left to divide among other creditors.

Sandler & Worth began closing stores, including those in Paramus, Nanuet, Roxbury, Fairfield, and Livingston, during the past three months and is holding auctions at its flagship store on Route 22 in Springfield.

Last month, one of the company's many creditors, a carpet wholesaler, filed a petition in federal court seeking to force the company into Chapter 7 bankruptcy. Sandler & Worth has until next week to respond. Meanwhile, at least 30 customers unable to reach anyone at the company have filed complaints with the state Division of Consumer Affairs. State officials have called a meeting with company representatives next week.

Most of the customers paid deposits of up to $2,000 for carpets or other floor coverings. When the carpets were not delivered as promised, they found the stores closed and could not get through to anyone in the company. Other customers fear losing up to $7,500 in carpeting after returning defective merchandise or giving rugs back for exchanges or cleaning.

"I'm really furious," said Raymond Paragian, a Westwood retiree who in January made a $1,500 down payment on a $3,500 carpeting order from Sandler & Worth in Paramus. He was told that the wall-to-wall carpeting for his living room, family room, and stairway would be delivered in three to four weeks. Ten weeks later, he went to the store and found it locked and empty, with the phone number of the Springfield store on the door. Many messages left at that store were not returned.

Copyright © 1995 by Bergen Record Corp. *Bergen Record*, Apr. 5, 1995, p.D1. Reprinted with permission.

"We are examining the situation and reviewing the options at our disposal to protect consumers fully," said Mark S. Herr, director of the Division of Consumer Affairs.

Greenberg said Sandler & Worth, which a few years ago posted more than $28 million in annual sales, has fallen on hard times. He cited competition, layoffs, unemployment, a downturn in new construction, and a drop in consumer spending on home furnishings. Asked why the company has not returned calls from customers, Greenberg said: "Right now, the company is not in a position to return the deposits to them. I can't tell you if they will or they won't."

Greenberg called the involuntary bankruptcy petition invalid. When companies have more than 12 creditors, he said, at least three must join the petition. Sandler & Worth may file for Chapter 11 protection, which would supersede an involuntary bankruptcy, he added.

Sandler & Worth's Springfield store is open Friday through Monday to hold auctions. Those auctions have angered several carpet suppliers. J. Harounian Oriental Rug Center in Manhattan, which filed the involuntary bankruptcy petition, says Sandler & Worth will not return $65,000 in carpeting that Harounian left with the company on consignment. "They're selling rugs that belong to wholesalers for far less than wholesale prices," said Harounian's lawyer, J. J. Longley of Summit. "Does that indicate they're ever going to pay the wholesalers? The chances of there being any money in this kind of situation is zero."

Greenberg denied that Harounian gave the carpeting to Sandler & Worth on consignment, saying it was sold on credit. "They're ours to sell," Greenberg said, though he could not say whether the wholesaler would get any of the proceeds. Another wholesaler, Noury and Sons Ltd. in Saddle Brook, said Sandler & Worth owes it payment for carpets "in the high six figures."

Sandler & Worth was founded in 1946 by Lou Sandler and Frank Worth, who opened their first store in a chicken barn not far from the present Springfield store. Since then, the chain has been owned and operated by members of the two families. The chain, which boomed in the 1980s, garnered a reputation for quality, value, and customer service.

If a judge grants Harounian's involuntary bankruptcy petition, a court-appointed trustee would oversee the listing and liquidation of assets. Any money would first go to pay bank debts, taxes, wages, lawyers, and the auctioneers, said Kenneth A. Rosen, a Roseland bankruptcy attorney not associated with Greenberg. The rest, if there is any more, would be divided on a pro-rated basis among unsecured creditors, such as wholesalers and customers, he said. However, customers and other individuals owed up to $1,800 would have priority over other unsecured creditors, Rosen said.

Customers should file a "proof of claim" form with Bankruptcy Court, including documentation such as invoices and canceled checks. The forms can be obtained from the court or at office-supply and stationery stores.

International Perspective

Secured transactions can have painful human consequences, as this Mexican case demonstrates. Is this farmer's plight a throwback to the days of debtor's prisons, or is it the inevitable result when someone breaks the rules?

Farmer Jailed for Months in Theft of His Own Tools

James Pinkerton, *Houston Chronicle*

Juan Kornelson Teicheroeb has spent nearly six months in a state prison after his bank accused him of stealing his own farm machinery. Teicheroeb, 30, said that last year he had fallen behind in repaying a $65,570 loan to a bank in Cuauhtemoc. When he asked his bankers for an extension to give him time to plant another crop, the bankers held his farm tools as collateral and forbade him from using them.

Teicheroeb, reluctant to rent equipment and unable to buy more, took his truck, a tractor, a planter and a harvester and planted another crop of beans. He was arrested before harvest. "How can I pay when they have me here, doing nothing?" Teicheroeb said at the prison, where he was awaiting trial.

Teicheroeb said the bankers withdrew $1,638 from another of his accounts and used it to pay their lawyers to bring legal action against him. "Look, I could act like a big shot, too, if I could use someone else's money to pay for lawyers," he said. Meanwhile, his wife is expecting a child, and is trying to feed two young sons.

Teicheroeb, a Mennonite—a member of an evangelical Christian sect founded in the Netherlands in the 16th century—said he has never been arrested for any other offense. Members of the militant Democratic Farmers Front have asked Chihuahua Gov. Francisco Barrios to free him.

Copyright © 1994 by The Houston Chronicle Publishing Co. *Houston Chronicle*, Feb. 20, 1994, §A, p.27. Reprinted with permission. All rights reserved.

Repossession

Repossession is common and entirely legal . . . usually.

Judge OKs Settlement with Used-Car Dealer Falk
Marc Davis, Staff Writer—*Virginian-Pilot (Norfolk)*

Used-car dealer Charlie Falk will change the way he repossesses customers' cars under a class-action settlement approved Monday by a federal judge. Falk also will forgive $10.5 million in defaulted loans, and give some cash back to customers who say he cheated them in a massive "churning" scheme since 1989.

As Judge John A. MacKenzie signed the settlement in Norfolk's federal court, one customer in the audience sobbed, "Yes! Yes! Yes!" When the hearing ended, the woman dashed to the front of the courtroom and hugged her lawyer. "We got what we wanted," said the customer, Laura Richards, one of four original plaintiffs against Falk. "He's going to have to change the way he does business so this doesn't happen to anyone else, so the little man doesn't get knocked around." Another original plaintiff, Nora Chisolm, also left court happy. "I think God answered my prayers. He's brought things out into the open that were done underhanded, the racketeering and all that," Chisolm said.

The customers' lead attorney, Kieron F. Quinn of Baltimore, said it is unlikely there will be another case like it in Hampton Roads or elsewhere. Such a scheme, Quinn said, requires a large-volume used-car dealer who can sell cars, make loans, repossess cars from defaulting customers, obtain court judgments against those customers, then resell the cars over and over. "You don't run into very many Charlie Falks," Quinn said. "There aren't that many massive used-car dealers around."

Falk is the biggest used-car dealer in Hampton Roads, with 11 locations in the area. He caters mainly to people with little money and poor credit. He is best known for his TV ads in which a goat eats customers' credit reports. About one-fourth of all Falk customers default on their loans, Falk's lawyer said in a 1993 court hearing. Falk sells more than 3,000 cars a year.

The lawsuit was filed in 1993 by four women in Norfolk and Portsmouth who bought cars from Falk, defaulted on loans, lost the cars to repossession, and were threatened with "deficiency judgments" in court. A deficiency judgment is what a borrower owes after subtracting the value of the repossessed car from the defaulted loan. Lawyers said Falk put artifi-

Copyright © 1995 by Landmark Communications, Inc. *Virginian-Pilot (Norfolk)*, Jan. 24, 1995, p.B3. Reprinted with permission.

cially low values on repossessed cars, then got artificially high deficiency judgments against customers.

Under the settlement, Falk will wipe out $10.5 million in deficiency judgments. Much of that debt was not collectible anyway—about $1 million was still on Falk's books, his lawyer said—but it is worth every penny to customers who have the debts on their credit records. "Getting the judgments wiped out for thousands of people, that's the best part," Chisolm said.

Falk also agreed to give customers more notice on repossessions, and more value for cars that are repossessed. The agreement could become a model for other used-car dealers, lawyers said. "It should end several years of disputes between Legal Aid and several dealers in the area over how cars should be appraised," said Falk's lead attorney, F. Whitten Peters of Washington. "Our hope is this will substantially make life much easier for everybody."

Falk also agreed to pay $400,000 in cash damages, but most of that will go to Quinn's law firm in Baltimore, which charges up to $250 an hour. Lawyers will get $265,000, including a small portion for Tidewater Legal Aid, which did most of the local work. Related court costs are $33,000. Each of the four original plaintiffs will get $2,000 damages. About 1,228 customers will split the remaining $94,000, or about $76 each.

Chapter 27

Bankruptcy

Introduction to Bankruptcy

Chapter 7

Chapter 11

Introduction to Bankruptcy

From the text, we know why the actress Kim Basinger filed for bankruptcy protection. This article explains why she switched from Chapter 11 to Chapter 7.

Main Line Strikes Back; Basinger's Ch. 7 Filing Angers "Boxing Helena" Producers
Dan Cox, *Daily Variety*

Lawyers and execs for Main Line Pictures lashed back at Kim Basinger Tuesday, claiming the sultry thesp is using bankruptcy court to avoid payment on the $8.1 mil judgment against her for breach of contract on the pic *Boxing Helena*. Basinger switched her bankruptcy petition Monday from Chapter 11 to Chapter 7. If approved, that will allow her to have a court-appointed trustee liquidate her current assets and distrib them to creditors.

Problem is, says Main Line lawyer Joel Samuels of the firm Sidley & Austin, Basinger's assets of roughly $2 mil to $3 mil don't cover the size of her debt, which has been targeted at more than $10 million. "She wants to use the bankruptcy process to insulate herself and keep her post-bankruptcy earnings," said Samuels. "Conversion of their case to Chapter 7 is an indication by her that she was not willing to put forward a plan that would meet the criteria of the court that her plan be found in good faith."

Basinger's attorneys initially pitched a reorganization plan under Chapter 11 that offered three years' worth of future earnings to creditors. Main Line nixed the formula, saying that she might work lightly or choose not to work at all during those three years. "It could be a hollow commitment," said Samuels. "It could be illusory if she chose not to work. She could choose not to work for a variety of reasons."

Basinger's team responded this week with the Chapter 7 declaration. "Our amended plan for reorganization provided for substantially higher distributions than a Chapter 7, and more than the law requires for Chapter 11," said Leslie Cohen, Basinger's bankruptcy attorney from the firm Levene & Eisenberg. "But nothing was good enough for Main Line." Cohen claimed that Main Line had worried in court whether Basinger might get pregnant in the next three years, thus avoiding more work. Cohen said such an infringement on Basinger's private life was "the last straw" in her decision to file Chapter 7.

Copyright © 1993 by Daily Variety Ltd. *Daily Variety*, Dec. 29, 1993, p.3. Reprinted by permission.

"It really doesn't matter to us one way or the other whether she has a family or not," responded Samuels. "The issue for us and the court is whether she disclosed what she intended to do with the three-year period of time during which she was promising to pay creditors."

Carl Mazzocone, Main Line president, called the move a "calculated manipulation of the judicial system" by Basinger to delay the proceeding. "Now we're back at the beginning, where we started seven months ago," he said. Samuels identified several options for the indie, two of which included objecting to any discharge of debt a court might rule for the actress or legally seeking to dismiss the Chapter 7 case.

Meanwhile, Cohen says Basinger is still carrying on her appeal attempt, which she expects to win when it comes before the California State Court of Appeal in the next 12–18 months. Basinger was ordered to pay $8.1 mil to the small indie after an L.A. Superior Court held her to a verbal pact to star in *Boxing Helena*.

Chapter 7

In this article, a doctor describes his travails in bankruptcy court.

"I Started a New Practice To Save My Old One"; How a Doctor Avoided Bankruptcy
Burritt Newton, *Medical Economics*

I was prepared to say goodbye to my toys—the plane, boats, camper, guns, fishing equipment. I was prepared to lose my property and investments. But when I filed for bankruptcy, I was determined to hold on to my practice.

It all started in December 1984, when an ill-advised fishing lodge venture finally exhausted both my personal resources and those of my lucrative solo practice in obstetrics and gynecology. I spent 1985 filing stacks of financial documents, meeting with creditors, attending court hearings, and turning my assets over to a bankruptcy trustee for liquidation.

Had my practice been a sole proprietorship, the trustee would have

Copyright © 1990 by Information Access Co., a division of Ziff Communications Co.; Medical Economics Publishing 1990. *Medical Economics*, May 21, 1990, vol. 67, no. 10, p.182.

slated it for liquidation along with everything else. But it was incorporated, and I thought it was safe from my financial misadventures. I was wrong. I owned all the shares in the corporation, and stock shares are a personal asset. I had to hand them over.

Once the trustee took control of the stock, I became his employee. His first step as boss: to claim that I'd been overpaying myself during the previous year. I'd been drawing $5,000 a month more than he claimed I was worth. He demanded that I cut my salary and pay him $60,000 for the "excess" payments of the previous year. When we went before a judge on the issue, the trustee's lawyer claimed that nurse midwives and nurse practitioners ran the office and saw the patients. Where was I? I spent all my time on California beaches. He couldn't substantiate this, however, and the judge told him to come back when he had supporting evidence.

Meanwhile, I prepared some evidence of my own. I documented the number of deliveries, operations, and office visits I'd handled, and got affidavits from my colleagues confirming the annual income an obstetrician-gynecologist in this area would receive from that workload. As it turned out, I never needed that evidence. The trustee's next attack was not on my salary. Instead, he offered to sell back my shares for $100,000. Now I had to prove that that figure wildly overvalued the stock. I began another round of documentation, gathering more financial records, adjusting obstetrical fees for undelivered patients and other uncompleted care, estimating collectibility of accounts receivable, and valuing office equipment. Based on these records, my accountant concluded that the shares were worth no more than $20,000. I offered $10,000.

The trustee scoffed at the offer. Then he tried an arm-twisting tactic. The IRS had placed a $40,000 lien on my plane to cover back payroll taxes. That money was sitting in the trustee's account. We'd tried to get the IRS to force him to hand it over, but the IRS knew it would collect the money from me in time and refused. Meanwhile, penalties and interest were piling up. The trustee's lawyer now threatened that if I didn't agree to their price for the shares, he'd keep delaying the proceedings. "You'll lose the entire $40,000 to legal fees if we wait long enough," he warned over the phone. I understand the consequences: I'd have to pay the IRS out of my own funds after the bankruptcy settlement. But I refused to give in to this legalized blackmail.

"My offer still stands," I said, and hung up.

The trustee then began sending formal demands that I turn over my practice—office records, accounts receivable, financial records, and patient charts. His plan: to hire another physician to take over my practice. Yet he seemed confused. At one point, he said he was going to sell my patients' medical records to other OBGs in town; at another point, that he planned to advertise the entire practice for sale.

My attorney, Cabot Christianson, and I began our counter-attack. We pointed out that medical records are confidential. Several of my patients, we added, were influential in the legal and political community, and would be interested to know that the trustee was seeking their records. If he obtained them through a court order, I'd urge all my patients to demand copies of their charts—at the trustee's expense.

Next, we informed him that since he owned the practice, he was subject to any of its liabilities. We also pointed out that I had no medical-liability insurance. I had no claims pending against me, but I hinted that some dissatisfied patients might be ready to sue. Malpractice wouldn't be the only liability, we added. Patients who switched to another practice after I left would be entitled to refunds for uncompleted diagnostic workups and prepaid deliveries.

Later, we invoked a state law that required a professional corporation to be owned by a member of the relevant profession, such as doctor, lawyer, or accountant.

The trustee seldom responded. He'd simply wait several weeks and then repeat his demands that we turn over the corporation to him. We spent pointless months in motions and counter-motions, court hearings, and negotiations. But while our defensive tactics bought us time, they weren't saving my practice. I found myself lying awake at night, going over the problem and running into the same dead ends.

One night I got up and began scribbling notes, summarizing events so far and reviewing the motives of everyone involved. During the next four hours, I covered 14 pages. Then I began to see the flaw in my tactics. The trustee was convinced that I was superfluous to my practice. In his mind the nurse practitioners and nurse midwives did most of the work. All the figures that my lawyer and accountant presented to the contrary didn't shake this belief. Why not use his misconception to my advantage?

The next day, Cabot and I prepared our plan of action. It was simplicity itself: I'd start an entirely new practice as a sole proprietorship. Under bankruptcy rules, the new practice wouldn't be liable for my personal debts or those of my old corporation.

I rented a new office, bought a few essential pieces of equipment from the old corporation, and leased the rest. I took with me three of my employees—a nurse, a receptionist, and an accounts clerk. The four of us would serve as consultants to the corporation at reduced salaries until the trustee found replacements. My patients, I hoped, would follow me to the new office. We notified them by a newspaper ad, newsletter, telephone, and in person. Meanwhile, my three employees set up new patient records, appointment books, and a computerized billing system. They ordered new forms and stationery, and arranged for the lab work to be rerouted. My account set up a separate system for the new office, and Cabot drew up a new contract for my salary and my employees'.

Cabot insisted that we inform the trustee, which worried me. My new practice wouldn't begin making money for about three months, because of the time lag between billing and payment. Until then, I needed my consulting salary from the corporation to pay bills for the new practice. But as my patients switched, the corporations accounts receivable dwindled. The trustee wanted that money to apply to my debts, and I was afraid he'd run to court for an order preventing me from drawing a salary from the receivables. But he didn't interfere. Convinced as he was that I contributed little to the original practice, he must have concluded that my reduced hours didn't matter. Although the corporate records were available to him, he never asked to see the books.

After three months, the corporation didn't bring in enough cash to pay its bills. One by one, the rest of my employees resigned from the corporation and came to work for me. My new practice began making money, and by the time the trustee called us for another meeting, there was little left of the old corporation for him to take over.

The next time we saw the trustee was in court. Before the hearing began, Cabot suggested that the trustee and I take a walk to work out a solution. As we walked, he explained that he'd been under pressure to squeeze the rich doctor for everything. I told him that "everything" was less than he thought. I showed him the corporation's current financial statement, with collectible accounts receivable down to about $10,000 from $150,000 a few months earlier.

"We still think the shares are worth $100,000," he said.

"I'll go up to $15,000," I told him. "Or you can take the practice itself—what's left of it."

He shook his head. "This has gone on too long," he said. "Give me the $15,000, and get it over with."

With the shares back in my hands, I had no reason to continue consulting to the corporation, and closed the old office. On paper, though, it continued to exist a few months longer, while we closed out patient records, bills, and taxes, and transferred the last of the equipment and remaining employees over to my sole proprietorship.

My practice has been thriving ever since. My employees managed the transition with hardly a glitch, and my patients never knew that the move involved anything more than a bigger office. I'm afraid, however, that other physicians in the area may not be able to use the same strategy. The local lawyers seem to have learned from my trustee's mistakes. In several bankruptcies since mine, the grapevine tells me, the trustees have moved to take over the practice—books, records, and accounts—at the very first meeting.

Chapter 11

For the creditors of 47th Street Photo, bankruptcy was a disaster. What went wrong? How could this debacle have been prevented?

Chapter 11 Debacle Fades 47th Street Photo
Emily DeNitto, Crain's New York Business

47th Street Photo Inc. was on the minds of merchants all along that bustling street after the electronics retailer's landmark store closed last month. The closing leaves just one open outlet for a chain that once had five stores, a 150,000-square-foot warehouse and a thriving mail order business. "I can't believe it," said one diamond retailer, staring at the 47th Street store's gated windows. "How could this be allowed to happen?" asked another.

That's a good question for the bankruptcy court to answer. 47th Street Photo has spent three and a half years operating under the protection of Chapter 11. In that time, the company's revenues have declined steadily and dramatically. But the owners of the electronics chain have never come up with a court-approved reorganization plan. And now a trustee will either liquidate the company or sell its well-known name in an effort to recoup some of the losses.

Meanwhile, creditors have stood by in frustration as charges of fraud were leveled against both the company and its founders, Irving and Leah Goldstein. Twice, there have been demands for a court-appointed trustee, including one by the U.S. Attorney for the Southern District of New York, who has charged the Goldsteins with "massive self-dealing, fraud and misconduct." The judge in the case ignored both motions, including one filed in 1992, before finally appointing Alan Cohen of Manhattan-based Alco Capital Group as trustee last month. "This is probably one of the most bizarre cases I've ever worked on. We resigned from the creditors committee many moons ago, because absolutely nothing was going on," says Michael J. Deutsch, a lawyer for Hachette Magazines Inc., one of the firm's creditors. "You started this bankruptcy with a $300 million company that at its height was the most successful electronics firm in the world, and you end up like this. It's like being in never-never land."

The Goldsteins, 47th Street's lawyer and the judge, Cornelius Blackshear, would not comment on the case.

Copyright © 1995 by Crain Communications, Inc. Reprinted with permission from *Crain's New York Business*, July 10, 1995, p.1.

Chapter 11 was never meant to be this way. Introduced as part of the Bankruptcy Reform Act of 1978, Chapter 11 was devised as a way for struggling firms to reorganize under the court's protection. The act also allows judges to limit how long a company can stay in Chapter 11 with old management in place. Otherwise, firms may fall deeper into debt, so that creditors find little left if a business is eventually liquidated. In the case of 47th Street Photo, the judge renewed exclusivity—the exclusive right of management to file a reorganization plan—a dozen times, even though management was consistently unable to come up with a workable strategy for getting out of bankruptcy. Now as 47th Street nears liquidation, the only winners will be the professional firms that have collected fees for the past three and a half years. The bankruptcy court docket shows that the judge has already authorized $1.7 million in fees for the lawyers and accountants representing the company and its creditors.

47th Street once employed 750 people; today, only about 200 work there. Most are likely to lose their jobs whether the company is liquidated or sold. Even if the trustee can find a buyer for 47th Street's remaining assets—the company's name, its leases and its flagging mail order business—creditors expect to receive pennies on the dollar for their claims, at best.

47th Street Photo is an extreme example of how Chapter 11 has evolved over the years. Bankruptcies last an average of three years, according to Michael Bradley, a professor of law and business at the University of Michigan. In the end, most companies liquidate.

A Disaster in the Making

47th Street Photo's tale of woe began about five years ago. The retailer was hit hard by the recession and by management turmoil following disputes between Mr. Goldstein and a former top executive. A shakeout in consumer electronics felled other chains, too, including Newmark & Lewis Inc., Brick Church and Crazy Eddie Inc. In January 1992, the company filed for bankruptcy protection, listing $46 million in liabilities owed to 200 creditors.

The Goldsteins brought in advisers to help put the company back on track. A chief executive, Gani Perolli, was hired in January 1993. He focused on closing stores and paring other expenses, but his work had little effect on the company's prospects. After making a modest profit in 1993, the company started falling further into debt. Court papers show that as of January 1995, the company had lost money in 26 of the 36 months it had spent in bankruptcy. Total losses for those three years were $2.47 million.

One of the company's biggest problems, both before and after its bankruptcy filing, was its disorganized bookkeeping and its unusual financing, which included funds from friends and community groups near the Goldsteins' Brooklyn home. "They operated under completely unconventional financing," says Ted Berkowitz, a partner in the bankruptcy group of Meltzer Lippe Goldstein Wolf Schlissel & Sazar, which represents the unsecured creditors. "It wasn't run like Macy's. The books were in shambles. We had a line of conventional lenders come in to consider financing, but every one of them passed."

The company's last major stab at reorganizing came six months ago, when the creditors committee proposed a plan that would have given them about 25 cents on the dollar. But 47th Street Photo's management was unable to find financing.

The firm's bookkeeping problems also attracted the government, which began several investigations. In September 1994, the Internal Revenue Service said that based on an audit of 47th Street Photo's operations from 1988 through 1991, the company owed a whopping $44 million in back taxes to the federal government.

The U.S. Attorney's office calculates that since filing for bankruptcy, the company has incurred $5.98 million in unpaid "administrative" expenses on top of its other debt. "After three years in bankruptcy, the debtor continues to sustain millions of dollars in losses and is no closer to being financially able to effectuate a plan of reorganization than it was on petition date," wrote the U.S. Attorney's office in a March 1995 court filing. At that time, the U.S. Attorney's office also charged that the Goldsteins wrongfully removed $4.5 million from the company. The U.S. Attorney at that point asked for a trustee to run the company. "What you have in this case is the proverbial fox guarding the henhouse," Assistant U.S. Attorney Edward Smith noted in court.

In a bankruptcy court hearing, a lawyer for 47th Street Photo denied both allegations. The court refused the request to appoint a trustee.

Lawsuit the Last Straw

Then on June 14, Tuttnauer Co.—an Israeli medical manufacturer that had provided financing to 47th Street Photo in exchange for a stake in the electronics firm—filed suit. Tuttnauer claimed that nearly $2 million in 47th Street Photo inventory is not accounted for. Two days later, the judge finally appointed Mr. Cohen as trustee. Some creditors suggest it was a move that should have come much sooner. Others say Mr. Blackshear's decisions were simply typical of Chapter 11 bankruptcy proceedings. "It's like walking by drug dealers day after day. After a while, you get used to it. This is just business as usual," says one creditor.

Mr. Bradley, the professor, is so critical of the process that he has called for an end to Chapter 11. He argues instead for a market-driven system for liquidating the assets of insolvent companies. "Chapter 11 is a judicial process, where markets can't work," he says. "That's what we're seeing in the 47th Street Photo case."

Mr. Deutsch, Hachette's lawyer, agrees: "The only ones making money are those who are getting administrative fees. This case was significantly worse than most, however."

Unit 4

Agency and Employment Law

Chapter 28

Agency: The Inside Relationship

Creating an Agency Relationship

Duties of Agents to Principals

Creating an Agency Relationship

When Fred is transferred to a quarry in Hollyrock, the Flintstones use a relocation agent. Is the relocation expert an agent for the Flintstones . . . or for Fred's employer?

Is Your Relocation Policy as Old as the Flintstones? Don't Let a Primitive Relocation Strategy Create an Implied Agency Situation
John Foltz, *Real Estate Today*

"Wilmaaaaaaah!" shouts Fred Flintstone as he runs up the walk to the couple's cave in Bedrock. "Wilmaaaaaaah!"

"What is it, Fred?" Wilma asks, running toward him.

"Wilma," gasps Fred, out of breath and excited, "I've been transferred to the quarry in Hollyrock, and we need to move."

Wilma begins to plan. "Let's see," she says almost to herself. "We'll need to sell this cave and buy a new one in Hollyrock. There's the mover to arrange, and we'll have to find a good school for Pebbles and a new veterinarian for Dino. . . ."

Fortunately, Fred's employer has a relocation program to help make the move more bearable and has already contacted the relocation consultant, Bob Boulder, to help the couple. "Bob Boulder will help us," Fred explains. "He'll oversee both transactions and take care of every detail. He'll handpick an agent to sell our cave here in Bedrock and select another agent to help us buy in Hollyrock. He'll advise us so that we don't make any mistakes. I know we can count on and trust him because the company chose him to work just for us."

Meet the Flintstones—Modern Stone Age Transferees

By now your agency alarm is probably screaming: ISN'T FRED TALKING ABOUT BOB BOULDER AS THOUGH BOB'S THE FLINTSTONES' AGENT? Yes, even though the reality is, of course, that Bob's relationship isn't with the Flintstones but with Fred's employer. The fact that Bob is the quarry's relocation consultant doesn't make him an agent for the Flintstones. Bob would become the Flintstones' agent if his company listed

Copyright © 1992 by Information Access Co., a division of Ziff Communications Co.; National Association of Realtors 1992. *Real Estate Today,* July 1992, vol. 25, no. 6, p.45.

the Flintstones' current cave or if he acted as a buyers' broker when the couple looked for another cave in Hollyrock. But Fred obviously believes Bob is already his and Wilma's agent.

Fred's misperception may become worse when he and Wilma go to Hollyrock on a cave-finding trip. They'll be referred to Randy Rock, an agent they also believe works for them. They may or may not be advised that Randy is the sellers' subagent.

The Flintstones, who've been told Bob Boulder will "take care of every detail," are unrepresented. Ironically, if asked, Fred and Wilma will probably say they're represented by both Randy Rock and Bob Boulder.

When Fred and Wilma discover a huge crack in the foundation of their new cave, they naturally claim they should have been protected by "their agents." They sue the sellers for 5,000 stones—the amount of the repairs—and Randy Rock and Bob Boulder, who the Flintstones claim assumed agency duties through their actions, also for 5,000 stones.

Bob Boulder and Randy Rock probably didn't intend to create an agency relationship, but they did through their actions and activities. Just ask Fred and Wilma. They'll be happy to testify in court that they trusted Bob and Randy and relied on their advice, guidance, and protection from pitfalls in the transaction.

No Yabba Doo Time for the Flintstones

"Wilmaaaaaaah!" Fred screams as he leaps up the stairs of the couple's new tri-level cave. "You won't believe what has happened!"

"What is it, Fred?" comes Wilma's usual calming voice. Fred, still out of breath, says, "Barney and Betty have been transferred to Hollyrock, too. We've got to warn them so that they don't run into the same problem we did!"

Barney Rubble is also being transferred by his employer (the Brontosaurus Bakery), but his experience turns out to be completely different from the Flintstones'. "Relax, Fred," Barney says confidently when he arrives in Hollyrock. "The personal director told me the bakery has an agency relationship with a relocation consultant, Greta Gravel."

"We talked to Greta on the telephone," Betty explains. "And she sent us a letter that clearly states she works for the bakery. It says that although she can give us information and referrals, she can't be our agent in either transaction. Greta referred us to a listing agent in Bedrock and a buyers' agent in Hollyrock."

"The great part," Barney adds, "is that the agent here in Hollyrock is required to work for us instead of as a subagent of the sellers. Greta does a good job of staying abreast of both the listing agents and the buyers' agent's activities and has made sure that both we and the bakery are satisfied."

Wilma looks at Fred and says, "Don't worry, honey. We'll win the lawsuit and be more satisfied then."

Fred and Wilma Aren't Alone in Their Ignorance

Even though they're cave people, Fred and Wilma aren't stupid. And they're not alone. Many transferees aren't represented when they buy a destination home. When brokers work as relocation consultants, their relationship is with the corporate employer, not the transferees. Through employers, brokers provide transferees with relocation services and function purely as a source of referral to other brokers.

In some instances, you might function as a relocation consultant to employers and list transferees' property or represent transferees when they buy a home in a new area. In those cases, you volunteer to become a fiduciary of the transferees. When you define your agency relationship with transferees by becoming the listing broker or a buyers' broker, your agency liability becomes manageable.

The problem is, relocation consultants' and referral-receiving agents' actions—combined with transferees' misunderstandings—create risky agency relationships. And transferees, their employers, and real estate professionals alike suffer the consequences.

Avoid Trouble Like the Trouble in Hollyrock

To avoid those consequences, establish a company policy on agency that's logical, that serves the corporate client and transferees, and that protects you from unwanted agency liability. Transferees will know your role and won't rely on your advice when they can get it from agents directly responsible to them. Employers benefit by having more satisfied and better-served transferees, your company develops increased loyalty from corporate clients, and you avoid or control agency risks.

Your first move should be to clearly define your relationship with the employer by identifying the services you'll provide. Require that the policies you suggest be reviewed by the employer's counsel and that you be relieved of liability for the policy the company eventually adopts. In other words, you'll give the company good information, but it'll make all decisions.

When the company's human resources manager refers you to transferees, explain your function as a facilitator of services on behalf of the employer. And explain that you can refer transferees to agents who'll establish an agency relationship with them both for the sale of their existing home and for the purchase of their new home.

"I'm Happy to Help, but I Don't Represent You"

Regardless of whom you refer transferees to, you want the transferees to look to that person—not you—as their agent. And whether you refer transferees to an agent in your company or in another, send them a letter that confirms their understanding of the agency relationships you've explained. Ask them to sign it and return a copy for your files.

But remember that, despite the written disclaimer, you may still be liable if your actions imply an agency relationship. So rather than provide direct advice to transferees, say you'll help them "on behalf of" the employer or "through" the listing agent or the buyers' broker. If an agent in your company lists the property, be sure transferees know they should look to that agent for service. But remember to follow up with listing agents so that you know that transferees receive the best service possible.

When you refer transferees to an agent at another company, use a written referral agreement that covers compensation and also includes an agency disclaimer. You'll need the listing broker to indemnify you against any claims that arise from the transferees' sale of their existing home. You should probably also confirm that the listing broker has errors and omissions insurance. That type of arrangement not only makes transferees aware that the other agent is their direct representative but also insulates you against claims arising from that agency relationship.

Come Out of the Relocation Stone Age

When I refer transferees to someone to help them buy a home in their new location, I try to choose a buyers' broker whenever possible so that transferees are directly represented by another real estate practitioner. Then my liability decreases.

If you refer transferees to a buyers' broker from another company, again use a written agreement. This time it should include the amount of the referral fee, an agency disclaimer between you and the buyers' broker, an agreement under which the buyers' broker will indemnify you against losses or claims the transferees make, and a confirmation that the buyers' broker has E&O insurance.

If a buyers' broker isn't available in the area the transferees are moving to, advise them to work with a subagent to find a property but to seek legal counsel for advice during the actual purchase, as they would in any other transaction. (In this case, you could make an indemnity from the subagent a condition of referral.)

Both the Flintstones and the Rubbles are settled in Hollyrock, but their relocation experiences were substantially different. That has probably affected the Brontosaurus Bakery, where Barney is happy and probably willing to transfer again, and the quarry, where Fred is considerably less happy and probably more reluctant to transfer again.

Bob Boulder now spends his time defending himself in a lawsuit, but Greta Gravel is being congratulated for orchestrating another successful move. Who would you rather be?

Duties of Agents to Principals

Brenda Exline arrived in her office one Monday morning to discover that half her staff had resigned without notice. How do employees balance their duty to their employers with their desire to advance their own careers? Did these agents go too far?

Turncoat Workers Trade in Experience for Greener Pasture
Tom Locke, *Denver Business Journal*

Mondays are bad enough for most people, but Monday, July 23, was worse than usual for Brenda Exline, founder of the Denver advertising and public relations firm The Exline Agency Inc. When Exline arrived in her office that morning, four letters of resignation greeted her. Nearly half her staff, including key creative and management people, had left her in the lurch without notice. Even worse, the group had taken more than half of her business to a new agency incorporated several days before. Exline would have to scramble.

What happened to Exline is an age-old problem for employers and is not uncommon in metro Denver. Gary Rasmussen, president of Golden-based Telecom Equipment Corp., for example, has seen departing employees form four competing companies within the last three years.

"I see a fair amount of it," said Lynn Feiger, a Denver lawyer specializing in employment law. Colorado law wrestles with competing values in such situations, Feiger said. For example, the law must balance the employee's "absolute duty to the employer" while employed with the recognition of "a privilege (of the employee) for preparing to leave," she said.

There are two particularly sticky areas in the law, Feiger said, including solicitation of other employees and solicitation of clients before departure. "The day after you leave you can do this stuff, but not while you're still working there," she said.

Rasmussen, whose company brokers used telephone equipment, said some departures are more amicable than others. "There's a good way to leave and a bad way to leave," he said.

Exline apparently feels that her ex-employees chose a bad way. She filed suit against them and their new competing agency, The Denali Group Inc., on Aug. 31. Among the allegations in the complaint were Feiger's two

Copyright © 1990 by Denver Business Times, Inc. *Denver Business Journal*, Sep. 21, 1990, vol. 43, no. 1, §1, p.1. Reprinted with permission.

sticky areas: solicitation of co-employees and solicitation of clients. The latter cost Exline at least $250,000 in lost accounts and business, according to the complaint. The suit also alleges the defendants removed computer equipment, files, supplies and artwork, causing damages of at least $32,300, and that the defendants failed to devote their time to Exline's business interests.

"There are a lot of things in that suit that I think are ridiculous," said Paul Shamon, president of The Denali Group and one of the defendants. "We never solicited any of the other employees to come with us, and we never solicited any of the clients," said Shamon. All the employees that joined him had decided to leave before the idea of a new agency surfaced, he said. Concerning the computer equipment, "all the equipment belonged to Wayne and Jody (Rigsby)," said Shamon, so they had the right to take it for use at The Denali Group, where they direct creativity and production.

Exline, who called the police when she discovered the missing equipment, said, "The reason I went to the police is because I had things gone." Criminal charges were not filed, she said, because "there was a question of who owned the rights to the computers." As for the client artwork that was taken, Shamon said that it was the property of the clients and it was taken from Exline's offices at the clients' requests. He denies they took any files. He also denies the suit's allegation that he verbally agreed to a non-compete agreement that he did not sign.

But why the departure? Shamon said he decided to leave because three employees had recently left the agency and another three, the Rigsbys and account executive Victor Chayet, had told him of plans to leave. "I left for the betterment of the clients," said Shamon. Chayet, who also joined The Denali Group, said the departures were due to a growing feeling of "our hard efforts supplying her (Exline) with her leisure time." And they didn't supply notice, said Shamon, because, "it's not an industry standard in advertising for the two-week notice." He added, "I feel uncomfortable about doing that, but it's very common in that industry."

Exline's suit alleges that the defendants solicited three restaurant accounts away from Exline while employed there—including Bagel Deli, Psghetti's and Iliff Park—with combined 1990 past billings of $68,000 and potential 1990 billings of $95,000. The biggest loss, however, was Denver-based Professional Travel Corp., which provided Exline with $75,000 in 1990 past billings and represented $150,000 in 1990 potential billings, said the complaint.

"I chose to go with the people (The Denali Group) who know my company inside out," said Margie Grimes Adams, senior vice president of business development for Professional Travel. Adams said Exline is "a very fine business person," and added, "I think the world of her and wish her the very best." Nevertheless, she decided to go with Denali because she had come to rely heavily on its members and had invested time with them. "It took a good six months for them to get to know our business," she said.

That customer reaction is not unusual, said Feiger. "Who are you going to be loyal to?" she said. "You (the customer) don't know the abstract entity." The competing ex-employee problem "seems to be mainly a problem with sales," said Feiger.

Rasmussen's examples would appear to verify that view, since all four of his employee/entrepreneur cases involved salespeople. The most recent involved two salespeople who gave little notice, cut his sales force in half in a single blow, and weren't working hard for him before their departure, Rasmussen said. "They were basically planning the futures on my time," he said.

In the earliest case, about two and a half years ago, Rasmussen lost an employee who was "an old friend from the Bell system," he said. Particularly disturbing was his financing the employee's trip to a convention to meet people in the industry, which helped the employee's new business. Rasmussen said his friend knew he would leave prior to the trip, but lied to him about when he had received the offer to be backed in his own business.

In one amicable departure, Rasmussen trained an employee with the idea that he would establish a franchise in California, but there was a misunderstanding about how the franchise would be financed, the deal fell apart, and the employee started his own competing business in Denver. But in this case, the employee had given 30 days notice, and "he's trying to stay out of our territory," said Rasmussen. The two firms also conduct a large amount of wholesale business with each other.

At the other extreme, Rasmussen said, is a salesperson who left with no notice, took certain confidential lists with him and tried to take some of Rasmussen's major accounts. In addition, this ex-employee threatened to sue Rasmussen for one year's worth of commission on an equipment-rental deal, even though he had provided only a month's service on the deal. He backed off after Rasmussen threatened to bring his own suit, based in part on the customer lists that were taken.

Rasmussen has taken two major steps to improve the competing ex-employee dilemma. For one, he has added to his employment "confidentiality agreement," which protects information about pricing and customer lists and prohibits solicitation of clients or co-employees for a year. Now it also states that if salespeople leave, "every one of their accounts receivable will fall into a house account," said Rasmussen. The payment of commission on those accounts then is "up to my discretion," and an amicable departure is more likely. The other strategy has been a screening out of entrepreneurial types in the interview process in favor of "team players," he said.

The contractual right to withhold commissions, as in Rasmussen's contracts, is a "really, really hot area," said Feiger. Depending on the wording and circumstances, those contracts can be unenforceable, she said. In certain instances of solicitation, however, an employer may be justified in withholding commissions, she said. Employers try to deal with the situation through non-compete agreements, said Feiger, but a large number of such contracts are illegal, either because they don't come under the exceptions allowed under Colorado law or they aren't reasonable.

As for solicitation, said Feiger, It's really a difficult area of the law." If the employee goes far beyond a simple statement to the client about imminent departure and says something like, "here's how we service our clients and here's our price list," then solicitation might be inferred even without a direct request for business, said Feiger.

With respect to solicitation of co-employees, if 50 percent of the staff walks out on the same day, "that looks like solicitation," said Feiger. "There's a strong inference there." Plus, if an employee starts a business the day after leaving, it might create an inference of breach of duty to the employer while employed. In a March 1989 case, Jet Courier Service v. Mulei, the Colorado Supreme Court overturned the Colorado Court of Appeals in ruling for a strong interpretation of the employer's right to a duty of loyalty from an employee.

Denali's Shamon, however, appears confident. "We feel fairly comfortable that she doesn't have a case. While Exline said the parties are "kind of in negotiations right now," Shamon expressed little interest in a settlement. Meanwhile, Exline said she is placing less emphasis on the case because she is very busy, having added "six new clients in the last two weeks." Shamon said The Denali Group is also "doing very well," and adding new clients. It's a good thing. The litigation, said Shamon, is costing "quite a bite of time and money."

Chapter 29

Agency: The Outside Relationship

Apparent Authority

Acting Within the Scope of Employment

Principal's Liability for Torts

Apparent Authority

Selecting the right roommate is always important, especially if he has apparent authority.

Double-Cross; Lies and Fast Exit Leave Roommate Out in the Cold
Robert A. Boron, *Chicago Tribune*

Q. I signed a lease and lived with a roommate. He had financial trouble and, as a result, we didn't pay the rent for the past month. One night I went back to my apartment and found the locks changed. The landlord informed me that my roommate had told him that we had moved out and that my roommate had returned the apartment keys to him.

My roommate has moved out of town and I don't know where he is. The landlord refuses to let me back into the apartment, where all my belongings are located. Can he lock me out and can he hold me responsible for the half of the rent that normally would be paid by my roommate?

A. In such situations, you normally would be bound by the actions of your roommate, just as he would be bound by yours. Either roommate would have the right to enter into an agreement with the landlord that would bind both tenants because each tenant is, in essence, the agent for the other tenant.

Your roommate normally would have the "apparent authority" to act as your agent with the landlord. "Apparent authority" means that to the outside person, in this case the landlord, one tenant would seem to have the right to deal with the landlord, whether or not he had the authorization from the other party, in this case yourself. If this apparent authority appeared to exist, the landlord didn't have to ask whether your roommate had the authority to act on your behalf.

In this situation, your roommate normally would have the right to tell the landlord that you've both moved out and to surrender possession of the apartment on behalf of both of you. However, an examination of your apartment should have revealed to the landlord that considerable property was still there and that this was not a true abandonment of possession. Therefore, your landlord probably doesn't have the right to lock you out of your apartment. If he wants you out, he should file an eviction action.

Unfortunately, you remain responsible for the full rent for the apartment. When leases are signed by two parties, barring a specific statement in the

---

Copyrighted © 1994 by Chicago Tribune Co. All rights reserved. *Chicago Tribune,* June 24, 1994, p.34, by Robert A. Boron. Special to the Tribune. Robert A. Boron is a Chicago attorney who specializes in leasing matters. Used with permission.

lease to the contrary, both parties are jointly and individually liable for the obligations under the lease, including paying the rent. The landlord is not bound by any agreement you might have had with your roommate regarding splitting the rent payments.

If your roommate has moved away and can't be located, the landlord probably will proceed against you for the rent. Nothing prevents you from suing your roommate for his portion of the lease obligation, if you are able to find him. However, the fact that you can't locate your roommate needn't delay the landlord in his efforts to collect the rent from you.

Acting Within the Scope of Employment

When employees drink too much at an office party, is the employer liable for the harm they cause? Is the intoxicated employee acting within the scope of employment?

Employer Liability Has Sobering Effect on Holiday Parties
Sally Roberts, *Business Insurance*

On Dec. 11, 1987, a Raytheon Co. manager had too much to drink at a company Christmas party. Driving home on a Massachusetts highway, the manager hit Wayne R. Mosko, who was changing a tire in the breakdown lane. Raytheon, which had rented a room at a restaurant for the party and paid part of the food bill, soon faced a suit alleging it was responsible for Mr. Mosko's serious injuries. Only now, six years later, is the electronics and defense firm off the hook. On Nov. 10, the Supreme Judicial Court of Massachusetts held that Raytheon was not liable because restaurant employees, rather than company employees, mixed the drinks that night and Raytheon employees, not the company, paid for them.

Other companies have been less fortunate and that has some worried this holiday season. Many are wondering whether courts are growing more willing to hold companies liable when employees drive drunk after company

Reprinted with permission from *Business Insurance,* Issue of Dec. 13, 1993, p.3. Copyright © 1993, Crain Communications Inc. All rights reserved.

functions. Management attorneys say they are flooded with calls for advice on how to curb potential liability from holiday parties.

Thousands of companies will hold holiday parties over the next few weeks and where alcohol is served, employers could be at risk. In 43 states and the District of Columbia, commercial servers of alcohol face possible liability for accidents caused by intoxicated patrons. A few states have extended liability to non-commercial servers or social hosts, which could include employers.

To reduce their potential exposure, employers should first shift responsibility for alcohol to liquor licensees, say lawyers familiar with this area of liability. This means holding parties at restaurants, nightclubs, bars or other places and having the staff of those establishments serve any drinks.

And if employers are adamant about holding he function on site, "they ought to hire an independent catering service with trained bartenders," said Ron Beitman, a partner with Kistin, Babitsky, Latimer & Beitman in Falmouth, Mass. "So long as the employer exercises no control over alcohol beverages, it will not be held liable," he contends. But if employers continue to allow their own employees to act as bartenders they will "sooner or later end up defending a social host liquor liability case."

Serving food can also be important in reducing potential liability. For instance, employers can stop serving alcohol early and leave food out for another hour. Employers must also bear in mind that times have changed and drinking and driving is no longer socially acceptable. Make alternative transportation modes available for employees after a party, lawyers advise. "The Christmas party without designated drivers is now a thing of the past," said Jeffrey D. Fisher, a lawyer in West Palm Beach, Fla.

Before any holiday parties, companies should set a tone of moderation, experts say. This can be expressed through pamphlets or at meetings prior to a celebration. Employers need to make clear that the party is not intended to allow the employee to get back at the employer by "drinking up what he didn't get for a raise," Mr. Beitman said.

One company that seems to have taken that advice to heart is Ben & Jerry's Homemade Inc. A few years ago, people ate and drank all they wanted at the holiday parties, said a spokesman for the Waterbury, Vt., ice cream maker. Now Ben & Jerry's passes out coupons for three free drinks. After that, employees are on their own. The company also provides more food than it used to at the parties, which are held off site. All non-alcoholic beverages are free the whole night. Prior to the holiday party, employees are reminded through posters and pay check inserts to be responsible drinkers and to think ahead, the spokesman said. Ben & Jerry's reserves a block of rooms at a local hotel and gets reduced rates for employees who decide to stay the night. It also provides taxi services.

Heightened liability concerns or not, little has changed at The Stroh Brewery Co. in Detroit. Holiday parties are held every year in the atrium of the headquarters building and Stroh products and other drinks are served by outside bartenders, a spokeswoman said. "We've had the holiday party for years and have never had any incident of misuse or abuse," she said. "We have always taken the steps to ensure our employees have a good time and consume in moderation."

Employers planning holiday parties should check their general liability policies to see if there are any alcohol-related exclusions, said Steve June, general council for North Point Insurance Co. in Southfield, Mich. About 50 percent of all general liability policies exclude coverage for damage or injury arising from the sale or furnishing of alcohol. If employers are sponsoring a function and plan to serve alcohol and have no coverage for it in their policy, they can obtain a special events policy that will cover them for the one event, Mr. June said.

"Serving liquor is a big gamble today," warns Alan Jay Kaufman, a lawyer at Kaufman & Payton in suburban Detroit who specializes in liquor liability. Carroll Air Systems Inc. took that gamble in 1985, when it bought drinks for some of its employees and clients at a trade show dinner dance. After the party, a drunken employee was driving about 90 mph when he ran a stop sign and plowed into a car, killing a man. The victim's mother sued Carroll Air and in 1991 won $85,000 in compensatory damages and $800,000 in punitive damages. That award was upheld by a Florida appeals court on Dec. 1.

Even though no business was discussed during the imbibing, the court foung that the social gathering was for the company's benefit and the employee was in the scope of his employment. Therefore the company was liable for his conduct. One factor working against Carroll Air: It paid the employee's mileage to and from the meeting.

In contrast, Raytheon escaped liability when the court found that its party was not within the scope of the manager's employment. Among the factors working in Raytheon's favor: The party was off premises and outside normal working hours.

Ultimately, though, there may be only one foolproof way to eliminate all potential liability from alcohol consumption: Prohibit drinking altogether. "It doesn't matter if the employer sells (alcohol), buys it or gives it away," contends Mr. Fisher, the lawyer for the Carroll Air victim. If the function itself is a purpose of good will and done to benefit the employer, it is liable, he said. Holiday parties are held as a way to induce loyalty among employees, to give employees a Christmas present and to make employees feel they are liked by the company.

"As far as I'm concerned, I could win any case if an employee hurt someone" after drinking at a corporate function, Mr. Fisher said. Name one company that doesn't deduct holiday party expenses, he challenged. "As soon as they deduct, they're dead."

Principal's Liability for Torts

In this case, the employer was held liable for negligent hiring. What obligation does a potential employer have to check references?

Who's Minding the Store? Cases Against Companies That Do Not Screen Applicants
Security Management

Elizabeth Harrison was brutally attacked in her apartment by a delivery man employed by Tallahassee Furniture. Although the delivery man was not on duty, he knew where the victim lived because he had previously delivered furniture to her apartment. He had a criminal record and a history of mental illness. Tallahassee Furniture hired him without a job application, without collecting references, and without conducting a preemployment interview.

After the attack, Harrison sued Tallahassee Furniture alleging that the store was negligent in hiring the delivery man. The jury's verdict favored her; it found the delivery man unfit for employment that involved entry into customers' homes and decided that Tallahassee Furniture was negligent for not checking his background. A verdict for $1.9 million in compensatory damages and $600,000 in punitive damages was awarded.

Elizabeth Holland Harrison v. Tallahassee Furniture is just one of many such cases nationwide. Companies that do not properly screen applicants can be held responsible for the actions of that applicant should he or she be hired. Those companies are also exposing themselves to what could be financially devastating losses from employee theft and drug use.

To keep liability and costs in check, many employers are turning to preemployment screening. Should an employee commit a criminal act, the employer will not be held liable if it can prove in court that a thorough screening process was used.

The expression "an ounce of prevention is worth a pound of cure" definitely applies to preemployment screening, says Christopher Cavello, vice president of Records Search, Inc., in Davie, Florida, a screening company. Cavello says that comprehensive preemployment background screening should include previous employment verifications, workers' compensation histories, employers and earnings histories, professional license verifications, social security number verifications, criminal histories, credit reports, driving records, educational verifications, and personal reference verifications.

Copyright © 1993 American Society for Industrial Security, 1655 North Fort Myer Drive, Suite 1200, Arlington VA 22209. Reprinted by permission from the December 1993 issue of *Security Management*.

Long John Silver's, a national fast-food chain that uses Records Search to conduct criminal background checks on all managers, found that 110 of its 2,006 management candidates in 1992 had criminal records they hid or misrepresented to the company. Following are a few examples of what those checks revealed that an interview and quick reference check did not:

- A shop manager in Florida suspected of underreporting sales was found to have been fired from and prosecuted by another fast-food company for taking more than $7,000 in a similar manner.
- A criminal check of a new manager in North Carolina revealed several problems with law enforcement that were not reported on the employment application. These included child molestation and three counts of writing bad checks.
- A convicted murderer was removed from the company's payroll in Illinois. A background check revealed the man was incarcerated while his employment application showed self-employment.

Cavello says that applicants with criminal backgrounds usually stay within industries in which they have already worked. This is especially true in public contact positions, such as food service, security, and cable installation.

Principal's Liability for Torts

To avoid liability, many employers are now drafting cyberspace guidelines for their employees.

Firms Draft Cyber-Safeguards
Mitch Betts and Ellis Booker, *Computerworld*

Fears that an employee's outburst in cyberspace will land the company in court are prompting many companies to set some rules. Several major corporations such as The Chase Manhattan Bank NA, Johnson Controls, Inc. and Monsanto Co. confirmed last week that they are crafting "appropriate usage policies" on what employees can or cannot do on the Internet and on-line services. Some have finished writing their cyberspace policies, while

Copyright © 1995 by Computerworld, Inc., Framingham MA 10701. Reprinted from *Computerworld*, Mar. 6, 1995, p.1. Reprinted with permission.

others are still drafting them. In all cases, corporate information systems, security and legal departments are heavily involved.

For example, Johnson Controls in Milwaukee wrote a draft policy, dated Jan. 20, for internal and external electronic-mail networks. The policy prohibits the following activities:

- Operating a business for personal gain, searching for jobs outside Johnson Controls, sending chain letters or soliciting money for religious or political causes.
- Offensive or harassing statements, including "disparagement of others based on their race, national origin, sex, sexual orientation, age, disability, religious or political beliefs."
- Sending or soliciting sexually oriented messages or images.
- Dissemination or printing copyrighted materials (including articles and software) in violation of copyright laws.

The Johnson Controls' policy, which is awaiting possible revisions and executive approval, was prompted by "the expolosion of user interest in the Internet," said Thomas McCullough, project leader for electronic messaging.

Employers are concerned about a variety of legal entanglements such as employees downloading copyrighted software without authorization or sending flaming E-mail messages that could lead to charges of libel or harassment [CW, Feb. 13]. A big fear is that outsiders will view an employee's posting as an offical company statement. This could open the door for a harmed party to file suit against both the individual and his employer.

Joseph Rosenbaum, a technology lawyer in New York, said firms can help insulate themselves by answering three simple questions: Is there a guideline? Do employees know about it? Is it enforced?

Making an effort to enforce such policies is important if a court is to take usage policies seriously, legal experts agreed. "If it only exists on paper, without any record that it is reinforced with spot checks and action on complaints, I'm not sure it will mitigate the damages," warned Neal J. Friedman, a telecommunications attorney in Washington.

At Eastman Kodak Co. in Rochester, N.Y., E-mail abuse is rare, but there have been some internal investigations, said Robert L. Mirguet, an information security manager, at a recent conference. "Posting information on [Internet] newsgroups is becoming a problem now because it's going out there with a Kodak address on it, and people get the [wrong] impression that the opinions reflect Kodak's opinions," he said.

When a new Internet account is switched on at Baxter International in Deerfield, Ill., the user automatically receives an E-mail message reiterating the company's policies regarding appropriate use. The message includes a warning not to use the Internet to transmit sensitive company documents or data. Automating the delivery of the E-mail policy, which was updated six months ago to include Internet E-mail, was necessary because Baxter is preparing to offer Internet access to a larger number of users. Other companies such as Deloitte & Touche and Monsanto are in various stages of writing E-mail usage policies.

Liability for employee misbehavior stems from a body of corporate law called the "law of agency." It holds that employers are liable for employee deeds if the employee is acting as an authorized agent. The principle also covers job-related actions that appear to outsiders to be authorized. Many Internet users include a disclaimer when posting to newsgroups saying they do not speak for their employer, but that is only a partial solution. "The disclaimer will be just one factor that a court will look at. It can't hurt, and it might help, but corporations shouldn't get a false sense of security," said Dan L. Burk, an expert on cyberlaw at George Mason University School of Law in Arlington, Va.

Employees chattering in cyberspace might be better off avoiding all mention of their employer unless they have the same kind of management clearance they would need to write a press release, suggested Eugene Volokh, a law professor at the University of California at Los Angeles. Chase Manhattan in New York has a new Internet policy that makes the same point, said Steve Lutz, manager of information security and risk management. Information posted on behalf of Chase must be cleared by the corporate communications office and personal messages must have a disclaimer stating that the views expressed are not those of Chase.

At Johnson Controls, the draft policy not only requires a disclaimer but spells out exactly what should be in the employee's E-mail signature: the person's name, Internet address and teletpone and fax numbers.

Oh, What a Legal Web We Weave

The American Bar Association will unveil a World-Wide Web site at the end of the month, packed with association information and links to legal resources elsewhere on the Internet. The site, as yet unnamed, will be open to anyone on the Internet, although the association is considering ways to create closed areas for its approximately 370,000 members.

Ironically, because the Web page will not include any new editorial material, its designers saw no need to check its content with the association's legal counsel.

Chapter 30

Employment Law

Public Policy

Employee Privacy

Sexual Harassment

Age Discrimination

Public Policy

A manager alleges that Firestone Tire and Rubber Co. fired him because he refused to sell parts and services that customers did not need. Did Firestone violate public policy? In answering this question, consider the standards set forth in Chapter 30 of the textbook.

Car-Repair Firm Accused of Lying
Sam Negri, *Arizona Republic*

A Superior Court jury will be asked to decide next month whether Firestone Tire and Rubber Co. fired one of its store managers for refusing to sell customers parts and services he says they did not need. The allegations are contained in a civil suit filed in Pima County Superior Court by Mark Lewis, 35, a master mechanic who managed Firestone's store in Tucson Mall until he was fired in February 1989.

Lewis maintains in a sworn statement that he was discharged because he refused to "cheat and steal" from customers. Court documents allege that Firestone required Lewis "to make false representations to customers" to boost his store's profits. Jim Smith, a spokesman at Firestone headquarters in Akron, Ohio, said the company will make no statements on matters under litigation.

At the center of the dispute are two of Firestone's marketing programs. One is called I.N.D.Y., which stands for "If Not Done Yet," and the other is the Vehicle Systems Analysis, or V.S.A.

Lewis' lawyer, Don Awerkamp of Tucson, said his client considered the I.N.D.Y. program fraudulent because it required telling customers that various parts and maintenance procedures were recommended by vehicle manufacturers when, in fact, they were not. For example, he said, the program falsely suggested that manufacturers recommend a front-end alignment and tire rotation after a car is six months old or has been driven 6,000 miles. According to the suit, the program also is wrong in saying manufacturers recommend those services, plus wheel-balancing, after one year or 12,000 miles.

Lewis, who is certified by the National Automotive Institute for Service Excellence as a specialist in eight areas of vehicle repair, said in a sworn statement that he knew such things were not recommended by vehicle manufacturers. When he brought his concerns to Larry Day, then regional man-

Copyright © 1991 by *Arizona Republic*, June 8, 1991, vol. 102, no. 21, §E, p.6. Sam Negri. Used with permission. Permission does not imply endorsement.

ager in Los Angeles for Firestone but who no longer is with the firm, he was told to give up his "ridiculous ideals" and become a part of "the real world," Lewis said in a deposition. Day could not be reached for comment.

Court documents filed by Awerkamp further charge that customers were told that under the V.S.A. plan, a certified technician had analyzed their vehicles and diagnosed the need for the service and parts, although "the technician was often not certified or even competent to make the diagnosis."

Awerkamp hired a professional research firm to survey Firestone stores nationally, court records show. Contacting 14 of the 30 stores in Arizona, the firm found that 12 tell their customers that all of the recommendations in the I.N.D.Y. program "are based solely on vehicle manufacturers' recommendations." He said the survey also showed that more than half of the Firestone stores contacted in Arizona "have technicians performing other diagnoses and repairs" than those for which they are not qualified.

Lewis filed suit against Firestone in November 1989 alleging wrongful discharge, breach of employment contract and interference with contract. The suit seeks a minimum of $500,000 in compensatory damages and unspecified punitive damages.

Firestone Tire and Rubber was purchased by a Japanese company in May 1988 and now is known as Bridgestone/Firestone Inc.

Employee Privacy

This employer mounted a video camera in the women's shower room. Was this a violation of the employees' right to privacy? Does it matter that the goal was to protect employees? Could the employer have used a less intrusive method to achieve the same goal?

Shower Surveillance Is Bound To Spring a Leak
Carol Kleiman, *Chicago Tribune*

Everyone knows men's rooms in offices and factories nationwide rank even higher than golf courses as the place where some of the best business deals are made. Many women believe if they could only get in the men's

Copyrighted © 1992 by Chicago Tribune Co. All rights reserved. *Chicago Tribune*, Mar. 23, 1992, "Business," p.5. Used with permission.

room, they'd be well on their way to running the company—or the world. But in the 1990s, the women's room also is becoming known as an important facility for the exchange of information among female members of the staff.

The fact is in our competitive society, washroom facilities for women and men are more than what they seem. And they're being joined in importance by another workplace facility, a place that most of the great unwashed would dismiss as a total washout: the women's shower room. Not all workplaces have a women's shower room, but in those that do, they're emerging as a hotbed of activity from which, many think, important information can be gleaned.

The importance of women's shower rooms came to a head recently as the subject of a $10 million lawsuit filed by Local 7-776 of the Oil, Chemical and Atomic Workers Union against the Amoco Corp. plant in Wood River, Ill. When it rains it pours, and allegedly there was a torrent of complaints from female workers who objected to the fact that Amoco considers their shower room so important the company put it under surveillance by installing a hidden camera. The camera was placed there, the company says, to trap a man making unauthorized visits to the shower-room area. The culprit was indeed detected and the camera removed. But the eight or so female laboratory workers who use the facility were outraged at being spied on and claim their privacy was invaded.

Howard Miller, representative for Amoco, says the hidden camera was not in the shower area itself but mounted in a fixed position in the entrance to the locker room. It was there four consecutive days and only for a portion of each day, Miller says. "Five to eight people were photographed—and they were all headshots only," Miller added. Despite these reassuring words, the women are not thrilled to be on hidden camera. And, one woman believes she was taped nude from the shoulders up—and the shoulders down.

When the lawsuit was filed last December on behalf of all female employees, a Madison County, Ill., judge issued a temporary order forbidding any further use of the camera—or tampering with the tapes. The case, which is pending, has since been moved to Federal District court. The flood of publicity about the case has resulted in the camera caper's being labeled in women's rooms and men's rooms alike as shower surveillance.

If you don't care a lot about people's constitutional rights, the idea of a hidden camera isn't so bad. A video camera complete with sound is even better. If women bumping up against the glass ceiling were allowed to train a video camera on the men's room in every major corporation in the world— from the shoulders up, of course—they'd be privy to corporate wheeling and dealing they've always been excluded from.

Talk about networking: The snippets of information women could learn from their male colleagues in only a few moments of surveillance would accelerate by months their tortuous climb up the career ladder and would give valuable insights into the Old Boy Network itself. If women only knew what's going on in the inner circles of the office, the outsiders would become insiders. They could make the most of inside information by being the first to take action that is to their own advantage, just like the men.

A typical men's room conversation, preserved on concealed video with audio, might sound like this:

Joe: "I'm going to be transferred to headquarters in a couple of months."
Jim: "Congratulations! That's an important step upward."

Now, that may not sound like very important stuff, but to Betty, who later views the tape of this casual conversation, it could make a big difference. Betty has been at the company as long as Joe and has the same credentials. In fact, she remembers training him for the job over her when he reported to her a few years back. But now he ranks above her, has more responsibility and makes more money.

The transfer is a few months off and it's possible Joe's replacement has not yet been named. This gives Betty a chance to apply for the job, and in one possible scenario, the boss might thank her for applying and offer her the job, saying, "I had no idea you were interested." Without shower surveillance, Betty might not have known there was an opening until Joe's replacement moved into his office, a done deal. And Amoco might not have been able to identify the shower invader, either.

But, let's face it, shower surveillance really doesn't smell good, and it's not entirely ethical to be a snoop. Even if you pick up needed information, it's an invasion of privacy. There's got to be another way to get information you need, whether you're a woman bound by glass ceiling and walls or a Fortune 500 corporation.

In fact, shower surveillance, whatever the end results, is all wet.

Sexual Harassment

Both men and women often complain that the rules on sexual harassment are too vague. The etiquette expert, Miss Manners, offers sure-fire guidelines for avoiding trouble in the office.

Miss Manners' Guide to Office Romance
Judith Martin

Gentlemen seem to have a renewed interest nowadays in learning the proper techniques for courting a lady. Put in their own gallant words, the question of the hour is, "How'm I supposed to get her attention without getting slapped with a sexual harassment suit?"

Simply cautioning workers not to engage in office romance at all is like telling people in a mosquito swamp that it is a mistake to scratch. Everybody acknowledges that this is sound advice, but nobody who is actually bitten will hesitate for a second before disobeying it.

And a generation that favors such socially unpromising leisure activities as watching television and working on improving its own bodies argues that the workplace is the only venue where people can respectably meet.

But after the charges aired in the Clarence Thomas confirmation hearings, gentlemen have been heard moaning about the impossibility of romance ever developing when its first tentative signs could be suspect.

As most of what has been legally charged as harassment involves grabbing, making threats, obscene remarks and vulgar suggestions, or flaunting an interest in pornography, one wonders what the newly panicked gentlemen's idea of initiating a courtship has been up until now.

It is certainly true that disgusting behavior is not permissible in the workplace, however successful its practitioners claim it to be elsewhere. Let us hope that doesn't put too much of a damper on true love. But milder advances, such as personal compliments, questions and invitations, can also qualify as workplace sexual harassment. And because these are permissible—indeed, often welcome—in the social arena, confusion has arisen as to why they can't be safely practiced at work.

The answer lies in a major difference between social manners and professional manners: Gender, so crucial to certain aspects of social life, is simply not a factor in the workplace. That is why it is wrong to assume that certain duties (such as the hostessy function of offering coffee) or courtesies

Copyright © 1991 by Judith Martin. Ms. Martin writes the syndicated Miss Manners newspaper column. Her latest book is "Miss Manners' Guide for the Turn-of-the-Millennium" (Pharos Books, 1989).

(such as standing when someone enters the room or picking up the check for a working lunch) pertain to gender, rather than rank. So is drawing attention to gender by discussing or complimenting anyone's personal attractiveness.

On the job, people are actually supposed to assume a professional demeanor, rather than to engage even in such socially harmless activities as listening to their favorite music or celebrating one another's birthdays. This may come as a shock, but they are supposed to act as if they had their minds on their work, not on their love lives.

In fact, those who best understand the necessity for keeping personal considerations out of professional behavior are the very people who actually have deep personal bonds with colleagues. A husband and wife team who engaged in sweet talk on the job, or a child in the family business who treated the boss as a parent in front of less privileged co-workers would have any office in an uproar.

But can a romance actually begin under such conditions? Well, sure. It happens all the time. Do you think there are no secret romances going on in your office among those who treat one another with careful formality?

One can even argue that restrictions can serve to make the possibilities more exciting, rather than less. There is decidedly less romance in the air at anything-goes singles bars than there used to be at gatherings when chaperonage existed to discourage it.

When romance flourished under such censorship, a gentleman understood the value of asking "Can you slip away and meet me later?" and a lady understood the necessity of supplying an answer that, allowing for the codes of the day, was easily understood to be positive or negative.

The modern business equivalent is a clearly nonprofessional invitation ("Would you like to have dinner after work?" rather than "Can we keep working over dinner?"). A positive response moves the relationship out of the office, where it can take a normal social course, and a definitive no, however politely phrased, kills any such possibility.

It is true that persistence after such discouragement is considered sexual harassment. But that should not be hard to understand. Being a pest—like opening a courtship by reaching out to grab body parts—has always been considered to be bad manners under any circumstances.

Age Discrimination

How could this employer legally justify firing a 56-year-old TV sportscaster? Does it matter if viewers prefer younger TV anchors? What if viewers prefer male or white newscasters? What if hospital patients or law firm clients prefer white male doctors and lawyers? Can an employer use customer preference as an excuse for discrimination?

Ryther Wins $715,777 in Age Bias Suit
Kevin Diaz, *Star Tribune*

Former KARE-TV sportscaster Tom Ryther, claiming he lost his job because the station thought he was too old, was vindicated Friday by a federal jury, which awarded him at least $715,777 in his age discrimination suit. Ryther, 56, once ranked the No. 2 sportscaster in the Twin Cities based on ratings, claimed he lost his job of 12 years because the station wanted a younger image.

KARE's liability in the case could reach more than $1 million, counting assessments for interest, attorneys' fees, claims under state law and an automatic doubling of the back-pay part of the award. Officials for KARE (Ch. 11) said they disagreed with the verdict and plan to appeal.

In an emotional climax to a bitter and protracted legal ordeal, Ryther's eyes welled with tears as the verdict was read, and he began to sob into a handkerchief provided by his attorney, Donna Roback. "I don't cry. I mean, I never cry. I don't get it. I guess it was because these emotions were bottled up for five years," Ryther said later.

After deliberating 2½ days, the jury of six women and two men decided that KARE discriminated against Ryther because of his age and that it willfully violated a federal law against age discrimination. Roback said the finding of a willful legal violation automatically doubles the back-pay part of the judgment, set by the jury at $272,444. The rest, $443,333, was to compensate Ryther for lost future earnings.

KARE's attorney, Tom Tinkham, said he would ask U.S. District Judge David Doty to overturn the verdict. That and other matters affecting the size of the award are now before Doty. A chief question is whether the award should be increased further on the basis of Minnesota discrimination law, which permits additional damages for pain and suffering.

The verdict is the second major discrimination award against a Twin

Copyright © 1993 by Star Tribune, Minneapolis-St. Paul. *Star Tribune*, Sep. 25, 1993, p.1A. Reprinted with permission.

Cities TV station in a year. In 1992, a Hennepin County jury awarded $382,000 to former KSTP-TV anchor Ruth Spencer in a sex discrimination suit against Hubbard Broadcasting.

"I'm absolutely thrilled beyond belief," Ryther said outside the courthouse in downtown Minneapolis. "For the first time in my life, I'm almost speechless." Ryther said he hoped the verdict would change the way television executives view on-the-air employees. "A message has been delivered here," he said. "I hope stations around the country get it—that ability should be the only thing that counts."

Henry Price, president and general manager of KARE, the Twin Cities' NBC affiliate, said the station was guilty of no wrongdoing and believes there should be no award. "We don't think anything was done that was incorrect. I think he was treated fairly and properly. "I agree with [Ryther's] message. That's what we've been saying all along—that age shouldn't matter and doesn't matter." KARE, owned by Gannett Co. Inc., said the decision not to renew Ryther's contract in July 1991 had nothing to do with age and was based on research that showed he was not attracting viewers. "It was a business decision based on sound business reasons," Tinkham told the jury.

Jurors, however, said the evidence supported Ryther. "I learned a lot about this business, and it's not a pretty picture," said one juror who asked not to be identified. "They step on each other." The juror, who described herself as an admirer of former WCCO-TV news anchor Dave Moore, said the verdict was also intended to make a point about television news. "That's not the way you treat people," she said. "If a guy wants to wear glasses to read the teleprompter, that's OK. I don't watch the news for beauty." (WCCO management decided in 1991 that Moore, then 67, should stop doing the 6 P.M. newscast, though he still hosts a Sunday morning program on WCCO.)

Jurors, she said, felt Ryther had not been given a fair chance. "We felt that if he were a younger man, maybe they would have renewed his contract and helped him along," she said. The juror noted that, compared with WCCO's Mark Rosen, the No. 1 rated sportscaster in the metro area, Ryther was not promoted to viewers. She also pointed out that Janet Mason, KARE vice president for news, testified that sports was not considered important at Channel 11.

Ryther, who joined the station in 1979, had been sports anchor for the 10 P.M. news and had anchored the 5 P.M. and 6 P.M. newscasts. He was replaced by Jeff Passolt, who is 36. In addition to age discrimination, Ryther claimed the station fired him in retaliation for filing a complaint with the federal Equal Employment Opportunity Commission, an allegation the jury rejected. Ryther, who sought $1.3 million, testified that in the last three years he worked at the station, he was taken off major assignments and had some tasks taken away.

KARE officials argued that Ryther resisted change, was not a hard worker, failed to take responsibility, had temper flareups and didn't get along with others. They said the shifts in assignments were because of those problems. "While there was a difference in his treatment, it related to the situation, not the age of the individuals," Tinkham said.

Mason also testified that the station's research showed that if Passolt had more exposure, he would attract more viewers, thus he had more potential than Ryther. Roback argued that that was simply a polite way of saying Ryther was too old. "They have been giving you a smokescreen," she told the jury.

After the verdict, Roback blasted what she said is a media tendency to favor image over substance. "The media have a very distorted view of what their viewers want," she said. "The audience is much more sophisticated than they think. Viewers are insulted and offended when it's assumed that they won't watch an anchor person who wears glasses or has bags under his eyes. We don't want the media to make us comfortable with our prejudices. We want the media to alleviate our prejudices."

During the trial, Roback emphasized that Ryther received a performance review from Mason in 1990 indicating that his performance was commendable. Ryther testified that his first clue that his contract would not be renewed was when he wasn't invited to be in a promotional photo.

Roback said that after earning $160,000 in his last year at Channel 11, Ryther's earnings have dropped to about $30,000 a year, and that he is still looking for a broadcasting job. He most recently worked for a metal fabricating company and now is a manufacturer's representative. But Ryther said after the verdict that he wants to get back into broadcasting. "It's in my blood."

Throughout the trial he carried a picture of his mother, Jean, who died on Jan. 3, 1992. "It hurt her bad [when he lost the job]," Ryther said. "But I know she's smiling today."

Chapter 31

Labor Law

Organizing

Collective Bargaining

Strikes

Organizing

Jimmy Hoffa was tough, colorful—and criminal.

They Knew Jimmy Hoffa, and Jimmy Hoffa Was no . . .
Patrick Goldstein, Los Angeles Times

In 1957, Jimmy Hoffa was acquitted of charges of bribing a government official, largely due to the efforts of criminal lawyer Edward Bennett Williams. After the trial, Hoffa left the courtroom without a word of thanks. When Williams complained of Hoffa's ingratitude to Frank Costello, another client, the Mafia don replied: "I told you Hoffa was no gentleman."

A tough guy among tough guys, Jimmy Hoffa was America's blue-collar samurai warrior. He took on all comers: big business tycoons, strikebreakers, Jack and Bobby Kennedy, mobsters from back East. With a head shaped like a bullet, arms like Cadillac bumpers, eyes like cold steel, Hoffa built the Teamsters into the nation's largest labor union the same way Al Davis' Oakland Raiders won championships—by any means necessary.

Like most of his Teamster brethren, Hoffa lived outside the law. Teamster elections were rigged. Union funds disappeared. Goons pummeled union dissidents into submission. Hoffa made no secret of his long-standing friendships with mobsters like Moe Dalitz, a key figure in Detroit's Purple Gang. In the 1950s and 1960s, the Teamsters Central States Pension Fund loaned hundreds of millions of dollars to various Las Vegas hotels, with much of the money going to casinos controlled by Dalitz. When Hoffa sought to take control of New York City's 30,000 taxi drivers, he allied himself with Johnny Dio, a convicted labor extortionist. His trusted special assignment expert was Barney Baker, a former underworld enforcer. Two of Hoffa's loyal Teamster business agents were Herman and Frank Kierdorf. Their previous area of expertise: armed robbery.

After years of battles with government adversaries, most notably arch-enemy Robert F. Kennedy, Hoffa went to prison in 1967 for mail fraud and jury tampering. (He hated the Kennedys so much that when John F. Kennedy was assassinated, Hoffa refused to lower the flag at Teamster headquarters, saying, "I hope the worms eat his eyes out.")

Five years later he obtained an early release after agreeing to step down

Copyright © 1992 by The Times Mirror Co. *Los Angeles Times*, Aug. 30, 1992, p.78. Reprinted with permission.

as Teamsters president, a title he continued to hold while in jail. On July 30, 1975, while waging a legal fight to regain his office, he left home to meet Anthony (Tony Pro) Provenzano and Anthony (Tony Jack) Giacalone, two organized crime figures who had fallen out with Hoffa. When the duo didn't show up at the Machus Red Fox restaurant, Hoffa called his wife to say the men were running late. Shortly thereafter, he disappeared. His body has never been found.

Dead but not forgotten. Red Fox waitresses say pranksters still phone the restaurant, asking them to page Jimmy Hoffa. What made Hoffa a legend was his tough-guy swagger, his shrewd negotiating skills and his fierce loyalty to the Teamster rank 'n' file. Hoffa took a barely existent union, run by local fiefdoms, and transformed it into America's most powerful labor organization.

No matter what they thought of his mob chums, Hoffa's men were impressed by the groundbreaking contracts he won for them. They also respected his frugal lifestyle—Hoffa had a modest Detroit home, he didn't smoke or drink and was faithful to his wife. When he died, he was driving a late-model Pontiac.

The media adored him, proclaiming him a beloved blue-collar battler. When Steven Brill started work on his much-admired 1978 history, *The Teamsters,* he found stacks of newspaper clips heralding Hoffa. "That was the myth, that he was this tough, can-do, can't be bought guy," says Brill, who now runs *American Lawyer* magazine and *Court TV.* "It reminds me of the way the press treated Ross Perot in the first month of his campaign. It's just not real. Hoffa was an owned-and-operated subsidiary of organized crime. The Teamsters weren't tied to organized crime. They were organized crime. And when Hoffa started to act independently, the mob simply killed him. If this movie makes Jimmy Hoffa into a hero, it would be a joke. Hoffa is a hero in the same sort of way John Gotti is a hero—it's totally manufactured."

Yet Hoffa remains a hero to many old-line Teamsters, especially Bobby Holmes Sr., a retired union official who first met Hoffa when they were teenagers, working in a produce warehouse. Now 80, Holmes ran Teamster Local 377 in Detroit for nearly 30 years. "I was on the picket line with Jimmy when he first met his wife, Josephine," Holmes recalls. "When we picketed in the 1930s, Detroit wasn't a union town. They'd hire strikebreakers to go after us. But nobody scared Jimmy. If they wanted a fistfight, they'd get one. He didn't back down to anyone."

Holmes acknowledges that Hoffa did business with the mob, but he insists the union was never under mob control. "Sure there were associations with questionable people. Mobsters did business with everyone—the linen-supply business, the soft-drink industry, even politicians. You couldn't avoid them. But our investments paid off."

Hoffa, Arthur Sloane's recent biography on the Teamster leader, supports this contention. He writes: "The unsavory character of so many of its loan recipients notwithstanding, the Teamster pension fund's assets virtually doubled in Hoffa's last four pre-prison years and there were relatively few loan defaults."

Steven Brill doesn't see it that way. "That's the Teamster myth again," he says. "When I was writing my book every story I read had the same phrase—that Hoffa made this 'Faustian bargain' with the mob to help his union. A Faustian bargain implies a case of good versus evil. With Hoffa and the mob, it was purely evil versus evil. The Teamsters pension fund was nearly bankrupt by the time he was killed. He negotiated terrible contracts. He didn't fight for his workers. Mostly, he screwed them."

Brill even has a beef with the movie's casting. Before the film started, Brill says he received a phone call from Armand Assante. The actor was researching the part of Sal D'Allesandro, a character based on Teamster hood Tony Provenzano. The two men never got together, but Brill found the casting choice puzzling. "Armand Assante's a great-looking guy, right?" Brill says. "He doesn't look anything like Tony Pro. I mean, if Tony looks like anyone, it's Lawrence Welk. And not just when he was old. Tony looked like Lawrence Welk for a long time."

Collective Bargaining

Ken Orsatti is as poised and legitimate as Jimmy Hoffa was raw. Orsatti heads a union that is smaller than Hoffa's, but even more visible: the Screen Actors Guild. Is there still a role for unions to play in the world of commerce?

He Speaks for the Actors: Ken Orsatti, as Chief Negotiator for the Screen Actors Guild, Represents the Financial Interests of Some 90,000 Actors in Contract Talks with Producers
Greg Spring, *Los Angeles Business Journal*

When Ken Orsatti was born on Jan. 31, 1932, he already had Hollywood in his blood. The Orsatti Agency, founded by his father and two uncles in 1932, went on to become one of Hollywood's largest talent agencies, with more than 900 clients at its peak. By 1948, his uncle had gotten into the production business, and Orsatti often worked on the sets of such television shows as *The Texan.*

It was as an executive producer that Orsatti planned to make his mark in the business. But as things turned out, he became just the opposite—heading the actors' union as the national executive director of the Screen Actors Guild, where he sits across the table from producers to fight for actors' wages and working conditions. In addition to representing SAG's 90,000 or so actors in contract negotiations, Orsatti is chief administrator for the union's 300 employees.

A native of the Los Angeles area, Orsatti has all the qualifications of a union leader—a degree in business administration from USC, followed by two more years of graduate school there and more than 30 years working his way up through the union's ranks. Yet, sitting in his modest eighth-floor office over Wilshire Boulevard, Orsatti seems anything but a wild-eyed union leader or grizzled veteran organizer. Nor is he a flamboyant, publicity hungry figure, the type of wheeler-dealer often associated with those in the acting profession. Dressed plainly in a simple white shirt, Orsatti has a gentle demeanor—taking time to praise his wife, Patti, lest she get left out of this article. Calm and thoughtful, he enjoys the simple pleasures of travel—which his job provides him ample opportunity to do—and reading.

Copyright © 1994 by Los Angeles Business Journal 1994. *Los Angeles Business Journal,* Dec. 19, 1994, vol. 16, no. 50, §1, p.15. Reprinted with permission.

Orsatti's presence is also surprisingly reassuring, as though he is well aware that he carries the responsibility of looking after the interest of some 90,000 actors. That responsibility will again be tested shortly, as Orsatti is preparing to lead a team of negotiators in renewing one of the guild's largest contracts—the theatrical and television contract, which covers wages and working conditions for theatrical films and TV productions. The contract is set to expire in June 1995. In 1993 alone, SAG members earned more than $713 million under this contract. As SAG's chief negotiator, Orsatti has the job of leading the union through the actual contract talks, at the direction of the union's membership. It is also his task to recommend to the union's membership whether to accept or turn down the producers' package.

Orsatti's easy demeanor is perhaps his greatest strength, as emotions can run high during such contract talks, and high emotions can just as easily impede the talks' progress. That is not to suggest Orsatti is a pushover, say those who have sat across the table from him.

"He does speak softly, but he knows how to bargain tough when he needs to," said Nick Counter, Orsatti's counterpart at the Alliance of Motion Picture and Television Producers. As president of the AMPTP, Counter represents producers in the theatrical and television contract talks and, with Orsatti, has managed to avoid a strike through the last four rounds of talks dating back to 1983. "He's very shrewd in figuring out where a deal is," Counter continued, "and when it will be acceptable to his membership and the other side."

Orsatti is also quick to point out SAG's decade-long no-strike record with the movie and TV producers. "The main thing I attempt never to lose sight of is that the whole idea of collective bargaining is to reach a deal," Orsatti says. "I have always had the conviction that I would do everything possible to work towards a deal before calling a work stoppage. It's very easy to put your members out on the streets," he says, before giving a knowing smile. "It's not so easy to get them back off the streets."

After *The Texan* was canceled in 1960, Orsatti got a job at the American Federation of Television & Radio Artists representing performers employed by NBC and KTLA. (AFTRA represents actors whose work is shot on videotape, while SAG represents actors who work on films. The two unions are currently in merger talks.) One year later, he joined the Screen Actors Guild as a business representative. Within months, Orsatti was sent to New York to the union in its contract talks with producers of commercials. It was then— going head-to-head with representatives from some of America's largest companies—that the labor bug bit for good.

"I became very excited and enamored with that kind of work," he says. "I think that piqued my interest to the point where I decided it would be a career I'd enjoy and find very fascinating and ever changing."

He moved up quickly thereafter, serving as the western regional director in 1966, Hollywood executive secretary in 1971 and the union's top job, national executive director, in 1981. As SAG's top man, his duties are broad and varied. As an administrator, Orsatti oversees a nationwide staff of 300 employees in 21 regional branches and an annual budget of more than $28 million. That staff, in turn, makes sure all the provisions in the union's various contracts with producers are met. That means minimum pay scales are honored, safety rules on sets are followed, meals are provided in an appropriate fashion and residual checks are mailed out promptly to performers.

But it is during contract negotiations that the spotlight most shines on Orsatti. The key to negotiating with the most influential producers in Hollywood? "Flexibility," Orsatti says, "and trying to find some creative solutions. Someone once said that the perfect negotiation is one where both sides are unhappy. I think there's some truth to that."

Strikes

As unions fight for their existence, management uses forceful measures to defeat strikers. Why do employment disputes become so fiercely antagonistic?

Detroit Strike Is no Closer to Resolution; Helicopters Used To Deliver Papers
Stephen Franklin, *Chicago Tribune*

As the sunlight faded and the crowd swelled, its howls growing fiercer, the driver of the newspaper delivery truck couldn't take his eyes off it. "I just have to think what I have to do to protect myself. If it's dangerous I'll do what I have to do," mumbled the paunchy, middle-aged driver, who kept a metal bar within reach.

Between him and the printing plant used by the jointly published *Detroit News* and *Detroit Free Press* stood about 1,000 people, many wearing goggles, masks or helmets, their arms locked defiantly against the 50 or so police facing them. "No Sunday paper," they screamed.

On this night, last Saturday, the nine-week strike by six unions against the two Detroit newspapers slipped into an eerie new phase. The confrontation had the aura of a staged battlefield with tactics and strategies, not just a long, abstract dispute. If the unions cannot stop the newspapers' delivery, they may be doomed. That is why the AFL-CIO has pumped in money and manpower, fearing it cannot lose on another front, and that what happens in Detroit may soon haunt it elsewhere.

So, too, the night had the feel of a blue-collar Woodstock, only it was grim and menacing. Families wandered among angry demonstrators. People sat on blankets. An ice-cream truck set up shop down the block. Folks from a middle-class complex across the way waited atop a grassy knoll. It was as if they were watching a parade go by. Besides striking workers from the Newspaper Guild, there were striking warehouse, delivery and newsroom workers. There were also members of other unions, many from the United Auto Workers, who said this was their fight, too, especially since the newspapers had begun permanently replacing strikers.

Early in the night, a group of clergy, led by Catholic Bishop Thomas Gumbleton of the Archdiocese of Detroit, asked the police to handle the situation non-violently. The week before, on Labor Day, there had been a

Copyrighted © 1995 by Chicago Tribune Co. All rights reserved. *Chicago Tribune*, Sep. 12, 1995, p.1. Used with permission.

bloody clash between rock-throwing demonstrators and police, who used pepper gas and clubs. The strikers insisted that radicals, trouble-hungry youths and motorcycle-gang types had brought on the clash.

Face-to-face with Sterling Heights police chief Thomas Derocha, Gumbleton, 65, softly pleaded the strikers' cause. "The violence done against these people by depriving them of their jobs is far greater than the violence they may have done," said the religious leader. The last thing he wanted, Derocha replied, was violence. He just wanted to carry out the law.

An hour later, several ambulances pulled up and flak-jacket-wearing workers set aside water bottles that would be needed if the police used tear gas. Since the crowd began building, none of the waiting trucks had been able to enter the plant.

Forming two lines, about 50 officers marched toward the plant gate and told the demonstrators to clear away. They didn't. The police waited and turned back. "I have enough men to push my way through the crowd, but it isn't worth the cost," said Derocha. He didn't want anyone hurt, or a bad image for his department, he explained.

One of those in front of the line was UAW member John Bolin, 40. He wore a union hat and windbreaker and held a dust mask in case the police used gas.

Around 9 P.M., two helicopters appeared—the Sunday edition would be airlifted out. Hours later company officials said they had gotten out about 900,000 papers, most by helicopter. The unions claimed the figure was half that amount. With the helicopters' roar in the background, Teamsters union member John Lee, 42, a massive man who carried a sign on a thick wood stick, looked furious. He said his circulation manager's job could be one of those the company wants to cut. Job cuts are one of the major issues in the strike. "Hopefully they'll never get a paper out of here," he said. "And that's a shame, too, because while it will hurt them it will hurt us, too. Nobody wins in a war."

Strikes

When a state government helps to settle a painful strike by becoming part owner of a gun manufacturer is it being creative, or foolhardy?

Colt's Strikers Return as Owners, but Deal Triggers Controversy; Connecticut Stake Under Fire
James Kim, USA Today

For four years, an angry Peter Moutafis walked the picket line at the Colt's firearms plant. Today he'll walk through the chain link gate and proudly reclaim his place on the assembly line. He'll be joined by about 800 fellow ex-strikers who are returning with more than good cheer: They're getting 13 percent higher wages, better benefits and $13 million in back pay. Best of all, they're returning as part owners of this historic gunmaker that Samuel Colt, inventor of the revolver, founded in 1836. "It'll be nice to go in and work just like I should have been for all these years," says Moutafis, 48, a 26-year Colt's veteran. "We survived."

Workers went on strike—the longest in the state's history—after 10 months without a contract. The deal that ended the walkout March 22: An investor group headed by Anthony Autorino, chairman of Shared Technologies Inc. of Wethersfield, Conn., teamed up with Connecticut's $8.5 billion-asset pension fund to buy the gun-making subsidiary of Colt Industries Inc. for about $75 million in cash. Rank-and-file United Auto Workers Local 376 members got a 12 percent stake through a stock-ownership plan. Managers own 12 percent of the firm, re-christened Colt's Manufacturing Co. Outside investors—including an Austrian bank and Scottish investment fund—own about 29 percent of Colt's. The state's stake is the biggest and most controversial—47 percent for its $25 million investment. Some lawmakers are bristling.

"Guns are bad," says state Rep. Robert Farr, R-West Hartford. "I don't want the state investing in them. We're the first state-owned manufacturer of assault rifles (M-16s)." He also wonders if the investment makes financial sense. "What happens in six months if Colt's starts losing money?" Farr plans to introduce legislation to force divestment.

"Look, I'm not crazy about guns, either," says Francisco Borges, the state treasurer who controls the pension fund. "But I am crazy about jobs and people going back to work." Indeed, workers returning to the com-

Copyright © 1990 by USA TODAY, Apr. 2, 1990, p.48. Reprinted with permission.

pany's two plants here and in nearby Hartford say the chance to once again man the presses, drills and grinders that fashion the M-16s and many Colt handguns comes none too soon. Most were living hand to mouth on $100-a-week strike benefits and whatever else they could muster. "If it weren't for my family giving me money," Moutafis says, "I'd be a street person."

Richard Rancourt, who has 25 years at Colt's tucked under his belt, couldn't manage. He broke the picket line soon after the strike began, joining 600 non-union replacement workers who lost their jobs last week. "I had to feed my family," he says. But now, even though he still has a job, "I feel like an outsider."

All told, 800 of the original 1,000 strikers stuck it out. The returning workers are solidly behind new management—led by Richard Gamble, president and chief executive; Autorino, chairman; and Ron Stilwell, a Colt's veteran who is chief operating officer. Gamble's first official act was to present a $10 million check to cheering union members. The check represents a first step toward complying with a September 1989 ruling by the National Labor Relations Board that found that the previous owners, guilty of unfair labor practices, owed employees $13 million—the largest settlement in the NLRB's 55-year history. Still, critics wonder if the Colt's deal best serves the state fund's beneficiaries—more than 40,000 retired state employees. Can Colt's match the state fund's 15 percent annual return?

Borges, who says he would rather be making widgets, is convinced Colt's is a financial winner. He believes that Colt's, which had $100 million in revenue in 1989, can yield an annual 25 percent return on the state's investment. Colt's strategy: Seek contracts with law-enforcement agencies, though its loss of a federal contract for M-16s in 1987 was a major blow. The company also wants to introduce new products, such as the forthcoming Colt Anaconda, a .44 magnum revolver. And Colt's is thinking about resuming sales of the Colt AR15 rifle to civilians. Colt's former owners halted sales last year after the federal government banned imports of similar weapons.

Says Bob Lesmeister, managing editor of American Firearms Industry, a trade publication: "There's no reason why they can't succeed. They have a name the public recognizes."

Unit 5

Business Organizations

Chapter 32

Starting a Business: Limited Liability

General Partnerships

Limited Partnerships

Limited Liability Companies

Franchises

General Partnerships

Raymond Hook's law partner committed suicide, leaving Hook with liability for crimes he never committed.

Lawyer's Suicide Unravels $8.5M Bank Theft
Linda Bean, *New Jersey Law Journal*

Raymond Hook doesn't want to speak ill of the dead. But the suicide of his partner, admitted thief Stephen Domenichetti, has plunged their Woodbridge firm into chaos, cast suspicion on those who worked there, cost Hook the use of the firm's business account and virtually guaranteed that Hook will have to defend himself against liability for Domenichetti's crimes. "I am devastated, shocked and angry over the fact that he could do this and ruin the lives of ten other people in this office," says Hook. "He has hurt the well-being of ten other people." In addition to Hook, two other lawyers and seven secretaries work at Domenichetti & Hook.

Domenichetti, 48, died in his car at the commuter parking lot of Cheesequake State Park off the Garden State Parkway on either July 7, the day he admitted to stealing $8.5 million from Pulse Savings Bank in South River, or July 8, the day his body was discovered in his Mercedes. Death spares Domenichetti—a well-connected Republican who served as counsel to the bank and to the town of Woodbridge—the certain disgrace that would have followed his impending arrest. But if the general pattern of fraud investigations holds true, the single shot Domenichetti fired inside that car will echo through courtrooms for years.

Position of Trust

George Hornyak, the bank's chief executive officer, says Domenichetti served the bank "in a variety of capacities" since 1988 and was appointed general counsel two years ago. From that position of trust, Domenichetti built an elaborate pyramid scheme that defrauded the institution of at least $8.5 million, the amount still outstanding. According to Middlesex County Prosecutor Robert Gluck and Jack Borrus, a lawyer retained by the bank to recover assets that Domenichetti may have concealed, the scheme worked like this:

For at least four years—from October 1990 through June 1994—Domenichetti falsified documents to support equally false applications for

---

Copyright © 1994 by American Lawyer Newspapers Group, Inc. *New Jersey Law Journal*, July 18, 1994, p.4. Reprinted with permission.

bridge or swing loans, funneled the proceeds through his client trust account, cut checks to fictitious clients and deposited them in other accounts or converted them to cash and concealed the money. Domenichetti paid the interest on time, and, when the notes came due, paid them off with the proceeds of other phony loans. It is not clear how many fraudulent loans Domenichetti ran through the bank and paid back in full.

According to other bankers, a bank analyst and real estate attorneys, bridge loans are relatively rare, shortterm commercial lending tools—generally reserved for the bank's best customers—that allow homebuyers to finance a new home while awaiting the sale of their old home. "If I have done 20 bridge loans in 20 years, I would be surprised," says a lender at one of the state's largest banks. "They are dangerous loans to make." Nevertheless, Domenichetti caused at least 250 and possibly more such loans to be made. A portion of the proceeds of each loan would go to service the interest on previous notes. No one is certain, says Gluck, what happened to the rest of the money.

No one knows, either, how long the scheme could have survived. According to a complaint filed by Borrus in Middlesex County Superior Court, the fraud was uncovered by the bank's chief lending officer, Ronald Vaughn. Vaughn began questioning how the number of bridge loans made by the bank could steadily increase in an otherwise stable real estate climate, says Borrus, of Borrus, Goldin, Foley, Vignuolo, Hyman & Stahl in North Brunswick. On July 5, Vaughn called a real estate salesman listed on one of the suspect documents and was told that the salesman had no knowledge of such a loan. He then reviewed several other files, discovered the loan applicants weren't listed in the telephone book and drove to one of the properties in question to find it did not exist at the address on the loan application.

At that point, says Borrus, the bank contacted the state Department of Banking, scheduled a directors' meeting for the next day and got in touch with the prosecutor. At 7:30 A.M. on July 7, investigators from the prosecutor's office met with Domenichetti at his office. They confronted him with the bank's information, and "he basically admitted it all," says Gluck. The investigators seized a number of files, and Domenichetti agreed, says Gluck, to turn himself in at 2 P.M. the same day.

According to Hook, Domenichetti left the office about 10 A.M. and told his wife, a part-time secretary for the firm, that there was trouble at the bank. "He said someone was stealing from the bank, and he had to go down there," says Hook, who was in court that morning and did not return until midafternoon. Hook learned about the morning's events in an afternoon telephone conversation with Domenichetti's wife, Irene.

"When I got to the office, he was gone, and no one really knew what was going on, so I called his wife. . . . While we were on the phone, investigators from the prosecutor's office showed up at her house, and I could hear her say 'I don't understand.' She asked me to come over and the investigators told me Steve was being charged with theft by deception in excess of

$75,000. They asked me if they could search the house—they were looking for him—and I said 'Sure, absolutely, but if his car's not here, I don't think you're going to find him.' You know what happened next."

Suicide Notes

Domenichetti's body was found at about 3:45 P.M. on July 8. Gluck says Domenichetti left two suicide notes in his car—one addressed to his wife and the other to the prosecutor. The note in the car indicated that Gluck could find a tape and other letters in Domenichetti's office.

On tape, Domenichetti sounded "very honest and very lucid," says Gluck. "He indicated he was sorry and upset and that he wanted to be a good, honest lawyer. I think he had tremendous regret and was distraught over the fact that he had this weakness. He blamed it on external forces, but he did put some blame on himself."

Autopsy reports that would indicate when Domenichetti killed himself were not available last week and no one can know when Domenichetti chose to kill himself.

Gluck, however, says he's confident that his office acted properly in giving Domenichetti the chance to turn himself in. "If this had been a case where we were contemplating a bail so high he couldn't have been released, then that would have been different. But in cases of theft, it is basically standard to do this. It is only in the more serious cases, crimes against a person, that we arrest an individual and take him into custody." Investigators are not "mental health professionals," Gluck notes, and they did not perceive Domenichetti as at risk for flight or suicide. They believed, he says, that Domenichetti had contacted a lawyer and they knew his wife was present in the building, although she was not privy to their discussion with Domenichetti.

Irene Domenichetti is represented by Carl Palmisano, a partner at Palmisano & Goodman in Woodbridge. Robert Goodman, the firm's other name partner, says their client, too, believes the prosecutor did nothing wrong. "You'd have to be a soothsayer," Goodman says. "I don't know what happened, but if they felt he was going to go out and shoot himself in the head, they would have done something about it."

The only thing that is certain is that Domenichetti considered, at least briefly, taking his chances in court. At 9:30 A.M., he called Barry Albin, a partner at Wilentz, Goldman & Spitzer in Woodbridge who specializes in criminal defense work. Albin was in court and didn't return to his office until later in the day. "It's a horrendous tragedy," Albin says. "But I don't know if it would have made any difference if I had been there."

Acted Alone?

In his taped confession, Domenichetti says he acted alone—an assertion that officially remains unchallenged. "But the investigation is continuing," says Gluck.

Last Monday, Borrus filed a complaint on behalf of the bank and obtained an order freezing all of Domenichetti's accounts. That includes accounts opened in Domenichetti's name, his wife's name, in the name of the firm, and the names of three apparently sham companies—Palm Cay Associates, F. Sid Associates and Armond Domenichetti & Associates Inc. The complaint names as defendants Domenichetti's estate, his wife, his law firm, the fictitious companies, National Westminster and First Financial Banks, where he had accounts or safe deposit boxes, and unnamed banks. The complaint details Domenichetti's wrongdoing and the bank's detective work. What it doesn't explain—and what bank CEO Hornyak won't discuss—is how the scam went undetected for so long.

Other lenders and real estate attorneys, none of whom wanted to be quoted by name, say two factors lead them to believe Domenichetti had an accomplice. The first, they say, is the extensive documentation that accompanied each loan application, which causes them to wonder if he had, at the least, some clerical assistance. Those documents, says Borrus, include fictitious letters from other attorneys, contracts, deeds stamped with a phony court clerk's seal and letters from other banks. "They were all fraudulent. It's very mysterious, and we don't know how he did it," Borrus says. The second factor is the sheer volume of the loans involved—the same factor that prompted Vaughn's investigation. At a time when real estate is stable, it only makes sense that bridge loans—rare when business is booming—would become only more rare, real estate professionals say. "He had to have inside help," says one.

Others are amazed that Domenichetti wasn't caught sooner. Elizabeth Summers, a bank analyst at Ryan Beck & Co. in West Orange, says that when the bank announced it was the victim of fraud, she expected some sort of mortgage scam. "But this is old. It goes back how far? And how come the internal auditors didn't catch it? My concern is that something went wrong," she says. Pulse is one of only three banks in New Jersey traded on the NASDAQ exchange that is not audited by one of the Big Eight accounting firms. Instead, its internal audits are reviewed by Stephen P. Radics & Co. of Haledon. When asked if he could explain how annual audits failed to turn up the fraud, Radics partner Raghu Gupta says, "Do you think you'll get an answer? No comment." CEO Hornyak is equally curt. "I can't comment on that," he says.

According to the first quarter analysis by Veribanc, Inc., a Wakefield, Mass., bank-rating firm. Pulse has assets of $447.3 million and produced $8.6 million in net income for the quarter. Loan loss reserves were $4.6 million, and the bank was given a three-star, green rating, the highest safety rating the company assigns. The same quarterly report indicates the bank has no outstanding loans to directors or other insiders.

Legal Battles Ahead

Domenichetti's crimes and his suicide create the potential for a number of legal struggles. Hook, who says he was Domenichetti's partner in name only, is hopeful that his arm's-length relationship will protect him from personal liability, but the firm's assets are on the line. With Domenichetti's death came the loss of the firm's two largest clients, the town of Woodbridge and the bank. Meanwhile, paychecks bounced at his office last week because the business account was frozen. "I'm hoping to at least get the freeze on the business account lifted so I can pay people," he says.

Pulse trades on the NASDAQ exchanges and it's possible—although not probable—that shareholders could institute an action against the bank's directors and officers. That's unlikely, as analyst Summers notes, because the bank's stock hasn't suffered a major hit. Although trading was suspended briefly and the price plunged when it reopened, it closed at $14 or better—to prescandal levels—four days last week.

Finally, if Gluck's investigation uncovers insider collusion, the bank could file a claim with its insurance carrier to recover at least a portion of the loss.

In life, Domenichetti was known as a confident, affable, able attorney. In death, local papers have reported rumors of a gambling addiction and his link to a second bank in Woodbridge that eventually failed. Now, it's the county's prosecutor who offers the most sympathetic portrait of Domenichetti. "I think he did want to be an honest lawyer," Gluck says. "I think he did feel remorse."

Limited Partnerships

Wayne Gretzky made some poor investment decisions. Luckily for him, he was only a limited partner—with limited liability.

Troubles of Owner Just Graze Gretzky; Bruce McNall's Losses Merely Trickle Down to Star Hockey Player
David Shoalts, *Toronto Globe & Mail*

When Bruce McNall was flying high, Wayne Gretzky was in the co-pilot's seat. Now McNall has had a spectacular financial crash, but hockey's greatest star has only a few bumps and bruises. That is not to say Gretzky has not lost a significant amount of money because of his partnership in investments with McNall, the former majority owner of the Los Angeles Kings. Gretzky's losses have been estimated as high as $5 million, but this is loose change given that McNall has been pushed into bankruptcy proceedings by creditors seeking more than $190 million.

What has cushioned Gretzky's financial plunge is his contract with the Kings, signed last February, which pays him $8 million a year over three NHL seasons. That contract will also help Gretzky through some expected turbulence ahead. His Los Angeles lawyer, Ron Fujikawa, said Gretzky has been threatened with several lawsuits by unhappy creditors of McNall's bankrupt Summa Stables Inc. Gretzky was not a partner in Summa, but he did own several Thoroughbred racehorses in partnership with McNall and could be held liable for part of their debt.

"Wayne now appears as the deep pocket" to horse trainers, feed suppliers and other creditors, Fujikawa said, "so the allegation is going to be that even though Wayne is a 50-50 partner or a 25-75 partner, he has to step in and pay (any debts) off. "There are those things looming out there, and I don't know that it's appropriate for me to comment on any litigation matters." Every other Gretzky friend and associate showed a similar reluctance to comment, at least on the record. A call to his agent, Mike Barnett, requesting an interview with Gretzky, was not returned.

Because of the tangled nature of McNall's finances, it is difficult to estimate how much money Gretzky has lost in his ventures with McNall. Estimates by associates range from a little more than $2 million to more than $5 million.

What Gretzky's associates can agree on is this: The player's investments

Copyright © 1994 by *The Toronto Globe & Mail*. Reprinted with permission.

with McNall were relatively few, and he was protected by his status as a limited partner. As a limited partner, Gretzky received protection from liability for any losses in exchange for investing a set amount of money. Gretzky's investments with McNall were a 20 percent ownership of the Toronto Argonauts of the Canadian Football League, a share of several racehorses and a portion of a sports-memorabilia collection that was highlighted by the 1910 Honus Wagner baseball card, which Gretzky and McNall bought for $451,000 in 1991.

All that remains are a few horses and some of the baseball cards, including the Wagner card. And the baseball card market isn't what it was a few years ago. Rich Klein, a price analyst for Beckett Publications of Dallas, which publishes several magazines for card collectors, said a 1910 Honus Wagner card in what he called "x-mint" condition has an estimated value of $250,000. Gretzky and McNall's card is said to be in a little better condition than x-mint, so it presumably would be worth more, although it's unlikely to be worth what they paid for it. Gretzky is having the card appraised and plans either to sell it or buy out the share held by McNall.

Gretzky's associates agree that his biggest losses came with the Argonauts, although they differ on the amount. Gretzky and the late John Candy each put up $1 million for 20 percent of McNall's 60 percent when they bought the team in 1991. When the Argos were sold to The Sports Network earlier this summer for about $6 million, all of the money went to the club's debts, with neither Gretzky nor Candy's estate receiving anything.

McNall's bankruptcy trustee is seeking to sell what's left of the racing stable, including the horses he owned with Gretzky. Gretzky will receive a share of those proceeds, according to Fujikawa, who said there are only "two or three or four" horses left that were co-owned with McNall. The racing stable may also be involved in criminal charges, as McNall has borrowed heavily against some of the horses. At least one bank has complained the horses it had taken as collateral were overvalued. However, Gretzky is not expected to face any charges.

The smallest loss will come in the sports memorabilia, which is estimated in the range of $250,000 to $350,000. Gretzky's losses also were limited by the fact he knew well ahead of almost anyone else that McNall's financial empire was headed for trouble. By 1992, he was directing a lot of his money into investments that didn't involve McNall. And in the early years Gretzky, despite signing a contract for $1.6 million a year when he was traded to the Kings in 1988 by the Edmonton Oilers, didn't have a lot of extra cash to invest with McNall. "Wayne's big money only started with the Kings," said one of Gretzky's associates. "There just wasn't that much capital to be putting around after buying a big house, the cars and paying for the (Hollywood) lifestyle. It gets spent, and that's typical. It happens a lot to athletes but more so to celebrities, and Wayne is both."

Now that Gretzky is in the second year of an $8-million-a-year contract, his losses in the McNall deals have become handy tax write-offs. Even if his losses prove to be as high as $5 million, Gretzky can use them to reduce the $4 million or so he owes in income tax each year. "This has been beneficial, frankly, the way the deals were structured," said someone who has spoken to Gretzky about the investments. "In a limited partnership, he had limited liability, and the tax losses flow through to him, which allows him to have all those other investments."

Limited Liability Companies

Limited liability companies are new and, as a result, some states do not regulate them as carefully as they regulate corporations or limited partnerships.

Is Theme Park Just a Fantasy?; Site Selected, Little Else Known
Edythe Jensen, *Arizona Republic*

Call it Secretland. The name fits a proposed 511-acre theme park near Higley and Pecos roads. No one except the promoter knows who's paying for it. Ulysses Sanchez, a 34-year-old former lobbyist and Mesa resident, is the public person behind the park plan. It was his idea.

Monday, Sanchez announced selection of the Gilbert site over unspecified alternates in Casa Grande and the west Valley. The announcement was a milestone in his effort to bring a theme park to Arizona, but Sanchez stresses it doesn't make the park a sure thing. He admits he has no background in the amusement park business. He was a lobbyist for the Maricopa Community College District. Sanchez dabbled in the entertainment business in 1989 when he entered the Johnny Walker National Comedy Search as a stand-up comedian. He didn't make the local finals.

He refuses to disclose where the hundreds of thousands of dollars are coming from to pay salaries—including his—to fund studies or to buy land. All he says is "money is available." "Investors believe in the idea, but they want to stay private," he added. For months, Sanchez' Ash Entertainment Development L.L.C. requested secrecy from Gilbert officials while he

Copyright © 1995 by *Arizona Republic*, Jan. 28, 1995, p.1. Edythe Jensen. Used with permission. Permission does not imply endorsement.

searched for real estate. A letter written to town officials in March by Ash Vice President Scott Ebert said, "any unauthorized release of information that may adversely affect these negotiations will be cause to seek alternative site locations."

While Ash demanded their silence, Economic Development Director Greg Tilque and his staff performed countless hours of research for Sanchez in an effort to lure his park to town. They researched all available land in town, how it was subdivided, and who owned it. Tilque isn't concerned about the secrecy. He said it's not unusual for business ventures to keep financial information private. Investors often want to remain anonymous when they're putting money into something that carries risk, he said.

The site selection was announced Monday, but Sanchez said he needs zoning approval and community support before he can seek more investors. Ash will host public meetings Wednesday and Feb. 7 in Gilbert Town Hall. Both sessions start at 7 P.M. and are billed as information sessions. "We want to build grass-roots support for this project. . . . [W]e're seeking public support before we look for more financing," Sanchez said.

When and if Sanchez gets more money and where it comes from won't have to be revealed thanks to a 1993 Arizona law that allowed Sanchez to form Ash as a Limited Liability Corporation. Under that law, Ash doesn't have to file public disclosure forms required of corporations or limited partnerships in Arizona. They don't have to file annual financial reports. Other Arizona corporations have to.

Opponents of the limited liability bill in 1993 told legislators the law could help businesses hide the identity of business operators with questionable backgrounds and could conceal financial information that would be of interest to law enforcement agencies and the public.

Sanchez talks freely about why he wants to build a theme park in Gilbert and why the Valley needs one. "I'm a local kid with a dream, and I've worked very hard on this for five years. Is it going to happen? I don't know. But there are investors out there, park operators out there, who are more than just interested in this project," he said.

When Sanchez did his homework, he discovered the Valley compares with San Antonio in population, climate and travel patterns, although Phoenix has a larger population. San Antonio's Fiesta Texas theme park is one of three successful Texas parks.

"There's nothing in Arizona except the Grand Canyon or Sedona that can draw the number of people an amusement park can draw," Sanchez said. "The Phoenix area is a major city that lacks a theme park. We're missing a big part of the entertainment pie," he added. Sanchez estimated half of the park's patrons would come from the Valley, half would be out-of-town or out-of-state tourists.

The Gilbert site was picked over others because the town is known as a growing residential, family area. The selected land is about a mile from the planned San Tan Freeway and eight miles from the Superstition Freeway.

It's surrounded by more vacant land, so developers won't have to worry about creating buffers between it and existing subdivisions.

Sanchez stresses his park won't be Disneyland, and it won't be the conglomeration of metal rides found in others. "We want to have a theme park reflecting the history, geography and character of Arizona. There will be some thrill elements but an emphasis on live shows. It won't be a cookie cutter of something else," Sanchez said.

When people dismiss Sanchez as young and inexperienced, he quickly replies: "Remember, Walt Disney was just a cartoonist."

Franchises

Franchises can be a risky business, but they also offer tremendous opportunity. This reporter shows how to research before buying.

Tax Shop? Gym? Finding a Franchise Without Losing Your Shirt
Earl C. Gottschalk, Jr., *New York Times*

After a long career as a broadcasting executive, Gene Swanzy decided to take early retirement five years ago to run his own business. Impressed by Mail Boxes Etc., a San Diego-based chain of postal and shipping stores, Mr. Swanzy and his wife, Mary Anna Severson, a public television executive, took action. They bought two of the postal and shipping service franchises in the Washington suburb of Arlington, Va.

Today, Mr. Swanzy is sorry he ever heard of franchising. So far, he and his wife have invested $300,000 in the two stores, and still are $250,000 in debt without taking out a dime in salary. "It's been a horrendous experience," said Mr. Swanzy, now 63. "I blew my retirement money, and now I'm trapped."

The couple has joined 29 other franchise operators in a fraud and misrepresentation suit against Mail Boxes Etc. The company, which vigorously denies the charges, has filed a cross complaint against the Swanzys.

Like the Swanzys, thousands of early retirees and victims of corporate downsizing have poured millions of dollars from their severance and retire-

Copyright © 1995 by The New York Times. *New York Times*, Mar. 26, 1995, §3, p.6. Reprinted with permission.

ment funds into franchises. Their investments have helped fuel the spectacular rise of the franchise business, which now accounts for one-third of retail sales in the United States, according to the Commerce Department.

But what has been a wonderful source of capital for franchise expansion hasn't always worked for the investors who've put their life savings on the line. Many have succeeded, but many have also failed because they haven't realized how risky buying a franchise truly is, say state regulators, franchise attorneys and business consultants.

"The industry sells itself on successes you and I could not possibly find," said Robert L. Purvin Jr., chairman of the American Association of Franchisees and Dealers, a San Diego-based group representing franchise operators. The top franchise businesses like McDonald's, Subway and Jiffy Lube are much too expensive for most people, and the smaller, less familiar franchises "are not the safe and secure absolute certainties that franchisers tout," Mr. Purvin said.

Nevertheless, the growing supply of jobless middle-aged people eager to buy a business have pushed the prices of established franchises drastically upward, said Donald D. Boroian, chairman of Francorp, a franchise consultant in Olympia Fields, Ill. This is particularly true in the fast food and beauty salon franchise businesses, he said. What's more, added Mr. Purvin, the quality of the franchises available has gone down as prices have risen. "It's an extremely overheated market," he said.

How should a potential investor proceed in this climate? First, remember that buying a franchise is very different from owning a business. The franchise operator puts up the bulk of the startup capital. In return, the franchising company provides training, business techniques, trade secrets, a recognizable name, a defined trade territory and promotional and advertising assistance. Once a franchise is up and running, the operator typically pays the company monthly royalties and advertising fees.

Theoretically, there is a symbiotic relationship between the franchise company and the franchise operator. But in reality, they are often at each other's throats. The franchise company wants royalties, and the franchise operator hates paying them. The franchise company wants as many outlets as possible, but the franchise operator does not want new competition.

All too often, people choose a franchise for emotional reasons instead of hard-headed financial ones. Look for a franchise that produces a 15 percent annual return on your capital within two years, plus a manager's salary, Mr. Boroian advised. If you invest $100,000 in a franchise, he said, "in two years, you should be making $15,000 a year in addition to your salary."

But there are some 3,000 different franchises in 65 industries, so where to begin? For a refugee from a managerial job, it's a good idea to stay on familiar turf, like business service franchises, said Mary E. Tomzack, the author of *Tips and Traps When Buying a Franchise* (McGraw Hill, 1994). The typical corporate person who goes into fast food franchising doesn't know what he's getting into, she said.

Such was the case for a former I.B.M. manager in suburban New York who bought a Subway sandwich franchise, Ms. Tomzack said. Since he bought just one outlet, he never got to the point where he could use any of his management skills. "All he was doing all day was throwing sandwiches together and cleaning up the place," she said.

Instead, corporate downsizing victims would be better off with accounting or tax service franchises, or others that provide service to corporations. "Hundreds of services once performed in-house are now being bought from outside businesses," Ms. Tomzack said. There are franchises that provide training programs, for example, as well as product design, data processing, advertising and corporate travel and legal services.

Or join up with several other corporate refugees and buy several locations of a franchise. "You take a marketing person, a finance person and a management person and divide up the duties," Ms. Tomzack explained. "That way you recreate a corporate situation and capitalize on people's strengths."

Also, look for growth fields, like child care. About 30 million children under age 13 live in either single-parent households where the parent is working, or in households where both parents work. Ms. Tomzack, who thinks women or couples do particularly well in the child care business, suggests franchises like exercise gyms, nanny services, day-care centers, and teaching programs.

Franchises that focus on the elderly are also likely to grow, she said. Examples include in-home health care services and personnel agencies that specialize in health workers. Travel and leisure activities geared to older people are also flourishing.

What do franchising professionals think you should avoid? Forget diet franchises, Ms. Tomzack said. "There have been too many articles on how diets don't work over the long run, and several national chains have run into difficulties." And think twice about buying franchises in shopping malls or strip centers. "Mall traffic is lower as they face heavy competition from the Wal-Marts and the Kmarts," said Mr. Boroian. Also, said Ms. Tomzack, mall and strip developers heavily regulate franchise operators. "You may have to keep your store open six to seven days a week and you may not be able to close until 10 P.M.," she said. In many cases, mall developers impose leases that raise rents for stores that do well.

Before buying, talk to other franchise operators also, and consult with lawyers and accountants who specialize in franchising. Volunteer to work in a franchise for a while. Most important, research franchises thoroughly before making a decision. "People spend more time researching a car before they buy one than they do when buying a franchise," said John Hayden, senior counsel for the California Department of Corporations.

Chapter 33

Life and Death of a Partnership

Creating a Partnership

Partnership by Estoppel

Dissolution

Creating a Partnership

These two friends went into a partnership together. In this article, they reveal what they consider to be the advantages and disadvantages of a partnership.

Friends Accept the Risks of Partnership
Thomas R. O'Donnell, *Des Moines Register*

When Dixie Cross and Felecia Hoff decided to start a company together, they first consulted lawyers, accountants and small-business experts. The experts were almost unanimous: Partnerships don't last. "It took that cold bath of reality with the lawyer," Hoff said. "He knew of absolutely no partnership that had ever lasted."

Undeterred, the longtime friends plunged ahead. Now, with their Ames marketing consulting company, Media Connection, more than a year old, they're sold on the partnership structure. At the same time, they're aware of traps many partnerships fall into.

Unique Strengths

Experts say the partnership form, while having some drawbacks, still is a common form of business structure. Partnerships also have some unique strengths. "I would be surprised at the statement that almost all partnerships fail," Iowa State University business professor Gary Maydew said. "It's a common form of entity." Maydew said the Internal Revenue Service reported that in 1981 there were 12.7 million sole proprietorships, 1.4 million partnerships involving 9 million partners, and 2.7 million corporations.

For Cross and Hoff, like many partners, the business grew out of their friendship. Both had sold advertising for a weekly newspaper in central Iowa and had known each other for years before deciding to form the marketing consulting company. Despite the discouraging advice, they also were told that a partnership was the best route for what they wanted to do.

Before heading down that road, however, they drew up a partnership agreement spelling out a number of things. Hoff said they both wanted to protect the other person, so they put it in writing.

Copyright © 1993 by The Des Moines Register Co. *Des Moines Register*, May 10, 1993, "Business." Reprinted with permission.

With Eyes Open

"No partnership will ever last," Hoff said, citing Sears and Roebuck, Montgomery Ward and other famous partnerships that broke up. "We structured it so that if it ends tomorrow, you can get out of it what you needed. In our case, we wanted to protect our friendship." Knowing that the contract allows either partner to walk away "makes us stronger because we don't feel like we're bound to each other," Cross said. Hoff added: "If I make a mistake, Dixie's house is on the line and her first born is on the line. . . . Those kind of pressures can break up a partnership if you don't go in with your eyes open."

Maydew said that pressure relates to one of the disadvantages of partnerships: unlimited liability. If the business goes under and one partner has more assets than another, the wealthier partner still could lose everything, he said.

Hoff and Cross also were careful to work out a way so that each is compensated for what she puts in. "In a partnership, if one partner is doing all the work and there's a 50-50 split in compensation," there can be hard feelings, Hoff said. The two women agreed that each would be paid according to the amount of business each brings into the firm.

That agreement also will help with lifestyle changes as the company, and the partners, mature. Cross, who is 20 years older than Hoff, may want to work less and spend time with grandchildren more. Hoff may want to work less to spend time with her young family. Each can do so without taking out of the company more than they put in.

"No Uncertainties"

Maydew said that's another important element to a good partnership. "It takes a very clearly defined, written partnership agreement where there are absolutely no uncertainties about how it's going to be managed, how much salary the partners are going to receive and who's going to keep the books," he said. An age difference also is an advantage, he said, because it boosts the chances the company will survive beyond the retirement or death of one partner.

That touches on another disadvantage of the partnership, Maydew said. Unlike a corporation, which is owned by stockholders and run by a board of directors, a partnership often dies with one of the partners. Hoff said she and Cross also tried to take that into consideration. "What's more debilitating to a partnership is when one partner is incapacitated," Hoff said. If one partner is unable to work, the company could skid to a stop.

There are advantages to a partnership structure from a business standpoint, Maydew said. They are cheaper to set up than corporations because they are less heavily regulated. They also don't have to issue public reports like corporations. Profits of a partnership are not taxed twice, as are corporate profits. If the business suffers a loss or incurs a debt, the partners share that loss or debt, decreasing their personal income taxes, Maydew said. But each partner also can enter into business agreements for the other. If one signs a contract for the business, even without the other partner's permission, it's the same as both signing. "If one partner is reckless or a spendthrift, that could create some problems," Maydew said.

Trust, Understanding

That, and all the other parts to a partnership, mean the business has to be built on a foundation of two or more people who trust and understand each other, Maydew said. It takes frequent meetings. . . . The kind of no-holds-barred meetings" where problems are aired freely, he said. "It's like any other relationship. A festering grievance just magnifies overtime."

Cross and Hoff couldn't agree more. "One of the big pitfalls is choosing each other on friendship alone," Cross said. "It's certainly a lot more than that. I have other friends, close friends and dear friends. We certainly shouldn't be in business together. We wouldn't last two weeks."

Cross said she and Hoff have strengths and weaknesses that complement each other. But more than that, Hoff said, is that "in a lot of ways, we have a fundamentally shared perspective." They have common goals for the company and talk frequently about them and how to reach them. It was scary, they said, when they hired an employee because that person didn't know or share that vision. They also needed to make the employee understand that their relationship as partners was central to the company's survival. "It's a lot like having children," Hoff said. "We've got to remember that we make this company go."

Partnership by Estoppel

Preventive Law: This article gives suggestions for avoiding partnership by estoppel.

Sharing Office Space and Sharing Malpractice Liability

Larry Bodine, *Illinois Legal Times*

Sole practitioners who share office space with other lawyers should bear in mind that they could be sharing more than rent, phone line and copier. They may also be sharing the risk of a malpractice claim, especially if clients get the impression that their colleagues are their partners.

Space sharing is popular among sole practitioners. It saves money, provides backup support and offers pleasant company. But it presents danger, too, when an unhappy client sues one lawyer for malpractice and tries to hold his or her office colleagues responsible for the responsible lawyer's actions. Lawyers who share office space, but who are not associated in law practice, should be very clear in advising their clients of this fact. Solos should also avoid conveying that they are partners in their letterhead door signs, directory listings and financial transactions.

Even when lawyers have not formed a true partnership, courts in Illinois and else-where have held them jointly liable under the doctrine of apparent partnership, sometimes called partnership by estoppel. Four cases illustrate the dangers:

In re Estate of Pinckard, 94 Ill. App. 3d 34 (1980), involved the four-lawyer firm Stradford, Lafontant, Fisher and Malkin. One lawyer converted $20,400 from a client estate to his own use. The administrator sued, winning an order holding the other three lawyers jointly and severally liable. The lawyers had asserted that their law firm was not a partnership, and that each member of the firm was a sole proprietor because:

- They had no partnership agreement.
- The money they received from the firm's account was based solely on the services they rendered to their individual clients.
- They did not share in the profits of the firm.
- The firm never filed an income tax return.
- The firm did not have an employer's tax account number.

Copyright © 1995. *Illinois Legal Times*, June 1995, p.14. Reprinted with permission.

However, the administrator pointed out the lawyers' acts that led to them being held jointly liable:

- The firm's letterhead showing the lawyers to be members of the firm;
- The acceptance of checks in the name of the firm;
- Oral representations made to the administrator that the law firm as named was acting as his attorneys;
- Prior oral references by one lawyer that another was a "partner" of the firm;
- A journalist's article referring to one lawyer as a "senior partner" of the firm; and
- A petition for attorney's fees that had been filed in the name of the firm.

The administrator argued successfully that the lawyers were at least partners by estoppel and thus were responsible for anything the defalcating lawyer had done. The ruling was reversed on appeal only because of a jurisdictional issue, but the lesson is clear to lawyers who share space.

The Term "Professional Association"

Solo lawyers elsewhere have also made mistakes that bound themselves together. The Appeals Court of Massachusetts recently revived a malpractice case against the two solos in Atlas Tack Corp. v. DiMasi, 637 N.E.2d 230 (1994), because their letterhead gave the impression that they were partners. The client sued lawyer Ralph A. Donabed along with two lawyers with whom he shared space, Salvatore F. DiMasi and Stephen Karll, even though they had done no work for the client. The court said a question of fact existed whether the two colleagues were vicariously liable for malpractice and whether a partnership by estoppel existed.

The lawyers argued in vain that they never actually formed a partnership nor they claimed to be partners. They kept separate files, had their own staff and paid their own expenses. However, they used stationery with the legend "DiMasi, Donabed & Karll, A Professional Association." The letterhead listed those three attorneys in addition to two more lawyers. The client was also billed on stationery with the "firm" letterhead.

"The term 'professional association' may well suggest a partnership to the public that is unlikely to distinguish among partnerships, professional corporations and professional associations," the court held.

The 4th U.S. Circuit Court also found that two lawyers had a "partnership by estoppel" with a Virginia lawyer, James Wampler, and thus were jointly liable with him for fraud and a $55,000 judgment, in Bonavire v. Wampler, 779 F.2d 1011 (4th Cir. 1985). All three of their names appeared on the door of the offices. An advertisement for "Dorfmeier, Stone and Wampler—A Full Service Law Firm" appeared in the telephone yellow pages. An escrow agreement between one fraud victim and Wampler was prepared on "Dorfmeier, Stone and Wampler" stationery. Wampler introduced lawyer Stone to one fraud victim as his "partner," and Stone did not disavow it.

Another court made a similar finding in Coleman v. Moody, 372 S.W.2d 306 (Tenn. 1963). Because the defendant attorneys practiced under a firm name composed of their three surnames, the court ruled that they held themselves out as a partnership.

Partnership by Estoppel

Michael Milken entered into a contract with UCLA for the sale of his videotaped lectures. Now it appears that this contract may have created a partnership by estoppel.

What a Deal; Milken Milks UCLA in One-Sided Contract
San Diego Union-Tribune

UCLA's lopsided business deal with Michael Milken is not a very good advertisement for its business school. UCLA definitely got the junk and the former junk bond king got the goods in his one-sided business contract with university administrators. Milken contracted for the right to sell videotapes of his series of 10 three-hour lectures, given at UCLA's Anderson Graduate School of Management last fall, through his fledgling company, Educational Entertainment Network (EEN). He gets 95 percent of profits and UCLA is left with 5 percent—only after EEN is reimbursed for all production, marketing and distribution costs, that is. Furthermore, Milken retains sole control of the tapes and gets to use the UCLA logo in perpetuity.

Unfortunately, by opting for a percentage instead of royalties, UCLA has inadvertently become a partner of Milken's and, as such, could be legally liable for Milken's actions. Some deal, huh?

Rightly, San Diego Regent John G. Davies has vowed "to leave no stone unturned" to get out of this arrangement. The problem is that UCLA

Copyright © 1994 by The San Diego Union-Tribune. *San Diego Union-Tribune*, Mar. 26, 1994, "Opinion," p.1.

boxed itself in when its shrewd negotiators gave up rights both to waive the contract and to file an injunction against Milken. About the only thing it can do now is go to Milken, hat-in-hand, and say "pretty please."

The whole Milken affair has been a major embarrassment to UCLA and the University of California system. It wasn't proper in the first place to invite a convicted felon who had just completed nearly two years in prison to teach graduate students. Some role model. Coupled with the fact that the Milken family had donated $3.3 million to UCLA and $40,000 to its business school before the deal was signed, the whole affair leaves the unsavory impression that the former junk bond king was buying back his reputation by riding on UCLA's good name.

But the deal is done. The jokes have been made. Milken may or may not decide to let the squirming regents off the hook. But the issue of contract oversight must be addressed. The fact that such a lopsided agreement got through in the first place makes one wonder not only about those doing the deals but about who is looking over their shoulders.

Dissolution

Like other American businesses, law firms are also downsizing. But what happens when a partner refuses to be fired? Does a partnership have the right to expel a partner?

"Outplacement" Gets Messy; Winston & Strawn Partner Refuses To Go Quietly
Jonathan Groner, Legal Times

In these tight times, a lot of law firms are pushing less-profitable partners out the door—or "outplacing" them, as the common euphemism has it. But what happens when an outplaced lawyer refuses to be fired? That's the question that Chicago's Winston & Strawn faced last week in dealing with D.C. partner Chester Nosal's head-on challenge to the firm's decision to let him go.

Nosal, 47, was one of 19 Winston & Strawn lawyers, four of them in the Washington office, whom the firm decided to cut in March. "Their talents

Copyright © 1992. *Legal Times*, May 11, 1992, p.2. Reprinted with permission.

were not sought at the present time by our client base," D.C. managing partner J. Michael McGarry III said at the time. McGarry added that some of the outplaced lawyers might be given until year's end to find new jobs.

But unlike the other 18, and unlike most lawyers who are told they are being terminated, Nosal, an international-transactions specialist, chose to force the partnership's hand. Exercising his right under the partnership agreement, he pressed for, and received, a vote of all 60 equity partners on his dismissal. If Nosal was hoping that he could save his job by forcing the vote, he was mistaken. On May 6, Winston & Strawn's equity partners ratified the executive committee's decision to dismiss him from the partnership. McGarry declines to say what the vote was, except that it exceeded the required two-thirds majority.

Nosal, who declines comment, may still not leave amicably. He has hired Robert Weinberg, a senior partner at D.C.'s Williams & Connolly, to represent him in his dealings with Winston & Strawn. Weinberg also declines comment, citing a Williams & Connolly policy against discussing non-public client matters.

Sounding a Warning

Earlier, according to an internal firm memorandum obtained by *Legal Times*, Nosal had undertaken an unusual lobbying campaign among the partners. In a futile attempt to stave off his dismissal, he portrayed himself as a dissenter whose views were being stifled. The firm's executive committee recommended expulsion, Nosal wrote, because of his "continued effort to clarify our Partnership Agreement" and his "insistence on an explanation for the attempted purge" of the partners. Nosal said he was being fired, in effect, for speaking up against the dismissals and for recommending that the partners accept lower compensation or retrain those in unprofitable areas rather than cutting their colleagues loose.

"If I can be expelled . . . no Partner is safe," he wrote. " . . . I am sure that each of you understand the terrible precedent it sets to permit expulsion without good and significant cause. Finally, the offer of a few months' compensation for a career partner's interest and retirement benefits in a law firm grossing $150 million annually (and probably worth twice that amount) is a taking without fair compensation which sets an equally bad precedent." Nosal urged the other partners to vote no or abstain on his expulsion. "In addition to helping me, your vote is a vote for yourself, the firm and your own professional future," he implored.

The backdrop to the Nosal dispute is the 1991 merger of Winston & Strawn and D.C.'s Bishop, Cook, Purcell & Reynolds, during which many Bishop, Cook partners were not made Winston & Strawn equity partners. Last month, four former Bishop, Cook partners left for D.C.'s Verner, Liipfert, Bernhard, McPherson and Hand because of a client conflict. Nosal, unlike two of the D.C. office's other terminated partners, is not a Bishop,

Cook veteran. He had been a partner in Winston & Strawn's small D.C. office before the merger.

Unexpected Opposition

Managing partner McGarry denies that Nosal's dismissal was ordered because Nosal disagreed with the other partners. "Chester was one of the attorneys that we decided should be outplaced from the firm. His practice was not best served in this office," McGarry says. "We presented him with a very generous compensation package. He was not satisfied with the decision or the package, and it looks like he's trying to position himself to negotiate a better package."

One laid-off Winston & Strawn partner said most partners are expecting lump-sum severance payments between $50,000 and $100,000, *The American Lawyer* reported this month.

"Chester had just refused to be reasonable," says McGarry. "It's the first time we've been faced with a man who wanted to escalate it that way."

Some law-firm consultants say that as more firms move to get rid of lawyers viewed as unprofitable, these sorts of messy disengagements may become more common. Janine Burns, managing director of the mid-Atlantic region for Jannotta Bray & Associates (who discussed outplacements generally rather than the specific Winston & Strawn dispute), says that partners who adopt Nosal's belligerent strategy usually do so "because of some pre-existing difference of opinion with the other partners." Burns, whose firm specializes in career transitions, adds that law firms are well advised to figure out how to ease people out gracefully.

"Law firms have a vested interest in an easy transition, as these people are likely to go into corporate or government roles, where there's an opportunity for continued contact with them," says Burns. "Ordinarily, the partner has the same interest."

Dissolution

A partner at one of Kansas City's oldest and largest law firms is trying to force the dissolution of his firm. Can one partner force the dissolution of a partnership?

Ex-Partner Seeks Receivership for Lathrop & Norquist

Dan Margolies, *Kansas City Business Journal*

The split between partner Richard Miller and Lathrop & Norquist has spilled over into a venomous lawsuit in which Miller is seeking to have the law firm, one of Kansas City's oldest and largest, placed in receivership and dissolved. The lawsuit, filed June 7 in Jackson County Circuit Court in Independence, lays bare Miller's version of the events that led to the dissolution last month of the 13-month-old merger between his firm and the much larger Lathrop firm.

The suit says Lathrop reneged on assurances the firm allegedly made when Miller Bash & Starrett and the Lathrop firm agreed to merge last year. Among those assurances, according to Miller, was that his base starting compensation in 1990 would be twice the percentage of the highest-paid partner at Lathrop and that it would be increased if he attracted new clients and business to Lathrop.

The lawsuit, which names most of Lathrop's partners, contends that Miller brought about 25 "new and substantial clients" to Lathrop; expanded business with existing clients; provided income-producing business to no less than 76 different attorneys at the firm; sparked an increase in productivity at all levels; and "reversed at least a three-year trend of stagnant or declining partner income" at Lathrop. Nonetheless, Miller says, his percentage share in the partnership was reduced "without cause or reason."

The suit also alleges that shortly after Thomas Stewart was appointed Lathrop's new managing partner last June, he fired an employee who had been with Miller more than 13 years. He then allegedly fired three more lawyers who had been with Miller's firm and had come to Lathrop as part of the merger. The suit says the lawyers were let go on a Friday afternoon, when Miller was out of the office preparing for an out-of-town trial. Lawyers

This article appeared in the 39th issue of the *Kansas City Business Journal* on June 14, 1991. It has been reprinted with permission from the Kansas City Business Journal and further reproduction by any other party is strictly prohibited. Copyright © 1995.

at Lathrop referred inquiries to the firm's attorney, Richard F. Adams of Slagle Bernard & Gorman. Adams declined to comment.

The lawsuit provides a rare glimpse into the strife besetting one of Kansas City's most established law firms, one that dates its founding to 1873. Among Lathrop's clients are The Kansas City Star, AT&T, Butler Manufacturing Co., the Chamber of Commerce of Greater Kansas City and Children's Mercy Hospital. The firm's lawyers include the current chairman of the Kansas City chamber, the former chairman of the Overland Park Chamber of Commerce, the current president of the Kansas City Board of Police Commissioners, two former Kansas City Council members, and several lawyers active in local and state politics.

Miller's lawsuit against Lathrop asks for a drastic remedy—the firm's dissolution. Although that request is not likely to be granted, it shows the degree to which matters had degenerated when Lathrop and Miller finally decided to call it quits last month.

The ten-count suit seeks up to $1 million in actual damages and $1 million in punitive damages per count. One count, for breach of fiduciary duty, is against three of Lathrop's partners personally. The three—Stewart, William Ray Price and William K. Waugh III—are members of the firm's executive committee. The count says they failed to honor agreements reached before the merger, failed to deal with Miller in good faith and excluded Miller from the firm's decision-making process.

The merger between Miller Bash & Starrett and Lathrop took place in April 1990, with all but one of Miller Bash's 14 lawyers joining Lathrop. Lathrop, which was named Lathrop Koontz & Norquist before the merger, changed its name to Lathrop Norquist & Miller after the merger, an indication of the importance the firm attached to the union. The combined firm had about 85 lawyers. Miller is a recognized expert in construction and surety law and represents two of the largest contractors in Kansas City, Clarkson Construction Co. and Massman Construction Co.

Among other allegations in his lawsuit, he contends that Lathrop reneged on its promise to lease an office building at 4310 Madison Ave. built and owned by Miller, at least until Lathrop obtained additional space to house the lawyers it couldn't fit in at its main office in Crown Center. On April 3, however, Stewart told Miller the firm was vacating the premises, exposing Miller to more than $225,000 in annual liabilities, according to the lawsuit.

In the following weeks, Miller says Stewart ordered the firm's furniture and equipment removed from the building, including furniture that was covered by leases to other tenants in the building. When Miller objected, Stewart "terminated the compensation" of Miller and his son, also a lawyer with the firm. Miller subsequently resigned, the lawsuit says, and though the firm offered to "amicably dissolve the merger," Miller alleges that partners with the firm were already calling longtime clients of Miller's and attempting to steal them away.

The suit says Lathrop then tried to strip him of his assets, attorneys and clients "in an effort to destroy his law practice and to damage him personally." Among other things, Miller says Lathrop refused to release client files; aggressively tried to persuade associate lawyers who worked for him to remain with the firm; and held onto the library he had accumulated over 25 years to prevent him from reopening his firm. Miller has retained one of the most prominent plaintiff's attorneys in Kansas City, Max Foust. Foust declined to comment on the lawsuit.

Chapter 34

Partnership in Operation

Fiduciary Duty to the Partnership

Right To Bind the Partnership

Joint and Several Liability

Fiduciary Duty to the Partnership

A partner in an accounting firm leaves to start his own firm. He takes with him big-ticket clients and 20 percent of the office staff. What duty of loyalty do partners owe to their firm?

Splintered Loyalties
Rami Grunbaum, *Business Journal—Sacramento*

When Rudy Croce, prominent accountant and pillar of the Stockton business community, resigned in September as partner in Grant Thornton's local office, the six remaining partners were stunned. That, however, was only half the surprise. In a mass defection two weeks later, 20 percent of the office staff announced they were joining Croce in forming a rival CPA firm. "The effect of that departure is staggering," declared Grant Thornton's local managing partner, in papers supporting the lawsuit that was slapped on Croce within days of the exodus.

Equally threatening to the firm were Croce's plans to lure away three-quarters of his own $630,000-a-year practice. Included were such big-ticket clients as the Indelicato family and their Delicato Winery, a $40,000-a-year account at Grant Thornton. It's a familiar scenario, played out at law firms, advertising agencies, brokerage houses and other kinds of professional firms. Partners or key employees, sensing better opportunities on their own, jump ship and carry as baggage whatever clients, colleagues and information they find useful. Wounded and angry, the jilted firm strikes back in court.

Examples abound. The prominent New York advertising agency of Lord, Geller, Federico & Einstein currently is battling a new firm comprised of former executives who wooed away such heavy-weight clients as Fuji Photo Film Co. and Ann Klein II. In Chicago, two partners in Arthur Young & Co.'s consulting practice recently were fired and sued after allegedly soliciting employees and possibly clients for a rival accounting firm they planned.

The Grant Thornton-Croce dispute serves as a good illustration of the legal issues that boil to the surface in such breakups. The CPA firm has accused him of breach of contract, misappropriation of trade secrets, and breach of fiduciary duties. Croce denies those charges, blaming his departure on policy disagreements with Grant Thornton's national management. One

---

Copyright © 1988 by Sacramento Business Journal, Inc. 1988. *Business Journal—Sacramento*, Aug. 8, 1988, vol. 5, no. 19, §2, p.4. Reprinted with permission.

reason for his discontent was that Grant Thornton dropped about 90 of his clients, many of them personal friends, because their annual tab was less than $1,000.

In the Croce case, as in others of its ilk, the stakes are high. Croce accounted for more than his share of the seven-partner office's $4 million in annual billings. His $630,000-a-year chunk would be sorely missed. Consider that, according to the managing partner's testimony, Grant Thornton's extensive efforts to cultivate new clients in Stockton annually brought in only $200,000 in fresh billings.

Small wonder that Grant Thornton sought to quash the new firm. Its lawsuit, which seeks more than $100,000 in actual damages and unspecified punitive damages, also requests a permanent court order barring Rudy Croce & Associates from serving any recent Grant Thornton clients. Grant Thornton argues that Croce's clients belong to the firm. In a sparring, daylong deposition of Croce, Grant Thornton's attorney pointed out that Croce originally inherited many of his clients as a young certified public accountant assisting senior partners in the firm. And managing partner Michael Burns noted in his affidavit that Grant Thornton "annually spends tens of thousands of dollars" on activities that help partners bring in clients.

Nonetheless, say legal experts, no matter what the investment, clients don't "belong" to the firm. "It would be difficult for a court to say, 'You have to stay (with a certain firm),' " says Paul Vapnek, an attorney at Townsend & Townsend in San Francisco and a member of the commission that rewrote the state bar's Code of Professional Conduct.

"There's plenty of things lawyers can have fights about when they break up, and they can be acrimonious," adds David Miller, a professor at McGeorge School of Law in Sacramento. But clients aren't on that list. "It's very clear that it's the clients choice who shall be the lawyer." As far as attorneys go, the state bar's code is explicit about the issue. Other professions may not have similar dictates, but the law's presumption is the same.

With no legal hold over their clients, professional firms often seek to tie the hands of would-be defectors by having partners sign non-competition agreements. Croce signed such an agreement in 1985 when Grant Thornton acquired the Stockton office of Fox & Co., the financially troubled national CPA firm that Croce had joined straight out of college. The agreement stipulated that if Croce left the firm, he wouldn't work as a CPA within 50 miles of Stockton, nor would he take on any clients served by the firm during the previous two years.

That might seem like an ironclad contract, but non-competition agreements are regularly thrown out by the courts. "You can't just completely lock a person out of a trade or profession," says Miller. "There are anti-trust implications, questions of restraint of trade." The experts say, however, that in some circumstances a carefully drafted non-competition clause may stand up in court. For instance, says Vapnek, "If you sell out your company, the buyer can extract an agreement not to compete."

Another charge frequently leveled by a stung professional firm is to claim that a departing colleague is taking its trade secrets. As Burns noted, Croce has "acquired a storehouse of intimate knowledge" about the firm's clients. Grant Thornton alleges that Croce's new firm will "use and disclose confidential, secret and proprietary information and trade secrets."

A client's files, however, belong to the client, says Vapnek, so that material is clearly not proprietary to the firm. And a departing professional with established relationships to clients would not be misappropriating anything by merely taking away the knowledge of who those clients are.

But there is a limit. If you're a securities broker, for instance, you're asking for trouble when you walk off with computer disks crammed with data on your clients' holdings and trading patterns, Vapnek says. "Even though they may have been your customers as a stockbroker, their records aren't yours, they belong to the company." And even such simple things as forms used in a law office can be considered proprietary, says Miller of McGeorge.

Perhaps the strongest line of attack against a defecting partner is the claim of a breach of fiduciary duties. Depending on how a partner's departure is planned and executed, it could indeed violate obligations to the firm. Burns asserted that Croce "secretly orchestrated" the defections before he left. The suit charges he capitalized on a partner's knowledge of staff salaries in "pirating key managers and employees."

In his deposition, Croce acknowledged meeting secretly with a half-dozen Grant Thornton staffers in the two months before his departure to discuss the new firm's medical benefits. He indicated the employees' salaries were agreed upon before he left Grant Thornton. It is also alleged that Croce hinted to some staff members that, once he took the accounts they worked on, their jobs at Grant Thornton would be eliminated anyhow. Grant Thornton's attorney also grilled Croce on how and when he informed clients of his plans. The CPA said that he had told some client groups in August, but without soliciting them.

Simply calling clients a couple weeks before moving to a new job is clearly not a problem, says Vapnek. "The fact is that you're entitled to change jobs, and you're entitled to let people know you've changed jobs and you'd be happy to take their business."

Again, however, there are limits. "Whether while you're working for a company you can actively solicit business (for a rival firm in the making), that's a more difficult question," Vapnek says. And it would be a clear-cut breach of fiduciary duty for a partner to urge a client to postpone its business until the partner hangs up a separate shingle.

Taking along one's staff also has its risks. "Recruiting employees, knowing their salaries and offering them a thousand or two more . . . that could create some liability on the part of the departing person," says Vapnek. "A partner clearly has fiduciary obligations. But if (the recruiter) were just one of the employees, then there are fewer obligations."

So far, the Croce case has been something of a standoff. In the first round, Grant Thornton won a temporary restraining order that bars Croce from removing additional documents from his former office or recruiting any Grant Thornton employees beyond the ten he'd already hired. But Gary Christopherson, one of Croce's attorneys, says that what Grant Thornton didn't get is more significant. "They sought to prevent him from practicing, which the court refused to permit," Christopherson says. "That was probably more a ruling in favor of Rudy Croce than in favor of Grant Thornton."

A ruling on Croce's motion for summary judgment against Grant Thornton is expected shortly. Otherwise, the case will go to trial in September. Whatever the outcome of this particular case, disputes over splintered partnerships will undoubtedly continue as long as lawyers, CPAs and other professionals ply their crafts. After all, professional partnerships are living organisms, and like the most basic of life forms, dividing and multiplying is a part of their natural cycle.

Right To Bind the Partnership

An associate is passed over for partnership but a group of partners promises him he will make it next year. Do these partners have the authority to bind the partnership?

Contract—No Breach
Michigan Lawyers Weekly

Where plaintiff's reliance on a promise was not reasonable, defendant was properly granted summary disposition.

Plaintiff worked for defendant-partnership. When he did not make partner, he told defendant he was quitting. Defendant persuaded plaintiff not to quit. Several partners told defendant if he did not make a major blunder he would make partner the next year. The next year plaintiff did not make partner. Plaintiff sued defendant for damages, breach of contract, fraudulent misrepresentation, or gross negligence or recklessness. The trial court granted defendant summary disposition. Plaintiff appeals.

The partners who convinced plaintiff to stay had no authority to bind the whole partnership. The partnership required a two-thirds majority to allow another partner into the firm. There were 60 partners when the promise was made to plaintiff. Only five partners made plaintiff that promise. Plaintiff admitted he knew the vote was required. It was unreasonable for plaintiff to rely on their promise. The court properly found plaintiff failed to state a cause of action.

However, the court improperly dismissed plaintiff's claim for bonus, vacation and personal leave benefits. The court found that plaintiff failed to exhaust his remedies under the Wages and Fringe Benefits Act. In Murphy v. Sears, 190 Mich. App. 384 (1991), this court held "that when an employee seeks redress for a common law right, such as enforcement of a contract, exhaustion is not required because the statutory remedy is deemed to be cumulative." Plaintiff was attempting to enforce a contract. Therefore, he was not required to pursue his administrative remedy first.

Affirmed in part and reversed in part.

Dorsey v. Plante & Moran.

Copyright © 1993 by Michigan Lawyers Weekly. *Michigan Lawyers Weekly*, Jan. 25, 1993, p.10. Reprinted with permission.

Joint and Several Liability

Although partners in accounting and law firms have always been jointly and severally liable for partnership debts, in the past these debts rarely exceeded the limits of modest malpractice insurance. Fueled by troubles in the savings and loan industry, and by a general increase in litigation, partners are now increasingly threatened with major liability.

$400 Million S&L Case Penalty; Accounting Firm Accused of Lax Audits
Michael Arndt, *Chicago Tribune*

Ernst & Young, one of the nation's Big Six accounting firms, paid the government $400 million Monday to settle federal complaints over audits of a dozen insolvent banks and savings and loans, including four of the most notorious—and costliest—failures of the 1980s. The sum was the second largest ever paid in connection with the collapse of the savings and loan industry, trailing only the more than $1 billion that junk-bond tycoon Michael Milken and Drexel Burnham Lambert Inc. remitted to resolve federal claims and criminal charges against them.

Ernst & Young audited the books of as many as 300 thrifts that failed over the last seven years, according to federal regulators. These included Charles Keating Jr.'s Lincoln Savings and Loan Association of Irvine, Calif., which cost taxpayers $2 billion after it was shut down. Also among the accounting firm's clients were Silverado Banking, Savings and Loan Association of Denver; Vernon Savings and Loan Association of Vernon, Texas; and Western Savings Association of Dallas. Reimbursing depositors of these three thrifts cost taxpayers an additional $3.5 billion.

The $400 million settlement was split between the Federal Deposit Insurance Corp., which regulates banks, and the Resolution Trust Corp., the federal agency created to salvage insolvent S&Ls, with roughly two-thirds of the money paid to the FDIC.

Regulators said they found evidence of improper auditing by Ernst & Young at roughly 12 institutions. If all of these cases had been brought to trial, the government would have been entitled to more than $1 billion, said Harris Weinstein, chief counsel for the Office of Thrift Supervision (OTS). In the firm's work for Western Savings alone, the FDIC had been seeking

Copyrighted © 1992 by Chicago Tribune Co. All rights reserved. *Chicago Tribune*, Nov. 24, 1992. p.1. Used with permission.

$560 million, alleging in a 1990 lawsuit that Ernst & Young accountants should have uncovered irregularities that hid the thrift's losses from regulators, thus allowing it to remain open and lose even more money.

But regulators decided to settle their complaints for $400 million to avoid having to take each case to court, which, Weinstein said, could have dragged on for as long as ten years and cost $150 million in legal fees—with no guarantee of receiving anything. Ernst & Young Chairman Ray Groves also cited the likely huge and drawn-out expense of litigation as the firm's reason for agreeing to pay. "Although this is a costly settlement, it is the only realistic solution to an endless stream of lawsuits that would have been even more expensive to defend," he said.

Ernst & Young offered to negotiate a settlement last March, shortly after a New York law firm, Kaye, Scholer, Fierman, Hays & Handler, agreed to pay $41 million to the OTS over its legal work for Keating. The government had sought $275 million from the firm and had moved to freeze its assets.

With Monday's settlement, the FDIC has recovered $585 million this year from operators of failed institutions and their outside professional help, and $1.7 billion since 1985. The S&L-regulating OTS has received more than $50 million this year. These sums pale, however, when compared to the taxpayers' overall bill for the bailout, now estimated to be $120 billion—excluding interest.

House Banking Committee Chairman Henry Gonzalez (D-Texas) called the settlement fair. "The American taxpayer should not be made to pay for oversights on the part of some accounting firms."

Ernst & Young was formed in 1989 through the merger of Arthur Young & Co. and Ernst & Whinney. Based in New York, the firm has 20,000 employees and about 2,000 partners, who are the company's owners. Under the settlement, these partners are liable for $100 million, while Ernst & Young's insurance policies, underwritten largely by Lloyd's of London, are responsible for $300 million. The firm's 1991 revenue was $2.24 billion, according to Public Accounting Report, an Atlanta newsletter. In addition, one current Ernst & Young partner and two former partners were permanently barred from working for federally insured lenders. Seven others agreed to orders requiring them to get further audit training.

One of the former partners, Jack Atchison, became a top executive at Lincoln Savings' parent company, American Continental Corp., only days after overseeing the audit of the thrift's books in 1987. Lincoln Savings and American Continental were headed by Keating, the Phoenix real estate developer who was convicted of fraud for selling uninsured junk bonds to investors, many of whom were elderly and who lost their savings when the thrift failed.

In its investigation of Ernst & Young, federal regulators said accountants often took the word of S&L operators without verification. They also didn't adequately review real estate appraisals, thus missing instances when these values were purposely exaggerated. Ernst & Young accountants also failed to detect or disclose transactions between thrifts and related entities that allowed S&L operators to hide losses on real estate developments from regulators. For example, Silverado set up a partnership in 1984 with Silverado-Elektra Venture Ltd. to develop real estate. But though Silverado was the sole owner of Silverado-Elektra, its losses weren't included in Silverado's books, the government said in court documents released Monday.

Though the Ernst & Young settlement is the largest among accounting firms, it is not the only such firm that regulators have accused of improperly auditing the financial statements of S&Ls and banks that later became insolvent. For example, Coopers & Lybrand, another Big Six firm based in New York, agreed to pay $20 million to the government two years ago over its audits of Silverado, where President Bush's son Neil had been a director. And Arthur Andersen & Co., the nation's biggest accounting firm, was cited for negligently auditing the books of Benjamin Franklin Savings Association of Houston, which was shut down in March, 1989. In a civil lawsuit filed last July, the RTC is seeking $400 million from the Chicago-based firm.

Chapter 35

Life and Death of a Corporation

Incorporation Process

Piercing the Corporate Veil

Incorporation Process

Corporation law offered these lawyers an entrepreneurial opportunity—they have formed a business to incorporate your business.

Firm Helps Companies Go Corporate
Lisa Baertlein, *Palm Beach Post*

Anyone can form a corporation. Just get a how-to book, fill out the necessary forms, send the required fees then wait a couple of weeks for your papers. Then you can file for your tax identification number and wait anywhere from a day to four weeks for that. Sounds easy, right? And it is—if you know the answers to questions like these: When is it best to form a limited partnership, a limited liability company or a non-profit? Who is eligible to elect S Corporation status? You could hire a lawyer but one look at the fees, ranging anywhere from $500 to $1,000, and you're likely to reconsider the do-it-yourself route.

A local company offers another option. Brothers Frank and Johnny Rodriguez head Corporate Creations, a business to incorporate your business. For about $195, or about $75 more than filing fees, they can set up a Florida corporation and check the availability of a corporate name in 24 hours. Both brothers are licensed to practice law in Florida, so they can answer some of those confounding questions. "It's not worth an entrepreneur's time and money when (this service) is available at such a cheap cost," said Johnny Rodriguez, vice president.

A Harvard University Law School graduate with dreams of being his own boss, Frank launched the business from his Palm Beach Gardens home in January 1993. And he left an associate position with Steel Hector & Davis to do it. In November, Johnny left the Miami firm of Shutts & Bowen and set up in his Miami Beach residence. Independence, that's the most important thing to us," said Frank Rodriguez.

But independence has not meant shunning the legal community they left. In fact, law firms now make up the bulk of their business. Last year Corporate Creations filed 200 corporate applications. This year, said Frank, they expect to hit their goal of 500 incorporations, or about $400,000 in gross annual sales. In the future they plan to capture an ever-increasing percentage of the 90,000 companies that incorporate in Florida each year.

"When I have to get something done quickly, I call Frank," said Richard B. Comiter of the West Palm Beach-based firm August Comiter Kulunas

Copyright © 1994 by Palm Beach Newspaper, Inc. *Palm Beach Post*, July 13, 1994, p.4B.

& Schepps. Comiter completes the paperwork and uses Corporate Creations for expedited electronic filings and tax lien searches.

The company can file corporations in all 50 states, but only those with electronic filing capabilities offer the potential for same-day service. Available in Florida, Delaware and a handful of other states, electronic filing with the secretary of state's office enables efficiency and quick turnaround times. That means businesses can get up and running faster.

While corporate filings make up the majority of their income, on-line trademark searches, with prices ranging from $99 to $550, is the company's emerging money maker, said Johnny Rodriguez.

Jim Tittle, partner in the law firm of Beverly & Tittle, uses Corporate Creations to clear out the busy work that takes time away from his legal work. "That's good for my clients who want everything done yesterday," Tittle said. Even better, he said, the work is done by a Harvard-educated lawyer, not a paralegal. Frank Rodriguez's success inspires a little envy, Tittle admits. "He told the firm to chuck it and now he works out of his house," he said.

Piercing the Corporate Veil

Incorporation is no guarantee against personal liability for a business owner.

Suits Go After Personal Assets Of Firm Owners
Barbara Marsh, *Wall Street Journal*

The shield of incorporation is wearing perilously thin for a growing number of small-business owners. Entrepreneurs often incorporate to limit their exposure to business litigation. But now, many owners risk losing their homes, cars, yachts and retirement savings as more courts held them responsible in lawsuits against their businesses. The recent proliferation of regulations protecting the environment and workers' rights has led many courts to tear down the corporate shield of owners regarding claims in these areas.

Shareholders of closely held companies "face increased liability for

---

Reprinted by permission of *Wall Street Journal*, © 1994, Dow Jones & Company, Inc. All Rights Reserved Worldwide.

environmental, pension and other claims against the corporation," cautions Robert Thompson, a law professor at Washington University in St. Louis.

Feeling Defenseless

Prof. Thompson says that the number of closely tracked cases attempting to pierce the "corporate veil" increased 75 percent to 286 over the past decade—and an estimated 60 percent of those involved private companies. In an earlier study, he had found that courts decided against sole shareholders of private firms in nearly half of 276 cases studied.

Entrepreneurs feel nearly defenseless against the threat of such litigation. "I'm scared to death," says Jonathan Sklar, an owner of Spexus Inc., a small computer consulting firm in Arlington, Va. "Is there anything we can do about it? No."

Such suits often surprise business owners because they chose the corporate form to shield themselves from liability. With few exceptions, courts historically have upheld the principle that a corporation is separate from its shareholders, officers and directors, legal scholars say. Shareholders generally only risked their investment in the corporation; their personal assets were beyond the reach of a lawsuit. By contrast, general partners in a partnership are personally liable for the business's obligations.

Personal Exposure

A lawsuit involving the Adkins family typifies the new ways that courts are broadening the personal exposure of small-business owners. The family operated a coal mine in Hippo, Ky. In June, Orville Adkins, his wife, Dixie, their son Adam and Adam's wife, Sally, got a jolt from a federal appeals court in Washington, D.C. Union pension plans for retired coal miners had sued the family and its holdings to recover nearly $2 million for the plans' unfunded pension liabilities plus interest, according to Kenneth Robbett, a Washington, D.C., attorney for the Adkinses.

A trial court previously decided that the pension plans couldn't impose personal liability on the family for their investment in several hundred acres of farming properties, where they hunt, fish and take vacations. But the appeals court disagreed. It ordered the trial court to reconsider whether the plans can go after the Adkinses' farm and other personal assets, Mr. Robbett says.

The case illustrates how far pension plans can go these days to recover claims, the attorney notes. "No one would expect that their hobby or recreation—in this case a glorified garden—would subject them to personal liability as a result of a technicality in pension law," he says. A lawyer for the pension plan declines to comment.

Shareholders of private firms are peculiarly vulnerable to such suits because they often own and manage their companies. That dual role gives courts dual reasons to hold them personally liable for a company's actions, legal experts say. "It is only the small entrepreneurs who get hit with this," says Stephen Presser, a Northwestern University law professor who has written extensively on the subject.

Defining an Owner

Many recent claims against private shareholders involve alleged violations of federal laws on cleanup of environmental hazards. Under those laws, an "owner" or "operator" of a facility where hazardous substances were disposed is liable for removal costs or other remedial action.

Some federal courts have interpreted the definition of owner or operator to include shareholders of private firms. Last March, a federal appeals court in Cincinnati held a sole shareholder of a defunct auto-parts maker liable for pollution at the firm's waste dump in the 1970s. For a time, barrels of manufacturing sludge had been discarded on land leased to the company by the owner's sister, according to the court's opinion. In 1987, a couple buying the waste-dump site—Richard Donahey and his wife, Patricia—sued the company, its owner and the owner's sister.

Seabourn Livingstone, the company's now-retired owner, didn't know about the waste disposal, the opinion notes. Still, the court found in March that he had "the authority to prevent the contamination of the property by his corporation" and therefore was one of several people responsible. "It's an awful finding," says Henry Carnaby, a Troy, Mich., attorney for Mr. Livingstone.

The opinion says the Donaheys should recover legal fees in an amount to be deemed "reasonable" by the lower court, which had originally ruled that Mr. Livingstone wasn't liable. The Donaheys sought to recover $279,000 in legal fees, though Mr. Carnaby says he may appeal the appellate ruling. A separate, even costlier issue looms: Mr. Livingstone and the others involved in the case have not learned yet who must pay the estimated $1 million-plus for the site's eventual cleanup.

Stiffer Penalties

In some fields, pressure on business owners has been building for a number of years. Owners of small businesses now face stiffer personal penalties in a widening array of cases involving state regulation of workers' welfare. Certain state courts gradually have extended corporations' traditional liability for workers' claims to their owners.

In an important 1987 ruling, an Illinois appeals court in Chicago upheld a trial court's $73,690 judgment against Joel Ross, an owner of a local movie theater, for his failure to pay employees' union dues and welfare contributions, according to the appellate opinion. A collective-bargaining agreement with the company had provided for such payments.

Mr. Ross sought to avoid personal liability by claiming that the union's trust fund didn't demonstrate that he had knowingly or willfully refused to make the payments, the opinion says. But as the company's president and chief operating officer, Mr. Ross had made payments and so knew about his obligation, the court ruled. Mr. Ross couldn't be reached for comment.

Chapter 36

Corporate Management

Duty of Care

Business Judgment Rule

Takeovers

Duty of Care

Who serves on boards of directors? What role do directors play in a company? Are directors more than "pet rocks," as Ross Perot once called them?

When Directors' Cheers Become Jeers, Execs on Hot Seat; New Assertiveness Challenges "Pet Rock," Rubber Stamp Images
Nancy Ryan, *Chicago Tribune*

Because it isn't often that the chief executive of one of the country's largest corporations gets the boot from the company board, small shareholders and top executives sometimes forget a simple fact: "All power in a corporation is in the board of directors. Corporate officers really serve at the pleasure of the board," said John C. Coffee Jr., professor of corporate and securities law at Columbia University School of Law. But because that authority usually lies dormant, boards often are cynically viewed as rubber stamps for a company's top executives—or "pet rocks," as Ross Perot once characterized the General Motors Corp. board.

Obviously that has changed at GM, as well as at other companies in crisis. The growing influence of institutional investors, mainly pensions and mutual funds, that own large blocks of stock and the higher proportion of directors from outside a corporation have led to more assertive boards in the last two decades. The owners of a company, after all, are the shareholders, not the executives—and the directors work for the owners. Nevertheless, most chief executives don't live in fear of boards, mainly because CEOs generally have a major hand in deciding who sits on boards.

Who does sit on boards? And what do directors do when they're not working under unusual pressure? The number of directors of a typical Fortune 500 company can range from 13 to 18. The average compensation, whether through stock or salary, is $30,000 to $40,000 a year, Coffee said; directors often are paid by the meeting. The chief executive always sits on the board. Other top executives usually are directors as well, but the declining proportion of company insiders is one of the major changes seen in boards and is a driving factor behind their growing activism. As recently as 15 years ago, half the directors on the average board were executives. Now about one-third are insiders.

Copyrighted © 1992 by Chicago Tribune Co. All rights reserved. *Chicago Tribune*, Oct. 28, 1992, p.1. Used with permission.

Sitting or retired chief executives or chief financial officers of other Fortune 500 companies make up the largest portion of large companies' outside directors, Coffee said. Next come university chancellors, business- and law-school deans, former holders of major government posts, such as Cabinet or Federal Reserve Board officers, and directors of major not-for-profit groups. The GM board includes the past and present presidents of the California Institute of Technology, a former U.S. secretary of labor and former GM chief executives.

"Then, there's some dim recognition of the desirability of getting people on the board who are not white males," Coffee said. "It's still at the level of one or two directors." GM's board includes two women and one black director, a retired Baptist minister.

Most chief executives usually only have time to sit on one or two other boards. But some outside directors, so-called professional directors, sit on as many as a dozen or more. GM director Ann D. McLaughlin lists board memberships at seven public and private concerns.

Most boards meet about six or eight times a year, though GM's meets monthly. Board committees meet separately. Major ones can include the nominating (for new directors), finance, executive-compensation, audit and social-responsibility committees.

As the forced resignation of GM Chairman Robert Stempel showed, the board's most important job is to oversee top managers and select a chief executive's successor. Directors also determine a chief executive's salary and other compensation. They evaluate whether the company is managed well, based on gauges such as stock price and quarterly earnings, said Steven Kaplan, a professor of finance at the University of Chicago Graduate School of Business. They take part in long-term strategy decisions, especially those that involve major capital expenditures and acquisitions and divestitures. Other responsibilities involve making sure the company is in compliance with audit, environmental and equal-opportunity laws and overseeing employee benefits such as health insurance.

Directors increasingly find themselves embroiled in public controversies as major shareholders cry foul over bloated executive salaries and hemorrhaging operations. Spearheading this movement are the giant funds, whose equity ownership in companies has grown from 33.1 percent in 1980 to 53.3 percent in 1990, according to a study by the Columbia University School of Law.

In the 1980s, however, boards' major preoccupations were threats of hostile takeovers. That's no longer true, meaning boards can focus on other issues, including the performance of CEOs. "Given that hostile takeovers have basically been severely regulated," Kaplan said, "I think you'll see more boards taking action—because you don't have that external pressure anymore."

Business Judgment Rule

This article suggests that an erosion in the business judgment rule has *reduced* executive responsibility.

"Not Me": The New Corporate Candor
Margot Slade, *International Herald Tribune*

Looking for an excuse? Relax. In a burst of innovation, imagination and, yes, desperation, American business has devised a collection of cop-outs to suit the harried executive who is performance impaired. Just try these "explanations" for recent foul-ups on for size:

- A missing minus sign is how Fidelity Investments explained a $2 billion-plus mistake in calculating Magellan Fund shareholder payments, saying an accountant omitted the minus from a spread sheet and no one noticed.
- Intel Corp., explaining to millions of owners of Pentium-equipped computers why it was not recalling and replacing the defective chip, said the device only rarely goofed at long division. (The company ultimately agreed to replace, but not recall, the chip, after howls of protest.)
- Among a long list of big-money losers in the derivatives debacle, blue-chip companies such as Gibson Greetings Inc. and Marion Merrell Dow Inc. are explaining their misfortune by saying they are financial rubes.

Don't worry if nothing fits. By all accounts, the market for excuses—good, bad and ridiculous—is growing, a veritable hotbed of corporate creativity. Scarcely a day goes by without a statement from a captain of industry or mover of money that tries to distance the person in charge—or even the one with the smoking gun—from the latest bottom-line disaster.

To be sure, excuses are a familiar fixture on the American business scene. Just look at William Agee, late of Bendix and now Morrison Knudsen Corp., whose explanations for management missteps over a 30-year career must be legend among a select but growing boardroom crowd. But students of blame say the corporate environment has changed, making excuse now a preferred mode of operation. Paradoxically, the change resulted from an effort to make executives more accountable for their actions, not less.

Copyright © 1995 by International Herald Tribune. *International Herald Tribune*, Feb. 20, 1995, "Finance." Reprinted with permission.

"There's been a chipping away at the business judgment rule, which states that just because a management decision turns out badly does not make it subject to litigation or regulation," said Clifford W. Smith Jr., the Clarey Professor of Finance at the University of Rochester's Simon School of Business Administration. The purpose of the rule, Mr. Smith said, was to free management to make decisions without being subjected to the crippling effects of Monday-morning quarterbacking.

But it has also been used to shield executives from valid criticism. "To the extent that plaintiffs' lawyers, the Securities and Exchange Commission or others say they'll scrutinize a company when things go badly and go after its managers with a class action or regulatory club," he said, "the market for excuses will grow."

Fueling that growth is the increased use of consultants, what many executives bluntly describe as expensive but convenient scapegoats. "My friends who work for Fortune 100 corporations say that whenever questioned a corporate type can say, 'But that's what the consultants told us to do,' " said Sarah A. B. Teslik, the executive director of the Council of Institutional Investors, an organization of 100 of the nation's largest pension funds.

And with more top and middle management coming from a kind of no-fault "Not Me Generation," that is precisely what contemporary corporate types are likely to say, according to Jeffrey Sonnenfeld, the director of the Center for Leadership and Career Studies at Emory Business School. "They are children of the '50s—conformists, not mavericks or creators," he said. "As a general rule, they want to duck responsibility, not embrace it."

The not-me attitude, which often translates into a blame-others approach, may indeed get an executive off the hook, for a while. But it could prove damaging to the executive's company and eventually the economy, experts say, since the problem in question may wind up being ignored or buried until it recurs or gets worse.

Analysts say that in today's competitive economy, business leaders are so error-averse that they offer euphemistic excuses for plant closings or sluggish sales when unvarnished truth will do. They know, for example, that on Wall Street "restructuring means never having to say you're sorry," said Jerry Sterner, a businessman-turned-playwright who wrote the Off-Broadway success "Other People's Money."

"Just talk about restructuring as positive and investors will buy it," Mr. Sterner said. "It's really an admission of failure: We're closing this operation and firing these people so that we can stay in business. But we ain't paying the price. The employees, the community—they pay the price. Meanwhile, the executives' salaries go up and their benefits increase because they are making the 'hard decisions.' "

Takeovers

Poison pills are among the most common anti-takeover device. Chrysler's pill helped protect the company from Kirk Kerkorian's takeover attempt.

Poison Pill Proves Bitter Medicine
Gareth Hewett, *South China Morning Post*

Poison pills are a hot topic of legal and corporate governance debate in the United States. The ambitious takeover bid by 77-year-old Kirk Kerkorian of car giant Chrysler Corp, valuing the company at US $22.8 billion, has brought many of these issues into strong relief. It was a poison pill put in place in 1990 that has restricted this acquisitive shareholder from holding more than 10 percent of Chrysler's stock.

According to reports, Mr. Kerkorian bought shares in Chrysler during 1990 in what was described then as passive investment. The poison pill provision was put in place when directors feared that his purchase of large numbers of Chrysler shares was the start of a takeover attempt. The provisions were intended to make a hostile takeover prohibitively expensive.

Mr. Kerkorian's beef with Chrysler is that while he is showing a pretty good paper profit over the period, he argues the price of his shares has not reflected the big leap in profits seen last year, after a turbulent three years of net earnings swinging wildly between profits and losses. Last November Mr. Kerkorian demanded better treatment as a shareholder and he got it in the form of a 60 percent rise in the dividend payout and a start in share buyback activity at the corporation.

Roger Monks and Nell Minow say in *Power and Accountability* that poison pills are the nuclear weapons of corporate control battles in the US. They are not common in Hong Kong and other major centres in Asia because on the whole the main shareholders or families behind the companies involved are controlling shareholders. There is a shareholder ownership restriction under the Hong Kong and Shanghai Banking Corporation Ordinance which requires investors of more than 10 percent of the issued shares of the bank to obtain approval from the central banking authority before they exercise their voting rights. Similar approval applies for a change in ownership involving more than 50 percent or more of a bank in the territory.

Poison pills, as they exist in the US, were first upheld in a famous court

Copyright © 1995 by South China Morning Post Ltd. *South China Morning Post*, Apr. 18, 1995, p.24.

case in Delaware called Moran v. Household in 1985. They have emerged as a means by which listed company management could effectively stave off contested takeovers. The initiative was triggered by the emergence of a plague of opportunist takeovers in the 1980s as new sources of money and new instruments came into being which enabled raiders to take on just about any corporation in the US of any size.

The investor may well ask exactly who was to benefit from these poison pills and to what end were they being put by the management. Many argued corporations needed protection from opportunist takeover because this type of activity was taking place without any cognisance of the target's qualities as a corporation doing real business and instead sought to tear the heart out of American commerce, all in favour of making a quick buck.

This ultimate deterrent has been behind effectively robbing the rights of ordinary shareholders in favour of the interests of management. Corporate jets, golf club memberships, club house parties and corporate holiday condos all appeared to be to the benefit of the management.

Where you stand on poison pills will depend on where you sit, say Monks and Minow. Their existence in the US is testament to the huge division in outlook and interest that has grown up in the US between a corporation's shareholders, its board and management.

Mr. Kerkorian is an extremely big fish able to not only express his dissatisfaction with circumstances, but is able to do something about it.

In the US, it is argued, the corporate interest—as identified by professional management—has subjugated the interests of the board and shareholders. In Hong Kong, one can observe, corporate interest—as identified by the controlling shareholders who are represented by the board—has total hegemony over the rights and interests of the shareholders.

In both cases there is a need for the legitimate rights of long-term investors to be protected to a greater extent, although the abusers of these rights and the tools that they use in their unwholesome deeds are quite different. The end result has tended to be the same.

Chapter 37

Shareholders

Shareholder Meetings

Rights of Shareholders

Right to Protection from Other Shareholders

Shareholder Meetings

Are annual meetings an idea whose time has passed? Is there a better forum in which management and shareholders could meet?

Companies Cut Back on Annual Meetings; Rite of Spring Pared To Save Time, Money
David Young, *Chicago Tribune*

Spring is a time of gentle showers, gaily colored flowers, budding bowers and that most unnatural of vernal wonders—the corporate annual meeting. In hotel ballrooms, dining halls and conference rooms nationwide, shareholders are now gathering to tell the corporations they own how to run the business. At least that's the way it's supposed to work.

But these days corporations are cutting annual meetings to the bone—to save money and because many executives and big institutional shareholders consider them 19th Century anachronisms. Even General Motors Corp. is scaling back. Indeed, officials of some companies admit privately they would do away with the meetings if stock-exchange regulations and, in many cases, state laws did not require them. The voting now is done by mailed-in proxies before the meetings are gaveled to order. And communication with shareholders, at least the big ones, is done by fax, computer or in private briefings.

Louis M. Thompson Jr., president of the National Investor Relations Institute in Washington, said a survey by his organization last year indicated companies believe annual meetings are no longer productive because of the time and expense involved. Though most corporations are reluctant to discuss how much they spend on annual meetings, executives with big companies indicated that the tab can run from $10,000 to several million dollars.

The annual meeting also is becoming increasingly difficult to justify for companies with shareholders scattered all over the world, said John D. Nichols, chairman of Illinois Tool Works Inc. in Glenview. "Just as the annual report is obsolete in the form we know it, so is the annual meeting," agreed Robert L. Heidrich, head of Heidrich Partners, a Chicago-based search firm. "Possibly 1 percent of the shares are represented at the annual meeting."

Still, the meetings provide "an opportunity for shareholders to discuss their opinions," said Jack Reichert, chairman of Lake Forest-based Bruns-

Copyrighted © 1995 by Chicago Tribune Co. All rights reserved. *Chicago Tribune*, Apr. 21, 1995, p.1. Used with permission.

wick Corp, "although we don't get too many comments. We get more retirees than investors."

Unlike many other companies, McDonald's Corp. packs 2,000 shareholders and employees into its suburban Oak Brook headquarters each year. The company has videotaped its meeting for several years and last year sent out 4,000 copies worldwide. Company officials have even talked about a live broadcast to offices and franchises worldwide, said Mary Healy, head of investor relations.

Another company that still attracts a crowd is ServiceMaster L.P. In May it puts up a circus tent on a parking lot next to its corporate headquarters in Downers Grove and holds what one official calls "a company celebration" that still includes a free lunch and shareholder gift. They welcome families with kids and have packed 1,000 people into the tent the last two years, said David P. Aldridge, vice president for educational development. This year they will enlarge the tent because they expect 1,200.

The annual meeting at most corporations, at the minimum, is a forum for shareholders to elect directors and approve the auditor for company books. Sometimes, shareholders will vote on stock-option or long-term incentive plans. Only rarely does the annual meeting serve as the scene of a proxy fight for control of the company. Still, it can happen, as it did last year at Elgin-based Katy Industries, though the effort was easily held off.

Critics note that the dwindling number of stockholders who go to annual meetings typically hear only a summary of the same financial data contained in the company's annual report, which they receive a month earlier. And while shareholders once received samples of company products and a nice lunch, those perks are few and far between today.

Furthermore, there is little likelihood shareholders will hear bombshells at the annual gathering. Securities and Exchange Commission rules require major announcements to be made to the public; even a good turnout at an annual meeting typically represents only a fraction of shareholders. "By the time the meeting is held, the annual reports and proxies are out, so there is nothing to announce," said Nichols of ITW, who also is a director of Philip Morris Companies, Rockwell International Corp. and Stone Container Corp.

Federal Signal Corp., just across the East-West Tollway from McDonald's, is a case in point. "About 1987, I sent out a 'dis-invitation,' " explained Chairman Joseph J. Ross. "We worried about what the reaction would be, but it was positive." He took the action to cut unnecessary costs after noticing that the annual meeting had become a free lunch and expensive three-projector slide show mostly for employees. Since getting rid of the lunch and slide show, attendance has dropped from a high of 250 to about 80, and Ross estimates he saves the company about $125,000 a year.

Critics claim a big factor in corporate America's interest in getting rid of the annual meetings is to avoid the "gadfly factor"—a term that can mean anything from a single individual who asks embarrassing questions to disenchanted labor unions. Legendary gadfly Wilma Soss showed up at U.S. Steel

Corp.'s meeting in 1949 dressed in Victorian attire to protest management's attitude toward shareholders. In 1960, she came to Columbia Broadcasting Co.'s meeting decked out as a charwoman to demand a cleanup of the network after the quiz-show scandals. Soss died in 1986. No replacement has emerged.

Even the giant California Public Employees Retirement System has largely abandoned the annual meeting as a platform to reform corporate America. The state pension fund, which in the 1980s engaged in several expensive proxy battles at annual meetings, now has enough clout to go directly to the boards.

Rights of Shareholders

Robert Monks is a well-known shareholder activist. In this article, he details his efforts to win a seat on the Sears Roebuck board of directors. Note that he failed, even though the Sears bylaws provide for cumulative voting.

My Battle for the Boardroom
Robert A. G. Monks, *Manhattan Lawyer*

A few months ago, I did something no other person has ever done before. I engaged in a proxy contest for one seat on the board of a public company. The company was Sears, Roebuck and Co. They defended me, this year. But the contest dramatized some of the critical concerns the Securities and Exchange Commission currently is addressing in its comprehensive review of proxy rules. And if the SEC levels the playing field, future contests might be very different.

The challenge began last November, when I submitted my name to the Sears board's nominating committee, along with my references—six CEOs of companies on whose boards I had served. I chose Sears because it was a major and highly visible U.S. company with an operating division in my field of expertise (financial services), because it was poorly managed (For-

---

Copyright © 1991 by American Lawyer Newspapers Group, Inc. *Manhattan Lawyer*, Sep. 1991, p.44. Reprinted with permission. Robert A. G. Monks is president of Washington, D.C.-based Institutional Shareholder Partners. He is the author, with Nell Minow, of *Power and Accountability*.

tune recently ranked it 297 out of 300 and not once in the last decade did it meet its own goal of a 15 percent return on equity), and because there was scheduled to be a vacancy on the board.

Sears did not call any of my references, and the directors did not discuss my candidacy at the November board meeting; they said it was because they did not have enough information. They did discuss my candidacy at the February meeting. It wasn't that they used the extra time to get more information; they didn't. They explained later that they decided additional information was not necessary, because my record, already well known to them, clearly qualified me for the job. But I was missing one important qualification. They did not come to me; I came to them.

The board turned me down. But Sears' own bylaws provide that a shareholder may nominate a candidate for the board. Apparently the corporate leaders think this is a fine system—as long as no one tries to use it. My old friend and business associate (and Sears shareholder), Arthur Dubow, nominated me. This threw Sears management into such a tizzy that the board hired Martin Lipton of Wachtell, Lipton, Rosen & Katz, filed suit to stop me, and budgeted $5.5 million over and above its usual solicitation expense just to defeat me (as Crain's Chicago Business pointed out, one out of every seven dollars made by the retail operation last year). The company also assigned 30 employees to spend their time working to defeat my candidacy.

Honey, I Shrunk the Board

The real outrage was that the board got rid of three of its own directors just to prevent me from winning one seat. With cumulative voting—allowing a shareholder to distribute his per-share votes the way he wants among the candidates, including casting them all for one candidate—and five directors up for election, I could have gotten a seat with only 16 percent of the vote, not impossible for someone with strong connections to large institutional holders. But Sears shrunk its board by eliminating three director seats, which meant that I needed 21 percent of the vote to win a seat; virtually impossible to obtain, because 25 percent of the vote was held by Sears employees (and voted by Sears trustees) and 37 percent was held by individuals whom I could not possibly solicit without spending millions of dollars.

The myth is that the officers of the company report to the board. The reality is that the board reports to the CEO, at least at Sears. When the CEO (who is also chairman of the board and head of the board's nominating committee) tells three directors they are off, they are off, especially, as in this case, when they are inside directors, full-time employees of the corporation.

Following approval and mailing of its own proxy statement, Sears was free to have press conferences and to comment to the press on my candidacy—but I was not permitted to respond. The weird world of SEC regulation prevented me from making any public statement for two crucial weeks, while the SEC reviewed my solicitation materials. SEC rules also prevented me from making clear to shareholders that I was not out to displace anyone. One of the reasons I picked Sears was that there was an opening on the board with the retirement of former CEO Edward Telling. Therefore, I wanted to put Sears' candidates on my proxy card, so that a shareholder could vote for me and for two of the incumbent directors. But the SEC said no.

An imposing obstacle for any outsider campaigning for shareholder votes is the problem of communicating with shareholders. Sears' suit against me was aimed at preventing me from getting a shareholder list, claiming I wanted it for an "improper purpose." The "improper purpose" alleged was promoting my new book.

I would have to be Kitty Kelley to make enough money on a book to pay for a proxy contest, but I would have to be Sears to finance both a proxy contest and a lawsuit to make that point. (Sears ultimately spent only half of what it budgeted and still outspent me ten to one.) The suit effectively stopped me from communicating with smaller shareholders. Even if it had not, though, the expense probably would have been prohibitive. I could not afford the roughly $1.5 million necessary to send my proxy materials to every shareholder. So my materials went only to institutional investors—those with large enough holdings to warrant public disclosure—other large holders, and investors who called to ask for it.

Iron Curtain

Perhaps the biggest frustration was that I could not reach the largest group of shareholders: Sears' own employees. Sears offered to mail my materials to them, if I would pay $300,000 in costs. That was more than my entire budget for the solicitation, so I declined.

More serious was that the trustees of the employee stock ownership plan (four out of five of whom were past and present members of the Sears board) would have voted the stock without even considering my candidacy, if not for the intervention of the Labor Department. That resulted in a pro forma meeting with the trustees, who proceeded to vote for their board colleagues.

Many Sears employees called me to say that they were unable to get any information about my candidacy, or that they wanted their stock voted for me but could not direct it. Sears refused my request for confidential voting to permit shareholders, including Sears employees and money managers with commercial relationships to Sears, to vote without Sears knowing how they voted. This would at least have allowed employees who held stock in their own names to vote for me without fear of reprisal.

In theory, of course, the directors are there to represent the shareholders, evaluate the performance of the chief executive officer, and oversee the overall direction of the company. If they have one obligation, it seems to me, it is to ask hard questions. But the current rules not only fail to ensure that directors ask questions, they prevent others from asking them as well.

Consider Sears. Edward Brennan, an undeniably capable man, wears many hats. He is CEO of the company as a whole, chairman of the board, and head of the company's flagship division, the retail operation. Part of the description for those jobs is that the people who fill them are supposed to communicate with each other, measure each other, ask questions of each other. One person simply can't do them all. On top of that, Brennan is head of the board's nominating committee. He gets to pick his own bosses, and, as my experience shows, when faced with someone he didn't pick, can bring all of the corporate resources to bear in opposition.

Pocketful of Directors

Where was the board in all this? The answer lies in another question: Who are the directors? "Independent director" is something of an oxymoron in today's companies. As business writer Edward Jay Epstein has pointed out, shareholder elections "are procedurally much more akin to the elections held by the Communist Party of North Korea than those held in Western democracies."

The directors are selected by the CEO. The candidates run unopposed, and management counts the votes. In the rare case of an opposing slate, management gets to use the shareholders' money to pay for its side of the contest, without regard for the interests of the shareholders, while the dissidents must use their own. The CEO determines the directors' pay, and the directors set the CEO's pay. It's a very cozy relationship, and one that has been most profitable for both parties, as CEO pay and director pay have skyrocketed over the past decade at many times the rate of increase in employee pay. This system does not promote accountability, or even the questions that are a necessary predicate for a climate of accountability.

At the annual meeting, after the votes were cast, I said that Sears had changed as a result of my contest. Brennan said, "Baloney." Time will tell. But I can think of three important changes already.

First, my arguments about the ability of Sears' investment banker to give an objective opinion about the value of remaining a conglomerate led to the disclosure that Goldman, Sachs & Co. had indeed advised the company that it could realize more value—as much as three times more—by spinning off the other entities. This may not have changed Sears—yet—but it certainly changed the perception of the company in the investor community.

Second, possibly as a result, there has been some evidence that Sears is "in play." (A company spokesperson declined comment.) If Sears wants to continue as a conglomerate, it will have to find a way to produce value for shareholders.

Finally, ironically, Sears is now left with a board with a higher percentage of outside directors, directors who can expect extra focus on their election next year. Brennan may just find that at least some of the extra accountability I was seeking may be the result of the actions he took to stop me.

More important, though, are the changes I hope my candidacy will bring to the current proxy rules. The SEC is responding to hundreds of letters on proxy reform with a comprehensive review, and it has already issued the first of what are expected to be several proposals for comment. If the next person to run a proxy contest for a single board seat can do it on a level playing field, the term "independent director" will start to mean something, and Sears will not be the only company to change.

Rights of Shareholders

Ekkehard Wenger is a shareholder activist in Germany.

The Outsider
Economist

Shareholders' meetings in Germany used to be like Communist Party conventions in lands further east. Dissent was rare; decisions were nearly unanimous; applause for the ageing row of worthies running the proceedings was obligatory. Then Ekkehard Wenger came along. This Wurzburg University economics professor has made a second career lobbying for shareholders' rights with a vigour that verges on civil disobedience.

Mr. Wenger typically shows up at an annual general meeting (AGM) with a gaggle of students in tow and spends most of the early part of the meeting consorting with the press and sniggering loudly at the propaganda doled out by management. Then in mid-afternoon, when things would otherwise be winding down, he strides to the podium and, in a voice that sounds like the controlled sob of an angry child, harangues management. At Deutsche Bank's recent AGM he demanded, among other things, that the bank sell its stakes in industrial companies, that it stop exercising proxy votes without specific permission from its clients, and that the chairman of its supervisory board resign to take responsibility for a "whole row of serious mistakes."

Copyright © 1995 by The Economist Newspaper, Ltd. *Economist*, June 3, 1995, p.66. Reprinted with permission.

The performance seems calculated as much to enrage as to edify. Mr. Wenger, who began ambushing AGMS in 1987, seems pleased when he can push a meeting past dark. At Daimler-Benz's AGM in 1993 he so provoked Hilmar Kopper, the Deutsche Bank chief executive who is also chairman of Daimler's supervisory board, that he was thrown out. Mr. Wenger claims to have been followed by private detectives, though he's not sure who sent them. Mr. Wenger's enemies accuse him of being a clownish self-promoter. Why should anyone listen to him?

Telling the Truth, Coarsely

Because, in most of the things that matter, Mr. Wenger has got it right; because the odds remain hopelessly stacked against him; and because his attacks are more subtle than they seem. Mr. Wenger's targets are the right ones: the excessive "influence of banks on industry, murky accounting rules, multiple voting rights and other things that help managers and exclude ordinary shareholders.

His enemies tend to pooh-pooh his claims. For example, Germany's Banking Association claims that between 1976 and 1994 big private banks' stakes in industry fell from a tiny 1.3 percent of total capital to a tinier 0.4 percent. That may be true, but banks' stakes in big companies are considerably bigger and their power is enhanced by proxy votes and cross shareholdings. For instance, Allianz, an insurer that owns many stakes in industrial companies, is 35 percent owned by four banks, including Deutsche, which hold stakes in the same companies. At many AGMS, banks have a lock on shareholder votes (see table).

Although Mr. Wenger wins few outright victories—none so far by shareholders' votes and rarely in court—his encyclopedic knowledge of German corporate law is helping him gradually find his foes' weak points. His 1992 proposal to liquidate a holding company that existed solely to protect Daimler-Benz from hostile takeover was rejected, but the holding company soon vanished to smooth Daimler's listing on the New York Stock Exchange. Now Mr. Wenger is pressing a suit claiming that companies violate shareholders' rights by withholding information about the value of their assets. If he wins, firms may reveal their hidden reserves.

Mr. Wenger has few natural allies because to attack the establishment in Germany is to offend virtually everybody. At Deutsche Bank's AGM his objections were recorded by one Gerold Bezzenberger, a prominent Berlin lawyer acting as the meeting's notary. The same Mr. Bezzenberger defended Siemens (and lost) in a court case brought by Mr. Wenger to force the company to disclose more of its shareholdings. Wearing yet another hat, Mr. Bezzenberger champions shareholders' interests as vice-president of the German Securities-Holders' Protection Association. Justifying his blunderbuss style, Mr. Wenger quotes Schiller: "One must tell the Germans the truth as coarsely as possible."

The closed ranks are beginning to buckle. A series of scandals, such as those involving Metallgesellschaft and Jurgen Schneider, have made banks look like indulgent overseers of German industry. Many Germans envy America, where lively capital markets and high-tech enterprise seem to go hand in hand. Liberals, who have long thought shareholders deserve a better deal, have been joined by leftists, who want to dethrone the banks.

The alliance is unnatural: leftists, after all, are fond of a system that puts the interests of "stakeholders" such as workers ahead of shareholders. Nevertheless, a government working group is likely to propose restricting the number of supervisory board seats one director can hold and making auditors more responsible to supervisory boards rather than to a company's managers. It is also likely to curb the proxy votes banks can exercise on behalf of clients. But the government's limp preference is to require banks to appoint an "independent" employee to vote the shares in clients'—rather than the bank's—interests. And the government will probably not restrict banks' holdings of non-financial companies. After all, few German politicians want to fight its biggest companies and banks.

The clique that runs German industry will not be broken by legislative fiat. Rather, it will be worn down slowly by unremitting pressure from the markets—and from Mr. Wenger. Long may he enliven AGMS.

Right to Protection from Other Shareholders

The role of minority shareholder is fraught with peril at the best of times. For the Nelson heirs, it was the worst of times.

Minority Stake Can Be Trap at Private Firms
David Young, *Chicago Tribune*

When O. T. Nelson retired in 1976 from College Craft Enterprises, a company he founded in 1969 and built into a going enterprise by using college students to paint houses, he set up a trust fund with 400 shares as an inheritance for his children. The majority block of 505 shares he sold to his

Copyrighted © 1993 by Chicago Tribune Co. All rights reserved. *Chicago Tribune*, Feb. 11, 1993, "Business," p.2. Used with permission.

associate, Scott Mennie, to continue the business. However, what Nelson's children discovered in 1988, when the trust expired, was that being a minority stockholder in a private, closely held corporation is not always the best investment. The grown Nelson children, Owen and Lisa, are engaged in a lawsuit with Mennie in Du Page County Circuit Court seeking to have the corporation's assets placed in a constructive trust.

Like almost all such suits, the real issue is the value of the investment of the minority shareholders. Such litigation is not unusual, said Charles W. Murdock, Loyola University law professor and a leading expert on minority stockholder rights in closely held corporations. It also is fraught with risks for all concerned. Protracted litigation can destroy a small company in which the principal value is that it is a going concern, the experts warn.

An estimated 12,000 to 15,000 publicly traded corporations are in existence at any time in the U.S., but in Illinois alone there are 255,021 total corporations, the vast majority of them private and small. "They are two radically different situations," said Murdock. "In a publicly held corporation, there is a market and you can get out. In a closely held corporation, the problem is that there is no market and you can't get out."

Corporate law experts call it the "locked-in, locked-out" phenomenon. Minority shareholders are locked into their investment because there is no market for their shares, but they are locked out of any decisions on the management of the company or jobs in it. That has given rise to a number of suits involving the value of minority holdings in such enterprises as the Chicago Bears, the M&R Theater chain, lumberyards and steamship companies. Often such disputes pit partners against one another, sisters against brothers, mothers against sons or nephews against nieces. That frequently means the minority shareholders are reluctant to talk publicly about their situations.

"I was surprised that people don't want their names known for fear their relatives (who often are the majority shareholders) will be offended," said Karen Lilleberg Goettsche of Inverness, a minority shareholder in a Chicago company she declined to identify. She feels so strongly about her situation that she organized a public lecture at 7:30 P.M. Thursday at the Hyatt Regency Woodfield in Schaumburg on the rights of minority shareholders. Their lot has been improving steadily, primarily because of pioneering legislation in Illinois in 1933 and more recent court decisions in Massachusetts and New York that have put curbs on the more abusive practices of the controlling stockholders.

It was not always so. Earlier in this century, penniless widows could be frozen out of corporations by their husbands' surviving partners. A majority stockholder almost with impunity could milk the company by paying himself an exorbitant salary, making loans to other enterprises he owned and setting inflated rents for property and equipment he owned but leased to the firm. As recently as last year, some of those abuses were alleged in the College Craft suit.

"Stockholders (now) have the right to see annual audits, but the company doesn't have to provide them unless you ask," said George C. Hook, a Chicago attorney practicing corporate law and editor of a forthcoming book on the Illinois Business Corporation Act. They also have the right to see the articles of incorporation and bylaws. "The first step when you become aware you are a shareholder is to sit down with the people in control and get as much information as possible," he said. Beyond that, the situation gets tricky.

Investors in public corporations get a return on the investment by means of dividends or capital gains when they sell the stock, but in most private corporations the return on investment comes mainly in the form of the salaries the firm pays stockholder-employees. Dividends, while not unknown, are rare. "When people invest in a publicly held corporation they are looking for a dollar return," said Murdock, who wrote a treatise on minority shareholders in the 1990 Notre Dame Law Review. "You don't buy stock in IBM to get a job there, but when you invest in a privately held corporation, you are looking for a job or managerial control."

Disputes frequently occur when partners gang up and fire a colleague, or when the majority stockholder dies, leaving his shares to several heirs. Goettsche said she was one of five children among whom the stock was split in the second generation of her family-owned business and the only one who did not get a job. The rest of the family has offered to buy her out, but the two sides can't agree on a price, said her uncle, who runs the company.

The Bears case makes Goettsche's look simple. Christine and Stephen Halas were by inheritance the third-generation stockholders in the Bears, an enterprise founded by their grandfather, George Halas Sr. When their father, George "Mugs" Halas Jr., died in 1979, George Sr. became trustee of his son's estate. At the same time, he reorganized the team's corporation under Delaware law to make it more difficult for minority shareholders to exercise control, said Stephen Fedo, attorney for the subsequent executor of Mugs' estate. Delaware law is less protective of minority shareholders than the Illinois act.

After George Sr. died in 1983, the new executor for Mugs' estate was forced to file a suit charging that in reorganizing the corporation the way he did, George Sr. had breached his fiduciary responsibility to the minority shares he held in trust for his grandchildren. The court agreed he had erred but could not determine what the damages should be, "because there was no way to determine what the minority interest was worth," Fedo said. Determining the value of the minority interests is the big problem in most such cases, especially because a majority buyout of the minority often is the only way to resolve such disputes, according to the experts.

The Halas grandchildren came out better than most minority shareholders, however. Although control of the corporation remained with the family of the senior Halas' daughter, Virginia McCaskey, the McCaskeys ultimately had to buy back the 19.67 percent minority interest to prevent its sale to outsiders to cover the expenses of Mugs' estate. The Halas siblings walked away from the sale with an estimated $6 million to $7 million apiece.

Minority stockholders in smaller firms are usually less fortunate. The courts in rare instances have ordered the appointment of custodians or even the dissolution and sale of a firm when majority stockholders abuse their control at the expense of the minority. But that can destroy the value of a company, not to mention the jobs it provides. So when the Illinois Business Corporation Act was most recently upgraded in 1983, the option of a minority buyout was added.

That opened another can of worms—how to determine the value of minority shares. The College Craft suit is "a classic case," said Richard L. Williams, the attorney who represents the minority shareholders in it. "Can you get a cost-effective solution?" That often means getting a fair price for the minority shareholders without destroying the corporation and rendering the majority shares worthless.

Chapter 38

Securities Regulation

Public Offering

Liability

Insider Trading

Public Offering

This bagel company has found a creative new way to promote its initial public offering—it is giving away 100 free shares in each of its 28 stores.

Serving Lox, Stocks and Bagels
Nancy J. Kim, *Bergen Record*

Bagels, cream cheese, and stocks. Stocks? Manhattan Bagel Inc. is not content just to run a tombstone ad to assess investor interest in an initial public offering of the company's stock. Instead, as part of its strategy to promote its IPO, the company plans to give away 2,800 shares—100 shares in each of its 28 stores throughout New Jersey, New York, Pennsylvania, Connecticut, and Massachusetts.

Along with the giveaway, the Eatontown-based company will use in-store banners, place mats, and bag stuffers designed to resemble stock certificates to assess interest. "Our securities lawyers thought it was a bit weird, giving away stock, so they checked it out with the SEC who never heard of such a thing, but couldn't find anything wrong with the idea," said Jack Grumet, president of Manhattan Bagel.

The offbeat promotional campaign was the brainchild of the company's financial adviser, Charter Financial Network Inc. in Montville, led by Louis Perosi Jr. The campaign was outlined Thursday at a Secaucus news conference given by officials of Eatontown-based Manhattan Bagel and Charter Financial. "There will be postage-paid reply cards attached to the place mats and bag stuffers that customers can fill out and mail or drop right in the boxes at the stores," Perosi said. "On the cards, you check whether or not you're interested in receiving more information on the company." The returned cards will be collected for a random drawing, the winners of which will receive shares of stock, if the company does go ahead with the sale.

Manhattan Bagel is taking advantage of the Securities and Exchange Commission's Small Business Initiatives Regulation "A" program. Before the SEC changed the regulations in June 1992, companies could not advertise their stock; only the underwriters could. Under the revised regulations, small companies that want to raise up to $5 million through the sale of stock can "test the waters" of public interest without absorbing the expenses asso-

Copyright © 1993 by Bergen Record Corp. *Bergen Record*, Dec. 10, 1993, "Business." Reprinted with permission.

ciated with conventional underwritings. "Underwriters would mandate a deposit of $300,000 up front," said Grumet.

Liability

What can Congress and the SEC do to prevent people like Robert E. Brennan from stealing innocent peoples' money?

His Long, Lucrative Run May Be Over
Steve Adubato, Jr., *Asbury Park Press*

Robert E. Brennan has been buying good will and dodging legal bullets for years. After years of investigating Brennan's business practices, the Securities and Exchange Commission finally concluded a couple of months ago they had nailed the wily stock salesman-horse breeder-racetrack owner-guy who wanted to buy the Meadowlands Sports Complex-philanthropist-political contributor.

In June, a federal judge found that during the mid-'80s, Brennan headed up a "massive and continuing fraud" against countless investors who had put their money into First Jersey Securities. Remember First Jersey? Those incessant TV commercials? A prosperous-looking Brennan getting off a helicopter, asking investors to come grow with him and his "emerging growth companies?" That same prosperous-looking guy, whom securities officials say swindled thousands of working stiffs out of millions, has filed for bankruptcy.

By filing for Chapter 11 protection, Brennan avoids having to shell out $75 million to satisfy a judgment against him for securities fraud. The judgment was to be paid by this weekend. He's got the best lawyers, and appeals can go on for years. But that's Brennan's modus operandi. He has had this uncanny ability to make millions while putting up a few pennies out of his own pocket. Some might say that's just smart business. If it were only that simple.

In my Brennan file is the Oct. 26, 1992 edition of *Forbes* magazine. In it

Copyright © 1995 by Asbury Park Press, Inc. *Asbury Park Press*, Aug. 13, 1995, §C, p.3. Steve Adubato, Jr. is an instructor of public administration and mass media at Rutgers University, a television commentator and former legislator.

was a detailed account of how a typical Brennan securities scheme worked. Here's the short version:

A brokerage firm named Hibbard Brown & Co. (the feds say Brennan has extremely close ties to the firm) had its salesmen on the phones trying to sell stock on something called Site-based Media Inc. The stock was selling for about $7 a share. The salesmen were telling potential investors that the company, specializing in in-store video advertising, would revolutionize the supermarket industry. "Get in now," they said. One detail the salesmen didn't disclose was that Site-based was in the hole for about $8 million and had sales of only $673,000 over three years. Another fact they withheld was that the company's chairman was Robert Landau, who had been convicted a few years earlier of trying to defraud the U.S. Olympic Committee. But these salesmen were good. During a single week in October 1991, they sold $28 million in Site-based Media stock. At the time of the *Forbes* article, shares bought at $7 were selling for $1.50.

Where does Brennan fit into this all too typical junk-stock story? It seems that the other detail investors weren't told about was that the biggest shareholder in Site-based was Brennan. According to government documents, Brennan bought shares in the company's predecessor (called Future Funding) for between 10 cents and 38 cents. Soon afterward, he sold his shares for between $4 and $6. In 18 months, it is estimated that in return for putting out $2.8 million, Brennan made $70 million on this one deal.

The *Forbes* article describes in graphic detail how insiders at Future Funding/Site-based Media were able to artificially pump up the stock price of this virtually worthless company through an intricate web of insider trading and highly questionable sales practices. The insiders, including Brennan, knew exactly when to get out—before the stock nearly went belly-up. They made a fortune and the non-insiders were left holding the bag.

The Site-based deal isn't isolated. Brennan and his shady securities buddies (many of whom have been barred from ever selling stocks) have allegedly had a long and lucrative run of fraudulent deals financed by unsuspecting investors. Brennan likes to say the SEC is just picking on him. Why, then, did he settle for $10 million in 1987 a class action suit filed by investors who said they were gouged and defrauded by a Brennan deal?

Brennan's story isn't just about sleazy securities dealings and his most recent effort at dodging the SEC's judgment. It's about the powerful politicians (including presidential candidates, governors and U.S. senators) and educational and civic institutions to which he has contributed tens of millions. (Brennan's generosity has made him the chairman of the Seton Hall University Board of Regents.) It's about the fact that despite all the investigations, shady deals and out-of-court settlements, those same people and institutions have had nothing but nice things to say about this less-than-reputable guy who has hurt so many people.

How many of our public officials and educational-religious leaders knew where the money was coming from to finance their campaigns or build their schools? Most, I suspect, if not all. What do these folks think about Brennan and his latest cry of poverty and his effort to dodge the feds? Hard to tell. None of them will say a word on the subject.

It's easy to criticize these beneficiaries of Brennan's generosity. But the fact is that most of us would probably do the same thing if we were in their shoes. In fact, the public television program I host and produce actually sought a grant from Brennan and First Jersey in 1987. If we had gotten the grant, I would have felt guilty, but probably would have accepted the contribution. Pretty sad, isn't it?

Insider Trading

The rules on insider trading are complex. Here is a good overview of the law.

Insider Trading: When A Tip Becomes A Trap
Geanne Perlman Rosenberg, *Investor's Business Daily*

You're in line at the grocery store when you overhear a stranger say: "That new widget is going to make XYZ Co. a fortune. I can't wait until the product launch tomorrow." What do you do? (A) Nothing. (B) Call your broker and buy as much XYZ Co. stock as you possibly can. In this case, answer "B" shouldn't get you into trouble. But if that stranger happens to be talking to you and he's not a stranger at all, but a neighbor and XYZ's president, watch out. Sometimes the rules can be confusing. But one thing's for sure: If you get caught, the penalties are heavy. And getting caught is easier than ever.

Insider trading may not be getting the media play it got in the days of Ivan Boesky and Dennis Levine. But with the recent surge in mergers and acquisitions—notably, the IBM-Lotus Development takeover deal—insider-trading investigations are at levels unseen since the 1980s, according to Thomas C. Newkirk. Newkirk, who is associate director of the division of enforcement at the Securities and Exchange Commission, says increased M&A activity can be an invitation to unscrupulous traders. He also notes that both the SEC and the stock exchanges have beefed up their investigating

Copyright © 1995 by Investor's Business Daily, Inc. *Investor's Business Daily*, June 14, 1995, p.A1. Reprinted with permission.

staffs, and that this has brought a rash of cases. Unlike the '80s, when insider-trading mainly involved kingpins on Wall Street, the action has spread to Main Street, Newkirk says. "We're seeing more cases involving people away from the financial centers," he says. Recent cases have involved corporate officers and their families, rather than investment bankers.

How do investigations usually begin? Each time a merger deal is announced, Newkirk says, regulators look at trading in the period before the announcement. If they spot any suspicious activity, like unusual volume or price movements, the next step is to find out who did the trading.

Determining whether trading on non-public information is illegal can be dicey. One rule of thumb: If you overhear inside information, you can trade on it; but if you hear the same information from a friendly neighbor and trade on it, you risk ending up in jail. You may also be hit with criminal fines, career damage, public humiliation and civil damages three times the amount you made on trading.

Here are some other scenarios:

■ *The tender offer*. Say that stranger in line at the food store is talking about a tender. And say you recognize him as XYZ Co.'s president. If you trade, even if you don't know him personally and he has no idea you're listening, you could be in serious trouble because of special tender-offer rules.

■ *The strapped executive*. Say you're an executive at XYZ. You know the president hasn't been feeling well and may take a leave of absence. On any given day, you know a lot of information that hasn't been released to the public. Meanwhile, your kid's going to medical school and the tuition's due. You want to sell some of the stock you've had for decades to pay the bill. Can you trade? Not if any of the non-public information in your possession is important enough to be found "material" under the law.

The motivation of "bills to pay," Newkirk says, "is something that people advance to use in a lot of cases." But that won't keep you out of trouble, he says, because it's "possession of the information" that gives rise to a violation, not your motive for raising money.

■ *The "smart" corporate insider*. Say you and a co-worker are looking through travel receipts and figure out your company is going to be involved in a merger. You buy options and make a lot of money on your observation. You also risk a long prison sentence, according to Newkirk.

■ *The broker tip*. Your broker tells you he's heard XYZ Co. may be subject to a takeover. According to Ira Lee Sorkin, a nationally known attorney who has both defended and prosecuted major SEC actions, as long as you don't know and have no reason to know the tip may be derived from a company insider, you're in the clear. When trading on a tip, always ask yourself where it originated, says Sorkin, who is a partner at Squadron, Ellenoff, Plesent, Sheinfeld & Sorkin, and former head of the New York regional office of the SEC.

If you know the tipper is the son of the chairman and you trade, you're "going to have a big problem," Sorkin says. "There's nothing illegal about buying on rumors," he explains. "There is something illegal if you're buying on tips and you know or have reason to know the person giving the tip is getting the information from an insider or is an insider himself."

If you know the source of the tip is an insider, even when the content of the information contained in the tip is vague, the "circumstances" can spell trouble, says Harvey J. Goldschmid, professor of law at Columbia University. "The difficulty is, you don't have to know the specifics," he says. "If the person you're getting it from has a senior position and the context is one where receiving it would be important to a reasonable investor, that can be enough" to qualify as illegal insider information.

Corporate insiders who are routinely privy to non-public information have to be especially careful about buying or selling their company's stock. An insider can't buy or sell stock in his company if he has "material" non-public information, explains Joel Seligman, professor of law at the University of Michigan. Advance knowledge of a tender offer can easily be characterized as important enough to be considered material in other situations, he says. But judging whether information is important enough to render trades illegal can be a close call.

Counsels Newkirk: "You need to think through how it's going to look in hindsight."

Chapter 39

Accountants' Liability

Liability to Clients

Fraud

Liability to Clients

Increased liability has caused accountants to decrease their client rosters.

Walking a Fine Line; Accountant-Client Relations Are Being Strained
Jay Greene, *Plain Dealer*

The division president was incensed. He jumped on the polished boardroom table and stomped from one end to the other. With each step, he kicked the paperwork of his outside auditors, who had just criticized his bookkeeping on a series of transactions. "The guy went ballistic," said Richard J. Kaplan, a Price Waterhouse partner. "He got up on the table and started kicking everybody's papers all over." As the documents settled on the floor, Kaplan's colleague, who handled the audit, remained unmoved. "He said, 'If you're through, we have two more points to cover,'" Kaplan said.

Accountants are finding that they need to keep a cool head now more than ever. The fine line of giving corporate executives bad news and keeping them as clients is becoming ever more delicate. In the last few years, accountants have faced a mountain of liability lawsuits, the collapse of one of the industry's biggest firms and threats of increased regulation. To make matters worse, high-profile cases from Phar-Mor Inc. to the Bank of Credit and Commerce International have shined a spotlight on the industry for failing to do what many claim they should have been doing all along—accurately determining the financial health of a company.

All of this has strained the relationship between accountant and client that many see as too comfortable. "Things have become too cozy," said Arthur Bowman, editor of *Bowman's Accounting Report*, a newsletter. Traditionally, an accountant's role has been to test whether management has fairly presented its financial statements. Investors and suppliers consider an accounting firm's seal of approval a green light to do business with a company. But, increasingly, accountants have also been expected to warn of pending financial problems and fraud. Had accountants detected the alleged $499 million fraud at Phar-Mor, for example, they could have saved investors and suppliers of the Youngstown discount drugstore chain millions of dollars and prevented worker layoffs.

The difference between perception and reality is something the industry

Copyright © 1993 by Plain Dealer Publishing Co. *Plain Dealer*, Apr. 4, 1993, p.1E. Reprinted with permission.

refers to as the "expectations gap." And as that gap has become a gorge, pressure has built to increase auditors' responsibilities.

Rep. Ron Wyden, D.-Ore., recently introduced a bill to make accountants the first line of defense against fraud at publicly held companies. But beyond its narrow legal changes, many believe the Wyden bill, which is expected to pass, will alter the accounting industry's role. "The philosophy behind this bill is that accountants work for investors, not managers," said Mark J. Usellis, a Wyden legislative aide.

While the industry says it's been doing that all along, others see that message as a radical departure from past practices. "Now the government wants them to come in there with a badge on," Bowman said. "It changes the relationship." And even some accountants acknowledge a shift in their roles. "One impact of the Wyden bill is that accountants will be more firm about drawing that line in the sand," Kaplan said.

The implications of that change are unclear. That's because the pressure to attract new clients and retain old ones outweighs any congressional concerns about getting tough. The reality is that clients keep firms in business and partners on golf courses. "I'm not sure I've seen accounting firms get a lot tougher with their clients," said Scott Cowan, dean of Case Western Reserve University's Weatherhead School of Management and a member of several corporate boards.

Accountants insist, though, that the times have forced them to rethink their relationships with some clients. Firms say they are dumping more and more clients who make them uncomfortable. "I believe we're putting a greater emphasis on character," said David J. Sibits, managing partner at Cleveland-based Hausser & Taylor. He recalled landing a client recently that the firm was thrilled to have. "It was an account that looked like it could be a home run," Sibits said. But shortly into the audit, he got a queasy feeling. The numbers added up, and the client wasn't cooking its books or even warming them over a low flame. It just didn't feel right, Sibits said.

"Did you ever have a situation where you're talking but you know they aren't listening?" Sibits asked. "At that time, they weren't doing anything wrong; it was just a concern that the situation could become out of control." So Sibits dropped the account. More than anything, he said, the client felt "hurt and abandoned." Since then, the company has had some legal problems that Sibits declined to discuss.

In addition to dropping old clients, firms say they are increasingly turning away potential business that looks risky. Price Waterhouse's Kaplan said he was excited not too long ago to take on an account of a friend's company. But looking over the books, Kaplan didn't find what he expected. "Almost every assertion he made to us turned out to be untrue," Kaplan said. Essentially, the company wanted to book its leases earlier than Kaplan thought it should. That, in turn, inflated its income. "The truth of the matter is I really like this guy," Kaplan said, who still goes to Cleveland Lumberjack games with the executive. "But I told him that I didn't think he was ready for a Price Waterhouse audit."

Firms figure that being more selective with clients may be as close to a panacea as they can find. "The big donnybrooks don't usually come with the clients who want to do the right things," said Robert J. Huefner, an Arthur Andersen & Co. partner. "They're with the ones that want to push the envelope."

But as noble as turning away business sounds, it's rare. The industry keeps no data on client rejections. But, like any business, accounting firms are reluctant to shun clients. "You work so hard to get them," Sibits said. It's that delicate balance—counting on accountants to bite the hand that feeds them—that keeps industry critics wary.

All their testimonials to the contrary, accountants simply aren't as skeptical as they ought to be, said A. A. Sommer Jr. A former commissioner at the Securities and Exchange Commission, Sommer now chairs the Public Oversight Board, an independent panel created by the American Institute of Certified Public Accountants, the industry's trade group. "They should not assume that everything is in order," Sommer said. "Part of it is habit. They know their clients, and they are comfortable with them."

The board released a report last month suggesting the industry take a close look at recent corporate frauds, such as the Phar-Mor debacle, and learn from its mistakes. "Management can pull the wool over the auditors' eyes," Sommer said. "But can the auditor do more? Our report says they can." The board recommended establishing well-defined auditing standards, which, had they been in place, could have prevented past problems. One of those suggestions, surprise inventory audits, could have impeded the Phar-Mor fraud. Phar-Mor's auditors followed standard industry practice of notifying management when and where they would check inventory. But that, in turn, gave the alleged perpetrators of the fraud a chance to conceal it.

Those sorts of standards may make for a more adversarial relationship between auditor and client. But, Sommer said, so be it. "Auditors do not want to do things that are offensive. That's why we ought to have standards," Sommer said. "Clients may not like it. But they won't be able to go to another auditor and get different treatment."

Perhaps the only way real change will come is from those who foot the bill. While clients may not be itching for tougher auditors, increasingly, they have come to expect more from auditors, Weatherhead's Cowan said. Directors on a board that Cowan sits on recently asked the company's accountants if the internal financial department was doing a thorough job. The company had recently laid off staff. "I don't remember the auditors ever saying anything other than things were fine," Cowan said. "Now, they were saying we could use a few more people."

Cowan thinks the change is tied, at least in part, to increased concern over liability. Instead of being sued later for not disclosing shortcomings to the board, auditors are coming clean on any problems they may have encountered. "In the past, they might have perceived that as some disloyalty to management. They had this dual master," Cowan said. "But because of the liability, they are more likely to say those sorts of things than not."

Without question, the issues are ones the industry must cope with quickly. Lawsuits charging auditor malpractice continue to grow. According to Bowman, accounting firms spent about $540 million, roughly 9.5 percent of the revenue from their auditing and accounting business, on litigation and settlements in 1992. That's up from $477 million, or 8.7 percent of that revenue in 1991, and $405 million, or 7.5 percent, in 1990.

And for nearly every Big Six firm, the problem is getting out of hand. In 1990, Laventhol & Horwath, at the time the nation's seventh largest accounting firm, collapsed, largely under the weight of expensive judgments and settlements. Last year, Ernst & Young agreed to pay $400 million, the largest settlement ever for a professional firm, to government regulators with regard to its audits of hundreds of failed banks and savings and loans.

Accountants, though, say answers may not be as simple as lining up specific standards or forcing auditors to turn in fraudulent clients. The kinds of issues accountants are taken to task for are often less specific than straight math. "It's highly subjective," said Bret W. Wise, a senior manager in KPMG Peat Marwick's Cleveland office. "Accounting, in many instances, is an art rather than a science."

Fraud

Charles Ponzi is one of the most infamous con men ever—the term "Ponzi scheme" is often used to describe the kind of pyramid program he developed. Can accountants prevent modern-day Ponzis?

Comment: Legislation Needed To Beef Up Fraud Detection
Thomas R. Creal, *American Banker*

In June 1920, Charles Ponzi boldly challenged the public to lend him their money for 45 days, promising he would return it with 50 percent inter-

Copyright © 1994 by American Banker, Inc. *American Banker*, Mar. 16, 1994, p.17. Mr. Creal is president of Checkmate Consulting in Chicago, a division of the accounting firm Checkers, Simon & Rosner.

est. For a 90-day loan, he would double the money. It was all very simple. Ponzi could buy a stamp from Spain for 1 cent and then exchange it at the U.S. Post Office for 6 cents. And it worked! In December, 15 people gave Charles Ponzi $870, and each received $1,218 at the end of 45 days. By June of the following year, 7,824 people had trudged up the stairs to Ponzi's office to give him more money.

Ponzi never bought one stamp. Those who received a "return on their investment" were simply receiving the dollars of later investors. Only when Barron's published news stories about Ponzi did the truth emerge—followed by the inevitable collapse.

Smoke and Mirrors

In 1982, Barry Minkow started ZZZZ Best in his garage. In 1987, he took it public, had reported revenues of $50 million, and a market value of $200 million. He was referred to as "Wonder Boy." Minkow was in the business of restoring fire- and flood-ravaged buildings. There was one problem: Most of his sales were only smoke and mirrors. ZZZZ Best eventually collapsed, leaving lenders empty-handed.

In 1992, U.S. News and World Report estimated that crimes against business amounted to $128 billion in one year. That was 69 percent of the after tax corporate profits earned by U.S. companies.

Liable for Millions

As the ugly truth about the savings and loan debacle unfolded, Judge Stanley Sporkin was quoted as saying, "Where were the professionals?" He decried the fact that the audit and legal professionals had not identified and publicized the fraudulent activities. And in the courts of law and public opinion, the audit profession was judged accountable for hundreds of millions of dollars. The adherence to professional standards seemed almost superfluous to the fact that frauds were occurring and auditors failed to blow the whistle. The message to the audit profession was clear. The investing public expects fraud detection as part of the attestation process.

Investors' Needs

During the first half of the 20th century, the auditor's historical role shifted. First, the excesses of the 1920s and the resulting enactment of the Securities Act of 1933 and Securities Exchange Act of 1934 required attestation. Investors needed audited statements to protect their resources and to weigh risks and rewards. They required assurance that the financial statements fairly represented changes in financial position. Second, with the advent of federal income taxes in 1913, the government became interested in the fairness of reported income. Fraud detection increasingly was seen as a byproduct of the audit and tax work rather than the primary focus.

Trained Skeptics

There is little doubt that auditors have unparalleled insight into the operations and finances of a business. Their training focuses on a skeptical review of all transactions and the documents that support them. And their professional standards still include directives on detecting and reporting fraud.

To help refocus the audit profession on fraud, Rep. Ron Wyden of Oregon introduced the Financial Fraud Detection and Disclosure Act with the cosponsorship of 16 members of the House Energy and Commerce Committee. The American Institute of Certified Public Accounts has endorsed the legislation. The bill uses the carrot-and-stick approach. The stick is the long arm of government that, through the law, would tell audit professionals that detecting fraud is their job. The carrot is the attempt to change the audit client's perception of value. Auditors can be trained to ferret out fraud, and such procedures can be part of an audit engagement. But the end users (businesses, investors, lenders, et al.) must understand and be willing to pay for the added value of such a service.

Stronger Assurances

The new audit engagement will deliver a much higher level of assurance that any material fraud has been uncovered or does not exist. The adoption of new procedures can be an opportunity for the profession to focus public attention on the purpose and value of the audit. Investors seeing the additional level of attestation will place more reliance on the report and insist on such procedures in future reports. Eventually, such procedures will be a routine part of all audit engagements.

Auditors are in the best position to detect fraud. But while the courts and investors are demanding fraud detection, and while the government and the profession recognize the need, it is by no means certain that the profession can deliver. Much of the fraud today is in transactions that exist for nanoseconds in the memory of computers. The perpetrators are often so devious that the results may remain hidden for years or be stolen with no evidence that anything is missing.

Unrealistic Expectations

While a new focus on fraud detection is long overdue, the expectation that even the most astute investigators can uncover all fraud is naive. No amount of procedures or training can deliver that level of assurance. Some improvement can be achieved through the kind of attention that news reports of frauds and settlements have created. Additional improvements can be achieved through training in detection techniques we already know. Still more improvement will come through research into fraudulent schemes, psychodemographics of perpetrators, and characteristics of successful investigations. When such research is translated into training and practice exercises, investigators will be better equipped to find sophisticated fraudulent activity.

Unit 6

Government Regulation

Chapter 40

Antitrust: Law and Competitive Strategy, Part I

Price-Fixing

Cooperative Strategies

Price-Fixing

Fashion designers agreed to reduce the fees they were paying runway models. This price-fixing was "never intended to be malicious," they said. Does intent matter in a price-fixing case?

Is This Face Worth $10,000 a Day?
Pamela Reynolds, *Boston Globe*

Naomi Campbell and Linda Evangelista must be dancing down the runways. The two-year struggle between such $10,000-a-day supermodels and wage-weary New York fashion designers is finally over. The models won.

The Council of Fashion Designers of America Inc. and Seventh on Sixth Inc., the group of designers who tried to reduce runway fees—which have been known to hit $18,000 per show for some top models—recently reached an agreement with the Federal Trade Commission, according to the council. There will be no cap on modeling fees. Fern Mallis, the executive director of both CFDA and Seventh on Sixth, said the organizations decided to settle to avoid the time and expense of responding to the FTC's investigation.

The FTC began an investigation a year ago into whether the industry had been price-fixing after the two organizations proposed that designers limit models' runway fees to a few hundred dollars an hour. Fees were slashed before the 1993 Bryant Park Tent Shows in New York, and during the 1994 shows designers refused to pay more than $750 an hour for supermodels, $600 for second-tier models and $500 for cub models. Annoyed by such ceilings, many top models decided that the latest round of shows in New York wasn't worth their time, or the money. Other supermodels, like Campbell, sharply curtailed their participation in the shows.

The fee limit, according to the CFDA, was never intended to be malicious. The idea was simply to give young designers a chance to compete with established designers who had the advantage of spicing up an otherwise stale show with the hot—and pricey—face of the moment. While admitting no wrongdoing, the CFDA and Seventh on Sixth have agreed that, as a group, they will never again set modeling fees.

John Casablancas of Elite Models, which represents both Campbell and Evangelista, told Newsday: "We feel models should be paid as much as the market will bear. No one is saying that designers should have a limit on the

Copyright © 1995 by Globe Newspaper Co. *Boston Globe*, May 3, 1995, p.33. Reprinted courtesy of The Boston Globe.

price they sell their clothes for." So if designers are willing to pay Campbell and Evangelista $10,000 to strut down a runway for three or four hours, so be it.

Cooperative Strategies

Catfish farmers announced that they would limit catfish production until prices rise. Do the catfish farmers really want the Justice Department to read about this in the paper?

Catfish Cartel Plans Boycott To Buoy Price
Charles Haddad, *Atlanta Journal and Constitution*

The South Africans control the diamond market. The Arabs rule the world of oil. But can Mississippi Delta farmers control the price of catfish? Beginning Feb. 8, catfish farmers plan to boycott supermarkets, restaurants and food processors in a desperate attempt to boost plummeting prices. They say they will withhold their catfish until prices hit 65 cents a pound—or 17 cents above the current market.

"This is not about trying to maximize profits—it's about trying to keep farmers alive," said Bill Allen, executive director of the Catfish Bargaining Association. "A lot of farmers are facing bankruptcy." Indeed, about 14 of the country's roughly 1,400 catfish farmers have gone out of business in the past year, according to the Catfish Farmers Association.

What's whittling down the ranks of catfish farmers is the whipsaw of supply and demand. Last year alone, the industry produced 290 million pounds of catfish. And it did so at a time when demand for the fish, served mainly at restaurants, fell as people ate out less. The result: "Prices have crashed," Mr. Allen said. Since July, the price of catfish per pound has fallen from 70 cents to 48 cents, or about 12 cents less than the cost of producing the fish. That's good news for consumers and retailers such as supermarkets and restaurants. Paul Jones, owner of Atlanta's popular Colonnade Restaurant, says the price he pays for catfish has fallen 20 cents a pound in the past month alone.

Now the catfish cartel, as the CBA is known, hopes to stop the decline. It

Copyright © 1992 by The Atlanta Constitution. *Atlanta Journal and Constitution*, Jan. 27, 1992, §A, p.3. Reprinted by permission.

did just that in 1989, when members agreed to limit the amount of fish they sold, pushing prices up 17 cents a pound in two years. But price-fixing ultimately fails, some economists say. Explains Mississippi State University agricultural economist DeWitt Calliavet: "No sooner has the cartel agreed to a boycott than some small farmer decides to unload his catfish on the market."

Indeed, Mr. Allen says CBA was forced to abandon its price-fixing efforts earlier this year because so many farmers were undercutting it on the market. Now, out of desperation, CBA members are willing to give it another try. "If it [price] doesn't go up, then I'll just let my fish die," said Charlie Stephens, a Wisner, La., farmer who is president of the Louisiana Catfish Farmers Association.

Chapter 41

Antitrust: Law and Competitive Strategy, Part II

Monopolization

Predatory Pricing

Tying Arrangements

Monopolization

Steve Bacon, a small-town pharmacist, is trying to prevent the giant drug company Merck & Co. from merging with Medco Containment Services Inc., a mail-order pharmacy. What must Bacon prove to win his monopolization suit?

Small Pharmacist Battles the Giants; Mill Valley Man's Suit Calls Merck Merger a Monopoly
Kathleen Sullivan, *San Francisco Examiner*

As a child, Steve Bacon used to sweep the parking lot at his father's Mill Valley pharmacy in the morning, then spend all his wages, 25 cents, on an afternoon matinee. In high school, he worked as a delivery boy. Bacon, who earned a doctor of pharmacy degree at UC-San Francisco in 1988, bought the store two years ago. Now, like his father before him, he works behind the counter, filling prescriptions. "I was groomed to be a pharmacist," said the 38-year-old Bacon, noting that his father's godfather worked as a pharmacist in Placerville in the late 1800s.

Last year, Bacon also became a crusading pharmacist, when he filed a lawsuit challenging the 1993 merger of Merck & Co., cited in the suit as the world's biggest manufacturer of prescription drugs, and Medco Containment Services Inc., a mail-order pharmacy that provides "managed prescription drug programs" to employers. The suit, filed in U.S. District Court in San Francisco, goes to trial next month. In it, Bacon charges that the merger will lessen competition and create a monopoly in the sale and distribution of prescription drugs, "inevitably resulting in damage to independent community pharmacies in the United States, and maintaining high and arbitrary prices to American consumers for prescription drugs."

If successful, the suit filed by Bacon's small pharmacy could reverberate across the industry, threatening similar mergers, experts say. It would also be a boost to other small pharmacists, many of whom are fighting to protect their profit margins in an age of chain stores and giant health plans. Asked why he filed the lawsuit, Bacon said: "I'm serving a community I care about. If the only way to bring prices down is to fight the guys that are raising them, then I'll do it."

The lawsuit says the nation's 60,000 community pharmacies, which employ about 112,000 pharmacists, dispense more than 2 billion prescrip-

Copyright © 1994 by *San Francisco Examiner*, Oct. 6, 1994, p.E-1. Reprinted with permission.

tions a year. "It is essential to the preservation of a competitive community pharmacy marketplace that widespread price discrimination by manufacturers of prescription drugs be eliminated, because the favored buyers compete with community pharmacists for the same group of customers," the suit charged. The suit cites figures from a 1992 drug company invoice to illustrate the disparity in pricing on 11 drugs, including an inhaler that costs an independent pharmacist $33.61, but costs a mail-order firm only $2.58.

Bacon said business at his Lawson-Dyer Pharmacy, the store retained the names of its original owners, has dropped 20 percent since the Merck merger. "Prices have gone up consistently and reimbursement for services has decreased in proportion to the increase in the cost of living," he said. "The level of service I have to provide is going up; it takes more intensive work to process these things." Bacon recently turned down a settlement offer from Merck, saying he would have been "mortgaging his self-esteem" by accepting the money. Merck executives had no immediate comment but have stated that the New Jersey company does not comment on pending litigation. A trial has been set for Nov. 14.

Issue of Market Share

At issue is whether drug companies have the right to control a significant share in the distribution market by purchasing what are known as "pharmacy benefits managers," or PBMs, of which Medco is one of the largest. Typically, a benefits manager will only reimburse outlays for prescription drugs if they are bought from an approved pharmacy, usually one in a large chain. At present, an estimated 50 million Americans are covered by pharmacy benefits managers, which offer consumers and health care providers cut-rate drugs by pressuring manufacturers and pharmacists to drop their prices in return for volume. By 2000, that number could grow to 100 million, experts say.

The market is driven by demands for lower-cost health care by corporations, consumers and governments. But small pharmacists complain that they are either being forced to play along with the growing power of PBMs and slash their margins or be left out altogether. They say that PBMs are exercising de facto price control over the market, particularly when they link with drug companies to set prices.

If the suit succeeds, similar mergers by British drug powerhouse SmithKline Beecham PLC and Indianapolis-based Eli Lilly and Co. could be threatened, analysts say.

FTC Approved Merger

The Federal Trade Commission, which evaluates whether merger activity has monopoly implications, approved the Merck-Medco merger. But the FTC has yet to approve Eli Lilly's proposed $4 billion purchase of

McKesson Corp.'s PCS Health Systems Inc., another major PBM, in July. "It is a skirmish, but the pharmacists are obviously fighting a rear-guard action," said analyst Bill Blair.

Predatory Pricing

Dave Hooper owns a compact disc store. He has accused Best Buy Co. of setting predatory prices on CDs to drive him out of business. Are CD prices too low? Is predatory pricing bad, if it leads to lower prices?

Small Record Stores Lament Best Buy Barrage
Brett Chase, *Business Record*

Dave Hooper was convinced compact discs would be the next big thing. He kept reading magazines predicting records would eventually become a thing of the past. Recording companies would stop manufacturing them. CD players were outselling video cassette recorders. Convinced the CD business was a sure thing, he took time off from his family's warehousing business and opened the Compact Disc Shoppe in Des Moines. It was the only independent record store in the land where malls and strip centers rule. That was 1987.

1994 was much different. Other independent stores—Music Circuit, Archives Records and Tapes and Cop Records—all went out of business. Sales at Hooper's store, which is now in Urbandale, dropped 25 percent. The only other remaining independent record store in Des Moines, Peeples Music, also reported sagging sales. "It was also the year big chains decided to double their inventory, and practically give away discs," Hooper said.

Like many other small businesses, record stores are facing new challenges from the corporate behemoths. Best Buy Co. Inc. of Minneapolis is cited by most record store owners as the reason sales are down. The company—the nation's third-largest CD retailer—has two stores in Des Moines. Like many other music stores, Best Buy got heavily into CD sales in the late 1980s, and has continued to expand its offerings ever since, said Laurie Bauer, a Best Buy spokeswoman.

Small merchants like Hooper and his store manager, Ned Rood, who has

Copyright © 1995 by *Business Record*, Apr. 24, 1995, vol. 91, no. 17, §1, p.8. Reprinted by permission of the Des Moines Business Record.

worked at record stores since 1978, charge Best Buy with predatory pricing. They claim the chain uses CDs as loss leaders to bring customers in to buy big-ticket items, such as appliances, stereos and TV sets. Best Buy's Bauer disputes the charge, saying CDs are the company's fastest-growing product line. "We don't use our CDs as loss leaders. They're one of our most profitable areas."

What no one disputes about Best Buy is that the chain has tremendous buying power because it can purchase CDs directly from distributors. Many small stores have to go through wholesalers which adds to a CD's price. And Best Buy is large enough that it can buy at deep discounts and pass the savings on to consumers. There are more than 200 Best Buy stores, each carrying between 40,000 and 60,000 CD titles.

What small retailers are concerned about is that customers will overlook the services they can offer—musical knowledge, special orders, collectors' items—and go straight for the lower prices. And there's no way small merchants like Hooper can compete in a price war. The problem, he said, is the independent store's slim margin. If Hooper buys a CD for $11, he needs to sell it for $16. "If I sold CDs the same way furniture is marked up, or clothing is marked up, they'd be $40 apiece. Obviously, I can't sell CDs for $40 apiece." Peeples owner Mike Enlo tried to match Best Buy's prices on new releases last year. But Enlo saw no new business; the move did little more than cut his cash flow.

Distributors used to deal directly with the small record stores, said Steve White, who closed his Music Circuit store after more than 22 years in business. For White, there was nothing sentimental about closing. He knew in the late '80s the record business would not be profitable for small stores. Part of the blame, he says, rests with the advent of CDs. The discs were priced much higher than vinyl records, which meant many of his customers couldn't buy recorded music as frequently as they once did.

Enlo disagrees. He says his store's peak years were in the late 1980s and early 1990s when audiophiles started replacing their favorite records with compact discs. Enlo, who has been in business for 19 years, says he stays afloat by attracting the customers who want knowledgeable salespeople—he says he hires his best customers—and by stocking the oddities that a major retail chain might ignore.

Best Buy itself started as a small operation in 1966 when it opened as Sound of Music. The company now has stores in 27 states and is expanding rapidly.

Conventional wisdom says record stores, like other small businesses, can survive if they find their niche. They have found that niche in used CDs. The record companies tried to squash this burgeoning market two years ago by threatening to withhold cooperative advertising money from stores that sold used CDs. Neither record companies nor artists receive royalties from secondhand discs.

But small stores, recognizing a potential market Best Buy wouldn't touch, continued to sell used CDs. "Screw 'em," said Hooper. The record companies eventually backed off—sort of. They still withhold cooperative funds from some stores, but they've toned down their threats. Nonetheless, it remains to be seen whether the small stores' battle cry of service, musical knowledge and collectors' items will carry the day. "The whole name of the game is volume. You need numerous locations. I had one," said White. "The day of the so-called record store is over."

Tying Arrangements

Bob Drake is not allowed to join the Citrus Hills Golf and Country Club unless he hires Citrus Hills Construction Co. to build his home. This arrangement may sound unfair, but is it illegal?

New Rules Restrict Who May Join Club
Collins Conner, St. Petersburg Times

For the 30 years he drove Stella D'Oro Biscuit trucks in New York, Bob Drake fantasized about retiring to Florida and playing golf in his back yard. Last January, he thought his fantasy was coming true. He discovered Citrus Hills, loved it, and bought a $17,000 lot overlooking the sixth green. His joy lasted less than a month.

Under the development's new rules, Drake can't join the Citrus Hills Golf and Country Club unless he hires Citrus Hills Construction Co. to build his home. He doesn't want to hire that company; he doesn't like the quality or cost of its work. But that is the condition he must meet if he wants to be a member of the course where he lives. "It just aggravated me that they kind of killed my dream a little," Drake said. He put his lot up for sale.

Drake is not the only one chaffing over the recent restrictions to club membership. Citrus Hills resident Ken Travis, a lawyer, told the developers if they did not stop linking membership to home construction, he would report them to the state Attorney General for using tie-in sales, a practice he said is illegal. The developers' representatives responded by yanking Travis' golf privileges, and the Citrus Hills lawyer accused Travis of engaging "in

Copyright © 1995 by *St. Petersburg Times*, June 19, 1995, p.1. Reprinted with permission.

felonious activity, i.e., extortion." The lawyer then filed a complaint against Travis with the Florida Bar.

Travis was astonished. "They're playing hardball," he said. "We're not trying to hurt the company. If the company flourishes, we flourish. I'm not a vengeful guy. I just want them to stop this."

The Citrus Hills Golf and Country Club is open to anyone who wants to pay user fees. Until 1993, the club did not even sell charter memberships. The change in club access followed a shift in Citrus Hills' business strategy. The developers, Gerald Nash and the late Sam Tamposi, designed the golfing community, then pegged their profit to lot sales. They flew potential customers from New England to Citrus Hills, sold them lots and gave them a list of "approved builders." In 1991, they formed their own home-building company, Citrus Hills Construction Co.

Two years later, they created the country club membership plan. For a limited time, they offered Citrus Hills property owners the chance to buy one of 900 "charter memberships" in the club for $2,000. Months later, the fee went to $3,000, then open membership sales stopped. For their money, the charter members would get "reduced greens fees and . . . preferred tee times," said Eric Abel, the Citrus Hills attorney. "The memberships were non-equity memberships, which means they have the right to use the facility, but no ownership interest," Abel said. Non-members also can use the club by paying greens fees, Abel said. The difference between members and non-members is that should the club be sold, a member would have the right to buy 1/900th of the club, Abel said.

After the two membership offerings ended in 1994, the unsold memberships "were assigned or transferred to the Citrus Hills Construction Company," Abel said. "And now, when Citrus Hills Construction Company constructs a home for a person, that person is able to apply for membership." Memberships, which now cost $7,000, are also available to buyers of an existing home if the seller hires a sister company, CHIP Realty, to market the property. Abel will not say how many unsold memberships are held by the Citrus Hills companies.

Two area builders, who joined Travis in his complaint to the Attorney General, claim Citrus Hills has a competitive advantage, since it holds the club memberships. Several area Realtors said they were blocked from the resale market in Citrus Hills, since club memberships also are tied to the use of CHIP Realty for the resale of existing homes. Those Realtors said customers are not well served by CHIP Realty. "CHIP is not an MLS (multiple listing service), which means the sellers don't get exposure around the county for their house," said real estate saleswoman Marie Richmond. She also questioned why CHIP would aggressively market a resale home, when its sister company, Citrus Hills Construction, builds new homes. "If you owned a whole farm and you were producing eggs, would you sell someone else's eggs when you can sell your own?" she said.

Abel said CHIP Realty had a "fiduciary responsibility" to aggressively market the resales. He said the memberships were not a significant marketing tool. He also said Citrus Hills' companies do not have an unfair advantage by getting all the unsold memberships. "Sam (Tamposi) and Jerry (Nash) already owned every membership out there," Abel said of the community's developers. "They own the club. They could have given all the unsold memberships to anyone they wanted. They could have given them to St. Pete Times if they wanted."

Abel said that when the club was selling memberships, the area builders and realtors could have purchased memberships to provide to their customers, as Citrus Hills Construction is now doing. Abel later said Citrus Hills Construction bought the unsold memberships for an undisclosed amount. "They gave consideration to the golf club, which the golf club thought was fair consideration," he said. But he would not say what the consideration, or payment, was. "It was intercompany. I couldn't tell you," he said.

Travis, who already has a club membership, said he is fighting for the people banned from membership. When he heard about Drake's problem, Travis told a Citrus Hills official that he thought the linking of memberships to the use of Citrus Hills companies was a "tie-in sale," which is prohibited by law. Abel responded to Travis' complaint by sending Travis excerpts from a letter from a Boca Raton law firm, which declared that no tie-in violation existed. " . . . We do not believe that the developer has sufficient market power in the sale of memberships to constitute the arrangement of illegal tying arrangement," said attorney James E. Wanless of Boca Raton.

On April 30, Travis wrote Abel, giving the developers two weeks to stop linking memberships to the use of Citrus Hills companies. If they did not stop, he warned, "I will refer the case to the Attorney General of Florida." That is when the club immediately suspended him and his access to the community's tennis courts, pro shop, swimming pool, clubhouse, dining room, lounge, banquet rooms, function rooms, locker rooms, administrative offices and golf-cart storage facilities. Abel also contacted the state attorney's office, accusing Travis of extortion. Assistant state attorney Mark Simpson said he saw no evidence of extortion. "After reading the statute on tie-in sales, my belief is there is possibly just cause on (Travis') part, or at least his complaint was not just made out of thin air." Simpson declined to prosecute. Abel then wrote the Florida Bar, the lawyer-policing arm of the Supreme Court, accusing Travis of unprofessional conduct. The complaint is pending. Meanwhile, Travis sent his complaint of the alleged tie-in sale to the Attorney General's office, where it is being reviewed.

Abel said the country club directors lifted Travis' suspension June 6. He declined to further discuss company action against Travis. "I think he has a misunderstanding of the facts," Abel said of Travis.

Drake, in the meantime, hasn't been able to sell his lot. "If worse comes to worse, and we can't sell the lot, we'll build on it," he said. "We won't use Citrus Hills Construction. We'll join a country club someplace else. We'll live on one golf course and be a member of another."

Abel says Drake has only himself to blame. "I would think that anyone who was interested in buying a home site on a golf course would check the rules and regulations for membership before he bought the property," Abel said. "Yes, it's 'caveat emptor' to a degree." "Caveat emptor" means "Let the buyer beware."

Chapter 42

Consumer Law and Truth in Advertising

Right to Privacy

Credit Cards

Consumer Product Safety Act

Right to Privacy

Preventive Law: Here are some tips for protecting your privacy.

Others Mind Your Business; Personal Data Goes Public on Information Highway
Jeffrey Rothfeder, *Dallas Morning News*

It was one of the most alarming phone conversations Karen Hochman of New York City had ever had. A long-distance company had called to persuade her to switch carriers. But Ms. Hochman wasn't interested. "I told him that I didn't make many out-of-town calls, but thanks anyway."

"I'm surprised to hear you say that," the salesman interjected. "I see from your phone records that you frequently call New Jersey, Delaware and Connecticut."

Ms. Hochman was shocked and scared by the salesman's invasion of her privacy. She asked how he had obtained her phone records and then threatened legal action. The salesman quickly hung up. "If strangers are able to find out the numbers I call, what else could they find out about me?" Ms. Hochman wondered.

A lot, as it turns out. The types of data available are mind-boggling: credit files, work history, driving records, health reports, bank balances, nonpublished phone numbers, phone records, criminal convictions, Social Security earnings, family makeup, personal tastes and buying habits. Enterprising marketers, and most anyone with a computer and the required fee, can purchase general information from original sources, such as credit or government agencies. And though they won't sell the most sensitive information to just anyone, there are dozens of information resellers, known as superbureaus, that often will.

The worst thing about this information blitzkrieg is that even though errors abound, what computers say about us is usually considered accurate. Often those affected are unaware of the process and are given no chance to offer explanations. For example, insurers use computerized data to decide who should get life, disability and medical coverage—and who should be denied it. Employers make hiring decisions based on computer-compiled reports. Those who have access to these files could share this private information, causing damage that can range from embarrassment to ruined repu-

---

Copyright © 1994 by The Dallas Morning News. *Dallas Morning News.* June 21, 1994, p.1C. Jeffrey Rothfeder, an editor at Bloomberg Business News, is author of the book *Privacy for Sale* (Simon & Schuster, 1992). This story was distributed by New York Times Special Features.

tations. Criminals also use databases to take on the identity of others and get car loans, mortgages, credit cards and a lot more.

Don't expect the law to shield you. There's no federal legislation protecting medical, telephone, employment, insurance and bank records. And the few privacy laws on the books—such as the 1970 Fair Credit Reporting Act or the 1974 Privacy Act—are outmoded vestiges. Some state statutes exist, but they're hard to enforce.

Each time you book a flight, your name, address, credit-card number and where and when you're going are entered into the airline's reservation computers. This data is sold to rental-car companies, travel agents and others. Warranty cards are another key source for marketers.

Here are some of the things strangers know about you—and how you can protect yourself.

What You Earn, Owe

The nation's three biggest credit bureaus—TRW, Equifax and Trans Union—store 500 million records on more than 160 million people. The financial data in their files includes: employment and salary histories; credit-card numbers, transactions and balances; mortgage records; bankruptcies; and tax liens. The credit bureaus constantly comb bank, credit-card and other records for unusual signs—for instance, late payments, an increase in salary, a higher mortgage. Then, without permission, they share these tidbits with banks, retailers and marketers.

Superbureaus subscribe to the credit bureaus and sell credit reports via computer to virtually anyone who pays the sign-up fee, from $100 to $500, plus $20 to $50 extra for each specific report. Marketers use credit-bureau data for targeted junk-mail campaigns—so your mailbox may be flooded with unwanted solicitations. Creditors use credit-bureau tips to unfairly shut off the accounts of people whose general solvency appears to be slipping—even if they are still paying their bills on time—to avoid getting stiffed down the road. It's legal for them to do this because having a credit card is a privilege, not a right. Criminals access credit data to steal money using the identity of others.

Privacy precaution: Get your credit report once a year from each credit bureau to look for inaccuracies, transactions you haven't made and the names of people who have accessed it. Call TRW at (800) 682-7654 (they offer one free report a year) and Equifax at (800) 685-1111 ($8). Write to Trans Union, P.O. Box 7000, North Olmsted, Ohio 44070 (include $8 and your Social Security number, previous address and any previous name).

To stop receiving junk mail, write to the Direct Marketing Association, Mail Preference Service, P.O. Box 3861, New York, N.Y. 10163.

To delete your name from credit bureau marketing lists, contact Consumer Relations, TRW Target Marketing Services, 901 N. International

Parkway, Richardson, Texas 75081; and Trans Union Corp., TransMark Div., Name Removal Option, 555 W. Adams St., Chicago, Ill. 60661.

To get your name off lists sold by your credit-card companies, contact them directly.

Your Medical History

Medical records aren't private. The Medical Information Bureau (MIB), an insurance consortium, collects physician and hospital records on millions of Americans and Canadians. No federal laws restrict when and to whom a medical record can be revealed.

Two dozen states have laws allowing for the release of medical records only with a patient's approval, but people give their consent almost every time they sign an application for insurance, loans, credit or employment. In fine print these applications usually state that a background check, including looking at an MIB file, may be conducted. Many of these forms have no expiration date, so they can be used to access your medical records at any time. The information contained in your medical profile—accurate or not—can affect your reputation, employment, insurance and licenses.

Privacy precaution: You can ask your doctor not to give out information unless you approve. Limit blanket medical-record release forms by writing in that your OK is only for the specific purpose.

Though it can be expensive, some employees pay for their drug- or alcohol-abuse treatments and programs to keep their employer from finding out.

For a free copy or your MIB file, call (617) 426-3660.

Credit Cards

What can you do if you get a wrong charge on your credit card bill?

Cutting Through Credit-Card Bureaucracy—Charge!
Sharon Stangenes, *Chicago Tribune*

It was a tale from credit-card hell. The caller had moved to Chicago from Florida in August, and even after notifying the credit-card company of his new address, he had yet to receive a monthly statement by late February. Repeated calls to the company's 1-800 number resulted mostly in conversations with service representatives who blamed the computer. He spoke—once—to a supervisor who later sent a letter outlining how the company would rectify the situation. But nearly three months later, nothing had changed. He then tried the card issuer's corporate headquarters, estimating that he spent "well over $100" on telephone calls, but all that got him was rude treatment by a vice president's assistant. "All this," he said with a great exasperation, "because I want to pay my bill!"

Credit cards are a fact of life for most Americans. An estimated 1.1 billion of them are in circulation, including 280 million bank cards, according to Robert B. McKinley, president of RAM Research Corp., which tracks the credit-card industry. And not only is the number of credit cards increasing, says McKinley, but Americans are using them more. Although the vast majority of these transactions go without a hitch, it takes only one bad experience to turn what usually works like a dream into a nightmare. Since few people have much extra time or energy to spend unsnarling a problem, knowing how to cut the red tape to get a speedy resolution is important.

"There are pretty concrete steps to take when there is an error in billing," says Michelle Meier, counsel for government affairs for *Consumers Union*, a consumer advocacy association and publisher of Consumer Reports magazine. Thanks to the Fair Credit Billing Act, consumers who question a charge can challenge it with a reasonable chance of success. "Put in writing what the error is," says Meier. Mail a copy of the letter and a copy, not the original, of the statement with the error to the address designated on the bill. It is vital to "retain the original statement" in case the problem is not immediately resolved, Meier notes.

Under the law, the credit-card issuer has 60 days to respond and get back to the consumer with a clarification. During this time, the issuer is not

Copyrighted © 1993 by Chicago Tribune Co. All rights reserved. *Chicago Tribune*, Mar. 26, 1993, "Your Money," p.1. Used with permission.

allowed to report a late payment to a credit bureau. "Don't pay the bill during this time until you hear from the issuer," advises Meier. "Don't worry about getting reported." These steps apply to charges that you don't believe are yours and to charges that you don't feel you deserve because you were displeased with the quality or the service. Under the Fair Credit Billing Act, a consumer can demand that the bank that issues the card not pay a merchant. One example of when this might be useful is when the car conks out five blocks from the shop after you have paid $500 for it to be repaired.

There Are Limitations

Most bank cards don't promote the fact that this can be done and there are limitations on how this works. The charges must cost more than $50, the purchase must have been made in your state or within 100 miles of your billing address, and you must make a good-faith effort to work out the problem with the merchant or service provider before taking this step.

For the thornier question of misdirected or unreceived statements, the game plan is more complicated and the law not as clear-cut. For those reasons, experts do not agree on which tactics to use—for example, whether it will help or hurt to try to go straight to the top with a complaint. "I think that writing to a chief executive can be helpful," says Meier. "I have found it effective." But James Daly, editor of Chicago-based *Credit Card News*, an industry newsletter, disagrees with that strategy. "I'm not convinced it gets solved any faster that way."

Experts do agree, however, that the wise credit-card customer, like the Boy Scouts, must be prepared. "It's best to forestall the problem if you can," says Daly. McKinley suggests asking about service before you sign a credit-card contract.

Check Out the Service

While the cost of the card, both in interest rates and annual fees, is the top priority for most consumers, the service the company offers should be the next concern. "Do they have a 24-hours-a-day number you can call about a problem? Is there a person who answers the phone when you call? Some of the cards with rock-bottom rates have lousy service. That's not true of all of them. Some low-rate cards have very good service. But it is one of the things a consumer should know," McKinley says.

Once the signature is dry on the contract's dotted line, smart credit-card consumers will:

- Hold onto and really read those cardholder agreements sent with the card. Daly acknowledges that most agreements "are pretty dry reading," but "you should keep those because it spells out your rights as a cardholder" and may help you avoid the runaround should you encounter a problem. Another good reason for reading the fine print is that billing contracts vary by issuer and may give different procedures to resolve a problem, says Brad Hennig, spokesman for San Francisco-based Visa U.S.A.

- Keep and file the statements and charge slips. These documents become invaluable when there is a dispute. Send the change of address in an appropriate and timely manner before you actually move. "It is important that the change of address contains the account numbers," Daly points out.

- Act immediately when you do not receive a statement. "The one basic overriding thing is notification," stresses Hennig. "Notify the issuer right away," he urged. "Do not let the dispute go over 30 days." Hennig suggests it is appropriate to call the 1-800 service number and then follow up that call as soon as possible with a letter. Daly says acting promptly helps forestall other complications such as "late charges that could end up on your credit record."

- If all else fails, get outside help. Hennig suggests that frustrated Visa consumers might call the association's customer service line, 1-800-336-3386. Meier and Daly suggest enlisting government agencies or organizations such as Herndon, Va.-based Bankcard Holders of America to help your cause.

Consumer Product Safety Act

This article details how one parent used the Consumer Product Safety Act to force the recall of a toy that almost killed her child.

Birth of an Advocate; Housewife Helps Get Kids Hamper Recalled
Debbi Snook, *Plain Dealer*

Kathy Ridenour can tell you it takes seconds to become a vigilant consumer advocate—a few harrowing seconds. After she had such an experience, she helped lead the recall of more than 150,000 items designed for children.

Here's what happened: The Maple Heights mother of three was at home with her family last October when they heard a thump in the room where her 14-month-old son, Brett, was playing. "But it didn't sound like a play

Copyright © 1995 by Plain Dealer Publishing Co. *Plain Dealer*, May 9, 1995, p.1E. Reprinted with permission.

thump," she said. Ray Rogers, her brother-in-law, went in to find the child caught in the round space inside his whale-shaped, plastic hamper. Brett's face was wedged so tightly into the hollow of the whale's tail that it was hard to hear his crying. He was also sweating. Ray tried to get him out but couldn't. Ray called for help, and Jeff, Brett's father, rushed in. They tipped the hamper, swiftly, carefully maneuvering Brett out. "His face was a purple-red color, then it went red and pinked up," said his mother. "Then he really started screaming, so I knew he was doing good." "It only lasted a minute," she added, "but it felt like forever."

Ridenour called Rubbermaid, the makers of the Li'l Roughneck "Bubbles the Whale" hamper and told them about the problem. She called a few other times over the next couple of weeks to find out what action might be taking place. Rubbermaid staffers always seemed genuinely concerned, she said, but couldn't tell her exactly what was going on. "Maybe they were working on this every day, but I felt it went on a little too long," Ridenour said. "I'd go into the stores and see it on the shelf and start getting upset. I didn't want to see another child hurt. The hamper was cute, and with Christmas coming, it was a very appealing gift."

One day her husband, Jeff, heard a Rubbermaid spokesman being interviewed on a radio talk show, and called Kathy. She called the radio show, but was unable to get through. She later talked to someone on the station, who got a message to the spokesman. She got a call from another Rubbermaid staffer the next day. The product was being recalled. Ridenour hadn't known it, but she had helped spark what turned out to be the first recall in the Rubbermaid division's history.

About two weeks later, on Christmas Eve, a friend showed her a copy of the *Plain Dealer* business section, which announced the recall. She had missed the story. "I don't read the business section," she said. "I'm a housewife." It showed she wasn't alone in her complaint. The family of a 10-month-old had a similar experience with a Li'l Roughneck "Humphrey the Dinosaur" hamper. It, too, was recalled.

Ridenour believes Rubbermaid ultimately did right by its customers—offering to send a carton, postage and a $30 check to buy the product back—but she didn't know why it had taken two months to announce the recall.

So why did it take that long? Linda Whyte, press relations supervisor for the home products division of Rubbermaid in Wooster, said it was a new situation for the division. "And in light of never having had a recall, and never having anything of this type to occur, we wanted to get everybody's input from every department and determine how much of a threat this was. The children were apparently not seriously injured, but we still know it was not a pleasant circumstance to go through. So we re-evaluated all the data and went to the U.S. Consumer Products Safety Division with the information." The determination, after further testing, was that a potential hazard did exist. The recall was announced about two weeks later.

It's still unclear, however, when Rubbermaid notified the government of the complaints. By law, the company is expected to report any complaints regarding substantial hazards within 24 hours. But on Monday, Whyte said she had not yet determined when the company made its report. And that 24-hour rule may not apply in every case, according to Ken Giles, spokesman for the U.S. Consumer Products' safety division. Nor could Giles release the date on which Rubbermaid contacted the safety division. In an attempt to protect manufacturer's trade secrets, the Consumer Product Safety Act restricts access to recall documents unless formally requested through the Freedom of Information Act. The process takes about a month. Giles said recall investigations can be done in an afternoon, but that it's not uncommon for them to take several weeks. "It depends on how much work we need to do to identify the hazard," he said. "We also need to identify the problem and what will solve it."

Since Rubbermaid's recall on the animal-shaped hampers was voluntary, the timetable to declare the recall was negotiated between the company and the government. The intent is to give manufacturers time to prepare for calls from customers and to set up systems that will handle the return or repair of recalled products.

Apparently, the design flaw that caused the problem was overlooked, despite the company's attempt to have the product tested more than once. Whyte said the whale and the dinosaur hampers were both initially tested by Rubbermaid's Li'l Tykes division as well as by an outside contractor, which, by company policy, she declined to name. The original determination was that the cavity of the whale's tail and the dinosaur's neck "were actually designed in a cone shape so that anything that might head that way would fall right out." But after the complaints, further tests revealed that a small child could get stuck by kicking and pushing against the opposite wall of the hamper.

"It was a very unusual circumstance," Whyte said, noting that the company received only two complaints on the product. "But it was worthy of recall. Rubbermaid has a reputation for high quality, safe products, and this is something we were not happy about having out there." Several thousand hampers have been returned, she said, but she did not have an exact figure. She said the company has taken extra steps to notify consumers of the problem, by sending notices to consumer news reporters around the country, and by individually contacting consumers who had filled out a product response card that was attached to the product. She expects a future recall might not take as much time. "I think the fact that we've had this experience prepares us for perhaps a faster response time," she said.

Kathy Ridenour hopes more people who own the hampers will find out about the recall. She said she's more aware of recalls in general, and recently chastised a chain store for still having a recalled pacifier on the shelf. She's happy she's speaking up. "I couldn't have lived with myself if I had done nothing and another child got hurt," she said.

Chapter 43

Environmental Law

Clean Water Act

Clean Air Act

Superfund

Clean Water Act

Are the fines under the Clean Water Act large enough to discourage violations?

Dean Foods Fined $50,000 for Ammonia Spill in 1992

Andrew Melnykovych, *Courier-Journal* (*Louisville*)

Dean Foods was fined $50,000 yesterday for a July 1992 ammonia spill that killed 14,000 fish in Beargrass Creek. A U.S. District Court jury in December convicted the company—which had been charged with a felony—of a misdemeanor violation of the Clean Water Act. Winfred Smith, the maintenance supervisor for the dairy plant at 4420 Bishop Lane, was acquitted.

Assistant U.S. Attorney Randy Ream, who had sought a $175,000 fine, said he was satisfied with the sentence imposed by U.S. District Judge Edward Johnstone. "It's sufficient to let Dean Foods know they need to be more careful about how they handle ammonia," he said. The spill occurred when Dean Foods workers, under Smith's supervision, vented ammonia vapors from a cooling unit into a drain that eventually empties into a tributary of Beargrass Creek. Enough ammonia reached the creek to kill fish, turtles and other aquatic life for more than a mile.

Ream argued for a high fine—only $25,000 less than the maximum allowed—because Dean Foods twice had ammonia vapor leaks at the plant, which he said showed a pattern of carelessness. The company recently has been charged with civil violations of the Clean Water Act in connection with dumping of ammonia into sewers at a plant in Pennsylvania, he said. A small fine "would be nothing more than the cost of doing business," while a substantial penalty "fits a $2 billion corporation which uses tons of ammonia each day and has a history of not using (it) safely," Ream said.

Defense lawyer David Lambertus countered that Dean Foods has no prior history of environmental violations and accepted responsibility for the spill "in every way imaginable," including paying the state compensation for the dead fish. "This was an accident for which they have paid restitution," he said in asking for a fine of about $11,000.

Johnstone imposed a total fine of $50,000, but suspended $40,000 on the condition that Dean Foods pay that amount to the Kentucky Nature Preser-

Copyright © 1994 by The Courier-Journal. *Courier-Journal* (*Louisville*), May 20, 1994, p.6B. Reprinted with permission.

vation Fund, a state fund used to acquire nature preserves. Neither Lambertus nor Dean Foods plant manager Carl Powell would comment on the penalty.

Clean Air Act

Under the Clean Air Act, utilities can in theory buy and sell the right to pollute. In practice, well, that's a different matter.

Acid-Rain Pollution Credits Are Not Enticing Utilities
Matthew L. Wald, *New York Times*

What do you get when you cross a free-market economist with an environmentalist? First, a Federal law that allows companies to buy and sell the right to pollute. Next, a market for the right to pollute—and a price tag on the value of that right. But in the end, maybe a lot less than was predicted.

Five years after the system was passed into law, trading in pollution rights is slow, and the price for the right to put a ton of acid-rain pollutants into the atmosphere, which had started low, has collapsed. In fact, the price is now so low—a tenth of what some utility lobbyists had predicted—that it raises questions about the assumptions that Congress used when it established the system and accompanying pollution limits. Another interpretation is that the market is simply not working.

The Clean Air Act of 1990 cut the allowable emissions of sulfur dioxide by roughly half. And it created a new regulatory system to reach that goal, a system described by proponents as bringing the efficiency of a free-market economy to the expensive problem of pollution control.

Here is an example of how it was supposed to work: To comply with the new Federal sulfur dioxide limits, Plant A and Plant B each have to cut one ton of the pollutant. The reduction would cost $1,200 at Plant A and $1,500 at Plant B, or $2,700 total. But under the system, Plant A is allowed to reduce its pollution by two tons and sell Plant B the right to emit the second ton. The result is equal pollution reduction for $2,400, for a savings of $300.

Copyright © 1995 by The New York Times Co. *New York Times*, June 5, 1995, §A, p.11, col. 1. Reprinted with permission.

On a national basis, the savings could total billions of dollars on the cost of cutting emissions by about 10 million tons annually.

"It's one of those things that looked terrific in theory," said Peter Jump, a spokesman for the Edison Electric Institute, the Washington-based trade association for the utility industry. "But once you get into the practice of it, some things don't turn out the way you expected."

One clear difference is price. When Congress was debating the emission limits, utilities predicted that a one-ton allowance would sell for $1,000 or more; some said $1,500. The Environmental Protection Agency said $500 to $600. The price of a one-ton allowance is now less than $140. In 1992, when the first trades were made, it was about $250, and it has fallen every year. "Everybody was stunned," said Brian J. McLean, director of the Environmental Protection Agency's acid rain division. The industry estimates during debate on the bill, he said, may have involved some "gaming," meaning utility executives picked high numbers in an effort to dissuade Congress from imposing stricter standards. But no one thought the price would be so low, he said.

The economists' theory was that if the price was low, utilities whose costs were higher would rush to buy the right to pollute. But utilities appear reluctant to buy or sell, even though the General Accounting Office said earlier this year that the utilities could cut costs if they participated more. "The lesson so far is its potential has not been realized," said Peter Guerrero, an author of a December 1994 report by the accounting office on trading pollution rights. "Trading has effectively reduced the cost of compliance, but there are far greater reductions that could result."

According to the G.A.O., the annual cost of compliance in 2009, when the stricter pollution standards are fully phased in, will be about $2 billion, assuming heavy use of trading. In 1990, when Congress was debating the law, the environmental agency put the cost at twice that. In other words, the amount that Congress thought it was committing the power companies to spend—a cost to be picked up by electricity consumers—was fiction. The nation will achieve the pollution reduction for far less, while spending what Congress thought it was requiring would have bought far more pollution reduction.

If Congress was striking a balance between environmental toughness and financial mercy, it could have required tougher standards for the amount it had agreed to make utilities spend. And some environmentalists say that the trades have made the acid rain problem worse than it would have been with a simple order that each plant reduce its pollution. New York State tried unsuccessfully to intervene when one utility cleaned up more than required and made the excess emission credits available to utilities in the Midwest—a region whose emissions blow back into New York, aggravating the state's acid rain problem.

The unanticipated twist in the market may have implications for other trading schemes that are proposed or now beginning. On Thursday, a New

Jersey utility, Public Service Electric and Gas, announced a sale to a drug company, Merck, of the right to emit nitrogen oxides, which cause smog.

The E.P.A. is supposed to issue regulations soon on a trading system for nitrogen oxides, and economically minded environmentalists—or perhaps, environmentally minded economists—are predicting all kinds of permutations, including entrepreneurs who will generate credits by, for example, buying up and junking old, polluting cars. They would then sell the credits to hordes of waiting buyers.

But if the utilities are an example, that kind of market is far in the future. For one thing, utilities are still choosing in-house solutions, like building scrubbers or switching to cleaner fuel, even if the cost is more than the market price of an emission credit. "You have a lot of really bright engineers who have a preference for technology over financial tools," said Christian J. Colton, a vice president of Cantor Fitzgerald, a New York firm that is a broker for emissions trades. The engineers have been helped by a drop in the price of natural gas, which produces less sulfur dioxide than coal. Coal producers have also found lower-sulfur sources. And scrubber manufacturers have cut their prices.

This is not bad, said Mr. McLean of the E.P.A. "Trading is not the bottom line," he said. "Tons coming out of stacks is the relevant piece of information. My goal was to reduce emissions at the lowest possible cost, not to see 1,000 trades occur." As far as he is concerned, the cheaper an allowance gets, the better.

But the price means little if utilities are reluctant to enter the market to buy or sell. They face two problems. One could be called the Robert Citron effect: they fear becoming like the former treasurer of Orange County, Calif., who put public money into complex financial instruments and lost it. If the utilities buy allowances now to stockpile for later use, and the price drops later, state regulators could argue that the purchases were imprudent and the financial loss should not be borne by customers, but by shareholders. Conversely, if they sell now and prices go up later, they could also look dumb.

If utilities cut costs through the trading system, they could lower their rates, or raise their dividends to shareholders. But Mr. Colton said that only Connecticut has so far agreed to let any of the benefit flow back to shareholders. Faced with risking a loss to shareholders and no possibility of benefit, many have apparently decided not to bother.

Second, the industry itself is in turmoil as it moves toward open competition in electricity, where customers can leave their utilities for the lowest-priced supplier. As a result many old plants may be retired in the next few years. "They don't know if they're going to be using the plants in a year or two," said Mr. Jump of the trade group.

The market could pick up in the next few years. Many utilities are believed to be stockpiling allowances for Jan. 1, 2000, when a second phase of the acid rain program takes effect and the emission limits become stricter.

But some attitudes have to change first. "Toes have got to be stuck in the water," said Mr. Jump, "and that's taking some time to do."

Superfund

Does Superfund need to be reformed?

Makers, Dealers Push for Superfund Changes
Donna Lawrence, *Automotive News*

Larry Abbott wanted to do the right thing. That's where Abbott says he went wrong. The fixed operations director for the Ed Voyles Family of Dealerships in Marietta, Ga., sent used antifreeze to a recycler. If the shop had simply dumped it down a drain, the Voyles chain wouldn't be embroiled in a costly Superfund cleanup battle, Abbott says. Used antifreeze got contaminated with oil in an accident five years ago at the Daytona Recycling Group plant in Marietta. The recycler didn't have the money to clean up the $450,000 spill, so the EPA went after about 30 dealers that recycled used antifreeze at the facility, Abbott says.

The dealers and a few independent garages are responsible for about 25 percent of the gallons of antifreeze spilled, but EPA has asked them for 100 percent of the cleanup cost. Under Superfund law, the dealers must locate the other contributors and sue them for the rest of the cleanup cost, Abbott says. "I never felt so helpless in my life. We have already paid the attorney $20,000 to $25,000 in legal fees. The EPA wants $450,000, and it doesn't care who it comes from," says Abbott, adding that his share of the cleanup comes to almost $20,000.

Industry Wants Reforms

Abbott is not alone. His case is an example of what the auto industry says is wrong with the 15-year-old Comprehensive Environmental Response Compensation and Liability Act, or Superfund law. Automakers and dealers are lobbying for reforms this year after an unsuccessful bid to change Superfund law last year. They charge that although the law was created to clean up toxic waste sites, most of the money is spent on litigation.

Copyright © 1995 by Crain Communications, Inc. *Automotive News*, Aug. 14, 1995, p.6. Reprinted with permission.

The reforms are more likely to pass this session, since "the taxes (to fund Superfund) expire at the end of this year. We suspect some people will be reluctant to extend those taxes given the track record of the program as it is right now," says Tim Johnson, legislative assistant to Rep. Michael Oxley, R-Ohio. Oxley plans to introduce reforms in the fall. Reforms will make reinstating the tax palatable to more members of Congress, Johnson says.

The Blame Game

Reformists refer to the Superfund as "the blame game." The law calls for "joint and several liability," which makes the pack of potential polluters of a site liable for the entire cleanup even if some of them go belly up, says Bill Funderburk, a Los Angeles attorney for two dealers involved in a California Superfund case. "If you try to beat one of these cases, you wind up getting steamrolled," Funderburk says.

The law's retroactive liability provision makes potential polluters liable for contamination before 1980, when the Comprehensive Environmental Response Compensation and Liability Act took effect. Industry lobbyists claim this is unfair, since many Superfund cases involve contamination dating back to the 1960s and 1970s. Many companies—particularly smaller firms—don't keep records that long, says Mike Wascom, a lobbyist for the National Automobile Dealers Association. In some cases, dealers have been drawn into a Superfund case when there's no evidence that they contributed to the pollution, Wascom explains. Small waste generators such as dealers weren't required to keep disposal records until 1986, he says.

Here's generally what happens: The EPA orders large polluters to clean up a contaminated site. These companies locate smaller contributors to the site and sue them for their share of the cleanup cost. But without records, there's no way to determine whether a dealer contributed to a site and, if so, how much, Wascom explains.

The cleanup process itself is a mess, automakers maintain. The American Automobile Manufacturers Association wants the EPA to use less expensive cleanup methods.

Chances for Reform

Just 5 percent of the more than 1,300 sites on the federal government's national priorities Superfund list have been cleaned up for a total $60 billion, Oxley says. More than 25 cents of each dollar spent for Superfund goes to administrative and legal costs—not cleanup. Per-site costs average more than $30 million, and cleanup takes more than 10 years to complete, Oxley says. Oxley's aides expect to have a bill drafted next month. Superfund reform also has supporters in the Senate: Sen. Robert Smith, R-N.H., has outlined reforms.

Congressional support, however, isn't the main stumbling block, Johnson concedes. A tough Superfund reform bill could face a presidential veto. President Clinton supported a Superfund reform bill last year, but only because it kept a provision for "retroactive liability" intact, he says. Dealers and automakers want retroactive liability eliminated. Manufacturers want liability to kick in in 1981; dealers want the clock to start in 1987, after they were required to keep waste disposal records.

The Administration argues that axing retroactive liability would ultimately put the cost of cleaning up earlier sites on the taxpayers' shoulders. "We are deeply concerned about proposals to roll back the 'polluter pays' principle in Superfund (using federal funds to pay for cleanup). This administration firmly believes that the polluters who made the mess must be responsible for cleaning it up. The taxpayer should not be stuck with the bill," says Carol Browner, EPA administrator.

The House passed a $1 billion Superfund budget on July 31 as part of an appropriations bill. That's down from last year's budget of $1.4 billion, a House Appropriations Committee source says. "Instead of reforming Superfund to make it faster, fairer and more efficient, the cutbacks will make the program slower and less fair," Browner maintains.

But reformists believe straightening out Superfund will more than offset proposed cutbacks, since reforms will require more cost-efficient cleanup and end costly legal squabbles. Says Wascom: "About $1.3 billion a year—money that should be spent on cleanups or job creation and economic development—pays for the attorneys' fees, litigation and other transaction costs that result from disputes over retroactive liability."

Unit 7

Property

… Chapter 44

Intellectual Property

Ownership of Intellectual Property

Intellectual Property in Cyberspace

Patents

Ownership of Intellectual Property

NBC tried to prevent David Letterman from using his "Top Ten Lists" on CBS, claiming that it was intellectual property belong to NBC.

You Can't Take It With You; Employees' Ideas, Contacts Are Often Company Property
Joe Ross Edelheit, *Newsday*

If you're thinking about quitting your job like Jose Ignacio Lopez de Arriortua, you'd better think twice about taking your files with you. It could make you a spy. Lopez, the former General Motors purchasing chief who defected to Volkswagen, was noted for his zeal in cost cutting and manufacturing efficiency. But GM contends that when Lopez resigned last March, he smuggled out confidential business plans to use at his new employer.

The issue is one of intellectual property and who owns it—and it's not just for top executives. Your files—not to mention your Rolodex, the memos you write and the business strategies you design—may in fact belong to the company you work for. If you take them to a second employer, you might be guilty of theft.

Intellectual property refers to "creations of the mind" such as ideas, inventions and writings, said Ralph Brown, a professor emeritus at Yale Law School. And intellectual property created by employees on the job often belongs to their employers. Passing it on can amount to corporate espionage—a charge leveled against Lopez by GM and some in the German media. VW has promised an announcement concerning the dispute today.

In a separate controversy over intellectual property, NBC is trying to prevent David Letterman from taking his well-known Top 10 lists to CBS. "We think that the things like the Top 10 list were created by people who are being paid by NBC and therefore they are the property of NBC," said Curt Block, an NBC spokesman. It's not certain whether NBC has a case, but in general, "Works created by employees belong to employers," said Daniel Kaufman, a California lawyer specializing in intellectual property.

The upshot is your employer owns the copyrights on what you write and the patents on what you invent. "If you were hired to design software, then the software belongs to the company unless there's an express agreement to the contrary," said Charles Sims, a copyright lawyer in New York City. That's why taking your files when you quit a job might amount to stealing.

Copyright © 1993 by Newsday, Inc. *Newsday*, July 28, 1993, "Business," p.39. Reprinted with permission.

But in the real world, Kaufman notes, employers don't usually demand that resigning employees leave their memos at the door.

As the Lopez case shows, "trade secrets" are another matter. Such secrets can include customer lists, production methods or business strategies. Unlike other kinds of intellectual property, trade secrets are not protected by copyrights or patents. But if you learn trade secrets at work, lawyers say, you cannot legally take them from one job to another—even if the secrets are your own creations.

"The formula for Coke belongs to Coke . . . even if you're the employee at Coke that created that formula," said Lewis Malty, a lawyer specializing in workplace rights for the American Civil Liberties Union. Coke's formula is the classic example, lawyers say. But it's not always easy to know what is and what isn't a trade secret. The reason: In many states, including New York, the prohibition against revealing trade secrets is based on "common law"—the tradition of court precedents dating from pre-colonial times, Brown said. As a result, legislatures have not specifically said what constitutes trade secrets, Brown said, and defining them amounts to "a very slippery business." It's not enough, for instance, for a company to declare some materials confidential. Courts tend to define trade secrets only as "highly secret methods and plans" that a company makes an explicit effort to protect, said Sims.

To protect their secrets, some businesses make employees sign agreements not to divulge company information. But courts often throw out these agreements because they are overreaching, protecting what is effectively public information, Sims said. "Look in the files or the employee manual to see what it is you have signed," Sims said. If you possess genuinely confidential information, "you should not divulge it . . . unless you're prepared to be engaged in a lawsuit."

Are You an Industrial Spy?

Whether you're entitled to use what you know when you switch jobs depends on the circumstances. Take this quiz; the answers are based on interviews with some legal experts.

Can I take copies of memos and other documents that I wrote?
Yes   No   Maybe

NO. Whether or not your company says the material you produced is confidential, you have no legal right to take them to a second employer. Material penned by employees belongs to their employers.

If I don't take copies of anything, but remember certain trade secrets, is that okay?
Yes   No   Maybe

NO, it's not okay. If an employee quits Coca-Cola and goes to work for Pepsi, he or she cannot legally reveal Coke's secret formula. But the employee can reveal information that's not a trade secret—that is, what the company does not explicitly deem confidential.

Can I take my Rolodex of phone numbers that I built up while working at the company I'm leaving?
Yes   No   Maybe

MAYBE. The answer is no if your company provided you with the contacts, and if the company expressly said the names and numbers were confidential. But if you build up a list of contacts through the course of your work, their names and numbers belong to you.

Can I use ideas that I suggested to my old employer at my new job?
Yes   No   Maybe

MAYBE. Orally expressed ideas generally do not belong to the old employer. But remember that your company owns the copyright to anything you wrote on the job. And if the company adopted your idea and expressly told you not to give it away, then your idea may constitute a trade secret that you cannot reveal to a second employer.

When I know I'm leaving but haven't yet resigned, can I call or attend meetings where confidential business is discussed?
Yes   No   Maybe

YES. But . . . There's nothing wrong with obtaining confidential information as you go about your job, even if you know you're about to resign. But that doesn't mean you can reveal secrets after you leave.

Intellectual Property in Cyberspace

Companies are fighting vigorously over the right to use certain e-mail names on the Internet. Cyberspace brings new challenges to intellectual property.

E-mail Addresses Being Grabbed for Resale to Top Bidders
L. A. Lorek, *Fort Lauderdale Sun-Sentinel*

A digital name game has been playing on the Internet, and the stakes are high. More and more businesses are snapping up electronic mail addresses as interest in the Internet, the global computer network that reaches an estimated 20 million people, escalates. The names include everything from (victoriasecret.com) by Victoria's Secret Stores in Ohio to (unholy.com) registered by The Devil Himself Inc. of Beverly Hills, Calif., to (cosmopolitan.com) registered by Coconut Grove, Fla.-based Coral Technologies.

A domain name is the part of an Internet electronic mail address that lets people know where the message is coming from. The domain is everything to the right of the "@" sign, for example, (userid@domain). The practice of registering domain names has caused quite a fuss in the business community, especially with companies that have earned a reputation with their copyrighted name and now find themselves fighting for those rights in cyberspace.

"It's first come, first served," said Mark Costers, spokesman with Network Solutions of Herndon, Va. The company is part of InterNic, a network supported by the National Science Foundation, which registers commercial, organizational and network names on the Internet. As a result of early-bird-gets-the-name policy, some technology-savvy entrepreneurs have been able to register well-known names. L. Q. White's House of Guns in Summerville, S.C., registered (whitehouse.com). The government owns "whitehouse.gov" but it failed to register the commercial domain name "whitehouse.com." Now it has to negotiate with L. Q. White's House of Guns for the rights.

Different kinds of domains exist, including org. for organizations, mil. for military, gov. for government, net. for computer networks. But the fastest growing has been "com" for commercial businesses, said Jayne Levin, editor of NetGain, a database service in Washington that tracks new Internet domain registrations. Problems over trademarks have arisen because many

Copyright © 1995. Fort Lauderdale Sun-Sentinel. Reprinted in *Denver Post*, Sep. 11, 1995, "Business," p.F-108. Reprinted with permission.

companies have registered for the paper rights to their trademark but have failed to register for the electronic rights, Levin said. So some entrepreneurs have seized on the loophole to register such well-known trademarks as (coke.com), (mcdonalds.com), (fox.com), (abc.com) and (bbb.com).

"The situation as it currently exists is ripe for confusion," said Robert Baskins, Coca Cola Co. spokesman based in Atlanta. Coca Cola has asked the person that registered (coke.com) to sign over the electronic mail address, Baskins said. Last April, Coca Cola opened its World Wide Web site on the Internet under the domain address of (cocacola.com), but it would also like the rights to (coke.com) to cut down on any confusion, he said.

"The line is very blurry over trademarks in cyberspace—it's not a cut-and-dried situation," Levin said. So far, the electronic trademark disputes have been settled out of court. A lot of the people who hold the electronic rights to the names are small, obscure companies or individuals that don't have the financial resources to battle corporate America, she said.

Since the early '80s, Network Solutions has issued more than 60,000 commercial domain names, Costers said. That number has skyrocketed in the past year from a few hundred a month last year to more than 1,000 a day this year. It doesn't cost anything to register a name and anyone can do it as long as the name isn't in use, Costers said. The overwhelming business demand for domain names has forced Network Solutions to limit domains to one per company, Costers said.

However, Chris and Sarah Riley, husband and wife lawyers who run Coral Technologies, managed to register 65 commercial domain names, including (casino.com), (palmbeach.com) and (boating.com). Coral Technologies, an Internet marketing service, registered the names last year before Network Solutions began restricting the number, Chris Riley said. Coral Technologies plans to lease or sell the domain names to its clients to market their products on the Internet's World Wide Web. It has received interest from resorts wanting to list their business under (honeymoon.com) and cruise ships under (cruising.com).

Patents

Reggie Baker patented a great idea—a play house for cats. It was such a great idea that Kmart began producing a very similar product. What can Baker do to protect his idea?

Cat "Castle" Shows Patent Field Tough To Hoe
John Kostrzewa, *Times Union (Albany)*

His buddy called with congratulations. "I saw your invention in Kmart," he said. "You must be rolling in money." Reggie Baker didn't know what his friend was talking about. He got in his car, drove to the nearest Kmart and went to the pet section. There it was—an indoor playhouse for cats.

But it wasn't his "Kat Kingdom." It was called "Kitty Apartment" and to Baker, it looked like a knockoff of the patent he had been granted two years before. "Steam was coming out of my ears," Baker says. "I asked myself how this could have happened."

How it happened is what Baker now calls "Reggie's Horrible Kmart Adventure" to anybody who will listen. It's a story about how a merchant mariner became an inventor and tried to navigate the treacherous waters of mass merchandising. "Everybody's dream is to get this lottery ticket called a patent," he said. "But it doesn't necessarily work out."

Baker, 40, got the idea for Kat Kingdom in 1989 when he was between jobs as a deck officer on commercial ships. He was at a Christmas party when he noticed Tiki, his brother's cat, running up and down a mattress box bent into a square shape and propped against the wall. "That's a pretty smart idea," he told another partygoer. "Somebody should market that." Baker decided to try. He designed a cardboard playhouse in the style of a medieval castle and called it "Kat Kingdom." "It was for a cat's exercise and entertainment," he said.

Baker went to the public library to study how to patent an invention. He also researched existing patents and found one for a "cat condo," a small habitat that did not resemble in form or function his multi-level structure. He hired a patent lawyer and after doing more research, drawings and schematics, applied for a patent in April 1990.

While waiting for approval from the Patent and Trademark office, he went back to sea and invested the money he made in building a prototype of

Copyright © 1995 by *Times Union (Albany)*, June 18, 1995, p.G7. Reprinted with permission.

the Kat Kingdom. Baker shaped corrugated cardboard into a 40-inch tall rectangle that is 20 inches square at the top. He put in three carpeted floors and a roof supported with wooden struts. He cut three arched doors and slits in the sides. When the design was finished, he hired a manufacturer to make a dye to chop the cardboard preprinted with a gray fieldstone design into the right sizes. Baker then spent $25,000 to manufacture 1,200 Kat Kingdoms. He spent another $6,000 for publicity posters of a friend's daughter playing with kittens in the kingdom.

In September 1991, Baker said he was granted a utility patent because Kat Kingdom has a function—the structure collapses into a display box for easy packaging. "It was my first invention," he said. "I thought I was on my way." Baker contacted five distributors to try to place the product in department stores. But they told Baker the estimated price of $30, including the markup was too expensive.

Baker decided to test Kat Kingdom himself. He removed the back seat from his VW Rabbit to make room for the boxes, drove across New England and peddled Kat Kingdoms for $10 to $16 each to mom-and-pop pet stores. "They loved it," he said. "But I was running out of product and killing myself on the road."

He thought he had enough of a track record to approach national department stores. He sent samples and visited Wal-Mart in Bentonville, Ark., and Target in Minneapolis. He traveled to Troy, Mich., in late 1992 to see a buyer at Kmart's headquarters.

Baker said a Kmart representative suggested that he contact a vendor in Florida that Kmart had worked with in the past. The vendor might manufacture the product for placement on Kmart's shelves under a licensing deal. In return, Baker might receive a royalty fee for each Kat Kingdom sold. With the potential sale of hundreds of thousands at Kmart, Baker thought he could hit the jackpot.

Baker said he called Purr-fect Products, the Florida company, and a representative asked Baker to send a Kat Kingdom. "I waited but nothing happened," Baker said. "No one ever called me back and I couldn't get through to them."

It was in early 1993 when his friend called to congratulate him on his success. At Kmart, he found the Kitty Apartment was about the same size and shape as Kat Kingdom. Both were made of cardboard and had three floors and three holes. While Kat Kingdom is designed as a medieval tower, Kitty Apartment looked like a brick building with blue-and-white striped awnings. Baker said he called Purr-fect in Florida but nobody there would return his phone calls.

After complaining to Kmart, the department store in February 1993 offered to purchase 5,000 Kat Kingdoms on a trial basis. If the product sold well, Kmart said it would consider buying more. In exchange, Baker agreed to waive any claims against Kmart regarding any patent infringement. Baker signed the agreement. "I thought it was the best I could do because it was the only alternative I had," he said.

But Baker said he has not been able to find a manufacturer who would extend him credit to make 5,000 Kat Kingdoms with no assurance that Kmart would ever order any. He doesn't have the money himself to finance another production run and he can't borrow any more because he already has taken out a second mortgage on his house. Since realizing he couldn't deliver the 5,000 Kat Kingdoms, Baker has barraged Kmart executives, corporate communications staff and intellectual property lawyers with letters and phone calls, seeking a new arrangement.

"Kmart has a strict policy to observe all patent rights," says Mary Lorenz, a Kmart spokeswoman. "We made an agreement with Reggie Baker in 1993 to purchase 5,000 of his product and we are still willing to uphold our end of the agreement. However, it appears Baker has been unable to provide the product."

Sam Jacobson, Purr-fect's president, and Sue Mohr, its director of marketing and new product development, were not available for comment.

"I want to call attention to the tremendous pitfalls that can befall somebody, even if you have a patent," Baker said. "It's a tough game to play because it's hard to crack the network of vendors, manufacturers and department stores."

Chapter 45

Real Property

Sales

Adverse Possession

Eminent Domain

Sales

Even an honest seller can make the costly mistake of failing to disclose. Is it fair to put such pressure on sellers?

Full Disclosure; Lawmakers' Proposal Would Force Sellers To Reveal Property Defects
William Hathaway, *Hartford Courant*

The family looking at the Litchfield house in the summer of 1989 wanted to know the location of the septic system. Unsure, the sellers showed the family a spot within their property lines, where they said they thought the system was buried. The sellers apparently didn't realize that when the septic system was installed in 1985, it was placed partially on a neighbor's property. After moving in, the new owners discovered the mistake and had to replace the septic system. They sued the former owners. Who is responsible for the cost of replacement?

After six years of litigation, a Connecticut appellate court ruled in March that the sellers must pick up the cost, even if they did not deliberately mislead the buyer. The moral of the case: "Don't tell, if you don't know," said David Burke, the New Milford lawyer who represented the buyers in the lawsuit.

The parallel in real estate law is that if you do know, do tell, real estate lawyers say. "Sellers can be held liable for misrepresentation if it leaves the buyer on the hook," said Mimi Lines, a Hartford lawyer who has studied the subject. "And it does not matter even if there is no fraud, bad faith or deceit."

Many property owners don't know it, but "seller beware" may be more of an apt description of Connecticut common law regarding real estate transactions than "buyer beware." In court case after court case, sellers have been forced to make restitution or even take back property after misrepresenting the property's condition or omitting crucial facts in real estate transactions.

The General Assembly is reviewing a bill that would require sellers to divulge in writing known defects with their property. The bill would formalize what is already firmly established in case law, lawyers say. The bill, which unanimously passed the real estate and insurance committee, would require sellers to credit buyers $300 if they did not provide buyers written

Copyright © 1995 by The Hartford Courant Co. *Hartford Courant*, Apr. 9, 1995, p.J1. Reprinted with permission.

disclosures at the signing of the purchase agreement. The legislation would require disclosure of a variety of property issues, including, structural quality, environmental hazards, and zoning or code problems. The state Department of Consumer Protection would be required to develop disclosure forms by Jan. 1.

If these mandatory property disclosure rules are passed by the legislature, Connecticut would join 24 other states which have imposed such requirements. The bill has the backing of the Connecticut Association of Realtors, which offers members voluntary disclosure forms. "It gives buyers the information they always want to know about a house," said Chip Kunde, executive vice-president of the association. "For sellers, it gets everything out on the table early and no one can question whether the problem was disclosed or not."

Disclosure is an issue of great concern to real estate agents, who have found themselves named in lawsuits along with home sellers. In some ways, agents' exposure to lawsuits is greater than sellers', said Katherine Pancak, assistant director of the Center for Real Estate and Urban Economic Studies at the University of Connecticut. In some state courts, agents have been held liable for damages if they omit vital information they should have known, such as the existence of lead paint in an older house. These responsibilities lie with the agents even if they represent sellers, and the responsibility remains even if buyers do not ask questions. "Even if the couple buying never asks about lead paint, you can't leave that information out," Pancak said.

Lines, of Robinson & Cole, cites a Connecticut case in which the seller failed to disclose that the town had denied permission to build a septic system on the property, even though the buyer had told him he was planning to build a house. The buyer sued and won, even though the buyer apparently never asked the town or the seller whether the lot was suitable for a septic system.

Omission of vital information by agents can lead to severe consequences. For instance, a Vermont real estate agent selling his own house failed to disclose that his house had a faulty driveway heater. He was convicted of manslaughter after members of a family that bought the house died of carbon monoxide poisoning traced to a malfunctioning driveway heater.

Disclosure helps the real estate agent by reducing the risk of last minute disputes that can derail deals, Kunde said. In general, the obligation of sellers and buyers is to disclose "material facts" of importance to the buyer. The definition of material facts has been decided case by case in court. But in general, it is the unrevealed property flaws that cause severe problems for the buyer that generally win for plaintiffs. Some of the main causes of litigation are undisclosed problems with "water in the basement, leaking underground storage tanks, faulty septic systems, asbestos wrapping around pipes, "or general conditions not obvious to the buyer," Pancak said.

A good checklist for sellers is the voluntary disclosure forms now available at both the Connecticut Association of Realtors and some local boards, such as the Greater Hartford Association of Realtors. The forms should help jog sellers' memories about work they have or haven't done on their house. They will then be better prepared to answer questions. "People sometimes just don't remember things. With the forms they might say, 'Oh yeah, I serviced that furnace three years ago,' " Lines said. "It will also give the buyer more facts that might be important to them. It might not be important, but it should be their decision to make. It's usually the biggest investment people make in a lifetime, but you usually can get more information on a car than an existing dwelling," she added.

Mandatory disclosure will "level the playing field" for both buyers and sellers because options and their costs will be clear to everyone, Pancak said. "Sellers should be happy about this. It may be an initial burden to have to comply, but they will be protecting themselves because they fully disclosed," she said. Lines also said that full disclosure by all sellers should have a minimal effect on home values.

Buyers, meanwhile, should ask for voluntary disclosure forms before making an offer. While not yet mandatory, they provide a good basis to ask questions about the condition of a property. Lines said buyers should get written representations of the property by the seller. These can be included in the purchase agreement, which is a sales contract with certain contingencies. And even with such representation and disclosure forms, sellers can be honestly unaware of some problems, and buyers should also hire home inspectors or other professionals to inspect the house before purchases, Kunde advises.

The National Association of Realtors says that most mandatory disclosure laws have been passed in recent years, and it is not known whether they have reduced the number of lawsuits filed. When fully practiced, disclosure should reduce botched real estate deals, lawyers and real estate professionals say. No one wants the lawsuits and acrimony involved.

Adverse Possession

It was noxious enough for a town to use someone else's property as a dump. But can the town then claim that the dumping *made it the property owner?* What is the rationale for the adverse possession rule?

Developer and a Town Dispute Dump
Kate Stone Lombardi, *New York Times*

Peter D. Gache claims that he has lost everything from his dispute with the town of Harrison. Once the owner of 104 acres of valuable undeveloped land in this town's exclusive Purchase section, along with properties and homes elsewhere in the United States, Mr. Gache says he now has no assets and can barely pay for his own lunch. His financial ruin came at the hands of Harrison town officials, who he says knowingly created a hazardous dump on a five-acre parcel of Mr. Gache's property, rendering the rest of land—on which he had planned to develop multi-million dollar estates—valueless. All of this has given rise to a web of lawsuits.

Town officials of Harrison have a different story to tell. They maintain that the town acquired ownership of the parcel through a legal principle called adverse possession. Legal documents claim that Mr. Gache (pronounced gash-AY) lost possession of the land by failing to take actions like "inspecting, fencing, maintaining or attending to his property" over 14 years, a period during which the town admitted it was dumping there without permission. The town made its claim despite the fact that Mr. Gache continued to pay his property taxes during that period.

But town officials have said the town dumped only "organic material" on the property, which lies directly behind a town-owned garage on Barnes Lane, and maintains that there is nothing of a toxic or hazardous nature there. They say that Mr. Gache's surrounding property was not harmed, and that if he has experienced financial ruin, it is as a result of his own actions, not the town's. "If Mr. Gache had spent as much energy marketing the property as he has fighting the town of Harrison, he might not be in the situation he's in now," said Philip A. Marraccini, the Supervisor of Harrison. "The value of his property may have been ruined as the result of the publicity he gave it." Mr. Gache's story has been covered extensively in The Westchester Business Journal by Don Dzikowski.

A walk along the property in dispute shows a huge discrepancy between

---

Copyright © 1995 by The New York Times Co. *New York Times*, June 25, 1995, §13WC, p.1, col. 1. Reprinted with permission.

the Purchase Imperial Garden Estates—the development that Mr. Gache envisioned years ago—and the present state of the wooded area. In lieu of stately homes nestled on cul-de-sacs, dotted with ponds and tennis courts, there sit empty and rusting 55-gallon drums, tires, drainage pipes, car bumpers, plastic buckets and construction debris. An old dishwasher and toilet lie overturned with ferns and weeds growing inside them. A discarded doll's hand pokes through some underbrush. A 20-foot-high landfill juts over a meandering brook.

The town says that it only discarded brush and other natural material at the site, and that it is not responsible for what private citizens may have put there. Mr. Gache scoffs at such talk. Pointing to a rusting refrigerator, he said: "How did this get here? Did someone bring this in on their back?" Whether the material is hazardous is also in dispute. Mr. Gache says an environmental engineering firm he hired, Malcolm Pirnie Inc., found evidence of lead, cadmium and chromium, which had contaminated surrounding wetlands. The town says that it has conducted its own tests, which show no hazardous materials on the site. Mr. Gache says he lacks the money for additional tests to further prove his point.

Mr. Gache, who is 54, has a $26 million lawsuit pending against the town, which he filed in 1990. He filed for bankruptcy in 1991, after the Bank of Kuwait moved to foreclose on the Purchase property. Mr. Gache's request to have his suit against Harrison heard in bankruptcy court as part of his Chapter 11 filing was granted. Last month, Mr. Gache filed another suit—this one for $100 million, claiming that the town had violated his civil rights. In a surprise move, Mr. Gache also moved to dismiss his lawyers—the firm Sidley & Austin, which is based in Chicago—and to represent himself. Mr. Gache said his lawyers were more interested in settling the case than in preparing for trial. "Their goals and my goals seemed to be on divergent tracks," Mr. Gache said. "My goal was to be made whole on this thing. Their goal was to get paid and get out."

Richard Stanley, one of Mr. Gache's former lawyers at Sidley & Austin, said the firm would have no comment on Mr. Gache's assertions but noted that they had made an application to withdraw from the case, citing "irreconcilable differences." Bob Weininger, Harrison's Town Attorney, said the fact that Mr. Gache dismissed a reputable law firm suggested that he simply didn't like the advice he was getting, particularly concerning the evaluation of his chances for success. "This case has been characterized as an environmental case, but it is really a case of a property owner of a very large parcel in an exclusive area of town who, for whatever reason, wasn't developing his property and latched on to the idea that it might be more profitable to sue the town in which he owns it for millions of dollars," Mr. Weininger said. "If you scream 'toxic dump' long enough, you'll get people to believe you, but the facts just don't bear out the sensational claims he has been making."

Both sides say they would like a negotiated settlement but seem to be millions of dollars apart on what such an agreement would be. Mr. Gache says he has not met with accountants to determine what "being made whole" would constitute, but that he owes his creditors $7 million and that his property was once appraised at nearly $14 million. His home in Ketchum, Idaho, is also in foreclosure, and property he owned in Hawaii was recently auctioned. "This has caused my financial ruin, the loss of my reputation, and it has totally taken my life away," Mr. Gache said.

Mr. Weininger said that the kind of money Mr. Gache is looking for is more than the annual budget for the town of Harrison. "Obviously the town disputes Mr. Gache's charges," he said. "Just because he says it's a hazardous site in the face of clear, compelling, contrary evidence, does not mean that the town ought to roll over and play dead, accept his solution and offer up the coffers of the town treasury to him. That's just not realistic."

Mr. Gache and the town of Harrison have each spent close to $1 million in legal fees on the case already, they said. Neither party would estimate how much a trial would cost. The town of Harrison has also filed suit against its insurers, the North River Insurance Company of Parsippany, N.J., which asserted that a pollution exclusion clause in the town's policy allows them to decline to give the town coverage. The town sought a declaratory judgment for coverage in State Supreme Court in White Plains, but lost. It is appealing the decision.

Mr. Gache maintains that the town has engaged in a "conspiracy of cover-ups." He points to the discrepancy between how the town handled the discovery of another town dump on Kenilworth Lane and the Barnes Lane dump. "I feel like I've been singled out," Mr. Gache said. "They did everything in their power to clean up Kenilworth, and all they did in my situation was spend money on legal fees to fight me."

Mr. Marraccini, the Supervisor, said that when Mr. Gache originally brought suit against Harrison, during a previous administration, there may have been a tactical decision made to clean up one dump and defend against another. But he denied that there was a cover-up. "At best, something was done that should not have been," Mr. Marraccini said. "But there was no conspiracy. Mr. Gache would like to see this as a case of a poor citizen being oppressed by government. I prefer to view this as saying there's a dispute here, and what's the best way to resolve it so that Mr. Gache is provided with some relief and that taxpayers are not on the hook for something unreasonable?"

Mr. Marraccini said he believed the property could still be developed. Mr. Gache called the town's attitude "arrogant beyond belief." "As long as that dump exists, nothing can be done with the property," he continued. "Even after it's clean, how am I going to develop my property? My credit is mud. People don't want to live near where a dump has been. And anyway, I'd need approval from the people I'm suing."

Eminent Domain

Widening a road seems like a good idea to commuters, but the idea is less attractive if the new bit of road used to be your backyard. Are there any limits to the government's power of eminent domain?

E. Memphians Fear Roadwork's Impact, Plans Include 9-Lane Walnut Grove
Sarah A. Derks, *Commercial Appeal (Memphis)*

Road planners want to make it easier for cars to travel Walnut Grove and to create a shortcut from Walnut Grove to Bartlett. But along the way, homeowners in the Brierwood subdivision in East Memphis would lose their immediate access to the interstate, their already diminished peace and tranquility, and, in some cases, big chunks of their backyards. And the shortcut to Bartlett calls for extensions of Sycamore View and Kirby Parkway through Shelby Farms, a path expected to draw protests.

The plans, which will be aired at a public hearing Nov. 17, call for widening Walnut Grove to nine lanes from Interstate 240 to Humphreys Boulevard, and widening it to six lanes from Humphreys to Kirby Parkway. Widening Walnut Grove is part of a federally funded $30 million project that also involves work on other roads. "I am not happy about losing my yard," said Martha Martin, 41, who lives on Lynnfield in Brierwood. "You wouldn't be either."

The plans are in an intermediate stage, and the public hearing is to inform residents of changes, allow them to ask questions and suggest alternative designs. If residents raise enough concern or take legal action, designs could be altered. The state will use easements and pay residents for whatever property they take, said Brierwood Association president Steve Rhea. The state has yet to offer a price.

Plans also call for closing Brierview to all but right-hand turns onto Walnut Grove, causing concern among residents about emergency access for ambulances and fire and police vehicles. "I do not like it," said Betty Kaiser, 62, who has lived on Lynnfield for about a decade.

A 6-foot tall wood privacy fence divides the subdivision, shaded by maple, elm and other mature trees, from bustling Walnut Grove, a main east-west thoroughfare. The sight of boys playing hockey on rollerblades Thursday afternoon in a quiet Brierwood cul-de-sac was broken by the sound of

Copyright © 1994 by The Commercial Appeal, Memphis TN. Used by permission. *Commercial Appeal (Memphis)*, Oct. 31, 1994, p.1A.

cars and trucks rushing by on the other side of the fence. "We have enough traffic as it is," Kaiser said. The privacy fence, if demolished by construction, will have to be rebuilt at city expense, but the Martins' children will lose their play area, which will be uprooted and paved.

About 14 homeowners on Lynnfield have expressed concern over appearance and noise the newer, wider Walnut Grove will create and the possible dangers of closing Brierview. Residents plan to talk with state officials and ask for the addition of a sound-muffling buffer. They also have some concerns about rainfall drainage. As far as changing overall plans, though, "I don't know that there's a great deal we can do at this point," Rhea said. "All we care about is having a nice neighborhood and a place to live. We want them to preserve as many trees as possible."

The Martins and their children, 9 and 7, are among two families who stand to lose about 20 feet—as well as trees, play area and a child's rope swing—from their backyards. The Martins' backyard is about the size of three tennis courts, while the other resident's yard could hold about one tennis court.

Christian Brothers High School stands to lose 12 to 15 feet from its front yard when extra lanes are added, but Brother Chris Englert, school principal, said the widening is badly needed. The road project will leave the traffic signal outside CBHS. In 1996, state traffic surveys indicate, Walnut Grove from I-240 to Brierview will carry an average of 50,900 cars a day. By 2016, 76,200 cars, a 67 percent increase, will travel the road daily.

The project will take more land from the road's south side, where Brierwood residents live, than from the north side, where the school stands, because of the road's curves, said City Engineer James Collins. "It's just the way the alignment of the road works out," Collins said. With the new road, traffic on Walnut Grove won't stop at Humphreys Boulevard, so that "should reduce a lot of congestion. The bridge where Walnut Grove crosses the interstate will be replaced, and lanes will be added for cars exiting the interstate eastbound. "Cars won't have to merge so quickly," he said. Construction is scheduled to start in 1997. But property owners in Brierwood are still in the dark on exact construction details because the state has yet to finalize design plans.

Although the state handles design and construction, the city initiated and devised funding for the projects, making Walnut Grove a city project. Besides widening Walnut Grove, the project also involves limiting access to Brierwood subdivision. Plans call for partially closing Brierview so cars cannot turn west on Walnut Grove or enter the subdivision from Walnut Grove. The closing is to reduce the amount of traffic cutting through residential neighborhoods to Poplar. To get to the interstate, just scant yards from Brierview, residents will have to drive to Shady Grove, head west across the interstate to Yates, then north to Walnut Grove and back east to the interstate.

Homeowners are concerned that the changes will hinder fire, police and ambulance access, as well as block in residents if there's a wreck on Shady Grove. "It's going to be a madhouse. We'll be locked in," said Pattie Crafton, 60, who has lived on Brierfield for 28 years. "The two projects are squeezing us."

State officials expect opposition to plans to extend Kirby Parkway through Shelby Farms, said Luanne Grandinetti, spokesman for the Tennessee Department of Transportation. The plan already was redesigned once, after environmentalists objected to the extension through Shelby Farms Forest. The state projects 34,200 cars a day will travel on Kirby Parkway near Walnut Grove in 1996, and 53,400 cars a day in 2016. The public hearing on Walnut Grove and Kirby Parkway will be from 5 to 8 p.m. Nov. 17 in the Agricenter Amphitheater, 7777 Walnut Grove. No presentations are planned.

Chapter 46

Landlord-Tenant

Creation

Use

Crime

Rent

Creation

This article shows the flip side of creating a tenancy. Public housing tenants and the government are working to make renters into owners and squalid projects into healthy communities. Why might a neighborhood benefit from a greater number of home owners?

A Place With a View and a Dream
Alan Lupo, *Boston Globe*

The rich would fork over big bucks for a condo with the nighttime view from the East Boston waterfront. The multicolored lights of high rises sparkle and preen in the mirror of the bluish gray harbor, and all that's missing is a saxophone solo. But this is not fat city. This is the Maverick projects, built in 1942 and home to 1,200 people in 434 units. For most of that time, most of those apartment dwellers were white. These days, 73 percent of them are Hispanic, Asian or black, and most of the white folks are aging.

The projects are also home to a dream, one shared by increasing numbers of housing advocates and politicians. The dream is that tenants will run the projects, which will become home not just for the very poor but also for working stiffs and maybe even middle-income folks.

One dreamer is Marty Coughlin, a lifelong Eastie guy who has never been shy about pursuing longshots, be it the successful fight in the late '60s to limit Logan Airport growth or his many failed campaigns for political office. Coughlin grew up in the Maverick projects, and he has come back as director of the Maverick Tenants Organization. The MTO office is across the hall from the apartment where he grew up. He fantasizes that he'll return someday as a tenant in a mixed-income community of fewer apartments, one controlled perhaps by a joint venture of tenants and a private developer. "We've received a federal grant to train tenants on how to operate the development on their own," Coughlin says, "but we're looking toward the day when we will . . . take it out of the hands of the Boston Housing Authority altogether. Hopefully, this summer, we'll sign a contract with the BHA to manage it ourselves."

For an example of what the future could be, Coughlin figuratively looks across the harbor to Dorchester's Harbor Point, the mixed-income development of 1,283 units, managed jointly by residents and the developer, Corcoran-Jennison. Once, it was Columbia Point, a textbook example of

Copyright © 1995 by Globe Newspaper Co. *Boston Globe*, Feb. 26, 1995, "City Weekly," p.2. Reprinted courtesy of The Boston Globe.

how not to build and maintain public housing. Harbor Point would be an example of class coexistence, the dream of British "new towns." But it went up as the real estate boom went down. What resulted was an award-winning urban development beset with financial problems that were addressed only with a financial restructuring. Harbor Point today, says a housing industry source familiar with the development, "is very stable, well-managed and maintained." If the Clinton administration reinvents public housing, it could generate the capital funds to make clones of Harbor Point less complicated.

Meanwhile, the Maverick tenants make progress. "We want to get people on payrolls," Coughlin says. "We have English-as-a-second-language classes here four days a week, hopefully getting people ready for the job market. We've got funding to build a child care center for 24 children and hopefully get their parents into job training. We've just started a computer program for kids age 10 and 11. We want to start a few local businesses in the development itself. We have a thrift shop and a surplus food program now—the food's available for a buck a bag. We want to take that concept and start a food co-op, cheaper than the normal supermarket or dry goods store."

Crime is not the problem it once was, he contends. Six police officers have been assigned to Maverick, he says, providing 24-hour-a-day coverage, and a mental health program with three staffers deals with drug and alcohol dependency and child and spouse abuse. What Coughlin says he won't do is displace poor tenants to make way for market-rate renters. There are buildings nearby that could be converted into housing before any existing apartments are demolished.

Bill McGonagle, BHA deputy administrator, says the agency is in the MTO's corner. He notes that the BHA supplemented the $100,000 federal training grant with $50,000. The BHA would not rule out a joint venture between tenants and a private developer, though the ultimate call on tenant management belongs with the US Department of Housing and Urban Development. "Personally," he says, "the MTO is one of the better organized, more sophisticated residents' organizations in the city. I think they are poised, very close to where they can self-manage and self-determine their own destiny."

That's the message from downtown to East Boston—not a bad view either.

Use

Use is not supposed to include *abuse*, but according to some landlords, the two are synonymous. What can a landlord do to avoid, or limit, such problems?

Landlords Weary of Their Trashed Reputations
Chuck Haga, *Star Tribune*

Ed Johnston and Joe Kilen, landlords, showed an apartment Wednesday in the 3100 block of Pleasant Av. S. The apartment was vacated Tuesday. But it won't be available until March. Maybe April. A partial to-do list: Food covers the apartment as if exploded from cupboard shelves—spaghetti by the box, flour by the bag, coffee, rice, vinegar, oatmeal. Holes punched in walls, doors battered from joists. Windows broken, furniture smashed. Electrical outlets, light fixtures, the security system—destroyed. Carpets soaked with urine and overflow from hot water left on in the bathroom overnight. Johnston kicked at a smashed chunk of plastic and wire on a bedroom floor. "Some landlord you are, Joe," he told Kilen. "Look where you have your smoke detector."

They are weary of the landlord-as-bum stereotype. Some landlords are bad, Johnston said. Some gouge tenants and neglect their properties. "Human beings are human beings," he said. "Some people are irresponsible—some landlords and some tenants."

Kilen, who works out of Johnston's office and manages some apartment buildings of his own, told the Pleasant Av. tenant in November that she'd have to leave at the end of December. Neighbors had complained about noise. Police suspected drug activity. But when Kilen warned the tenant this week that he would have her thrown out, she laughed at him. She told him how many days it would take, going through the courts, to force her out. "She gave me the precise day," he said. So he paid her to leave. He wrote off a month's rent, $454. He paid a mover $150 and gave the woman $80 for other moving expenses. Now he's estimating cleanup and repair at $4,000 to $5,000.

The tenant left behind cans of peas and cranberry sauce, a sink full of dirty dishes, a smashed electrical fan, a broken ironing board, soiled clothes, a vase of drooping tulips, bowls of uncooked chicken, plates of baked beans. She left behind two books—"Alcoholics Anonymous" and "Narcotics

Copyright © 1994 by Star Tribune, Minneapolis-St. Paul. *Star Tribune*, Jan. 7, 1994, p.1B. Reprinted with permission.

Anonymous"—and a pamphlet from Hennepin County: "There are laws to protect your rights as a client of the Community Services Department." She left behind a child's winter jacket, gloves and shoes, a box of toys, a Homer Simpson doll, a book bag, and a letter from the Minneapolis Public Schools. "Dear parent," the letter says, and it goes on to say that one of her children is eligible to receive extra help with reading and math. It's a federal program. Sign if that's OK. Nobody signed.

Johnston, 58, owns 30 buildings—about 200 apartments—in Minneapolis. He has been in the rental business for 25 years. If he could, he said, he would get out tomorrow. "In the 1960s and '70s, I had mostly working people and retired people," he said. "You never got a call then that somebody had torn doors apart or pulled out all the wires to the furnace. My biggest cost now, next to taxes, is deliberate damage."

Almost all of Johnston's tenants receive some kind of public assistance, and many fall behind on their rent. When he takes steps to collect, he said, about one in four responds by damaging the apartment. Johnston and other landlords fault a welfare system that they say imposes few restrictions on clients and requires little accountability. They also allege harassment by city housing inspectors. "What's wrong with saying, 'We're going to help you get a place to live, and we expect you to behave like responsible adults'?" Johnston asked.

Charlie Disney, who has six duplexes in south Minneapolis, said that good landlords are selling out and leaving the inner city because of increasingly irresponsible tenants. "The welfare system has to be changed so you get less if you screw up," he said.

It's a sensitive issue. When he complains about welfare tenants, some people think he's talking race. He insists that isn't true. "I've had good black tenants and bad black tenants," he said. "I've had good white tenants and bad white tenants." Same for other races. "Nobody's working together," he said. "The welfare system encourages irresponsibility. The inspections department harasses landlords and doesn't hold tenants responsible. If we can't talk about these issues honestly, how are we going to change anything in this society?"

Jo Ann Rockwell, manager of the Family Assistance Division of Hennepin County's Department of Economic Assistance, has heard horror stories from both sides in the landlord-tenant area. "I've seen pictures of rental units that have been trashed," she said. "But we've also watched landlords taking down 'condemned' signs [and showing apartments] right after the inspectors were there."

Social workers are involved in the Community and Resource Exchange program, a collaborative effort of public agencies, neighborhood residents, police, landlords and others. Rockwell said they do indeed screen welfare clients to see if they will be responsible tenants. "We're saying to people, 'You need to be responsible. Your life is going to be easier if you're not trashing your apartment.' And we're seeing some successes here. We've applied for grants for more staff."

Penalizing welfare recipients for getting into trouble with their landlords isn't the answer, she said. "You have people already living well below the poverty line, and you're taking some more money away. If anything, that is going to increase their sense of anger and hopelessness. It would be strictly punishment," she said. "There must be people who work at Sears who have a bunch of people over, have a party and ruin a unit," and nothing will happen to them. "But you have this little captive group of people on public assistance, and you can get to them. It feels like you're getting at the problem, but it's the wrong way."

Michael Osmonson, Minneapolis housing inspections supervisor, denied that his people try to make life difficult for landlords. "Tenants often accuse us of taking bribes from landlords," he said. "But neither allegation is true. Absolutely, emphatically no way. We are neither tenant advocates nor landlord advocates." There are good and bad in both groups, Osmonson said. "Some tenants trash units. It has to be a great frustration. But I would say it's a small percentage."

It's one in four, Johnston said. "Once we go after them for rent, the damage starts. They bust windows, kick out doors and walls, throw crap on the carpeting, tear out light fixtures. I've got a dump truck sitting out here, and that dump truck is always full of crap I've had to haul out of apartments. We're stuck with all this crap, and there's rules—you can't just dump things anywhere today. I'm not just in the rental business. I'm in the junk business, too."

Johnston, who lives in Edina, has a clean record at the inspections department. He resents the stereotype of the absentee, neglectful landlord who sucks money from the poor. He bought many of his buildings 20 years ago. "Some of them I own free and clear, and I still don't make money on them," he said. "I'd love to get out of my investments in the inner city, but what do I do with these buildings? Nobody wants them. "I was raised on 25th and Chicago. I've worked my tail off; ask anybody who knows me. I started with absolutely nothing, and I've made something. But I did it in the wrong place. I did it in the city."

Crime

The ugliest of crimes occurred in the Chicago Bar Association building. Should the CBA be liable?

Victim Sues Employer, Site Owner Over Rape
Rebecca Carr, *Chicago Sun-Times*

Lynn Green was raped last August in an empty suite of offices in the Chicago Bar Association Building, where she was taking a break from her waitress job at the CBA's Corboy Hall dining room. Though a suspect has been arrested and charged, Green on Tuesday filed a civil suit against the CBA and Miglin-Beitler, the building's owner, saying they failed to take security measures that could have prevented the attack. The CBA declined comment, and Miglin-Beitler said the building has "state of art" security.

Green is the latest example of a new legal trend: More and more rape victims are seeking financial compensation for their trauma by suing employers, landlords and business owners where the rape occurred. "It's definitely a trend," said Corey L. Gordon, co-chairman of the Association of Trial Lawyers of America's inadequate security litigation group. Legal experts say that as violent crime spreads to places that were once considered sacrosanct—hospitals, churches, hotels, businesses and homes—more landlords are being held liable for crime-related injuries. "A building owner can't just provide bricks and mortar any more," said Jeffrey A. Newman, a Boston attorney and an expert in security law. Though no numbers are available on the number of suits rape victims are filing, Newman reports that a decade ago his firm handled about 20 cases like Green's. Today, his firm has more than 300 cases pending.

"Victims are realizing how permanently rape has affected their lives and they are starting to ask: Could this have been prevented?" said Kathleen T. Zellner, who is representing Green. "This rape could have been prevented with a $15 lock on the door." Green's suit, which will seek upward of $7 million, alleges that Miglin-Beitler provided lax security and that the CBA, even though it does not use or own the 17th floor, showed negligence for not warning employees that there was a serial rapist striking in the Loop at the time of Green's attack.

Rape victims are not usually identified in news stories. But Green said she wanted to go public with her story in the hopes that it would encourage other rape victims to come forward. "I feel like I have witnessed my own

Copyright © 1994 by Chicago Sun-Times, Inc. *Chicago Sun-Times*, Aug. 31, 1994, p.4. Reprinted with permission.

death, like a part of my soul has been ripped away," said Green in an interview about her experience.

The 17th floor, the building's top floor, was a place where CBA employees and their bosses would go to review employees, host cocktail parties, smoke cigarettes, take a break or even Rollerblade, according to interviews with employees. CBA employees said that Terrance M. Murphy, executive director of the association, held a staff meeting the day after the rape where he vowed to beef up security with locks on all of the bathroom doors. But seven CBA employees said the women's locker room in the basement and the executive offices on the 6th and 7th floors were the only bathrooms that got locks. The CBA declined to comment about the security of the building. But Miglin-Beitler said that all the bathrooms in the building have locks. "The security in terms of surveillance, internal systems and manpower is state of the art and is superior to most of the buildings in the Loop," said Mark L. Jarasek, vice president at Miglin-Beitler.

Green said she, unlike many victims of trauma, remembers every detail of the rape. As she emerged from a restroom, a man armed with an ice pick, pointed close to her midsection, said in a harsh tone: "Shut up! Shut up! Don't scream." The man threw her up on top of a cold marble sink counter, tied her hands with a cloth belt, placed a wider belt over her mouth and raped her three times. "I tried to just concentrate on staying alive," said Green. "I was scared he was going to kill me." The assault lasted 25 minutes, minutes that felt like hours to her.

She was taken to Northwestern Memorial Hospital and released. The following day she spent more than seven hours with Chicago Police piecing together a composite picture of her attacker, a composite they said was so detailed that it looked "like a painting." On May 27, police arrested a man who fit the description right outside the CBA building at 321 S. Plymouth. Green identified him in a lineup and he confessed, according to Det. Dave Kroll. But the suspect, Drake L. Sanders, 25, of Chicago, later denied that confession, his attorney said. He is pleading not guilty to a 30-count indictment that includes aggravated criminal sexual assault and armed robbery. He also was charged with sexually assaulting another woman at a different Loop building two weeks earlier.

Green says she is being supported financially by family and friends while undergoing therapy. She was denied workers compensation and is on an unpaid medical leave from the CBA. Her $196.30 take-home salary stopped coming after two weeks. The attack has left her so emotionally devastated, she said, that on some days she can't even leave her home. "I'm so separated from the world," she wrote in her diary. "How could anyone possibly know my heart is dead. I could just as easily close my eyes and say goodbye, even though I know I am alive and must try hard to carry on."

Rent

Rent strikes happen everywhere, but perhaps no city has as many simultaneously as New York.

Holding Back; Rent Strikes Are a City Institution—Even Among Wealthy Tenants
Lloyd Chrein, *Newsday*

For the third time, Clara Rivera has stopped making her monthly rent payments of $229. Rivera, who has lived in an apartment building at 45 Cook St. in Williamsburg, Brooklyn, for 17 years, says she has had to endure rotting windows, a leaky roof and poorly repaired bathroom fixtures for too long. Landlord Wayne Tabachnick, an optometrist who works in the building's storefront, claims he has offered to modernize Rivera's rent-regulated apartment to suit her, but she refused "because she doesn't want to pay higher rent." Landlords are entitled to rent increases for many improvements made to rent-regulated units. "That's the kind of nightmare this is," he added.

At 171 W. 57th St. in Manhattan, where rents range from $1,500 to $4,000 a month for sprawling three-bedroom, three-bathroom units, 40 percent of the tenants are on a rent strike. They say that landlords John and Nicky Venizelos have failed to furnish heat and hot water, and have harassed tenants with such tactics as dropping human excrement onto people's air conditioners—all in an effort, tenants say, to empty the building of lower-paying residents. The landlords declined to comment on the accusations.

In wealthy and not-so-wealthy neighborhoods, the rent strike has become a New York City institution. Depending on who you ask, the strikes can be blamed on greedy landlords who foster deplorable living conditions or on troublesome tenants who feel they are entitled to luxury at a bargain price. Whatever the cause, the number of strikes is overwhelming. In 1993, more than 10 percent of the city's 2.05 million rental units were the subject of rent-nonpayment suits by landlords. A little over half of those units are covered by rent control or rent stabilization, which protect a tenant's right to an apartment and limit yearly rent increases. Rent regulation, which has been in place in the city since the 1940s, is the cause of much of the animosity that leads to strikes. To bring rents closer to market rates, the best a landlord can hope for is rapid turnover of tenants so that rent increases for vacancy,

---

Copyright © 1994 by Newsday, Inc. *Newsday*, Dec. 2, 1994, p.D1. Reprinted with permission. Lloyd Chrein is a freelance writer in New York City.

and increases for renovations, can be tacked onto new leases. This often leads to a belief by tenants that the landlord wants to get them out and higher-paying tenants in—by any means possible.

"It is unlawful for a landlord to maintain the premises in a condition that is a threat to either health, safety or life," said William Rowen, a board member of the Metropolitan Council on Housing, a tenants' rights group. "Yet you see it all the time. Landlords not providing heat or hot water, not repairing leaks, and their attitude is, 'If you don't like it, then leave.'"

Landlord advocates contend that most owners strive to provide services required under the law and that it's the tenants who make trouble. "Many times a rent strike is motivated by tenant agendas rather than diminished conditions," said Paul Brensilber, president of Streamline Management. As an example, he said, tenants in a Brooklyn building wanted a 24-hour doorman. "They threatened a rent strike for no reason other than this was what they wanted," he said.

But for other tenants, a rent strike is the last resort. First steps generally include appeals to both the state Division of Housing and Community Renewal, which oversees rent regulation, and the city's Department of Housing Preservation and Development. Another option is a Housing Part proceeding, in which a tenant or group of tenants brings a housing court action against the landlord or managing agent. To give Housing Part proceedings more teeth, lawyers recommend that they be filed in conjunction with a rent strike. At 171 W. 57th St., the tenants have been on strike since spring, and hearings began on their Housing Part action in November. "This building has a lot of older tenants, including my 92-year-old mother, who I had come up from Texas," said John Oden, a tenant and member of the tenants' steering committee. "I've always been conscious of my credit rating, and it's always been my nature to pay on time. But it's really difficult to come home at night and find your 92-year-old mother lying under a pile of blankets because there's no heat. A rent strike hits them where they live."

While rent strikes can spur the landlord to action, they can also be fraught with hazards for tenants. Rule No. 1 is that a rent strike is doomed unless there is rock-solid organization. "Tenants who go into a rent strike without a close-knit group are asking for trouble," Rowen said. A landlord's legal response to a rent strike is to bring tenants into housing court for nonpayment of rent—a process that could lead to eviction if the judge doesn't accept the tenants' reasons for striking. A landlord is generally required to bring a separate nonpayment case against each striking tenant, rather than lumping all strikers into one case, according to Brooklyn housing court Judge Bruce Gould. That makes for a lot of cases. There were 295,451 nonpayment suits brought against tenants in 1993, according to Emesto Beizaguy, deputy chief clerk of the Housing Part of the City of New York Civil Court.

Some say that landlords work the one-at-a-time restriction to their advantage. "Often the landlord doesn't bring cases against everybody. He wants to single out key people or weaker people," Rowen said. "He attempts to break the ranks because if people see one or two others losing in court and getting evicted, they tend to lose heart. You have to discuss such possibilities before going on strike. You have to be prepared to stick together."

Another potential problem for tenants is a lack of knowledge of their rights. "Ninety percent of tenants who appear in housing court are not represented by attorneys, while almost all of the landlords are," said Angelita Anderson, executive director of the Citywide Force on Housing Court, a coalition of tenant advocates. "Not having an attorney can hurt you because it is easy to make errors in procedures. If the landlord is ordered to make repairs, the followup to make sure he does make those repairs is complicated."

"The collective feeling among housing court judges is that the court would work better if all tenants had attorneys," Gould said. Anderson noted that many low-income tenants are entitled to free representation from Legal Aid or Legal Services. For information on sources of free legal help, call the Citywide Task Force at (212) 982-5512.

Rent strikes often wind up being settled in housing court, with the landlord either making the required repairs or being ordered to reduce rent to reflect diminished services or conditions. The end of a strike usually means the tenants have to pay all or part of the back rent—and quickly. "If I rule that a tenant gets a 35 percent abatement, he must pay the rest of the rent back. Otherwise, he's going to be evicted," Gould said. Under city law, the landlord has to give the tenant only five days to come up with the money before eviction proceedings can be started.

Tenants who are on strike should establish a bank account for the money withheld, said Alison Cordero of the St. Nicholas Neighborhood Preservation Corp., which is helping the tenants at 45 Cook St. She said tenants have a legal right to pay utility bills if the landlord doesn't. Often, she said, utility companies will contact tenants to tell them that they can pay past-due bills to avoid a shut-off. Cordero said that in nonpayment-of-rent cases, judges usually deduct the amount paid for utilities and heating oil from the rent owed, as long as tenants can produce receipts. She said tenants should pay bills by check or money order and always get an invoice.

However, some lawyers caution against having a separate pool of money. David Rozenholc of Rozenholc & Associates, who represents the tenants at 171 W. 57th St., said a state appeals court recently ruled that a landlord has "a superior right to the money over the tenants' association. That means he might be able to tap into it, spoiling the purpose of the strike. My advice to tenants is to hold your own money, and just make sure it's available when it comes time to pay the rent."

Meanwhile, the standoff continues at 45 Cook St. Two previous rent strikes ended when the landlord made repairs, but now Rivera and two of the seven other tenants in this 16-unit building are sticking to their guns. Nine of their neighbors have moved out, and their units haven't been rented again. Tenants fear the landlord is trying to clear out the building.

But Tabachnick asserted that it doesn't make sense to rent out the other units until the current problems are resolved. And he says he wants to do the right thing for the remaining tenants. "I bought this building as an investment, an investment in my place of business," said Tabachnick, who is talking to a lawyer about possible action. "I have no intention of driving people out of the building. All I want to do is not lose too much money. I don't know how this will ever end."

Chapter 47

Personal Property and Bailments

Conditional Gifts

Bailments

Conditional Gifts

The love may be unconditional, but the gifts are not. A jilted veterinarian demands the return of money he had loaned his fiancée.

Love's Lost, But Not Loan
Cary Segall, *Wisconsin State Journal*

A jilted Westby veterinarian can recover the $14,000 he loaned a former La Crosse woman on condition of marriage, the 4th District Court of Appeals decided Wednesday. The court also said Joyce Temple must pay Paul Veum an additional $1,320 for the uninsured value of the engagement ring she lost in 1989, five months after Veum gave it to her in a glass of champagne.

Veum had given Temple $5,000 in 1989 to buy drapes and carpeting for her new condominium but had told her that if they didn't marry, the drapes were his. A short time later, on a romantic weekend in July, he gave her the ring, worth $5,570, and $9,000 more for furniture. "Temple was ecstatic," Judge Paul Gartzke elaborated, "accepted the ring and the check, and the parties bedded." But Temple's ecstasy inexplicably turned to fury just three days later. Veum said his intended drove from La Crosse to Westby to cash the check at his bank on Monday and then called him on Tuesday to tell him angrily that the engagement was off.

The change of heart was Temple's second that year. Earlier, in March, she had also called off the couple's engagement, returning a ring but keeping $9,000 Veum had given her in 1988, including $5,000 for a mink coat. Veum had forgiven those loans, he testified at trial last year, because he thought they would marry "and there was no sense having a loan with my wife." But the second time around, Veum, who had been married once before, wasn't about to be so forgiving. "Those were all pretty much conditional gifts and by March (1990) nothing was transpiring and I knew I'd been suckered in or misled," Veum said Wednesday. "I realized I was extremely foolish and that there was going to be no marriage proposals or vows resulting." He sued and won after a one-day trial before La Crosse County Circuit Judge Peter Pappas. The appeals court said Pappas had justifiably ruled the loans were conditioned on marriage, not courtship gifts.

"The amorous activities of the parties support (Pappas') description of their relationship," Gartzke wrote. "A factual basis exists for the court's inference that Veum's advances were loans conditioned on marriage." The

Copyright © 1992 by Madison Newspapers, Inc. *Wisconsin State Journal*, Nov. 27, 1992, p.1C. Reprinted with permission.

court said Temple might have won at trial if her lawyer had argued the loans weren't in writing, as required for agreements upon consideration of marriage. But, the court said, the lawyer had waited too long.

Veum said he agreed to talk about the case because he hopes others can learn from his mistakes. "I'm happy I won," he said. "I wish it hadn't occurred in the first place. By someone reading the story, I hope if they're involved in a similar situation, they can benefit from this." He apparently did. Veum found another woman and their happy marriage has already lasted more than two years, he said.

Bailments

In another sad tale of matrimonial woe, a couple sues a photographer who lost the negatives of their wedding pictures. Did the couple and the photographer have a bailment relationship?

Action for Lost Film Negatives Is Dismissed Under Bailment Theory
Lipman v. Hartman, Civil Court, Special term, Part I

JUDGE STALLMAN:

Lipman v. Hartman—In 1992, by a signed contract, plaintiffs hired defendant to photograph their wedding. After the wedding, defendant provided plaintiffs with approximately 300 color proofs and black and white contact sheets. It is undisputed that while defendant was assembling the albums, she discovered that approximately 100 black and white negatives were lost. Plaintiffs served an amended verified complaint in May 1994, asserting two causes of action: breach of contract and bailment. Defendant moves to dismiss the second cause of action of the complaint, sounding in bailment.

A bailment is a relationship by which the bailee, a non-owner of property, is permitted to acquire or retain possession of property under circumstances obligating him or her to deliver the property to another upon demand at a given time. Mays v. New York, N.H. and H.R. Co., 197 Misc. 2d 1062.

Reprinted with permission of the New York Law Journal. Copyright © 1991, the New York Law Publishing Co. *New York Law Journal*, Feb. 28, 1995, p.25.

While possession is transferred, title remains unchanged throughout the bailment. Cornelius v. Berinstein, 183 Misc. 2d 685.

Plaintiffs have not sufficiently alleged and cannot prove that a bailment ever existed between plaintiffs as bailors, and defendant as bailee, with regard to the black and white negatives. Plaintiffs have not demonstrated three elements required to prove a bailment: (1) an express or implied bailment contract; (2) ownership of the allegedly bailed property; (3) delivery of the subject property by plaintiffs to defendant. Plaintiffs have not shown any express or implied agreement of bailment of the negatives. The written contract between the parties says nothing about a bailment. To the contrary, the contract specifically provides for a sale of the negatives, i.e., that the negatives would become the property of plaintiffs only upon the payment of $150. Nor have plaintiffs alleged any facts to sustain a claim for implied bailment. It is well-settled that there cannot be an implied contract where an express contract existed between parties concerning the same subject matter. See 21 N.Y. Jur. 2d, Bailments and Chattel Leases §5 (1980). Since the contract provides terms for transfer of title and possession of negatives from defendant to plaintiffs upon payment, there can be no recovery upon a theory of bailment. See Nixon Gear and Machine Co. Inc. v. Nixon Gear Inc., 86 A.D.2d 746 (4th Dep't 1982).

Neither have plaintiffs demonstrated that they owned the black and white negatives. Plaintiffs did not have title to the negatives; title never passed to plaintiffs. Although plaintiffs did have a future interest in the negative under the contract, the negatives never became the plaintiffs' property because they never paid the separate contract fee for the negatives. The May 4, 1992 contract, which superceded a prior contract dated April 24, 1992, provided, "Negatives will become the property of the bridal couple upon completion of albums for a fee of $150."

Plaintiffs contend that they understood this language to mean that the negatives were always plaintiffs' property and would simply be returned to them after completion of the wedding albums. Plaintiffs further contend that they understood the term "fee" to mean a final payment of defendant's photography services and not to mean the purchase price for the negatives. Plaintiff Harry Lipman, who submits his affidavit in opposition to the motion to dismiss the second cause of action, is an attorney. Defendant contends that the negatives belonged to her when they were lost. The contract provided only for plaintiffs' acquisition, at a future time, upon completion of the album and when the $150 fee was paid. Indeed, the $150 negative fee was a separate purchase price for the negatives only and not a fee for photographic services. The contract itself provides that the total fee for photographic goods and services was $2,795. Plaintiffs cannot assert unilateral mistake to support their position that they had title to the black and white negatives; neither can they rely on parol evidence concerning their negotiations prior to signing the contract to vary the unambiguous, clear terms of their written contract.

Finally, plaintiffs have not demonstrated that they delivered the black and white negatives to defendant. Plaintiffs unpersuasively assert that they constructively delivered the negatives to defendant because they entrusted them to her. However, the only "entrusting" provable here is the assumption, as in any contract situation, that the parties will perform as promised. The contract obligated defendant to perform photographic services using her own property and equipment. Defendant owned the film before and after its exposure. At the time of loss of the black and white negatives, defendant retained title.

Constructive delivery has been interpreted as symbolic or substituted delivery, as by the transfer of a document of title. See Parshall v. Eggber, 54 N.Y. 18. Plaintiffs have not demonstrated any circumstances warranting application of this theory in the instant action.

The undisputed structure of the parties' contract provides no litigable basis for asserting that a bailment relationship existed. The remaining cause of action for breach of contract not only affords plaintiffs an adequate remedy, but is the appropriate legal theory for relief based on plaintiffs' own allegations of what transpired.

Accordingly, defendant's motion is granted and the second cause of action set forth in the complaint is hereby dismissed.

Chapter 48

Estate Planning

Wills

Living Wills

Wills

The late A. James Casner, an estate planning professor at Harvard Law School, used to say, "Only a fool would die without a will." This article gives a number of reasons why wills are important.

Going Without a Will Guarantees Problems
Steven M. Prye, *Commercial Appeal (Memphis)*

Where there's a will there's a way, but without a will there's no way you can be sure who gets your property and in what amounts after your death. Perhaps no other common legal document is shrouded in so much misunderstanding and ignorance as is a will. There are five widespread myths:

—*Myth No. 1.* Only rich people need wills. Not so. No matter how little you own, a will is not a luxury. Perhaps you own some family heirlooms or other trinkets that have no more than sentimental value. Unless you give them away before your death, it is only with a will that you can be sure the items will pass to those who also will treasure them instead of to someone who will toss the stuff in the nearest trash can.

A will also can effectively dispose of the hidden estate you may receive through employee pension plans, group life insurance and even accidental death insurance if these benefits are paid to your estate instead of to a particular beneficiary. This could happen automatically if your designated beneficiary dies before you.

—*Myth No. 2.* If I die without a will, my spouse inherits everything. Not necessarily. A person who dies without a will dies intestate. The state laws governing such estates are called intestacy laws, or laws of descent and distribution. These laws become your will if you don't have one. They don't hold a single advantage over a proper will. Depending on where you live, your spouse may receive only a third to a half of your estate when you die with the remainder going to the children or grandchildren or, if there are none, to other relatives.

In Tennessee, for example, a surviving spouse takes the entire estate only if there are no children. If there are children, the spouse takes the greater of one-third of the estate or a child's share. This scheme could create severe problems if your children are minors. The court would appoint a guardian to manage these funds comprising their share until the children reach 18. Thus, a substantial portion of the family funds could be tied up for years under court supervision, and would not be available to the spouse.

Copyright © 1994 by The Commercial Appeal, Memphis TN. Used with permission. *Commercial Appeal (Memphis)*, June 12, 1994, p.2C.

Under a will, you could leave your spouse your entire estate so that the spouse will have the maximum amount available for the support of the entire family, a far more sensible and convenient arrangement. If you want to provide separately for the children, you can set up the trust funds for them.

The really outrageous cases are those in which someone dies with no close blood relatives and the property passes to people so remotely related that they are referred to as "laughing heirs," people more likely to dance over your grave than weep. Perhaps you would like your property to pass to an old friend or charity. You can do so only through a will.

—*Myth No. 3*. The intestacy laws are fair. Yes siree. Coldly, blindly, rigidly inexorably fair. Intestacy laws make no distinction between a healthy, self-supporting child and a disabled child who may need special care for life, or the loving child who welcomes you into his home and the disrespectful child who slams the door in your face. Under these laws all children are equally deserving. The only person who can make these distinctions is you. Only you can reward and punish. These laws may be fair, but only you can render justice.

—*Myth No. 4*. My wife doesn't need a will. Wrong! Whether she is a homemaker or a business woman, a wife needs a will. If she outlives her husband and receives all his property, she certainly will need a will to distribute the couple's property after her death. But if the wife dies before doing a will, the couple's property would pass by law only to the wife's next of kin, which could be some cousin the husband never met. The husband's family could be cut off entirely. A husband and wife both need wills also to name a guardian for minor children in the event both die before the children reach adulthood.

—*Myth No. 5*. My wife and I own everything jointly, so we don't need wills. Big Mistake. Joint ownership is no substitute for a will. When the survivor owns all the joint property outright, he or she will certainly need a will at that point. If the couple were to die together in an accident and there were no wills, the joint property would be divided in half and distributed intestate. Again, the property could end up passing to relatives the couple didn't know or didn't like. Wills for both spouses are necessary.

Joint property can be simply disastrous for couples with children from prior marriages. In the absence of some binding agreement, the survivor is free to dispose of the joint property as he or she sees fit. This means stepchildren can be cut off in favor of the survivor's own children, family—or new spouse.

Living Wills

In life, Jacqueline Onassis and Richard Nixon both lived in the White House. In death, they also shared something in common.

Nixon, Onassis Deaths Spark Interest in Living Wills
Bill Briggs, *Denver Post*

Up to the end, they walked in contrary worlds: she soft and secluded, he open and opinionated. But in passing, Jackie Onassis and Richard Nixon both embraced a final, kindred cause—the right to die. Onassis, terminally ill with cancer, was allowed by doctors to return home to spend her last days without medical intrusion, as she requested in her living will. Reportedly, she even refused antibiotics to stave off pneumonia. Nixon also signed such a document before being felled by a massive stroke in April.

Living wills, long favored by a solid 10 percent to 20 percent of the American public, are basking in a new wave of acclaim, and some experts say the revelations about Onassis and Nixon are helping propel that sudden popularity. "We've had quite a bit of interest sparked," said Helen Voorhis, head of the Hemlock Society of Colorado, a right-to-die group. "I'm getting letters. I'm getting phone calls. People are really concerned about not wanting to get to the end of life and having themselves stuck on life-support equipment."

As always, some of the people drawing up living wills are facing certain death. About 30 percent of the calls to the Hemlock Society are made by people with AIDS or by friends of AIDS patients. But many more inquiries are coming from people who feel just fine.

Norma Shultz is one of the healthy ones. Days before embarking on a recent European vacation, Shultz, 62, decided it was time to put her ultimate wishes on paper. She penned another form of living will, something called medical durable power of attorney. In that document, people list an "agent" or a "proxy" to make health-care decisions should they become incapacitated. Slashing through the legalese: "I do not want any life-prolonging actions taken in case of a terminal illness or permanent coma," Shultz said. "Now my family's just aware" of those desires.

Shultz's overseas trip was the trigger for her decision but, she says, she's been thinking about an advance directive for years. Asked why, Shultz is fast

---

Copyright © 1994 by The Denver Post Corp. *Denver Post*, June 2, 1994, p.E1. Reprinted with permission from the author and The Denver Post.

to mention one of her relatives who has been kept alive by a pacemaker—three months after a stroke left her comatose. So the Hemlock Society's Voorhis met with Shultz to walk through the paperwork. "If I had sat down at my own desk (alone), I don't know that I would have done that or not," Shultz said. "I think for some people it does seem too weird to be taking time out of your life to do this."

"Weird, Dangerous"

When Colorado lawmakers first wrestled with this issue in 1984, "weird" was a word a lot of people were using. "Dangerous" was another. But the law passed and the dying were allowed to legally refuse life support such as respirators. "People were very concerned that this was going to open the door to euthanasia, that it would be a slippery slope to government intervention and mercy killings," said Denver attorney Mark Masters, who specializes in advance directives. "After a few years' experience using the living-will statute, and after seeing that a lot of the horrible abuse that was predicted never occurred, the (Colorado legal) stage was set for medical power of attorney," Masters said.

Nourishment Method

Today, Colorado doctors can withhold nourishment to terminally ill patients who have said in legal documents they don't want to prolong life through artificial means. And the state's "Right to Die" law, passed in 1992, allows relatives or friends to authorize that artificial feeding be stopped for patients in vegetative states.

As with any life-and-death issue, however, fights continue to flare. While some patients make it clear they don't want machines to sustain their ailing bodies, their desires may clash with family members who just can't pull the plug. When advance directives are too vague, loved ones and doctors sometimes quarrel over the best course of medical action. And there's always the fear among some that physicians will stop treatment when there's still the slightest glimmer of hope.

But advocates like Masters say the rules surrounding living wills are airtight. They can be had by any "competent" adult 18 or older. The will must be in writing, signed by you—or by another in your presence and at your request—and it must be done before two witnesses and a notary public.

Takes Two Doctors

Two doctors must certify a patient's terminal condition. The patient must also have been in a coma for at least seven days and cannot be pregnant, according to Colorado law. Free forms for living wills can be picked up at hospitals, health fairs and attorneys' offices. "There's no reason why people shouldn't take care of these options," Masters said, "particularly when they are so inexpensive and so simple." Yet until the deaths of Onassis and Nixon, the number of people with living wills remained virtually stagnant. The blame for that is most commonly leveled at doctors, many of whom are still afraid of advance directives like living wills, experts say. "The medical community needs to be more of an advocate for the documents but (worries about malpractice lawsuits) have that all tied up," said Judy Hutchison, project director for the DU/CU Health Ethics and Policy Consortium.

"My Health Wishes"

"If we had named it 'My Health Wishes' instead, we would have a lot of people filling them out. Why are so many doctors frightened of this? They see it as a legal instrument" that could be used against them if they let a patient die, Hutchison said.

A new study by the University of California at San Diego shows that physicians and their patients rarely talk about advance directives and most doctors don't know whether their patient has a living will. Yet it's a crucial medical topic that affects future treatment plans. Another recent study found that the people most likely to draw up living wills are those with Type-A personalities—those who must be utterly in control of their worlds.

Fits the Mold

Norma Shultz says she fits that mold. "Yes, I'm the type of person who likes to have my house in order, both literally and figuratively. I feel I'm one who wants to be prepared for things. And the reality is, we do not know what's around the corner."

Chapter 49

Insurance

Specialized Insurance

Specialized Insurance

What are Michael Jordan's legs worth? Or Pavarotti's vocal chords? Or Cindy Crawford's face?

Offbeat: Singers' Voices, Runners' Legs
Philip Crawford, *International Herald Tribune*

Imagine the following scenario: Your employer has temporarily assigned you to an area of the globe where social unrest and violence are prevalent. If you decline the posting, you're fired. You have an adequate package of health and life insurance benefits to protect you and your family, but moving into an area where the probability of physical injury is relatively high prompts you to seek some additional coverage. There's a small problem, however: None of the mainstream insurance companies will touch your situation because it's too risky. Where do you turn?

Enter the world of specialized insurance, or "surplus lines," where protection against anything from an executive kidnapping, the giving of bad financial advice, the spilling of nuclear waste to the deadening of a wine expert's taste buds can be bought if one is willing to pay the premium. The explosion of high technology, an increasingly litigious global society, and the high profits to be made from nonregulated contract insurance have made specialty underwriting a growth industry, valued at about $7 billion annually in the United States alone.

New things to insure crop up constantly, say experts. For example, how many individuals or companies 25 years ago would have needed to insure the crashing or burning of a computer data base? Now, it's a niche market. Professional investment advice and financial audits are more often charged with negligence amid today's legal climate, prompting some accountants, stockbrokers and investment advisers to insure themselves for protection. And those planning to take an exotic trip, such as an African safari, now often deem it prudent to buy ancillary medical coverage to provide for the financial consequences of being mauled by an animal or contracting a rare tropical fever. The possibilities are virtually unlimited.

"You can insure anything," said Nick Doak, a spokesman for the venerable insurer Lloyd's of London which, despite its recent well-publicized financial difficulties, is still acknowledged as the world leader in writing insurance for specialized risks. "Provided you can show an insurable interest." And what is an "insurable interest"? In the world of specialty under-

Copyright © 1994 by International Herald Tribune. *International Herald Tribune*, Apr. 2, 1994, "Money Report." Reprinted with permission.

writing, a rough definition might be anything deemed by an insurer to be a bona fide liability, of virtually any form, which through the course of possible events could cause someone financial damage. The key to executing a specialty contract, moreover, is the ability of a broker, acting on behalf the person seeking insurance, to come to an agreement with the insurer on the limits of a possible claim. The value of the asset being insured, be it a prize diamond, a rock star's timely appearance on stage, or one's ability to dunk a basketball, forms the basis for policy limits.

"Take the case of a professional athlete wanting to insure his body," said Mr. Doak. "A marginal player who sits on the bench would have a problem insuring his legs for, say, $10 million, because a broker would have difficulty convincing an insurer that the legs could ever be worth that much. But a star player who makes millions a year and has endorsement contracts might indeed be able to show that his potential loss of income would be huge if he were permanently disabled." In such a scenario, however, the star athlete's lifestyle would still be thoroughly examined before the policy could be written. "The underwriter might say, 'What's this fellow do in his spare time?' " Mr. Doak said. "If the answer is 'He skis,' the underwriter might say, 'Either he stops skiing or the premium doubles.' A person thus insured could not expose himself to undue risk."

The rise in white-collar crime has led financial institutions to start protecting themselves against what is referred to as "balance sheet risk," or anything that can catastrophically damage financial health. Such possibilities include invasion of computer systems, which can result in fraudulent transfer or theft of funds, sabotage of financial records, and the holding for ransom of a very valuable asset: the chief executive. "In analyzing such situations, one has to identify exactly what the risks are, how much they should be insured for and, of course, what is insurable," said Francis deZulueta, a director of Special Risk Services Ltd., a London insurance brokerage specializing in balance-sheet risk. Mr. deZulueta said that a large European financial institution involved in banking, stockbroking, and fund management might take out a blanket policy to provide, say, 1100 million in protection against a range of such risks. Such a policy, he added, would carry a premium of 12.5 million to 15 million.

In the United States, one reason for the growth in the specialty insurance industry is that, unlike in Britain, it is less regulated than traditional lines regarding premium rates and contract forms, and therefore often more profitable. According to the Insurance Information Institute, a U.S. trade group, the premiums for standard life, homeowner, and auto insurance policies are often a fraction of 1 percent of the amount of coverage bought. With specialty insurance, premiums can reach 10 percent of the coverage ceiling and even higher in some cases. "It's much more profitable to insure Phil Collins's voice than it is to insure Phil Collins's house," said Steve Goldstein, an institute spokesman, referring to the rock singer.

A trend, say U.S. industry sources, is for large, mainstream U.S. insurance concerns to form subsidiaries to tap into specialty markets. Among those to have done so are American International Group, Nationwide Mutual Insurance Co., and General Re Corp. State regulatory climates on standard markets, moreover, appear to be ever-tightening.

"In the U.S., insurance can't be placed in the surplus market unless it is not available in the licensed market," said Richard Bouhan, executive director of the National Association of Professional Surplus Lines Offices, known as NAPSLO, in Kansas City, Missouri, a trade group for specialty brokers and insurers. "And since regulation on standard markets is becoming more difficult, there are more opportunities for specialty lines." Mr. Bouhan said that liability insurance for day-care centers, amusement parks, and companies dealing with hazardous waste were other examples of specialty markets. "Take the example of nuclear waste," he said. "The people who generate the waste, haul it, and then store it all have to have coverage."